ANSELM OF CAN

THE MAJOR WORKS

ANSELM, monk and abbot of Bec in Normandy, and Archbishop of Canterbury from 1093 to 1109, was an author whose writings have been of profound importance to the development of theology in Western Christianity. He was born in Aosta in northern Italy in 1033. As a young man he travelled north as a wandering scholar and settled at Bec in 1059, where he studied under Lanfranc, then the Prior at Bec, and master of a famous school there. Anselm succeeded Lanfranc as master, and with his pupils explored problems of philosophy and theology, especially concerning the nature and existence of God. He began to write treatises on these subjects, as well as prayers and meditations for private rather than liturgical use.

On a visit to England in 1093 to inspect the English lands belonging to the Abbey of Bec, Anselm followed Lanfranc again, much against his wishes, and was appointed Archbishop of Canterbury. It was a job which brought him into a realm of politics where he was never comfortable. Problems of Church and State caused conflict with two kings in succession, and he had to go into exile in 1097–1100 and again in 1103–7.

During his years as Archbishop Anselm was always happiest engaged in theological discussion with his monastic community at Canterbury, or in writing his series of books on the incarnation, the problem of reconciling human freedom of choice with divine foreknowledge, predestination, and grace. In Canterbury at the time of his death, he was anxious to live a little longer so that he could finish a book on the origin of the soul.

BRIAN DAVIES is Professor of Philosophy, Fordham University, New York. He is the author of *The Thought of Thomas Aquinas* (Oxford, 1992), and *An Introduction to the Philosophy of Religion* (Revised Edition, Oxford, 1993), and editor of *Philosophy of Religion: A Guide to the Subject* (London, 1998).

GILLIAN EVANS lectures in the Faculty of History, University of Cambridge, and was British Academy Research Reader in Theology, 1986–8. Her books include *The Reception of the Faith* (London, 1997), *Method in Ecumenical Theology* (Cambridge, 1996), *Anselm and Thinking About God* (Oxford, 1978), and *Anselm* (London, 1989).

OXFORD WORLD'S CLASSICS

For over 100 years Oxford World's Classics have brought readers closer to the world's great literature. Now with over 700 titles—from the 4,000-year-old myths of Mesopotamia to the twentieth century's greatest novels—the series makes available lesser-known as well as celebrated writing.

The pocket-sized hardbacks of the early years contained introductions by Virginia Woolf, T. S. Eliot, Graham Greene, and other literary figures which enriched the experience of reading. Today the series is recognized for its fine scholarship and reliability in texts that span world literature, drama and poetry, religion, philosophy and politics. Each edition includes perceptive commentary and essential background information to meet the changing needs of readers.

OXFORD WORLD'S CLASSICS

══

ANSELM OF CANTERBURY

The Major Works

══

Edited with an Introduction by
BRIAN DAVIES *and* G. R. EVANS

OXFORD
UNIVERSITY PRESS

OXFORD
UNIVERSITY PRESS

Great Clarendon Street, Oxford OX2 6DP

Oxford University Press is a department of the University of Oxford.
It furthers the University's objective of excellence in research, scholarship,
and education by publishing worldwide in

Oxford New York

Athens Auckland Bangkok Bogotá Buenos Aires Calcutta
Cape Town Chennai Dar es Salaam Delhi Florence Hong Kong Istanbul
Karachi Kuala Lumpur Madrid Melbourne Mexico City Mumbai
Nairobi Paris São Paulo Shanghai Singapore Taipei Tokyo Toronto Warsaw

with associated companies in Berlin Ibadan

Oxford is a registered trade mark of Oxford University Press
in the UK and in certain other countries

Published in the United States
by Oxford University Press Inc., New York

British Library Cataloguing in Publication Data

Data available

Library of Congress Cataloging in Publication Data

Anselm, Saint, Archbishop of Canterbury, 1033–1109.
[Selections. English. 1998]
The major works / Anselm of Canterbury; edited with an introduction
and notes by Brian Davies and Gillian Evans.
(Oxford world's classics)
Includes bibliographical references and index.
1. Philosophy, Medieval.   2. Theology, Doctrinal—Early works to 1800.
I. Davies, Brian, 1951– .   II. Evans, G. R. (Gillian Rosemary).   III. Title.
IV. Series Oxford world's classics (Oxford University Press).
B765.A82E54 1998 189′.4—dc21 97–50479

ISBN 0–19–282525–9

5 7 9 10 8 6

Typeset by Best-set Typesetter Ltd., Hong Kong
Printed in Great Britain by
Clays Ltd, St Ives plc

CONTENTS

THE MAJOR WORKS

INTRODUCTION

Anselm's life and works

Anselm was an Italian from Aosta. He was born in 1033, at a time when a young man of enquiring mind would find others with similar interests travelling in search of education. Anselm began to travel after his mother's death, for at that time he quarrelled irrevocably with his father. For three years he wandered in Burgundy and the region of the Loire. He also spent time at Avranches, near Mont-Saint-Michel. By 1059 he had made his way to the monastery of Bec in central Normandy. This was a relatively new foundation, only twenty-five years old, and Herluin, its founder, was still abbot there. Anselm's reason for choosing it was probably that he had heard that Lanfranc (c.1005–89), then its Prior, was teaching there. A student 'wandering scholar' at this time could usually attach himself to any master he chose. Anselm's friend and biographer, Eadmer, tells us that Lanfranc's 'lofty fame had resounded everywhere and had drawn to him the best clerks from all parts of the world. Anselm therefore came to him and recognized the outstanding wisdom which shone forth in him. He placed himself under his guidance and in a short time became the most intimate of his disciples'.[1]

In 1060 Anselm became more than a visiting student at Bec. At the age of 27, after a good deal of soul-searching, he became a monk of the monastery. In 1063 Lanfranc left Bec to become abbot of the abbey of Saint Étienne at Caen. That left Anselm as the principal teacher at Bec, and under his tutelage the character of the 'school' there changed. Anselm did not encourage 'external' pupils. He was interested in training the minds of the monks of Bec in ways which would foster their spiritual as well as their intellectual development. His first major work reflects that concern directly. The *Monologion* begins with the explanation that it is a *meditation* on the 'divine essence', a subject Anselm had often discussed with his pupils, until they begged him to write down his teaching for them. The *Proslogion*, his next book, was written at the prompting of his own

---

[1] *The Life of St Anselm by Eadmer*, ed. R. W. Southern (Oxford, 1962), 8.

curiosity, but again he says his urge was to share with others the satisfaction it had given him to write it.

In 1075 Anselm would have thought of himself as someone little known in the world at large. In 1077–8 he was writing the *Proslogion*. In 1078 he became Abbot of Bec. By 1085, people were reading his *Monologion* and *Proslogion* in France, England, and probably in Rome. So by that year Anselm was gaining a reputation for himself which went well beyond the confines of his monastery. That brought him his first painful experience of controversy.

He was briefly engaged in disputation with someone outside Bec before 1089, when Gaunilo, a monk from Marmoutier, challenged some of the arguments in his *Proslogion*. Anselm thought that he could defend himself against Gaunilo, and he was so pleased with the exchange that he gave instructions that Gaunilo's argument and his own response should always be copied at the end when the *Proslogion* was circulated.

Anselm's second major controversy was with Roscelin, and was quite different from his engagement with Gaunilo. Now Anselm was dealing with an aggressive opponent, determined to treat him as an adversary. Roscelin (probably born about 1050 at Compiègne) was a teacher of theology and philosophy at various French schools. He was drawn to Anselm's attention in a letter from John, a monk at Beauvais, who said that Roscelin was claiming that the divine Trinity either included three distinct things, as three angels are three things, or that the Father and the Holy Spirit became incarnate with the Son. Anselm was distressed to find his name linked with unorthodox teaching. He wrote *On the Incarnation of the Word* to explain his true position.

Much against his inclination, Anselm had been chosen in 1093 to be Archbishop of Canterbury in succession to Lanfranc. He wrote on one occasion to Eulalia, Abbess of Shaftesbury, 'I am so harassed in the archbishopric that if it were possible to do so without guilt, I would rather die than continue in it.' The problems for him lay not only in his dislike of administration, although he always sought to do it conscientiously. It went deeper. He found his sense of order challenged when his duty of obedience to the Pope came into conflict with his duty of obedience to the King (William Rufus). Soon after Anselm became Archbishop William requested £1,000 from him to finance an expedition to Normandy. Anselm refused the sum because he felt that paying it would lead to hardship for his tenants. As Eadmer explains, he also took it upon himself 'to solicit the King for the relief of the Churches which were daily going to ruin, for the revival of the Christian law which was being violated in many ways, and for the reform of morals which every day and in every class of people showed too many corruptions'.[2] When William returned from Normandy, Anselm asked permission to go to Rome to receive his *pallium* (the symbol of his appointment as Archbishop) from Pope Urban II. But William did not wish to recognize Urban II as Pope and a majority of the English bishops sided with him.

Anselm was able to receive his *pallium* in 1095, and there ensued an uneasy peace between him and the King. But in the summer of 1097 William was complaining about the quality of the troops Anselm had provided under his duty to the King for a military exercise in Wales. Anselm begged to be allowed to go to Rome to ask Urban to resolve things, and when permission was given at last he reached Rome in April 1098. He stayed away from England until after William's death in 1100.

He had begun his major work *Why God Became Man* early in his Archbishopric, and perhaps a little before. He finished it in the high mountain air of his native Alps. On the same journey he worked on the treatise *On the Virgin Conception and Original Sin*, and after the Council of Bari in 1098 he began writing *On the Procession of the Holy Spirit*, which he finished in 1102. The Council at Bari was attended by a number of Greek Christians, anxious to discuss the issues on which the schism of East and West had occurred in 1054—although in fact there had been more politics than theology in the rift at the time. The most important of these was the question whether the Holy Spirit proceeded from God the Father alone or from both God the Father and God the Son. The Greeks maintained that the Spirit proceeded from God the Father alone; the Western Church held that the Spirit proceeded both from the Father and from the Son, and it was on this that the Pope asked Anselm to speak at the Council. Anselm asked for a day or two to prepare his thoughts and then sought to win round the Greeks to the Western view. He was unsuccessful but undaunted, and became sufficiently interested to want to write his treatise, which appeared four years later, in 1102.

---

[2] *The Life of St Anselm by Eadmer*, 69.

William Rufus's successor, Henry I, welcomed Anselm back to England. But it soon became clear that Anselm found his policies on the Church as unacceptable as those of William. Anselm thought that in loyalty to the Pope he ought to dispute the rights the King was claiming in the investiture of bishops. It was uncontentious that a king had a right to invest a new bishop with the lands or temporalities of his see. But it was becoming common for kings and emperors to go further into the sacramental domain and try to invest them with the spiritualities too, by giving them the ring and staff of their pastoral office. Anselm was conscious that an attempt had been made to do this to him, and glad that he had resisted, although at the time he had not yet understood the implications, and his objections had had more to do with his sincere reluctance to be made Archbishop at all.

Anselm left England again in the face of this disagreement, but Urban II's successor, Paschal II, made a compromise solution with Henry I, and although Anselm did not find it satisfactory, obedience required him to accept it. He returned to England in 1106. Eadmer says that Anselm was received 'with great joy and honour by the Church' and also that 'the King was heartily glad that he had made his peace with Anselm'.[3] But Anselm was now 73 years old, and his health was failing. At Easter 1107 he was seriously ill, and although he was working on the *De Concordia*, and said that he wanted to live long enough to write a study of the origin of the soul, his health broke down completely from this time. He died 'as dawn was breaking on the Wednesday before the institution of the Lord's Supper, on 21 April in the year of our Lord's Incarnation 1109, which was the sixteenth year of his pontificate, and the seventy-sixth of his life'.[4]

The *Monologion*

Anselm's *Monologion* is a reflection or 'meditation' on the divine essence (*divina essentia*), which he composed after years of teaching his monk-pupils at Bec and discussing the problem with them. He begins by postulating that there is something which is best (*optimum*), greatest (*maximum*), highest (*summum*). The task is to establish whether there really is any such thing and if so how we can get any

---

[3] *The Life of St Anselm by Eadmer*, 138.
[4] Ibid. 142.

idea of what it is like (what its attributes are). Anselm points out that everyone has an idea of what good is from the pleasures of everyday life. He likens it to the climbing of a ladder. One begins by contemplating something whose goodness one can easily understand, and then places in a hierarchy higher and higher familiar goods, and so climbs up, until one is able to begin to get an idea of what the highest Good may be like.

But the 'being of God' (*divina essentia*) in Christian thought is not only something with 'attributes', such as goodness and justice and mercy and truth, but also threefold, since the Godhead is Father, Son, and Holy Spirit. In the *Monologion* Anselm explores the ideas which lead him by pure reasoning to the doctrine of the Trinity. What he says owes a great deal to his reading of the *De Trinitate* (On the Trinity) of St Augustine of Hippo (354–430). Although he does not quote him, he borrows some of Augustine's 'psychological' images: of memory, will, and understanding (*memoria, voluntas, intellectus*); mind, knowledge, love (*mens, notitia, amor*). Like Augustine, Anselm was drawn to the idea that human beings have a single 'self' while having in their heads different faculties by which they inhabit or express that self. Now this is dangerous ground. If it is pressed too far one way, the persons of the Trinity look like mere aspects or faculties of the one God, and if it is pressed too far the other way, they begin to look like three Gods. Anselm had not yet met controversy, but he instinctively steered a finely adjusted course here. His main interest, like Augustine's, was in the *relationship* of the persons to one another, and there he was on the firm ground of being able to argue that it was entirely likely that the creation would reflect the Creator and that God would leave footprints in the minds of the rational creatures he had made to enable them to find their way to him by contemplation of their own deepest nature. His approach is to use pure reasoning, so as to show the rationality of the faith he is seeking to heighten in his readers. So this is a philosophical as well as a theological book.

The letter Anselm included for his old master Lanfranc, then Archbishop of Canterbury, when he sent him the *Monologion* for his approval, is translated below as an introduction to the text. Lanfranc was slow in responding, and Anselm sent reminders by former monks of Bec who were now in Lanfranc's household in Canterbury. Lanfranc's eventual reply and Anselm's reaction to it were important in fixing his habits of independence as a scholar. Lanfranc criticized the book, not for anything Anselm had said in it, but because he had not included quotations from authoritative authors to support what he had said. The *Monologion* was 'published' (that is, copied and circulated) as it stood.

The *Proslogion*

The *Proslogion* was a sequel to the *Monologion*. Anselm felt impelled to write it by the fact that he had been left with a sense of dissatisfaction when he had completed the *Monologion*. He recognized that the *Monologion* consisted of a chain of arguments, and his sense of economy and elegance of argumentation presented him with the idea that there ought to be just one argument (*unum argumentum*) on which all the themes of the *Monologion* could be made to depend. He suffered agonies of effort and a worrying distraction at prayer while he was trying to hit on this argument; when he found it, it burst upon him in a flood of pleasure.

The argument holds that nothing greater than God can be conceived to be and that God cannot even be conceived *not* to be. Sometimes called 'the Ontological Argument', it is probably that for which Anselm is best known today, for it has been very much discussed by philosophers of religion.[5] Its basic idea is that God is 'something-than-which-nothing-greater-can-be-thought'. Anyone who examines that idea will have to admit that for something-than-which-nothing-greater-can-be-thought to exist in reality would be greater than for it to exist in the mind alone. Something-than-which-nothing-greater-can-be-thought, Anselm argues, must therefore exist in reality as well as in the mind. For the modern reader that involves a considerable leap. But Anselm had a Platonic sense of what 'reality' is. In the Platonic tradition, what is in thought, in intellect, in idea, is more 'real' than what is concrete and measurable by the senses. So to move from having an idea in the mind to saying that there is a reality to which it corresponds is an altogether different kind of shift from that which would be made by saying that when-

---

[5] See John Hick and Arthur McGill (eds.), *The Many-Faced Argument* (London, 1967). See also Jonathan Barnes, *The Ontological Argument* (London, 1972).

ever I think of the 'best possible' of any kind of thing, it must follow that it really exists.

So according to Anselm, God cannot be thought of simply as a concept which people have. He thinks that people who deny God's existence can nevertheless be thought of as having some concept of God, for, so he says, they have some idea of what it is whose existence they deny. But, so Anselm suggests, reflection on the meaning of the word 'God' shows that God cannot fail to exist not only in the minds of those who have an idea of him but also in reality, and that someone who says 'there is no God' is ultimately propounding what must necessarily be a falsehood.[6]

Anselm saw this argument as paving the way for some serious reflection on what we might mean when we use the word 'God'. He thought of his *unum argumentum* as showing, not only that God exists, but also that God is what Christians believe God to be. So, from Chapter 3 of the *Proslogion* onwards, and drawing on the reasoning of that chapter and Chapter 2, Anselm reflects on the notion of God as 'something-than-which-nothing-greater-can-be-thought', to develop a defence of the teaching that God is omniscient, omnipotent, merciful, just, simple, limitless, and eternal. In doing so, Anselm presents a series of essays in philosophical theology remarkable for their rigour as well as for their clarity.

Here he began to develop an ingenuity made necessary by the constraints of truths which were hard to reconcile, but which nevertheless had to be included for the sake of orthodoxy. For example, if God is merciful it is hard to see how he can also be 'impassible', as orthodoxy required. The Supreme Being clearly could not be upset by human suffering in any way which disturbed his changelessness. On the other hand, he evidently minded about it enough to send his Son to redeem the world. Anselm argued that when God is merciful we 'feel' the effect of the mercy, but God does not 'feel' mercy in any way which disrupts the divine tranquillity.

The *Proslogion* is also remarkable among Anselm's treatises for the

---

[6] This is the drift of Chapters 2 and 3 of the *Proslogion*. Readers should note that there has been much scholarly discussion concerning the details of what is being argued in these chapters. For an introduction to this discussion, see Jasper Hopkins, *A New, Interpretive Translation of St Anselm's Monologion and Proslogion* (Minneapolis, 1986), 3–33.

way in which it alternates passages of prayer and passages of plain argument. The difference is reflected in the style, which is full of devices to be found in his prayers and meditations (as in Chapter 1); his style is entirely free of such literary devices in, for example, Chapters 2–4, which contain tight philosophical and theological arguments. Anselm meant it to be a devotional work, and that has a bearing on the question of what he was hoping to achieve in the ontological argument.

A token of this devotional purpose is the development in the last two chapters of Anselm's idea of what heaven will be like. He points out that heaven would not be heaven if it is not the best possible place to be, and he argues that even all innocent pleasures on earth, such as running fast, will for that reason necessarily have their heavenly counterpart.

Gaunilo, a monk of Marmoutiers, had objections to raise against some of the arguments of the *Proslogion*, and he put them to Anselm in his *Pro Insipiente* (On Behalf of the Fool). Anselm was delighted to have so intelligent a critic, and wrote a reply, explaining that the argument would work only for God because God has a reality of a unique kind. Anselm himself directed that his *Proslogion* should be published together with Gaunilo's reply to him and his reply to Gaunilo—and so they are in this volume. Readers should pay very special attention to Anselm's reply to Gaunilo, for it is, effectively, a commentary on the *Proslogion* from its author.

The *De Grammatico*

The *De Grammatico* is probably Anselm's earliest work. It is concerned with the question 'can an adjective such as "white", which in Latin is also a substantive or noun ("a white thing") signify a quality or accident only, or a substance as well?' In Latin there is no distinction between adjectives and nouns as parts of speech, and it is often hard to tell in a sentence whether *albus* is being used as one or the other. This was of interest to Anselm and his pupils for a number of reasons. Until the eleventh century there had been very little study of logic, although everyone had studied grammar in the process of learning Latin. It was therefore only when they began to compare the Roman grammar-books (by the late Roman grammarians Priscian and Donatus) with the textbooks on logic (by Boethius, who translated and commented on Porphyry and some of Aristotle's logical works in the sixth century) that they realized that these authorities disagreed. The treatise Anselm wrote *On the Incarnation of the Word* is about a variant of this same problem. Anselm had been using an image which played on the dilemma about whether (in Latin) 'white' merely describes a substance or signifies 'a white substance' in order to try to throw light on the question 'What are the Persons of the Trinity?' That led him into fierce controversy, as that treatise shows (see below). And Anselm was in any case strongly interested in the nature and working of language, as all his writings show.

Because this is the most technical of Anselm's treatises, it has a special introductory note in this translation.

The 'three treatises' *On Truth, On Free Will,* and *On the Fall of the Devil*

The 'three treatises pertaining to the study of Holy Scripture' were written between 1080 and 1086. Like the *De Grammatico*, they take the form of a dialogue between 'Teacher' and 'Student'. These dialogues are not like catechisms, in which the student gives formal, set answers. They are closer to the 'Socratic' dialogue form used by Plato, in which there is a real conversation, although Augustine, not Plato, was Anselm's immediate model. They all include close studies of one or two biblical texts, designed as models for students so that they could see how to apply the same methods to other texts.

The first treatise, *On Truth*, arose out of what Anselm felt to be some unfinished business in his *Monologion*. The 'student' asks him at the beginning of the book to explain what he had meant there when he spoke of 'truth'. Teacher and student together work out that truth—which can be in actions as well as in statements—has to do with things being as they ought to be. A true statement, for example, says that what is so is so or that what is not so is not so. This is an important theme in Anselm's thought. In the treatise *Why God Became Man* he writes of 'right order' (*rectus ordo*) and it is essential to his argument that there was something that fallen man ought to have done for his Creator, or owed to his Creator, and was not doing because of his sinful state.

The topic of the second treatise in the series followed naturally from the first, as teacher and student talk about 'freedom of choice'.

There is a difference between the title of Anselm's work and that of Augustine, who wrote a book 'On Free Will' (*De Libero Arbitrio*). Anselm is interested not only in the ways in which the wills of rational creatures can be free to choose, but also in the way they make choices and how it can be judged whether their choices are good or bad. Anselm and his pupil decide, in accordance with the principles they have worked out in the treatise *On Truth*, that choices made by creatures with free will are good if they are as they ought to be.

The subject-matter of the third treatise in the series, *On the Fall of the Devil* is also a natural sequel. The choice Satan made to do what he ought not to do was also a failure to 'stand fast in the truth', John 1: 44. Anselm was pioneering new ground here in certain respects. Much had been written about the fall of Adam and Eve, but the fall of the Devil is, if anything, a greater puzzle. These angels enjoyed the very presence of God before they fell and they were pure spirit, purely rational beings. Since God cannot be the author of evil and he made them, it is extremely difficult to explain how they can even have got the idea of disobedience. Anselm argues that what Satan did wrong was to desire something (to be like God) which was in itself a good thing, but which he wanted to a degree not possible for his created nature, high though it was. So his fault had to do with wanting something he ought not to have wanted. It was a breach of *rectus ordo*, which carried its own terrible inescapable consequences.

On the Incarnation of the Word

Anselm wrote the book *On the Incarnation of the Word* to try to meet Roscelin's claims. He first sought to explain that what had happened was that Roscelin had misunderstood some analogies which he had tried to draw between speaking of someone as 'white' and 'literate' and speaking of 'a white man' or 'a literate man'. This was of course exactly the same problem as the one he had written about in the *De Grammatico*, and it uses the same examples (*albus, grammaticus*). Anselm had merely thought it would be helpful for students to think, with the aid of this illustration, about the way the persons of the Trinity could be distinct persons without being three Gods. He had certainly not meant them to understand that there were three Gods in the Godhead. But his first response[7] was pounced upon with glee by Roscelin who said that Anselm had proved himself a heretic more thoroughly than ever. Anselm learned the hard way that not everyone was humbly in search of the truth and receptive to rational explanations. His final version of about 1094, the one translated here, is a careful exposition of what Anselm hoped would prove an uncontroversial position.

Among the ideas he looked at in this text were some which were to prove useful when he wrote *On the Procession of the Holy Spirit*.

Why God Became Man and *On the Virgin Conception and Original Sin*

It is probable that Anselm was prompted to address the question he tackles in the *Cur Deus Homo* (Why God Became Man) by conversations he had in the winter before his elevation to the archbishopric, while he was staying at the Abbey of Westminster. The Abbot who was his host was Gilbert Crispin, who had been a monk of Bec and was the only one of Anselm's former pupils to make his own mark as a theologian and writer. He wrote a *Disputation with a Jew*[8] about this time, in which he set about proving to a Jewish believer the necessity for the incarnation. Anselm uses a dialogue form—as he had done in the *De Grammatico* and the 'three treatises'—but whereas there the disputants had been 'Teacher and Student', Anselm now took the characters of himself and Boso, another of the monks of Bec who had formerly been his pupil. 'Boso' takes the part of the 'unbeliever'.

Anselm sets out to show that even if we know nothing about Christ through Christian revelation, it would be necessary to postulate that God became human in order to explain how the redemption of the human race could be possible. That is a bold attempt, because—as Hugh of St Victor in his *De Sacramentis Ecclesiae* in the next generation was to recognize—there had always been two departments of Christian theology. The first concerns the existence and nature of God, the doctrine of the Trinity, and the creation of the world. All these are subjects with which classical philosophy also deals, and in

[7] In *Anselmi Opera Omnia*, vol. I.
[8] In *The Works of Gilbert Crispin*, ed. A. S. A. Abulafia and G. R. Evans (Oxford, 1986).

large measure they can be approached by reasoning alone. These are what Hugh was to call 'the work of creation' (*opus creationis*). But there is also a part of Christian theology which depends upon a knowledge of historical events, the birth and life and death of Christ, his resurrection, the 'work of restoration' (*opus restaurationis*). What Anselm was proposing was to discuss the second by pure reasoning, without depending on the authority of Scripture, or any other authority, to support his argument at any crucial point.

The thrust of his argument is that God had been dishonoured by human sin. Anselm had a concept of 'honour' here which was feudal in origin. For him it meant that something much more than God's dignity was at stake. His very being was challenged by the falling away of humanity. Because he is all-powerful, he could not let that continue without doing something about it, or he would have been untrue to himself. He would not have been what he ought to be.

But if God himself had restored humanity to sinlessness by an action of his own (which he certainly had the power to do), that would not have restored right order, because it was humanity, not God, which owed the obligation to return to goodness. On the other hand, humanity could not put things right for itself, because although it owed the debt, it lacked the power. Anselm looks at the possibility that an angel could have acted on behalf of humanity to do what was necessary, but he dismisses it. There is not only the objection that an angel is not the debtor, but also the problem that while all human beings are linked together by birth, so that one man can act on behalf of the whole race, angels are separate individual creations, and cannot act together in one of their number in the same way. The only solution appears to be the one God used: for a God-man to be born who would both have the power to put things right and be a member of the race on whose behalf the putting-right needed to be done. Thus was God's honour restored.

Anselm thought it in one respect incomplete, because it did not give a full answer to the question about the manner in which it was possible for Christ to be fully human without being tainted with original sin. One area which contemporaries were telling him needed exploring was the related question whether the Virgin Mary was herself free of sin. *Why God Became Man* also has a *Meditation on Human Redemption* as a companion-piece which space does not allow us to include in this volume.

On the Procession of the Holy Spirit

Anselm found himself writing the treatise *On The Procession of the Holy Spirit* because something permanent seemed to be needed by way of a record of what he had said at the Council of Bari where the Greeks were raising objections to the addition to the creed of the clause 'and the Son' in the Western liturgy. His main argument is that only if the Holy Spirit proceeds from both Father and Son is there that symmetry in the relations of the persons of the Trinity which would seem to be required by what we know of the nature of God.

Anselm also wrote the *Letters on the Sacraments* (not included here[9]) as a result of his encounters with the Greek Christians at the Council of Bari. One of the grounds on which the schism with the Greeks had taken place was the difference of usage of leavened or unleavened bread in the Eucharist. Anselm argued that the bread was 'substantially' the same in both cases and that this should therefore not be a Church-dividing matter. The *Letters* are thus of some ecumenical importance.

De Concordia

Anselm's last major work was his attempt to bring together in a coherent way, and to complete, the various discussions of his earlier writings on the question of the relationship of divine predestination and foreknowledge with the work of grace and the operation of human freedom of choice.

Can there be genuine human freedom given that God is the all-knowing maker of the world of space and time? In the *De Concordia*, Anselm (echoing Augustine) argues that God can know only what is really the case and that, if people act freely, then God knows that they do so, from which it would seem to follow that God's knowledge is no threat to human freedom. In a tradition stemming from Boethius (*c.*480–524) to St Thomas Aquinas (*c.*1224–74), he also argues that since God's knowledge is timeless and is therefore not, strictly speaking, foreknowledge, it is compatible with the existence of human free agents. And he fills out his argument by suggesting that, though creatures achieve their good by virtue of God,

---

[9] They can be found in the translation of Hopkins and Richardson (Toronto and New York, 1974–6).

the good to which they rise is a good to which *they* rise by virtue of
God. On Anselm's account, God makes us what we are, and we could
not be what we are without God—from which, so Anselm thinks, it
follows that God is positively needed if we are to exist as free human
creatures.

The *Philosophical Fragments*

The translations in this volume end with the fragmentary 'philosophical' work which looks at the issues of 'will, power, and necessity', which Anselm addresses in *Why God Became Man*, and the
concepts of power and action, on which Anselm did not have the
advantage of knowing Aristotle's teaching, and which therefore
represent his own original explorations. These philosophical fragments[10] are authentic Anselm, but they represent an incomplete
work, or more probably, working notes towards writings which do
not survive in a finished form. Some of the ideas with which they
are concerned are developed in what Anselm says about 'will, power,
and necessity' in *Why God Became Man*. Their interest in the
problems about 'doing' and 'being able' runs through many of
Anselm's treatises.

Anselm's other writings

In addition to the works included in this volume, Anselm was also
the author of nineteen prayers, three meditations, and a large body
of letters. Anselm wrote the first group of his letters in the years
during which he was at Bec and before he became Archbishop. They
best reflect his private concerns and his personal sense of priorities.
They tell us a good deal about his gift for friendship. They also,
like the prayers and meditations and the chapters of the *Proslogion*
which are themselves prayers, show us the Anselm who wrote
Latin for its beauty as well as with clarity. They contain numerous
stylistic devices: antitheses, parallelisms, climaxes, paradoxes. The
remainder of the letters are mostly about business, and they may not
be Anselm's in every word, as the earlier ones certainly are.

---

[10] Edited in *Memorials of St Anselm*, ed. R. W. Southern and F. S. Schmitt (London,
1969).

Influence and achievement

As sources for his thinking, Anselm had the incomparable riches of the Bible and the writings of Augustine and other Western Fathers, such as Jerome (*c.*342–420), Gregory the Great (540–604), and Bede (*c.*673–735). He also had the advantage of ten years at Bec to read and absorb them before he began to write. The mode of reading taught in monastic schools was *lectio divina*, a slow, patient, reflective 'chewing' and ruminating which made the texts so studied ineradicably part of the furnishings of the minds which thus absorbed them. Anselm was unusual in that he responded not by quoting and citing authors he read as 'authorities', strung respectfully together, but by using them as points of departure for his own often wholly original thought.

Anselm had a remarkably limited range of books to draw upon in forming his mind as a philosopher. He lived at a period before even a complete set of the works of Aristotle on logic, let alone those on scientific subjects, was available in Latin, and he had no opportunity to learn Greek. There was almost no direct access to the other fundamental source of ancient Greek philosophy, Plato, except Calcidius' commentary on the *Timaeus*, and it is far from certain that Anselm can have read that. There was, however, a great deal of Platonism to be had, especially in the ideas transmitted by Augustine. And Anselm responded warmly and naturally to a Platonic way of thinking about the nature of reality.

He was never unorthodox. It was always his anxious care not to mislead those he sought to instruct. His special gift was clarity. He believed without reserve in the power of conviction of a rational argument, well set out, and, indeed, in the early days at Bec he evidently found this conviction to be justified because of the receptive pupils he had there. This method of simply explaining things clearly was the way he preferred to go on working in later life, although he came to recognize that it would be uphill work to convince those determined to resist his arguments. But a faith seeking understanding could, he remained certain, only be reinforced in its grasp of the truth by patient rational analysis. He was also profoundly drawn to the idea of 'order'. The right order in things, the 'oughtness' of truth and righteousness, of right willing and divine intention, form over and over again the basis on which he builds a solution to a problem.

As to evil, he held with Augustine that ultimately it is nothing, but he has some practical ways of treating it as a 'sort of something' for purposes of argument, so that he can take realistic account of its fearful impact on human lives in the form of sin.

This peculiar character of his work gave it a mixed reception in the next generation. There were those, especially monastic scholars, who continued to recognize its quality, and Anselm would often be included in sets of extracts from the Fathers in twelfth-century collections, along with Bernard of Clairvaux (1090–1153) and Hugh of St Victor (c. 1096–1141), as though he stood alongside Augustine and Gregory the Great as an 'authority'. But for the scholars working in the new contentious climate of the twelfth-century schools, which were growing into universities, the priorities were different. What was needed was teaching material which could be condensed and retailed efficiently in lecture-courses. Anselm's treatises do not lend themselves to that sort of treatment. They are always economical already and the highly integrated sequence of their argumentation does not readily permit the making of short extracts.

Although Peter Abelard (1079–1142) saw in the first half of the twelfth century that Anselm's account of why God became man had to be taken seriously before it was set aside in favour of his own view (that Christ came merely to set an example of the way the Christian life should be lived), it was not until the thirteenth and fourteenth centuries that scholars began to take Anselm seriously as a thinker of stature who had had a number of ideas of perennial value and importance.

Thomas Aquinas (c. 1225–74), though he is fundamentally out of sympathy with the line taken by Anselm in *Why God Became Man*, still invokes important elements of Anselm's arguments when talking of Christ and the salvation wrought by him. And, though sternly rejecting arguments which look similar to what Anselm offers in Chapters 2 and 3 of the *Proslogion*, Aquinas is in many ways at one with Anselm when it comes to the question of what can and cannot be known of God by reason.

Aquinas realized that the ontological argument was at root an argument that God's existence is self-evident, and that it therefore falls into a different category from arguments for the existence of God which depend on looking at his creation and drawing the conclusion that someone or something must have brought it into being.

In the twentieth century philosophers are still trying to discover where the flaw in the ontological argument may lie. The arguments of *Why God Became Man* still preoccupy theologians, for the doctrines of the incarnation and redemption are central to the Christian faith.[11] Philosophers of language continue to study the problems about signification-theory and the deep structure of language with which Anselm was grappling.[12]

Readers of the present translations will find in Anselm a mind of elegance and beauty and steady faith. He was a truly original thinker who wrote with a rigour and cogency which would put many theologians and philosophers to shame. He brought his mind to bear on the perennial questions of philosophers and theologians and his concerns are very much those of anyone thinking seriously about religion and philosophy today. His discussions of them are as well worth reading now as they were when he wrote them.

[11] See David Brown, '"Necessary" and "Fitting" Reasons in Christian Theology', in William J. Abraham and Steven W. Holtzer (eds.), *Festschrift for Basil Mitchell* (Oxford, 1987), 211–30.

[12] J. Hopkins, *A Companion to the Study of St. Anselm* (Minneapolis, 1972), gives a useful bibliography of studies in the first half of the 20th cent. and beyond.

NOTE ON THE TEXT AND TRANSLATORS

This book is the first English edition of all of Anselm's major works to appear in one convenient volume. In compiling it we invited several skilled Latinists to submit translations of various texts. The translators were given a relatively free hand, on the principle that we wanted renderings which were responsive to Anselm's qualities as a stylist and thinker and as unconstrained as possible by the imposition of a list of standard renderings. For, despite Anselm's own consistency of thought and usage, there are real difficulties with any attempt to translate the same word in the same way on every page. In the treatises he grouped together early in his career, on the study of Holy Scripture, *ratio* may often naturally be rendered as 'reason' in English. But in *Why God Became Man* the word *ratio* may more appropriately become 'logic'. Another term which presents huge difficulties is *iustitia*. It means both 'righteousness' and 'justice' and the play of that double meaning in the Vulgate translation of the Bible was of endless importance in Anselm's own thinking. Thinking of the age of Anselm, at no period of the development of Latin as a living language perhaps was there so strong an awareness of the equivocal character of many terms and the multiplicity of *usus loquendi* or 'ways of speaking'. To insist on one English word rather than the other at every point seemed to us to be a mistake. It would be to go back to a method of translation *de verbo ad verbum*, word for word, which turned out to have many disadvantages in the period shortly after Anselm's lifetime when scholars in the West set about bringing translations of Aristotle's writings into use in the schools. So we have encouraged our translators to follow their instincts and have sought to impose as light an editorial hand as possible.

All translations except that of the *Philosophical Fragments* are made from the edition by F. S. Schmitt, *Anselmi Opera Omnia* (6 vols., Rome and Edinburgh, 1936–68). The translation from the *Philosophical Fragments* comes from R. W. Southern and F. S. Schmitt, *Memorials of St Anselm* (London, 1969).

The Translators

Simon Harrison: *Letter to Archbishop Lanfranc*, *Monologion*; M. J. Charlesworth: *Proslogion*, *Pro Insipiente* (On Behalf of the Fool), by Gaunilo of Marmoutiers, *Reply to Gaunilo*; D. P. Henry: *De Grammatico* (*Dialogue on Literacy and the Literate*), *Philosophical Fragments*; Ralph McInerny: *On Truth*, *On Free Will*, *On the Fall of the Devil*; Richard Regan: *On the Incarnation of the Word*, *On the Procession of the Holy Spirit*; Janet Fairweather: *Why God Became Man*; Camilla McNab: *On the Virgin Conception and Original Sin*; Thomas Bermingham: *De Concordia* (The Compatibility of God's Foreknowledge, Predestination, and Grace with Human Freedom).

SELECT BIBLIOGRAPHY

Sources

Schmitt, F. S. (ed.), *Anselmi Opera Omnia* (6 vols., Rome and Edinburgh, 1938–68).

Southern, R. W., and Schmitt, F. S. (eds.), *Memorials of St Anselm* (London, 1969).

Southern, R. W. (ed.), *The Life of St Anselm by Eadmer* (Oxford, 1962).

Eadmer's History of Recent Events in England (*Historia Novorum in Anglia*), ed. M. Rule, Rolls Series (London, 1884) and trans. Geoffrey Bosanquet (London, 1964).

Other Translations and Collections

Charlesworth, M. J. (ed.), *St Anselm's Proslogion* (Notre Dame and London, 1979). Latin and English with introductory discussion. The English translation is reprinted in the present volume.

Colleran, Joseph M. (ed.), *Anselm of Canterbury: 'Why God Became Man' and 'The Virgin Conception and Original Sin'* (Albany, NY, 1969).

Deane, S. N. (ed.), *Saint Anselm: Basic Writings* (La Salle, Ill., 1962).

Hopkins, Jasper, and Richardson, Herbert (eds.), *Anselm of Canterbury: Truth, Freedom and Evil* (New York, 1967).

Hopkins, Jasper, and Richardson, Herbert (eds.), *Anselm of Canterbury: Trinity, Incarnation and Redemption* (New York, 1970).

Hopkins, Jasper, *A New Interpretative Translation of St. Anselm's Monologion and Proslogion* (Minneapolis, 1986).

Roques, René (ed.), *Pourquoi Dieu s'est fait Homme* (Paris, 1963).

Ward, Benedicta, SLG (ed.), *The Prayers and Meditations of Saint Anselm* (Harmondsworth, 1973).

The Letters of Saint Anselm of Canterbury, vol. 1, trans. and annotated Walter Fröhlich (Kalamazoo, Mich., 1990).

General Works on Anselm

Evans, G. R., *Anselm* (London, 1989).

—— *Anselm and Talking about God* (Oxford, 1978).

—— *Anselm and a New Generation* (Oxford, 1980).

Hopkins, Jasper, *A Companion to the Study of St. Anselm* (Minneapolis, 1972). This volume contains an extensive bibliography.

Luscombe, D. E., and Evans, G. R. (eds.), *Anselm, Aosta, Bec and Canterbury* (Sheffield, 1996).

Southern, R. W., *St. Anselm and his Biographer* (Cambridge, 1966).
—— *Saint Anselm: A Portrait in a Landscape* (Cambridge, 1991).

Other Relevant Reading

Barlow, Frank, *The English Church 1066–1154* (London and New York, 1979).

Fairweather, Eugene R. (ed.), *A Scholastic Miscellany: Anselm to Ockham* (Philadelphia, 1956).

Barth, Karl, *Anselm: Fides Quaerens Intellectum* (London, 1960).

Clover, Helen, and Gibson, Margaret (eds.), *The Letters of Lanfranc, Archbishop of Canterbury* (Oxford, 1979).

Colish, Marcia L., *The Mirror of Language: A Study in the Medieval Theory of Knowledge* (Revised edn., Lincoln, Neb., and London, 1983).

Gersh, Stephen, 'Anselm of Canterbury', in Peter Dronke (ed.), *A History of Twelfth-Century Philosophy* (Cambridge, 1988).

Gibson, Margaret, *Lanfranc of Bec* (Oxford, 1978).

Henry, D. P., *The Logic of St Anselm* (Oxford, 1967).

Schufreider, Geoffrey, *Confessions of a Rational Mystic: Anselm's Early Writings* (West Lafayette, Ind., 1993).

A CHRONOLOGY OF ANSELM'S LIFE

1033	Anselm born in Aosta in northern Italy.
1059	Anselm enters Bec.
	Early writings composed: prayers and meditations, letters, *Monologion*, *Proslogion*, *De Grammatico*, treatises on the study of the Scriptures.
1078	Anselm becomes Abbot of Bec.
Early 1090s	Controversy with Roscelin begins, leading to first version of *De Incarnatione Verbi*.
1093	Anselm nominated Archbishop of Canterbury by King William II. Problems arise over the respective roles of Church and State.
1097–1100	Anselm goes to Rome to ask the Pope's advice on resolving his dispute with the King. *Cur Deus Homo* completed.
1098	Anselm speaks at the Council of Bari, at the Pope's invitation, to try to mend the schism between the Eastern and Western Churches.
1102	*De processione Spiritus Sancti* and *Letters on the Sacraments* published.
1103–7	Anselm in exile again, over dispute with Henry I.
1109	Anselm dies at Canterbury.

ANSELM OF CANTERBURY

The Major Works

LETTER TO ARCHBISHOP LANFRANC

To Lanfranc, worthy of reverence and love, his master, father and teacher, Archbishop of Canterbury, primate of the English, most deservedly worthy, for his faithful service to the mother church catholic, to be, by her, embraced. Brother Anselm of Bec, a sinner by nature, a monk by religious profession.

Since in all that one does, one should seek advice, but not the advice of all—as it is written, 'do all things with advice' and 'let your advisers be one in a thousand' [Ecclus. 6: 6]—I have chosen one man, one, not in a thousand but from all that are mortal. A man whom you know. I have chosen one man to be my advisor when I am in uncertainty, to be my teacher whereof I am ignorant, to set me right where I go wrong, and to seal what I do right with his approval. Although, in accordance with your wishes I have been unable to avail myself of him, yet have I determined to do so as far as I am able. For although there are very many men, besides Your Prudence, from whom I, uneducated as I am, might be able to derive improvement and education, and to whose critical judgement I should submit myself, compelled by my very lack of education, yet there is not one of those whom I have encountered to whose teaching and appraisal I would as willingly and confidently submit as I would to yours. There is none who, if the matter required it, would behave to me with such fatherly affection, or who, if the matter demanded it, would so rejoice together with me. Whatever you may bestow on me from your fatherly heart and soul is chosen by wisdom, strengthened by authority, and seasoned with love. Therefore when I have taken in something of what you bestow, its sweetness is to me a source of delight, its guarantee a source of satisfaction. But I am telling all this to one who knows. Let me, then, pass over such things that I may set out the reason for my reminding you of this.

Some of the brethren, your servants and my fellow servants, have, by their many and frequent requests, compelled me to agree to write them something—as you may read in the preface to what I have

---

Having written his *Monologion*, Anselm sent it for approval to Lanfranc, by then Archbishop of Canterbury (cf. Editors' Introduction). This letter was his recommendation of the *Monologion* to Lanfranc.

written. It has turned out, without my expecting it, that many others, not just those at whose insistence I produced the treatise, want not only to read but also to copy it. I am uncertain, therefore, as to whether I ought to deny it them or allow them what they want. I do not want them to hate me, thinking that I have begrudged them it, or to laugh at me when they realize that I am a fool. So I turn to my one and only advisor. I send what I have written for examination, so that on the authority of your judgement it may either be kept from sight as something unsuitable or be corrected and offered to those who want it.

MONOLOGION

Prologue

Some of my brethren[1] have often and earnestly asked me to write
down, as a kind of model meditation, some of the things I have said,
in everyday language, on the subject of meditating upon the essence
of the divine; and on some other subjects bound up with such
meditation. They specified (on the basis more of their wishes than
of the task's feasibility or my capacity) the following form for this
written meditation: nothing whatsoever to be argued on the basis of
the authority of Scripture, but the constraints of reason concisely to
prove, and the clarity of truth clearly to show, in the plain style, with
everyday arguments, and down-to-earth dialectic, the conclusions of
distinct investigations. They also wanted me not to disdain to meet
the down-to-earth, or even downright silly, objections that I would
come up against.

For a long time I declined even to try. I considered how I mea-
sured up to what it involved, and I tried to excuse myself. I gave lots
of reasons. For the easier they wanted it to be to use, the harder they
made it to produce. But I was eventually overcome by the unassum-
ing persistence of their requests together with the sheer goodness,
which I could not fail to respect, of their earnestness. And so,
although I took it up quite against my will (in view of the difficulty
involved and the feebleness of my talents), I completed it (in view
of their love) willingly, to the best of my ability, and in accordance
with their specifications.

Now, I was induced to do this in the expectation that whatever
I produced would be read only by those who had asked for it. I
expected that they would soon scornfully and disdainfully consign
it to oblivion as something without value. (For I know that in this
work I have not been able to provide satisfaction for those that
entreated me. All I have been able to do was to put a stop to the
entreaties that pursued me.) But—and I do not know how it has
happened—despite that expectation, not only the aforementioned
brethren, but many others as well, each making a copy of this writing

---

[1] Monks in the Abbey of Bec.

for himself, have made it their business to preserve this treatise for posterity.

In the course of frequent rereadings of this treatise I have been unable to find anything which is inconsistent with the writings of the Catholic Fathers, and in particular with those of the Blessed Augustine. If, then, someone thinks that I have said here anything which is either too modern, or which departs from the truth, I would ask them not to denounce me as an arrogant modernizer or a maintainer of falsehood. Rather I ask that they first make a careful and thorough reading of the books *On the Trinity* of the aforementioned learned Augustine and then judge my little treatise on the basis of them.[2] When I say that the supreme Trinity can be spoken of as three substances I follow the Greeks, who confess three substances in one person but believe what we do when we confess three persons in one substance. For, with reference to God, the Greeks mean by substance what we mean by person. But what I say at that point is expressed in the person of someone who, by reasoning alone, is investigating and arguing through things to which they have not before turned their attention. For I was aware that this is what they—those whose request I was trying to comply with—wanted.

Now I entreat and earnestly implore anyone who wants to copy this work to be careful to set this preface at the front of the book, even before the chapter titles. For it will, I think, be of great help towards understanding what is written therein for the reader to know beforehand the aims and methods of the discussion. I think too that the reader who sees this preface first will not rush into passing judgement if he finds that I have uttered anything contrary to his own beliefs.

Chapters

---

[2] When Anselm sent a copy of the *Monologion* to Lanfranc he received a reply regretting that he did not do more to acknowledge the authority of St Augustine.

41. The supreme spirit most truly begets, and the Word most truly is begotten

42. The supreme spirit is truest begetter and Father, and the Word truest begotten and Son

43. What is common to both, and proper to each—a reconsideration

44. How one is the essence of the other

45. The Son is the Father's essence. This is a more appropriate possible claim than that the Father is the Son's essence. Likewise the Son is the Father's strength, wisdom and the like

46. Some of these claims can be taken in another way as well

47. The Son is the understanding of understanding, the truth of truth, and so on

48. It makes sense to think of the Father in terms of consciousness and the Son in terms of understanding. And how the Son is the understanding and wisdom of consciousness, the consciousness of the Father and the consciousness of consciousness

49. The supreme spirit loves itself

50. One and the same love proceeds equally from Father and Son

51. Each loves himself, and the other, with equal intensity

52. This love is as great as the supreme spirit is

53. This love is the very thing that the supreme spirit is. Yet Love plus Father plus Son, makes one spirit

54. All of it proceeds from the Father, and all of it proceeds from the Son, yet there is just one Love

55. Love is not their Son

56. The Father, only, is unbegotten begetter. The Son, only, is begotten. The love, only, is neither begotten nor unbegotten

57. Love, like Father and Son, is uncreated Creator. But they do not add up to three uncreated Creators, just one. Love can be called the Spirit of the Father and the Son

58. The Spirit is the Father's and the Son's essence, wisdom, and so forth—just as the Son is the Father's essence and wisdom,

8o. The supreme essence dominates and regulates all things. It alone
is God

1. *That of all the things that exist, there is one that is the best,
greatest and supreme*

Of all the things that exist, there is one nature that is supreme. It
alone is self-sufficient in its eternal happiness, yet through its all-
powerful goodness it creates and gives to all other things their very
existence and their goodness. Now, take someone who either has
never heard of, or does not believe in, and so does not know, this—
this, or indeed any of the numerous other things which we necessarily believe about God and his creation. I think that they can, even
if of average ability, convince themselves, to a large extent, of the
truth of these beliefs, simply by reason alone. Now, since this could
be done in several ways, I will set down here the one that I consider
to be the most readily available. For, given that all desire only what
they think is good, anyone can easily avail himself of the following
opportunity: he can at any time turn the mind's eye to look for the
source of the things that are good—things that one would not want
unless one judged them to be good. In this way, then, guided by
reason, he may make rational progress towards what he, unreason-
ingly, does not know.

But if I say something along the way that greater authority does
not teach, then I wish it to be taken in the following way: it is, indeed,
reached as a necessary conclusion from reasoning which seems right
to me. Nevertheless, it is not thereby asserted as necessary without
qualification. Rather I assert it as possible—for the present at least.

Anyone, then, can quite easily ask himself the following question:
'Given that there is such an uncountable number of good things, the
sheer multiplicity of which is simply a datum of bodily sense as well
as something we perceive by means of the rational mind—given this,
are we to believe that there is some one thing through which all good
things whatsoever are good? Or do different goods have their existence through different things?' Quite certain, indeed, and clear to
all who are willing to see, is the following: take some things that are
said to be (say) X, and relative to each other are said to be less, more,
or equally X. It is through this X that they are said to be so, and this
X is understood as the very same thing in the various cases and not

something different in each case (whether X is considered to be in them equally or not equally). Take, for example, some things that are said, relative to each other, to be, either equally, or more, or less just. They cannot be understood to be just except through justice, and justice is not something different in each of the various cases. Therefore, since it is certain that all good things when compared with each other are either equally or not equally good, necessarily all good things are good through something, and this something is understood to be the same thing in each of various good things.

Different good things may none the less appear to be called good through different things. Thus a horse may appear to be called good through one thing, because it is strong, and through something else, because it is swift. For it seems to be called good through strength and good through speed, and yet strength and speed do not seem to be the same thing. And if the horse is good because it is strong and swift, how come the thief that is swift and strong is bad? Rather, it is the case that the swift and strong thief is bad because he does harm, and the strong and swift horse is good because it is beneficial. (And indeed ordinarily nothing is thought to be good except on the grounds either of what is beneficial, e.g. health and what makes for it—or of what is excellent, e.g. beauty and what contributes to it.) Now, the reasoning above is irrefutable. Necessarily, therefore, everything beneficial or excellent is, if it is truly good, good through that same one thing, through which all good things necessarily are good, whatever that thing may be. And who would doubt that that through which all things are good is a great good?

Because, then, it is that through which every good thing is good, it is good through itself. It therefore follows that all the other good things are good through something other than what they themselves are, while this thing alone is good through itself. But nothing that is good through something other than itself is equal to or greater than that good which is good through itself. The one thing, therefore, that is good through itself is the one thing that is supremely good. For the supreme is that which so overtops the others that it has no equal and no superior. But what is supremely good is also supremely great. There is therefore one thing that is supremely good and supremely great, and this is of all the things that exist, the supreme.

2. *On the same subject*

We have found, then, that there is something supremely good (because all good things are good through some one thing, namely that which is good through itself). But in the same way we arrive at the necessary conclusion that there is something supremely great, since whatsoever is great is great through some one thing, namely that which is great through itself. I do not mean great in terms of size, like some sort of body; but something which, the greater it is, the better or more valuable it is, like wisdom. And since only that which is supremely good can be supremely great, it is necessary that there is something that is best and greatest—i.e. of everything that exists, the supreme.

3. *That there exists a nature, through which everything that exists exists, which exists through itself, and which is, of all things that exist, supreme*

Furthermore, not only is it the case that all good things are good, and all great things great, through one and the same thing, but also it would seem to be the case that whatever is, is through one thing. For everything that exists, exists either through something or through nothing. But nothing exists through nothing. For it is impossible even to conceive of something existing through nothing. Whatever exists, then, exists only through something.

Now since this is the case, there is either one or more than one thing through which all existing things exist. If there are more than one, then they are either themselves reducible to some one thing through which they exist, or each of them exists individually through itself, or they all exist mutually through one another. Suppose then, first, that they exist through some one thing, then all the existing things do exist through one, and not more than one, thing—that one thing through which the more than one exist. Suppose, then, secondly, that each of them exists individually through itself. In order for each to exist through itself, there must of course be some single power-to-exist-through-oneself (or some single nature-of-existing-through-oneself) that each possesses. And then, doubtless, they would exist through this one thing—that through which they possess the capacity to exist through oneself. It is therefore closer to the truth to say that all existing things exist through this one thing, than to say that they exist through things which, without it, are incapable of existing. The third possibility, that they should exist mutually through one another, defies reason. For the notion that something could exist through that to which it gives existence, is just irrational. For not even do things spoken of by means of mutually related terms exist mutually through one another. Master and servant are spoken of with reference to each other. Yet the human beings themselves who are thus spoken of do not exist through each other at all, nor do the relations themselves by which they are spoken of exist through each other at all. (The relations exist through the subjects.) Truth therefore rules out altogether the possibility that there is more than one thing through which everything exists. Therefore there is necessarily some one thing through which all existing things exist.

Therefore, since all things exist through this one thing, beyond a shadow of a doubt this one thing exists through itself. Therefore all the other things exist through something other than themselves, while this alone exists through itself. But what exists through something other than itself, is less than that through which all other things exist, and which alone exists through itself. Therefore, that which exists through itself, exists most of all. There exists, therefore, some one thing, which alone of all things most exists and exists supremely. But that which exists most of all, that through which whatever is good is good, whatever is great is great, and indeed through which whatever exists exists—this is necessarily supremely good, supremely great, and is of all the things that exist, the supreme. Therefore there is some thing which, whether it is called an essence, a substance, or a nature, is the best and the greatest, and of all the things that are, the supreme.

4. *On the same subject*

Furthermore, if one considers the natures of things, one cannot help realizing that they are not all of equal value, but differ by degrees. For the nature of a horse is better than that of a tree, and that of a human more excellent than that of a horse, and to doubt it is simply not human. It is undeniable that some natures can be better than others. None the less reason argues that there is some nature that so overtops the others that it is inferior to none. For if there is an infinite distinction of degrees, so that there is no degree which does not have a superior degree above it, then reason is led to conclude that the number of natures is endless. But this is senseless, and only the senseless would think it was not. Necessarily, then, there is some nature which is superior to others in such a way that it is inferior to none.

Now there is either only one of this kind of nature, or there is more than one and they are equal. Suppose there are many equal natures. They cannot be equal through different things, but are equal through one thing, that one thing through which they are equally as great as they are. This one thing, then, is either that which they themselves are (i.e. their essence), or something different from what they themselves are. But if it is simply their essence, then just as there is one essence, there is one nature, and not more than one. (For here I understand nature and essence to be the same.) If, on the other hand, it is something different from themselves, then they are, definitely, less than it—less than that through which they are great. For anything that is great through something else is less than that through which it is great. Therefore these natures are not so great that there is nothing greater than them. It is therefore quite impossible that there exist several natures than which nothing is more excellent, because a plurality of such natures cannot possibly exist either through that which they themselves are or through something different.

What this leaves, then, is that there is one and only one nature which is superior to others and inferior to none. But such a thing is the greatest and best of all existing things. There is therefore some nature which is of all that exists, supreme. But this is possible only if it is what it is through itself, and if all other things are what they are through it. Now that which exists through itself and through which all other things exist is the being that is of all beings supreme. This, reason has just taught us. Given that, either we can reverse the statement and say that the supreme being is that which exists through itself and through which all other things exist, or there exists more than one supreme being. More than one topmost thing? Clearly not. Therefore there is some nature (or substance or essence) which is good, great, and is what it is, through itself. And whatsoever truly is good, great and is a thing, exists through it. And it is the topmost good, the topmost great thing, the topmost being and reality, i.e. of all the things that exist, it is the supreme.

5. *That we can use 'out of' of the supreme being in the same way as 'through'*

So, then, we can agree on this result; what we need to do now, therefore, is to find out the answer to the following question. Everything that is anything, including the supreme nature, exists only 'through' the supreme nature: do they all likewise exist only 'out of' the supreme nature? Now, it is quite clear that when we say that something is 'out of' something we can also say that it is 'through' that same thing, and vice versa. Thus, for example, what exists 'out of' some material and 'through' a craftsman, can also be said to exist 'through' the material and 'out of' the craftsman. This is because it has its existence 'through and out of' both, that is by means of both—although the 'through and out of' the material is different to the 'through and out of' the craftsman. All things which exist are what they are through the supreme nature, and thus the supreme nature exists through itself while other things exist through it. It follows, then, that in exactly the same way, all things which exist exist 'out of' the supreme nature, and thus that the supreme nature exists 'out of' itself, whereas the other natures exist 'out of' something other than themselves.

6. *That there was no cause helping to bring the supreme nature into being, nor yet does it exist through or out of nothing. How its existence through and out of itself can be understood*

The reference then of 'that which exists through' and 'that which exists out of' something is not invariably the same thing. We must, therefore, investigate more precisely how it is that everything exists through and out of the supreme nature. And first of all we must start with the supreme nature itself, which exists through itself, and then afterwards go on to things which exist through something else. This is because what exists through itself and what exists through something other than itself, have not got the same explanation for their existence.

So then, we have ascertained that the supreme nature is what it is through itself, and that all other things are what they are through it.

But how does it exist 'through itself'? For, it would seem, existing through something is existing either through a maker, or through some material, or through something else, like a tool, that contributes. But something that exists in any one of these three ways—maker, material and tool—exists through something other than itself, and so is posterior to, and somehow less than, this other thing. The supreme nature, however, definitely does not exist through something other than itself, nor is it posterior to, or less than itself or any other thing. The supreme nature, therefore, cannot have been fabricated by itself, or by anything else. Nor was it the material from which it was made—and neither was anything else. Nor did it, or anything else, contribute in any way to its becoming what, before, it was not.

What then? Something that has come into existence without the existence of something that fashioned it, or some material for it to have been made out of, or some outside help, would seem to be nothing—or if not nothing, then to exist through and out of nothing. Now, this cannot not apply to the supreme nature. And, although the grounds for thinking this derive from what I have already, in the light of reason, pointed out, I am not going to leave out the step-by-step proof. For this meditation has all of a sudden brought me to something prodigious and fascinating, and so I do not want carelessly to skip any objection—no matter how down-to-earth or even downright silly—that I come up against. Two reasons: first, so that I can proceed with the argument more securely, leaving nothing uncertain behind. Secondly, so that (if I do want these insights to convince somebody) I can remove even the slightest of obstacles, so that even the slow of understanding will be able easily to assent to what they read.

So then, to assert that this nature (without which no nature would exist) is nothing is as false as the claim that 'whatever is, is nothing' is absurd. Is it through nothing? No, it is not, since it is completely unintelligible for something to exist through nothing. Is it in some way out of nothing? Then it is out of nothing either through itself, or through something else, or through nothing.

Now we have established that there is no way that something exists through nothing. If then it is out of nothing, then either through itself or through something else. But nothing can exist out of nothing through itself, since necessarily, what comes to exist (from nothing and through something) is posterior to that through which it comes to exist. But since the supreme essence is not prior to itself, it does not come to exist out of nothing through itself.

What if we say that it has come into being out of nothing through some other nature? But then it is not supreme, but is inferior to something; nor is it what it is through itself, but through something else. Furthermore that through which it exists would have to have been a great good, seeing as it is the cause of so great a good. But it is unintelligible that there should have been something good before that without which nothing is good. The supreme nature that we are talking about is the good without which there is no good. This is quite clear enough. There is, therefore, nothing prior to the supreme nature through which it might come into existence out of nothing— not even in thought.

In sum, if the supreme nature does exist either through or out of nothing, then, for sure, either it is not through or out of itself, or it may be said to be nothing. Both of which are, as I do not need to explain, quite false. It is clear, then, that the supreme nature does not exist through some maker or out of some material, nor was it helped into being by some contributing causes. Yet because it is what it is (whatever that is) through and out of itself, it is definitely not through or out of nothing.

But it did not make itself. Nor was it there as matter for itself. Nor did it assist itself into becoming what it was not. How, then, in the end, are we to understand its existence through and out of itself? There is, perhaps, a way to make sense of it: in the same way as we talk of brightness. Brightness through and from itself is bright and through and from itself brightens. For 'brightness', 'to brighten', and 'something that is bright' are related to each other, in the same way as are 'existence' and 'to exist' and 'something that exists' (i.e. something that has being or reality). Therefore supreme existence, supremely to exist, and the supreme existing thing (or supreme reality) go together rather like 'brightness', 'to brighten', and 'to be bright'.

7. *How all other things exist through and out of the supreme nature*

We still have to ask about the totality of things which exist through something other than themselves: in what way do they exist through the supreme nature? Was the supreme nature their maker or their material? We do not need to ask whether it merely contributed to their existence (with something other than the supreme nature as the maker and material). For, for everything to exist only secondarily, not primarily, through the supreme nature would go against what has already been made clear above.

The first question to ask, then, is this: does the totality of things which exist through something other than themselves, exist out of some sort of matter? Now this is not to call into question the composition out of earth, water, air, and fire of the universe, in its parts, and as a concrete and visibly formed whole. (We can separate, in thought, the four elements from the visible forms in formed things, and so we might think of the elements as having an unformed, unordered, nature, which might thus be the 'matter' of all bodies— bodies which are made distinct by their individual forms.) I am not, I repeat, calling this into question. What I am after is this: this thing that I called the matter of the concrete universe, where does this come from? If it comes from some other matter, then this other matter is more truly the matter of the corporeal universe.

If, therefore, the totality of things visible and invisible is out of some material, it can only be (indeed it can only be said to be) out of either the supreme nature, or out of itself, or out of some third essence.

But there just is no third essence. For nothing can even be thought of besides that which is supreme (which exists through itself), and everything that exists through that supreme being. That then which just does not exist, just cannot be matter for anything at all.

But can the totality of things which do not exist through themselves exist out of their own nature? No. If this were the case, then they would somehow exist through themselves, and through something other than that through which all things exist, which then would not be that through which all things exist. None of which is the case. Again, everything that is out of matter is out of something other than itself and is posterior to it. But since nothing is other than itself, or posterior to itself, it follows, therefore, that nothing is out of itself as material.

Can something less than the supreme nature exist out of the supreme nature as matter? But this would mean that the supreme good could be changed and made less good. One is just not allowed to say this. But everything that is not the supreme nature is less than it. It is therefore impossible that any non-supreme being should exist out of the supreme nature in this way. Furthermore, suppose that the supreme good were changed and corrupted through something. That thing would, without doubt, be something not at all good. Now if some lesser nature does exist out of the supreme good as matter (given that the only thing through which anything exists at all is the supreme essence), then it is the case that the supreme good is changed and corrupted through itself. Therefore the supreme essence—the supreme good—is something not at all good. Contradiction. No lesser nature, then, exists out of the supreme nature as matter.

We have therefore established that neither the supreme nature, nor the universe itself, nor anything else, is the matter out of which the universe exists. It is therefore clear that there is no matter out of which the universe exists.

So, whatever exists, exists through the supreme essence. Something exists through the supreme essence only if the supreme essence makes it, or if the supreme nature is the pre-existing matter. The necessary conclusion, therefore, is that, with the exception of the supreme essence itself, nothing exists that is not made by the supreme essence. The only things that exist, or have existed, are the supreme essence and the things made by the supreme essence. Therefore the supreme essence cannot have made anything through something else (i.e. using it as a tool or assistant)—it can only have acted through itself. Now there is no doubt that everything that the supreme essence made, it made either out of some matter, or out of nothing. But it is clearly, and most certainly, the case, first that the essence of everything that exists, apart from the supreme essence, is made by that supreme essence, and secondly, that it is made out of no material. It is therefore utterly evident, beyond a shadow of a doubt, that the supreme essence alone and through itself produced so much and so many things of such beauty—things so varied, yet ordered, so different, yet concordant—and produced them out of nothing.

8. *How to understand the creation of everything out of nothing*

But nothing gives us something of a problem. For when A is made out of B, B is a cause of A. And every cause contributes something to the essence of its effect. Everyone holds this to be true from experience, and cannot be argued or (at least most of them) inveigled out of it either by force or sleight of words. If, then, A is made out of nothing, nothing is a cause of A. But how can that which has no existence contribute to something's coming into existence? But if no contribution comes from nothing, who is going to be persuaded that something is effected out of nothing, and how?

Further: nothing either does or does not signify something. But if nothing is something, then what is made out of nothing is made from something. If, on the other hand, nothing is not something, then nothing comes to be out of nothing—since the thought that something should come out of what just does not exist is quite unintelligible. Nothing, as they say, will come of nothing.

It seems, then, to follow, that what comes to be, comes to be out of something. (Either, after all, out of something or out of nothing.) Whether, then, nothing is something or not, it seems to follow that whatever is made is made out of something. But if we set this down as true, then we upset everything that has already been established.

Hence nothing turns out to be something, and because of this the superlative something turns out to be nothing. What I mean is that I moved by a process of reasoning from the discovery of a superlatively existing substance to the conclusion that it made all other things, and made them from nothing. But if the nothing that it made them from is, in fact, something, then the tale I told about the supreme being . . . signifies nothing. What sense, then, are we to make of nothing? (I have already determined that I will leave nothing out of this meditation that could possibly present a problem, no matter how silly.)

There are, I think, three ways of taking the claim that a substance has been made out of nothing. First, when by 'it was made out of nothing' we mean 'it just was not made at all'. This is like answering 'nothing' when asked what a silent man is talking about, i.e. 'he is not talking'. What was the supreme essence made from? And that which just does not, and never did, exist—what was that made from? The correct answer to these questions is this sense of 'nothing', i.e. they just were not made at all. But this sense cannot be applied to any of those things that have been made. The second sense is when we really mean that it was made out of nothing, i.e. out of that which just does not exist at all. As if nothing were something that existed, out of which something could come into being. While this meaning can be expressed, it can never be true. And since it is always false, something impossible and inconsistent always follows every time it is asserted. Thirdly, we can mean that while something has indeed been made, there is not some thing from which it was made. This is like using the expression 'sad about nothing' of someone who is sad without a reason.

We concluded earlier that everything (except the supreme essence) is made out of nothing, i.e., not out of some thing. This conclusion followed consistently from its premises, and if we take it thus no inconsistency follows from it. We can use the expression 'made out of nothing' of things made by the creative substance—and we can do so without any inconsistency or contradiction whatsoever. Ordinary [Latin] language can talk of 'making a rich man out of a poor man' and of 'recovering one's health out of sickness'. The former refers to someone who has gone from rags to riches, i.e. someone who was formerly a pauper and is now a millionaire. He has become something which, before, he was not. The latter refers to someone who formerly had an illness, but who now has their health back. They now have something which, before, they did not.

'The creative essence made everything from nothing' and 'everything was made from nothing through the creative essence.' These claims are consistent and intelligible when understood in this sense, i.e., that which formerly was nothing, is now something. We say that it 'made' and that the others 'were made', and we understand that it made some thing, and that they were jolly well made to be some thing. Suppose that one man, A, has raised up another, B, from a humble position to great wealth and honour. We might say, referring to this, that A has made B from nothing and that B has been made by A from nothing, i.e., that he who before counted as nothing, is now, and through the action of B, thought to be really something.

9. *That before being made from nothing, they were not nothing—as far as the reason of the maker is concerned*

But I seem to see something which demands that we distinguish carefully the sense in which it is possible to say that created things were nothing before being created. For a maker makes something rationally if, and only if, there is already something there in his reasoning[3]—as a sort of exemplar. (Or perhaps terms like 'form', 'likeness' or 'rule' are more appropriate.) The following then is clear: before all things existed, the manner, features and fact of their future existence already existed, in the reasoning of the supreme nature. On the one hand, then, before being made, what was made was, clearly, nothing, inasmuch as it then was not what it now is, and inasmuch as there was nothing out of which it was made. Yet on the other hand, it was not nothing as far as the reason of the maker was concerned.

10. *This reasoning is the kind of verbalization of the object[4]*
    that a craftsman makes when he expresses in words to himself
    what he is going to make

But what is this form that is already there, in the maker's reasoning, before the things that are going to be created? Before a craftsman makes something by means of his craft, he first expresses it within himself by means of a mental conception. So, what is the form but this kind of verbalization of the things to be created in the maker's reason?

Now, there are linguistic signs which signify things, and we do, indeed, think with them. But this is not what I mean by the mind's or the reason's verbalization. What I mean is this: one sees the things themselves (whether they already exist or will, in the future, exist) in the mind by the eye of thought. Indeed ordinary usage recognizes three possible ways of expressing the same thing. First I can speak of a man, signifying him by the name 'man'. Secondly I can think the name 'man', but not say it aloud. Thirdly my mind can visualize the man himself. It can do so either by means of a bodily image (imagining, say, his perceptible shape), or by means of reason (thinking, say, of his universal essence—in this case 'rational mortal animal'). In the first case I am expressing something by means of perceptible signs. I am deploying, perceptibly, signs which the bodily senses can perceive. In the second case I am using the same outwardly perceptible signs, but I am thinking them, within myself, imperceptibly. In the third case I am not using these signs, either perceptibly or imperceptibly. I am expressing the thing itself inwardly within my

---

[3] Both 'reason' and 'reasoning' are used here to translate Anselm's *ratio*.
[4] 'Thing' and 'object' are used here to translate Anselm's *res*.

mind, either by imagination (in the case of bodily things) or by understanding (in the case of rational things).

Each of these three kinds of utterance consists of its own kind of word. The words of the third and last kind (since they express things that are known) are natural and the same for all peoples. It is because these words exist that all the other words have been invented. Hence, where there exists a natural word, one does not need any other word to pick the thing out, and where no natural word is possible, one cannot use any other word to point the thing out. We can also say without absurdity that natural words are truer, insofar as they resemble and designate their objects more manifestly. There are, of course, some things which we use as their own names to signify themselves, such as the vowel 'a'. But these are the exception. Apart from these, then, no other word appears so similar to and is so representative of its object, as this likeness by means of which the thing itself is represented to the thinking mind's eye. It is therefore the natural word that is correctly said to be the most proper and principal word for its object.

To conclude, then. There is no verbalization which gets as close to its object as that which consists in natural words. There is nothing in anyone's reason that can be as similar to any thing (be that thing future or present) as a natural word. Given this, it would seem possible that such a verbalization exists in the supreme substance, and that it existed before its objects, in order for things to be created through it, and which exists now, in order that through it things created may be known.

11. *There is, however, a lot of unlikeness in this likeness*

A craftsman first conceives in his mind what he is going to produce, and then produces it in accordance with that mental conception. Similarly, the supreme substance first said within itself, as it were, everything that it was going to create, and then brought it about in accordance with, and through, that inner verbalization. This we have agreed. I spy, however, a lot of unlikeness in this likeness.

A craftsman can only imagine bodily things on the basis of things he has already come across. And then he cannot realize his mental conception without material (or whatever is necessary to execute his plan). True, a human being can, indeed, come up with the thought or a picture of some animal that has never existed, but this can only be a composite of parts taken from other things experienced and remembered. But what did the supreme substance draw upon in order to sketch in itself the forms of what it was going to make? What did it requisition in order to make them into what they are? Absolutely nothing. This, then, is the difference between the inner verbalizations of the Creator substance and those of a craftsman: the former is neither taken from or given by anything external, and is the sole, sufficient and prime cause of its artificer's complete work of production. The latter is neither the prime, nor the sole, nor the sufficient cause—not even of the beginnings of its artificer's production. Therefore the creations of the supreme substance are what they are through the supreme substance alone. The creations of the craftsman, by contrast, would not exist at all unless they were something more than what they are through the craftsman.

12. *The supreme essence's word is the supreme essence*

The supreme substance has created everything through nothing other than itself. The supreme substance has created everything through its inner verbalization. (This is true, whether it creates individual things through individual words, or everything at once by speaking one word.) Given that these are equally certain, as reason has taught us, the supreme essence's verbalization is necessarily nothing other than the supreme essence. Can anything appear more necessary? It would be careless, therefore, not to stop and consider this verbalization. But if we are to go into it in depth, we must, I think, analyse some of the properties of this supreme substance.

13. *Through the supreme essence, all things flourish, just as they are created through it*

It is agreed, then, that whatever is not the same as the supreme nature was created through it. So then, only an unreasonable mind can doubt that all created things flourish and persist in their existence as long as they do, because they are sustained by what gave them that existence in the first place. The argument is simply the same as before. We have already reached the conclusion that all things that exist, exist through some one thing, and hence that this thing exists through itself while other things exist through something other than themselves. By the same argument it can be proved that all things that flourish, flourish through some one thing, and hence that this thing alone flourishes through itself while other things flourish through something other than themselves. This is the only possibility. Necessarily, therefore, nothing is created but through the creating and present essence. And just so, nothing flourishes but through this sustaining presence.

14. *The supreme essence is in and through all things. All things are through and in, and out of, the supreme essence*

And if so—no, rather, because it is necessarily so—it follows that where the supreme essence is not, there is nothing. The supreme essence, then, is everywhere. It is in and through all things. Now, no creature can, of course, go beyond the immensity of the Creator and Sustainer. And it would, thus, be absurd if the Creator and Sustainer were somehow prevented from transcending the totality of things made. Obviously, then, the supreme essence is what supports, overtops, encloses and pervades all other things. Add this to what we have already got, and: the very same thing is in and through all things, and is that out of, through, and in which all things are.

15. *What can and cannot be said about the supreme essence in terms of substance*

Of all the things that can be said of something, could any be appropriate to the substance of so wonderful a nature as this? This is the question to ask as carefully as possible at this point. I would be surprised if we could find anything from among the nouns and verbs which we apply to things created from nothing that could worthily be said of the substance that created all. None the less we must see where reason takes us.

Take relative terms then. No relative term applies in respect of substance to that of which it is said in respect of relation. No doubt about it. Something said, therefore, of the supreme nature in respect of relation does not signify its substance. Hence the mere fact that the supreme nature is greater than everything that it has created clearly does not specify its natural essence. For it is called 'greater' and 'supreme' in relation to other things, and, if they did not exist, it would not be intelligibly thought to be 'supreme' or 'greater than'. (But it would not be any less good, nor would its essential greatness be liable to any subtraction. This is because it is good and great through itself—not through something other than itself.) 'Supreme' therefore does not directly signify that essence which is, without qualification, greater and better than everything else. (Think of the nature that is, of all natures, the supreme. Now take away its being supreme. It is, nevertheless, still no greater and no less than it was.) And what goes for 'supreme' goes similarly for terms that are similarly relative.

No relational term, then, picks out the essence of anything without qualification. Let us therefore leave these to one side and turn our attention to other predicates. If one were to review each individually one could reach the following generalization. It is true of any non-relational predicate, P, that either P is better, without qualification, than not-P, or not-P is better, in some respect, than P. (I mean P and not-P to stand for things like 'true' and 'not true', 'body' and 'not-body', and so on.)[5]

P better without qualification than not-P: 'being wise' is better than 'not being wise'. The man who is wise is better than the man who is not wise. It may, of course, be true that a man who is just, although not wise, is better than a man who is unjust, but wise. This however, does not mean that the man who is not wise is better without qualification than the man who is wise. Indeed a not-wise X is always, insofar as it is not-wise, inferior without qualification to a wise X. And the same goes for 'true' and 'not-true', 'just' and 'not-just', 'living' and 'not-living'.

Not-P better in some respect than P: take gold, for example. It is better for a human being to be not gold than gold. Yet it may be better for something else, such as lead, to be gold than not gold. Neither the human nor lead are gold. The human is a better thing than gold insofar as the human is a superior nature. Likewise lead is worth less than gold, insofar as it would cost more if it were gold.

(There are, of course, plenty of relational predicates which do not fit into this scheme. As is clear from what we have just seen in the

---

[5] Anselm does not use symbolic devices to explain himself here or elsewhere in the *Monologion*. They have been added to assist the modern reader.

case of the supreme nature: the supreme (P) nature is not better in every way than the not-supreme (not-P) nature. The not-supreme (not-P) nature is not better in some respect than the supreme (P) nature. Are there at least some that do fit the scheme? I am not going to go into this question, since I already know all I need to know for the matter in hand: no relational predicate picks out the unqualified substance of the supreme nature.)

So then, for any non-relational predicate, P, either P is better than not-P, or not-P is better in some respect than P. Now it is quite out of bounds to imagine that there could be some P true of the substance of the supreme nature such that not-P would be better in some respect. So, in the same way, the supreme nature necessarily is any P that is better without qualification than not-P. This is because the substance of the supreme nature alone is better than everything else. It is that than which absolutely nothing is better.

Therefore it is not a body. Nor is it anything that can be perceived by the senses of the body. For there is something other than what they are that is better: namely, the rational mind. What the rational mind is, bodily sense does not perceive, nor what kind of thing it is, nor how great it is. Suppose it were an object of sense perception, how inferior would it be then! That is how much greater it is than any bodily object.

So, do not say that the supreme essence is one of those things than which something else is superior, and do say that it is one of those things than which everything else is inferior. This reason has taught us. The necessary conclusion is then: the supreme essence is alive, wise, powerful, all-powerful, true, just, happy, eternal . . . and whatever is likewise better without qualification than not-whatever. What the supreme nature, then, is and what it is not (of all the things that it might be) is now evident. Have I not got to the bottom of the 'what is it?' question?

16. *For the supreme nature, to be just is the same as to be justice. And the same goes for what can be said in the same way about it. But none of these terms answers the 'what kind?' and 'how great?' questions—only the 'what is it?' question*

But perhaps terms such as 'just' and 'great' do not pinpoint what the supreme nature is so much as tell us what kind of thing it is (its 'quality') and how great it is (its 'quantity'). For such terms would, after all, seem to be predicated through a quality or quantity. For it is through justice that what is just is just. And so on. Through justice, therefore, the supreme nature is just, and not otherwise. It would seem, then, that the supremely good substance is called 'just' by its participating in a quality (in this case, justice), rather than through itself.

But this is contrary to the already ascertained truth. The supreme nature is what it is—good, great, existing—precisely through itself and nothing else. So then, it is just through justice and it is just through itself. And if so, then what is more necessarily and clearly the case than that the supreme nature is justice itself? Thus 'just through justice' is and means the same as 'just through itself', and vice versa. And so if you ask 'what is this supreme nature we are talking about?', you may answer 'justice'. What could be truer?

What, then, does it mean to call this nature, justice itself, just? Now, since a man cannot be, but may possess, justice, a just man is intelligibly thought of not as 'being justice' but as 'possessing justice'. And since the supreme nature is strictly said not to possess, but to be, justice, when it is said to be just strictly it is intelligibly thought of as 'being justice', and not as 'possessing justice'. And if 'being justice' expresses what it is (and not a quality), then it follows that 'just' expresses what it is (and not a quality).

Further, it makes no difference whether it is said to be 'just' or 'justice'. This is because to say of the supreme essence that it is 'just' is the same as to say that it is 'being justice'. And 'it is being justice' is the same as 'it is justice'. And so when asked what the supreme nature is, 'just' is as appropriate an answer as 'justice'.

Justice is but one instance. The same conclusion applies to everything else that can be said in the same way of the supreme nature. Reason compels understanding to see this. All of these terms, then, indicate not a quality or quantity, but what the supreme nature is. And clearly any good thing that the supreme nature is, it is that thing supremely. It is, therefore, supreme essence, supreme life, supreme reason, supreme health, supreme justice, supreme wisdom, supreme truth, supreme goodness, supreme greatness, supreme beauty, supreme immortality, supreme incorruptibility, supreme immutability, supreme happiness, supreme eternity, supreme power, supreme

Monologion

unity. And all this is nothing other than being supremely, and living supremely. And so on.

17. *The supreme nature is simple: thus all the things which can be said of its essence are simply one and the same thing in it. And things can only be said of it in respect of substance with respect to what it is*

So the supreme nature is many good things. Is it then a composite of these many good things? Or is it not rather one good thing, signified by many names?

A composite requires, for its existence, its components and owes its being what it is to them. It is what it is through them. They, however, are not what they are through it. A composite, therefore, just is not supreme. If, then, the supreme nature is a composite of many goods, what belongs to a composite necessarily belongs to it also. But truth's whole and already manifest necessity destroys and overthrows by clear reason this, falsehood's blasphemy.

Since, then, the supreme nature is not composite at all, and yet really is all those good things, it is necessary that all those good things are not many, but one. So any one of them is the same thing as all of them (the same thing as all together and as each individually). So to call the supreme nature 'justice' or 'essence' signifies the same thing as the others (together and individually). So whatever is predicated of the supreme substance with respect to essence is one single thing. And just so, therefore, whatever the supreme substance is, it is with respect to essence, in one and the same way and respect.

Now a human being is said to be a body and rational and a human being. But these three things are not predicated in one and the same respect. A human being is a body in one sense, and rational in another. And neither of these on its own is the whole of what a human being is. The supreme nature, however, is not such as to be both X and, in another sense or respect, not-X. This is because what it is in respect of essence in any way, does add up to the whole of what it is.

Nothing, then, that is predicated truly of its essence is to be taken as a predicate of quality, or quantity, but of what it is. For anything that is of quality X or quantity Y is different in respect of what it is, and hence is not simple but a composite.

18. *Without beginning, without end*

This simple nature, that creates and sustains all things—when did it begin? When will it end? Or is it, rather, without beginning or end?

If it has a beginning, then it has it either out of (or through) itself, or out of (or through) something else, or out of (or through) nothing. In no way, however, is it out of (or through) something else. In no way is it out of (or through) nothing. This I have already established here. In no way, therefore, did it get a beginning out of (or through) something else, or out of (or through) nothing.

But, while it does exist out of (and through) itself, it cannot have its beginning out of (or through) itself. This is because its existing out of (and through) itself means that it exists out of (and through) no other essence. But if A begins to be out of (and through) B, B must be some thing other than A. The supreme nature, therefore, does not begin to be out of (or through) itself. So we have excluded all three possibilities (nothing, something else, and itself). Therefore it does not have a starting point at all.

Nor will it come to an end. For if it has an end, it is not supremely immortal or supremely incorruptible. But it is supremely immortal and incorruptible. (This has already been ascertained.) Therefore it does not have an end.

Another argument: if it has an end it is going to come to that end whether it wants to or not. But, indeed, that which wills the demise of the supreme good is no unalloyed good. But the supreme good is true and simple good. Therefore the supreme good does not come to an end of its own accord. And if it expires unwillingly? Then it is not supremely powerful or omnipotent. But rational necessity has already asserted that it is supremely powerful and omnipotent. Therefore it does not come to an end unwillingly. So if the supreme nature does not have an end either willingly or unwillingly, there is no way that it can have an end.

A further argument: if the supreme nature has either beginning or end, it is not true eternity. But that it is true eternity is something that we have already found out and it is quite irrefutable.

Further, try to think of an answer to this: 'X is going to happen in the future'; assuming this to be true, when does it start being true? When was it ever false? 'X is going to have happened.' Again, assuming this statement is true, when will it cease being true? There is no conceivable time 'when'. Add to this the fact that neither statement can be true without truth. Conclusion: Truth has no conceivable beginning or end.

Finally, suppose that truth did begin and is going to come to an end. In this case, before truth began it was true, then, that truth did not exist. And, after it has expired, it will, then, be true that truth will not exist. But the true cannot be true without truth. As a consequence, there was truth before truth was, and there will be truth after truth has come to an end. Quite a contradiction. Whether, therefore, we are talking about what we may say (that truth does come to a beginning or an end), or about what we may intelligibly think (that truth does not come to a beginning or an end), truth is not circumscribed by beginning and ending. And since it is supreme truth, this conclusion applies also to the supreme nature.

19. *Nothing before, nothing after*

But, again, nothing raises its head and alleges that everything that reason, truth, and necessity have together affirmed, is nothing. For if our results stand secure, fortified in the fastness of necessary truth, then it is the case that, before the supreme essence there was not, and after it there will not be, anything. And so there is nothing before, and will be nothing after it. (For necessarily either something or nothing precedes or follows it.)

But if you say that nothing was before it and nothing will be after it, you seem to be suggesting that there was a time, before the supreme essence, when nothing existed, and there will be a time after it when nothing will exist, i.e. nothing exists when the supreme essence does not exist. And how, then, does it not begin out of nothing, how does it not end up as nothing—given that when nothing already existed, it did not yet exist, given that when it no longer exists, nothing will still exist?

Have we raised up so mighty an argumentative structure only to see it effortlessly razed to the ground by nothing? Only decide that the supreme being follows on from, and gives way to, nothing, and the necessary truths already determined will all be undermined— and all by an aimless nothingness. Must we not rather strike back against nothing, lest it strike down what necessary reason has constructed? Lest the supreme good, which we sought and found by the light of truth, be lost for nothing? Indeed, rather than allowing some space for nothing before and after the supreme essence, it would be better to assert that there is not nothing before and after—if this is possible. Otherwise we bring to nothing, through nothing, that being which, through itself, brought what was nothing into being.

Now, the statement 'Nothing was before the supreme essence' has two senses. It can be taken to mean either: 'There was a time, before the supreme essence existed, when there was nothing,' or: 'There was not anything before the supreme essence.' An example: I say 'Nothing has taught me to fly'. Now I can interpret this as the— false—assertion, 'Nothing itself taught me to fly' ('nothing' here signifying 'not-something'). Alternatively I can interpret it as the— true—denial, 'It is not the case that something taught me to fly'. Our problem follows from the first interpretation. But this is the interpretation that reason always resists on the grounds that it is false. The second interpretation, however, fits unproblematically with our previous conclusions. Indeed as a whole they insist that it is true. So the claim 'nothing was before the supreme being' must be taken in the second way. It must not be taken to mean that there was a time when the supreme being did not, and when nothing did, exist. On the contrary, it means that before the supreme being it was not the case that there was something. And the same double meaning applies to the claim that nothing will exist after the supreme being.

So discriminate carefully the senses of nothing in this way, and you will reach deduction not destruction, our argument's solidity, not nothing's inanity: that neither nothing, nor something, went before or will come after the supreme essence; and that nothing existed before or will exist after it—this will be totally true.

20. *In every place and time*

The creative nature exists everywhere, in everything and through everything. This we have already concluded. That it always has existed, always exists, and always will exist, follows from its neither starting nor ceasing to exist. But listen! I think I hear the distant rumble of a contradiction. We must be more careful about the where and when of its existence.

The supreme essence exists either everywhere and always (i.e. in every place and time), or only somewhere and sometime (i.e. limited to some place and some time), or nowhere and never (i.e. in no place or time).

Never and nowhere? But it is that which exists supremely and most truly. A straightforward antithesis. 'Never and nowhere' must be false. Another argument: nothing is good, indeed nothing exists at all, without the supreme being. If, then, it exists never and nowhere, nothing will ever or anywhere be a good thing, or indeed be a thing at all. No need to explain the falsity of this conclusion, 'never and nowhere' is therefore false.

Is it, then, limited to somewhere and sometime, or is it everywhere and always? Suppose it is in some particular place and time. Now, something else is only able to exist where and when the supreme essence exists—there is absolutely no essence where and when it does not exist. This is because without it absolutely nothing exists. The consequence of the supposition: there is some place and some time where, and when, absolutely nothing exists. But this is false— because time is a thing and place is a thing. The supreme nature, therefore, cannot be limited to some place and time.

What about saying that it is limited to some place and time, through itself, but that through its power it exists wherever and whenever anything exists? Not true. Its power is not something different from itself. This is clear. No way, then, can there be its power without itself.

It does not exist, therefore, limited to some place and time. It must be the case, then, that it exists everywhere and always (i.e. in every place and time).

21. *In no place or time*

If it is the case that it exists in every time and place, then either the whole or part of it does. (And in the latter case the rest of it would exist outside every time and place.)

Now if part of it is in every time and place and part is not, then it has parts, which is false. It does not, therefore, partly exist in every time and place.

How then does it exist everywhere and always as a whole? There are two ways of taking this. (1) It exists as a whole only in the sum of all places and times, but in individual places and times it exists through its parts. (2) It exists as a whole both in the sum of all and in each individual place and time.

However, existing in individual times and places through its parts means that it does not escape being liable to division and composition. But we have already discovered that this is quite foreign to the supreme nature. Part (1), therefore, does not apply to the supreme nature. This leaves part (2) for consideration: how does the supreme nature exist in the sum of all and in each individual place and time? And it must do so either at the same or at different times.

So far we have been able to pursue our investigation taking time and place together. But now the laws of time and place seem to separate and thus slip, as it were, through our fingers. Let us therefore investigate them both individually. Let us first ask about individual places: can the supreme nature exist as a whole in individual places, either at one and the same time, or through different times? Then ask the same question about individual times.

Suppose it exists as a whole in individual places at one and the same time. Then you would have individual wholes throughout the individual places. One place is distinct from another (that is why they are individual places). But likewise, that which exists as a whole in one place is distinct from that which exists as a whole in another at the same time (so you get several individual wholes). But how can something be a whole in one place, and simultaneously be a whole in another place as well?

Proof that a whole has no parts which are simultaneously in a different place: take something that is whole, W, in some place, P. Now, nothing of W is not in P. Now take something, W′, such that nothing from W′ is not in some place P′: nothing from W′ is, at the same time, outside P′. It follows, then, that nothing of a whole, W, in a place, P, is at the same time outside P. Further, take this thing, W, such that nothing from it is outside some place, P: nothing of W will be, at the same time, in a place other than P (i.e. not-P). Therefore: nothing of a whole, W, in a place, P, is simultaneously in a place other than P.

How, then, can something be a whole in one place, and simultaneously be a whole in another place as well? (Nothing, after all, from it can be in another place.) One whole, therefore, cannot be simultaneously in several places as a whole. It follows, then, that if there is a whole in several individual places at the same time, then there is one individual whole for each of the several individual places. Suppose, then, the supreme nature exists as a whole at one and the same time in all the individual places. In this case there are as many individual supreme natures as there are individual places—an unreasonable thing to think. The supreme nature, therefore, does not exist as a whole in individual places at one time.

But suppose it does so at different times. In this case when it is in one place, in the meantime nothing good, indeed, no existence, can exist in the other places. (This is because things do not exist without it.) Absurd—as is guaranteed by the places themselves: they are not nothing, they exist. Not, then, at different times. Neither, then, at the same time nor at different times. Clearly therefore the supreme nature does not exist as a whole in individual things in any way at all.

Next question: times. Does the supreme nature exist as a whole in individual times? Does it do so simultaneously or distinctly throughout individual times?

But how can something exist as a whole simultaneously in individual times, unless those times are simultaneous? Suppose, on the other hand, that it exists as a whole in individual times severally and distinctly. (A human being, for instance, exists as a whole yesterday, today and tomorrow.) In this case we should, properly, say that it was, is and will be. In which case its time-span is not simultaneously a whole. Rather it is stretched out in parts through the parts of time. But its time-span is its eternity and its eternity is precisely itself. The supreme essence, therefore, would be cut up into parts along the divisions of time. For if its life span is drawn out along the course of time, it must have, as time does, a present, past and future. But what is its life span, the duration of its existence, but its eternity? So, since its eternity is nothing but its essence (as proved above), if its eternity has past, present, and future, then its essence also must have past, present, and future. And what is past is not present or future; what is present is neither future nor past; what is future is neither past nor present. But if it is one thing at one time, and a different thing at another, if it has parts scattered about throughout time, how will what rational and transparent necessity has already made clear still be true? I refer, of course, to the fact that the supreme nature is not composite, but supremely simple and supremely unchangeable.

Or rather, put it this way: if our earlier results are true—no, rather—given that they are clearly true, how are our latest results possible? Creative essence, its life span, its eternity, just does not admit of a past or future. For it must have a present—it is, after all, true. But 'was' indicates the past, and 'will be' indicates the future. Therefore the supreme essence never was, and never will be. Therefore not only does it not exist as a whole in different individual times, but also, it does not exist in different individual times severally.

To conclude, then. There is no way for the supreme essence to exist as a whole in every place and time. This is clear from our rejection of the two ways possible: first, that it exists as a whole in all times and places taken together, and in individual times and places through its parts. Secondly, that it exists as a whole in each individual time and place.

Similarly we have seen that it is not the case that part of it is in, while part of it is outside, every place and time. It only makes sense to think of it existing everywhere and always either as a whole or in part. Hence it is quite impossible for it to exist everywhere and always. It must, as a result, be either limited to some place and time, or in no place or time. We have already ruled out its being limited. So then it must be in no place or time. That is, it never and nowhere exists. (In order to exist, you see, it would have to exist in some time, or in every time.)

But then again, there is the irrefutable truth that it does exist through itself, without beginning, and without end. More than this, nothing ever, or anywhere, exists without it. Necessarily then it exists everywhere and always.

22. *How it is both in every place and time and in none*

Contradictory language—but ineluctable logic! How to reconcile all this? Well, perhaps there is a way for the supreme nature to exist in place and time. Perhaps it can exist as a whole in individual places and times, without there being lots of wholes, and without its life span (which is nothing other than true eternity) being divided into past, present and future.

For it would seem that only things that are limited to the time and place they are in are bound by the law of time and place. To such the rule that 'one and the same whole cannot simultaneously be a whole in several times and places' applies. But we are not necessarily confined to conclude this of things that are not so limited. It would seem to be within the letter of this law to say: 'X has a place if that place contains the extent of X by circumscribing it and circumscribes it by containing it.' And 'X has a time only if that time somehow delimits the duration of X by measuring it, and measures it by delimiting it.' So then, if we can adduce no limit to the spatial and temporal extent of Y, we may deduce that Y has no place or time. Place does not place it, time does not time it. So, we may reasonably say, its place is no place and its time no time. Now, to have been discovered not to possess time or place, is immediately to have been declared free from the jurisdiction of the time and place. What, therefore, no time or place defines, space and time do not confine.

The creator of all substances, the supreme substance, is necessarily free from the natures and laws of everything it has created from nothing. It is not subject to them. Is it then under the rules and regulations of time and place? All rational reflection, for every sort of reason, rules this out. Rather its power—and its power is just its essence—rules over and regulates everything it has made.

To say that some place circumscribes the extent of supreme truth, and that some time measures its duration—how brash, how rash! Supreme truth does not admit at all of the big and small, the long and the short, which belong to spatial and temporal distension.

This, then, is what time and space stipulate: that (and only that) which is enclosed in their limits, neither escapes the logic of (spatial and temporal) parts and wholes, nor exists as a whole in more than one place and time simultaneously. But as for what the long arm of space and time law does not encircle: this is neither condemned to the multiplicity of having parts, nor prohibited from being present as a whole in more than one place and time simultaneously.

Since, as I say, this is what time and space stipulate, I do not doubt that the supreme substance is exempt. No time or place, after all, contains it. Now, ineluctable necessity demands that the supreme essence be absent from no place or time. And, further, no space and time legality prohibits it from being present at every place and time simultaneously. I conclude, therefore, that it is necessary that it be present as a whole simultaneously to all places and times, and to each individual place and time.

It is not prohibited from being present simultaneously and similarly to place C and time D, just because it is present to place A and time B. Nor does part of its eternity leak away with the past into non-existence, or fly past, like the scarcely existing momentary present, or, with the future, wait, pending, in not-yet existence—just because it is, was and will be. That which does not commit its existence to a place and time is neither forbidden nor obliged, by the law of space and time, to be, or not to be, in some place and time.

Now we do say that the supreme essence is in place and time. But this is language we use of things which have their being in time and space. We use this language because it is ordinary language. Its significance, however, is different in each case. This is because what the language is about is different in each case. Used of temporal and spatial natures, it signifies two things. Namely, first, that they are present to the times and places they are said to be in, and secondly, that they are contained by these times and places. Used of the supreme essence, however, only the first applies, i.e., that it is present: that it is contained, does not.

So then, if ordinary usage allowed it, it would seem to be more appropriate to say that the supreme essence is with rather than in a place and time. ('In' having more of a sense of 'being contained by' than 'with'.) If we speak properly, on the other hand, we say that it is in no place or time. This is because it just is not contained by anything other than itself. And yet it may still be said to be in each and every place and time in its own way. This is because by its presence it sustains everything other than itself, preventing everything from falling into nothingness. It is in every place and time because it is absent from none. It is in no place or time because it has no place or time. It does not undergo spatial or temporal division: not here, there or somewhere; not now, not then, not whenever. It is, but it is not present—not our transient present. It was, but not in the past. It will be, but not in the future. For present, past and future belong to mutable things, to delimited things. Which it is not. And yet these things can still be said of it in some sense, since it is present to all delimited and mutable things as if delimited by the same places and changed by the same times.

The supreme essence, therefore, is always and everywhere and never and nowhere. It is in every place and every time and in no place and no time. Just how it is both, this we have now got clear about—

clear enough, at least, to have got rid of the rumble of contradiction, by distinguishing truth's harmony in the different senses of what we say.

23. *Why 'everywhere' makes better sense than 'in every place'*

The supreme nature exists in everything that exists, just as much as it exists in every place. It is not contained, but contains all, by permeating all. This we know. Why not say, then, that it is 'everywhere' (meaning in everything that exists) rather than 'in every place'. The intellect hereby grasps the clear truth about the object, without violating the proper use of locational words.

Locational language is often applied unobjectionably to things that are neither locations nor contained by locational circumscription. Thus I would say that where rationality is in the soul, there is the intellect. 'There' and 'where' are locational words, but the soul does not contain anything, nor are the intellect and rationality contained, by locational circumscription. 'Everywhere', then, in the sense of 'in everything that exists' is, as regards the truth, the more appropriate thing to say of the supreme nature.

And the supreme nature, as we have already learnt, cannot be other than as it is. Necessarily, therefore it is in all things that exist in such a way that it is in each individual thing as a whole, as one and the same, perfectly and simultaneously.

24. *Why 'always' makes better sense than 'in every time'*

We also know that the supreme substance is without beginning or end. It has no past, or future. It has no temporal present (not, that is, the transitory present that we experience). Its life span—its eternity—which is simply itself, is unalterable and partless. Suppose, then, we use the word 'always' of the supreme substance, a word which would seem to indicate the whole of time. Is this term not more accurately used here if taken to indicate 'eternity' rather than 'time passing'? Eternity is never unlike itself, but time passing is always, in some respect, unlike itself. Suppose, then, we say that it always exists. What we take this to mean, then, is that it exists eternally. And since for it to exist is to be alive, that it lives eternally. It has, that is, unending life, perfectly, simultaneously and as a whole. Nothing makes better sense. It would seem that its eternity is life unending, simultaneous, whole, and perfectly existing. Now its substance simply is its life, and its life simply is its eternity. Its eternity is quite without end; it is nothing but simultaneous and perfect existence. This is already sufficiently clear. True eternity, the eternity that applies to this one substance alone—what is it if it is not life unending, simultaneous, whole, and perfectly existing? True eternity pertains to one substance only—the uncreated Creator, a point that may be clearly appreciated from this one consideration alone: true eternity lacks the limits of beginning and end, which is something that does not apply to created things, precisely because they are created from nothing.

25. *That it is not alterable in terms of accidents*

This essence is, as is clear, entirely the same as itself, substantially. But is it not sometimes different from itself in terms of its accidents? Suppose you could even think of it as mutable (quite apart, I mean, from supposing it to be mutable). How would it, then, be supremely unalterable? But, on the other hand, does it not have accidents? It is, after all, greater than all other natures, and dissimilar to them, both of which would seem to be accidental to it.

Suppose that there are some accidents which, when taken on by a substance, do not entail any change in that substance. Being subject to such accidents would not negate the immutability of a nature. We may indeed divide all accidents into two kinds. There are those whose presence or absence implies some change in the subject: e.g. all colours. Others cause no change in that of which they are predicated: e.g. some relations.

Take someone who is going to be born next year. At the moment I am not taller than him, or smaller than him; nor the same height as, or similar to, him. When he is born, however, I will be able to have, and to lose, all these relations, without my changing at all, insofar as he grows and changes through different qualities. Some accidents, then, bring alterability with them in some respect. And other accidents do not take away inalterability in any respect whatsoever.

There is nothing, therefore, that can be accidental to the essence of the supreme nature so as to allow us to infer mutability. Sometimes, true, something may be predicated of it, in line with those accidents that do not impugn supreme immutability. This the supreme nature allows, just as it, in its simplicity, never allows room to any accident that causes change. Hence the further conclusion: it is not subject to any accident. Accidents that effect change really are accidents. In virtue of their effect they happen to the things they change.[6] Those, however, that do not have this effect are only accidents improperly so called.

The supreme essence is, therefore, never different from itself, not even accidentally. Just as substantially, it is always the same as itself. Whatever the rules are for using the term 'accident' properly, this is true and beyond doubt: nothing may be predicated of the supreme and immutable nature which might suggest that it is mutable.

26. *How it is to be called a substance. That it is beyond every substance. That it is what it is uniquely*

How is the supreme nature a substance, if what we have found out about its simplicity is true? Every substance has accidents and distinguishing features[7] (the former changing it, the latter being added on to it and combined with it). The supreme nature is, however, pure and unchangeable, and as such immune to combination and change. How then can we assert that it is a substance? Only if the term 'substance' is really standing in for 'essence'—the supreme essence being beyond, just as it is above, every substance. For there is, on the one hand, that essence which is what it is through itself, and which creates every other essence from nothing. And there is, on the other, that essence which becomes what it is from nothing through the action of something other than itself. The difference between these two is the distance between the supreme substance and the substances that are not as it is. Alone of all natures, the supreme nature has its being-what-it-is from itself—without the help of another nature. How, then, is it not unique? How can its being-what-it-is have

---

[6] 'Happen' here translates *accidere* which is the verb related to the noun *accidens* (plural: *accidentia*), here translated 'accident'.

[7] 'Distinguishing features' here translates *differentiae*.

anything in common with its creatures? Thus, while the same name (substance) may sometimes be shared by both, what it signifies must be understood in different ways.

27. *The general analysis of substance does not cover the supreme substance. Yet it is a substance and an individual spirit*

This, then, is established: a general analysis of substance does not include that substance whose essence is special and exclusive, having nothing in common with that of other natures. Now, substance is analysed into universal substance and individual substance. A universal substance is one whose essence is shared by several substances. Thus being human is what individual humans have in common. An individual substance shares in a universal essence. Thus individual humans share with individual humans their being human. But the supreme nature can neither be divided into several substances, nor can it be lumped together with other things in virtue of any shared essence. How then can one make sense of it as something included in the analysis of other substances? Nevertheless it most certainly exists. Indeed it exists supremely. And we do usually call the essence of anything a substance. And so, if any term is worth using at all, we may be allowed the term substance.

Now, we know no essence worth more than spirit or body, and of the two, spirit is worth more than body. Therefore we should assert that it is spirit rather than body. And since this spirit has no parts, and since there cannot be more than one of it, it is necessarily an individual spirit. And its absolute indivisibility can be concluded from what we have already established. Namely, that it is not composed of parts, and that it cannot make sense to think of it as changeable in virtue of distinguishing features and accidents.

28. *This spirit exists unqualifiedly. Compared to it, created things do not exist*

Thus this spirit exists in its own wonderfully unique and uniquely wonderful way. Indeed, it would seem to follow from the foregoing that this spirit is, for some reason, the only thing that exists: other things that seem to exist, in comparison, do not exist. It is the only thing that would seem, on careful examination, to exist without qualification, perfectly and absolutely, while all other things almost do not, and hardly do, exist.

Its immutable eternity means that it exists without qualification: you cannot talk of change, that it 'was' or 'will be'. It does not exist in a changeable way. It is not now something that it has not been, or will not be. It is not now not something that it has been, or will be. But it is what is, once, simultaneously and unendingly. And since, as I say, such is its being, it is correctly said to be without qualification, absolutely and perfectly.

As for all other things, it is correct to deny that they exist absolutely perfectly, and without qualification. It is correct to assert that they almost do not, and hardly do, exist. This is because they exist in a changeable way: in some respect they now are not what they were, or will be, and are what they have not been, or will not be. What they were, no longer exists. What they will be, does not yet exist. What they are in the fleeting, extremely brief and barely existing present, barely exists.

Again, all things that are other than this spirit, come into being from non-being, and through something other than themselves. And they return from being into non-being (as far as they themselves are concerned) unless sustained through something else. How does this fit with existing 'without qualification, perfectly and absolutely' rather than with 'almost not, and hardly'? Unqualified, perfect and absolute existence: does this not belong to the ineffable spirit alone? How can you make sense of it otherwise, given that you cannot make sense of the ineffable spirit (only the ineffable spirit) as something that arises out of non-being, or is able to sink from what it is into non-being; given that it is what-it-is, through what-it-is (i.e. not through something other than itself, but through itself).

It is perfect, unqualified and absolute. It is so unqualifiedly. It is so for every reason. It is so alone. Indisputably, then, there is a sense in which it can correctly be said to be the only thing that exists. By contrast, we have, through our foregoing reasoning, recognized things which do not exist without qualification, which do not exist perfectly, which do not exist absolutely, but which exist hardly and almost not. There is, then, a sense in which to say that all such things do not exist is right. For this reason, therefore, only the Creator spirit exists, and all created things do not exist. Its not that they just do not exist, however. They have been made into something from nothing, through the only thing that exists absolutely.

29. *Its verbalization is the same thing as itself. Yet they are not two spirits, but one spirit*

So far, following reason's lead, I have been working through the properties of the supreme nature. It is now, I think, the right moment to investigate, if I am able, the supreme nature's verbalization, through which all things were created. All the points that I have already been able to make about this verbalization have reason's unbending strength behind them. Nevertheless I am driven to go into it more carefully because it turns out that the supreme spirit's verbalization is the same thing as the supreme spirit. For if the spirit has created nothing but what it has created through itself, and if whatever has been created by the spirit has been created through its verbalization, then how is its verbalization anything other than what it is?

Further, what we have already discovered adds up to the following incontrovertible assertion: the only things that have ever been able to exist at all are the creating spirit and its creation. But you cannot possibly count the spirit's verbalization as something created. This is because everything created was made through it, and it cannot have been made through itself. And this is because nothing can be made through itself: whatever something is made into is later than that through which it is made, and nothing is later than itself. Therefore the verbalization of the supreme spirit cannot be a creature. This only leaves the possibility that it is nothing other than the supreme spirit.

Moreover we can only understand it as the spirit's understanding, the understanding by which it understands all things. When the spirit says something, in this kind of putting something into words, does it do anything other than understand it? It always says what it understands (unlike human beings). If, therefore, the supremely simple nature is the same thing as its understanding and wisdom, then, necessarily and likewise it is the same thing as its verbalization. And since it is already clear that the supreme spirit is just one complete individual, necessarily its verbalization is consubstantial with it. So there are not two spirits, but one spirit.

30. *This verbalization is not made up of several words, but is one Word*

This, then, resolves a question that I left open earlier: does this verbalization consist in several words, or in one? If it is consubstantial with the supreme nature, so that there is one spirit, not two, it is therefore as supremely simple as the supreme nature. Therefore it is not made up from several words. There is only one Word through which all things were made.

31. *The Word is not a likeness of created things, but is the truth of what is. It is created things that are imitations—imitations of the truth. Which natures are greater than, and more excellent than, others*

But this raises a further question. Not an easy question, but one we cannot leave undecided. All words of this kind, the kind we use to say things in our mind (i.e. to think), are likenesses and images of the things that they are the words of. And the degree of truth of every likeness and image depends on the degree of its imitation of its object. But what about the Word which says everything and through which everything was made? Is it, or is it not, a likeness of things made through it? For if it were a true likeness of mutable things, it would not be consubstantial with supreme immutability. Which would be false. But if it were not a completely true likeness (of mutable things), then the word of supreme truth would not be completely true. Which is absurd. And if it were not a likeness of mutable things at all, how could it be the model by which they were made?

Perhaps we may decide the question in the following way. Truth, we usually say, is in the sitter while the likeness and image of that truth is in the portrait. What if we took it that likewise, the truth is in the Word, and the imitation in created things? The essence of the Word exists supremely, so that, in some sense, it is the only thing that exists. Created things, by comparison, do not exist. Nevertheless they are created through and according to the Word. The truth of what exists is in the Word, and imitation of the supreme essence in created things. Thus it is not the Word (and the Word of the supreme truth is the supreme truth) that suffers increase or decrease in accordance with the degree of its similarity to creation, but the

other way round. Necessarily, for every creature, the degree of greatness of its existence and the degree of comparative excellence of
its existence is the degree of its similarity to that which exists
supremely, and is supremely great.

Perhaps this is why—no, rather, this certainly is why, everyone
with understanding ranks living natures (in whatever form) above
non-living, perceptive above non-perceptive, and rational above non-
rational. For the supreme nature does not just exist, it also lives,
senses and is rational in its own unique way. Clearly, then, of everything that exists, the living (in whatever form) are more similar to
the supreme nature than the non-living; and so too, the perceiving
(even things that perceive with bodily senses) more than the completely non-perceptive, and the rational more than things incapable
of reason. And for a similar reason, the same clearly goes for existence: some natures exist more than others. For a nature's comparative existence is the comparative similarity of its essence to the
supreme essence, in just the same way as its comparative excellence
is its comparative proximity, through its natural essence, to superlative excellence.

The point is easily grasped. Look at it this way: take a substance,
any substance, that lives, perceives and is rational. Now subtract, in
thought, first its rationality, then its perception, and then its life.
Take away finally the bare existence that is left. Who does not understand that the step by step dismantling of this substance is its reduc-
tion to gradually less existence, and ultimately to non-existence? And
the steps down to gradually less existence are the steps back up to
gradually more. So the living clearly exist more than the non-living,
the perceptive more than the non-perceptive, and the rational more
than the non-rational. There is no doubt then: for any essence to
exist more, and to exist more excellently, is precisely for it to be more
similar to that essence which exists and excels supremely. And this,
then, is quite clear enough: what is in the Word through which all
things were made is not the likeness to all things, but true and simple
essence. What is in the things made, on the other hand, is not simple
and absolute essence, but a pale imitation of it. Necessarily, as a
result, the Word is not more or less true, depending on its likeness
to created things. Rather it would seem that every created nature
stands at a higher stage of essence and worth the more it approxi-
mates to the Word.

32. *That the supreme spirit says itself with its coeternal Word*

Given all this, how can this simple truth be the Word for that of
which it is not the likeness? A word, of course, by which a thing is
said in the mind, is the likeness of that thing. So if it is not the word
for the things made through it, in what sense is it a word? A word,
after all, is a word for a thing. Indeed, if there was not a creature,
there would not be a word for it. What then? Should we conclude
that if no creature at all had ever existed, the Word would not have
existed at all? But this Word is the supreme and self-sufficient
essence. Or perhaps we should say that if nothing had ever been
created through the supreme essence, while the supreme essence
would not be a word, it would still be an eternal essence? You cannot
have a word for what does not exist, has not existed, and is not ever
going to exist.

However if we follow this reasoning through we reach utter absurdity. Suppose that no essence were to exist, apart from the supreme
spirit. Then there would be a word in it. True, but if there was not
a word in the supreme spirit, then it would not say anything to itself.
And if it did not say anything to itself, it would not understand anything. (For the supreme spirit, to say something is to understand it.)
And if it understood nothing, then, since the supreme spirit is
supreme wisdom, supreme wisdom would understand nothing.
Absurd! How could it be the supreme wisdom if it understood
nothing? And if there were nothing apart from the supreme wisdom,
what would there be for it to understand?

But would it not understand itself? Is it possible even to conceive
of supreme wisdom not understanding itself? The rational mind is
able, after all, to be conscious[8] both of itself and also of supreme
wisdom, and it can think intelligibly of both. (Moreover, if the
human mind could not, it could not tell itself apart from irrational
creatures by the kind of silent solitary self-argument that my mind
is now engaged in.)

Like the rational mind, therefore, the supreme spirit is conscious
of and understands itself. And, as it exists eternally, it does so eternally. (No, I take that back, the supreme spirit is not like anything.
It is the original. It is the rational mind that is like the supreme
spirit.) And if it understands itself eternally, it says itself eternally.

---

[8] Anselm's *memoria* and related words are generally translated here as 'consciousness'.

And if it says itself eternally, there is, eternally, a word for it, a word that is in it.

To conclude then, whether one thinks that the supreme spirit is the one and only thing that exists, or not, its internal and coeternal Word exists necessarily.

33. *With one Word it says both itself and what it has made*

But hold on. We have come across the Word by which the Creator of all says itself. But I was asking about the Word by which the Creator says all that it has made. Are there then two Words, one for itself, another for what it creates? Or does it say both its creation and itself by one and the same Word? Now, its Word for itself is, necessarily, the same thing as itself. And the same is true of its Word for its creatures. For, since its Word for itself exists necessarily (it would exist even if supreme spirit was the only thing that existed), its Word is nothing but itself. Reason demands it; what could be truer? And if its Word for itself and its Word for its creation are consubstantial with itself, clearly, then, they are one substance. So how can there be two Words?

Perhaps, however, identity of substance does not strictly imply singularity of Word. After all, the speaker here has the same substance as its Words, but is not a word. Yet the Word by which supreme wisdom says itself can most appropriately be said to be its Word, for the reason given above: it has its perfect likeness.

For there is no reason to deny that when a rational mind thinks and understands itself, an image of itself is produced in its thought. (Better: its very thinking of itself is its image; an image shaped to (moulded to, as it were, or impressed on) its likeness.) For when the mind wants to think accurately of something (whether by means of its bodily imagination or by means of reason), it tries to express, as far as it can, the thing's likeness in its thinking. The more accurately it expresses, the more accurately it thinks the thing. (This is particularly clear in the case of a mind thinking of something different from itself, and especially of something corporeal.) Suppose I am thinking of a man, known to me, but absent. The focus of my thought is shaped into his image, an image which I have already taken into and stored in my consciousness by means of my eyesight. This image in my thought is the word that I use for this man when I think of him. So then, when the rational mind thinks itself (and so understands itself) it has an image of itself. This image is inside it; it is born from it. That is, its thinking itself is formed into its own likeness (moulded, or impressed, as it were). And this image of itself is its word for itself.

Who would deny, therefore, that in this way, when the supreme wisdom says itself and so understands itself, it begets its own likeness, i.e. its Word? We cannot, of course, properly, or adequately enough, predicate anything of something as uniquely excellent as this. Nevertheless this word can, not inadequately, be called the image, figure and character, as well as the likeness, of supreme wisdom.

But note that the word by which it says what it creates, is not the word for what is created at all. This is because the word by which it says what it creates is not a likeness of what it creates. It is the original. So it follows, then, that it does not say what it creates by the word for what it creates. By what word, then, does it say what it creates? It can only be by the Word for itself. What it says, it says by a word and a word is a word for something, i.e. it is the likeness of something. Now, if it only says itself and its creation, it can only speak by its Word for itself, or the word for the created. But it does not speak by means of a word for the created. Therefore it says whatever it says, by its Word for itself. To conclude: it says itself and it says whatsoever it makes, by one and the same Word.

34. *How it is apparently possible for it to say its creation by means of its Word for itself*

But how can two such different things, creative and created essence, possibly be said by one Word? Especially given that the Word is coeternal with its speaker, while creatures are not.

Perhaps it is the case that when the supreme spirit says itself it says all created things. Take any product of any system or process (such as the product of a craftsman's expertise). Now that product has some existence in the system itself. And it exists in that system always—not just when it is produced, but before it is produced, and after it ceases to exist. And its existence in the system is nothing more than the existence of the system itself. This, then, is how all created things exist in the supreme wisdom and reason. Now the supreme spirit is the supreme wisdom and reason. Therefore when it says itself, it also says all created things.

All created things exist in the supreme spirit, before they are created, after creation and after they have come to an end, or in any way altered. But, in the supreme spirit, they are what the supreme spirit is, rather than what they are in themselves. This is because in themselves what they are is mutable essence, the product of immutable reason. What they are in the supreme spirit, however, is original essence and existence's original authenticity. And the degree of the truth and excellence of their existence is the degree of their similarity to this primary essence and primary existential truth. So then, it is possible to assert and to assert rationally that by one and the same Word the supreme spirit says both itself and what it has created.

35. *In the Word and knowledge of the supreme essence all creatures are life and truth*

Its Word is consubstantial with it, perfectly like it. This is agreed. It follows necessarily, therefore, that everything that is in it is, in the same way, in its Word. So then, everything created, be it alive or not, howsoever it is in itself is, in the supreme essence, life and truth itself. Now, for the supreme spirit, to know is the same as to understand and to speak. Necessarily, as a result, the supreme spirit knows everything that it knows in the same way as it understands and says everything. Conclusion: not only are all things life and truth in the supreme spirit's Word, they are also, likewise, life and truth in its knowledge.

36. *Its way of knowing and saying what it has created is beyond comprehension*

Human knowledge cannot comprehend the way in which the spirit says and knows what it creates. This fact, at least, is now clearly comprehensible. For what created substances are in themselves is not what they are in our knowledge—a fact no one doubts. This is because in themselves they exist each through its own essence, whereas in our knowledge they exist as their likenesses, not their own essences. And it follows that they exist more authentically in themselves than in our knowledge, just in proportion as they exist more authentically through their own essence than through their likeness.

And we have already established that they exist more authentically in the Word (i.e. in the Creator's understanding) than in themselves, just in proportion as creative essence exists more authentically than created essence. So then, how could the human mind comprehend the mode of saying and knowing of the supreme spirit? Our knowledge falls a long way short of created substances (by the gap between their essence and likeness), and they, in turn, fall so short of, and are so much less authentic than the saying and knowing of the supreme spirit.

37. *What the supreme spirit is, in relation to creation, its Word is too. Yet both together are not more than one*

The supreme spirit created all things through its Word. This I have clearly learnt from the preceding arguments. But did not the Word itself create them all as well? It is, after all, consubstantial with what it is the Word for, and so, necessarily, it is the supreme essence. But there is only one supreme essence, Creator, and first principle of everything that has been made. It created everything out of nothing by itself, through itself and nothing else. Therefore whatever the supreme spirit does, its Word does too, and likewise. And so what the spirit is, in relation to creation, its Word is too and likewise. Yet there are not several supreme creative essences. So both together are not more than one. Therefore the Word is Creator and first principle just as the supreme spirit is. Yet there are not two, but only one Creator and first principle.

38. *Just what there are two of, cannot be said, even though there must be two of them*

Here, then, I must proceed carefully: the case of the supreme spirit and its Word has turned up something rather out of the ordinary. Now, this is certain: we have got, on the one hand, what they are in essence, and, on the other, what they are in relation to creation. Now, these are present individually to each and simultaneously to both. But they are present in such a way that they are present as an individual whole to both, and yet there is not more than one thing in the two. For the supreme spirit is supreme truth and Creator, and its

Word, too, is supreme truth and Creator. Yet they are not both together two truths or two Creators.

This, then, is how it is. Nevertheless, astoundingly, the following too is crystal clear: the supreme spirit (whose Word it is) cannot be its own Word, and the Word cannot be that for which it is the Word (the supreme spirit). There are two upshots of this, namely unity and plurality: first, there is always one single unity with respect to the signs that signify what they are substantially and what they are in relation to creation. Secondly, insofar as the Word is derived from the supreme spirit, while the supreme spirit is not derived from the Word, there is an ineffable plurality.

And I do mean ineffable. For although there must be two of them, one just cannot express what they are. For even supposing that we could say that they were both equal (or related to each other in some way), if asked to say just what it was that was said to be equal, we could not answer in the plural. It is not like talking about two equal lines or two similar men. There just are not two equal spirits or two equal creators, nor two equal whatevers (where 'whatever' would signify either their essence or their relation to creation). Nor, indeed, can we say two equal 'whatevers' where 'whatever' would denote the proper relation of one to the other. There are not two Words or two images. The Word, in so far as it is a Word, or image, is related to the spirit, since it would not be a word, or image, unless it were a word for something. These relational terms are so proper to the one that they cannot be applied to the other. So what the Word is the word for, is not a word, and is not an image.

I reach the conclusion, then, that what these two things—the supreme spirit and its Word—are, is inexpressible, although they are distinguished from each other in thought by what is proper to each. Thus it is proper to the second to be derived from the first, and proper to the first to be that from which the second is derived.

39. *The Word derives from the supreme spirit by being born*

There is no more natural way of putting this conclusion in words than by using the term 'born': thus it is proper to the second to be born from the first, and proper to the first to be that from which the second is born. For I have already agreed that the Word does not derive from the supreme spirit in the same way as created things do, but that it derives as Creator from Creator, supreme from the supreme, and, to put the whole likeness in a nutshell, the very same from, and from nothing other than, the very same. This derivation can therefore most appropriately be thought of as a being born. This is because the Word derives from the supreme spirit alone, and has, as a result, a perfect likeness to it—like that of the child to the parent. Now we use this term, 'born', quite happily of countless things. We use it when the thing born gets its existence from that from which it is born, even when there is no likeness of the parent–child kind. For example we say [in Latin] that hairs are 'born' from the head and fruit from a tree, even though hairs are not like heads, nor fruit like trees. Given that this use of 'born' is not nonsensical, and given that the Word is very much more like the supreme spirit, this term is very much more appropriate to the derivation of the Word from the spirit.

40. *The supreme spirit is truest parent, and the Word truest child*

And if 'born' is the most appropriate term, and if the Word is so much like that from which it is born, why think of them as like parent and child? Why not rather assert that they truly are parent and child, in so far as the spirit alone suffices for the perfect birth of the Word, and in so far as the Word expresses the spirit's likeness? After all, in the case of other parent–child relations, no parent is able to beget a child entirely by itself, nor is any child completely like its parent.

If, then, the Word is the only child that is derived entirely from the essence of its parent alone, and the only child that is so uniquely like its parent, then the parent–child relationship must apply to nothing so much as to the supreme spirit and its Word. It is proper to the supreme spirit, therefore, to be the most true parent, and proper to the Word to be the most true child.

41. *The supreme spirit most truly begets, and the Word most truly is begotten*

But this conclusion requires, in turn, that the supreme spirit begets, and the Word is begotten, superlatively truly. This latter claim, therefore, is as necessarily certain as the former is clear. It is proper to the supreme spirit, therefore, most truly to beget and proper to the Word most truly to be begotten.

42. *The supreme spirit is truest begetter and Father, and the Word truest begotten and Son*

I would like now to state that the supreme spirit is truest Father and the Word truest Son. But there is a question that must, I think, be answered before I can. There is no sexual differentiation in them. Which, then, is the more appropriate terminology: Father and Son, or Mother and Daughter?

If 'Father and Son' because both are spirit—a noun [in Latin] of masculine gender—why not equally 'Mother and Daughter' on the grounds that both are truth and wisdom—feminine nouns [in Latin]? Perhaps grounds can be found in the claim that, in natures where there is sexual differentiation, the male is the better sex and the female inferior? But while this may often be true, there are, to the contrary, some natures, some birds for example, where the female is always bigger and stronger than the male.

This, however, is certainly the reason: the first and original cause of the child is always in the father. The paternal cause always, in some sense, precedes the maternal. And if this is the case, it would be most inappropriate to apply the name 'mother' to a parent that begets its child without any other cause either helping or preceding. The supreme spirit, therefore, is truest father of its child. Further, a son is always more similar to the father than a daughter. And nothing is more similar to anything than its offspring is to the supreme Father. Therefore this offspring is not truest daughter but truest Son.

Therefore, just as it is proper to the supreme spirit most truly to beget, and to the Son most truly to be begotten, just so, it is proper to the supreme spirit most truly to be the begetter, and to the Son most truly to be the begotten. And just as one is truest parent, and the other truest child, just so, one is truest Father and the other truest Son.

43. *What is common to both, and proper to each—a reconsideration*

So many properties of each! And such properties! Properties which prove that in the supreme unity there is such an amazing multiplicity, a multiplicity as inexpressible as it is irrepressible. This is what

I have found. Such an impenetrable mystery! What a delight to think it over and over again!

See now. On the one hand the impossibility of the one who begets and the one begotten, of the parent and child, being one and the same, entails the necessity of one being the begetter and the other the begotten, of one being Father and the other Son. On the other hand it is necessary that the one who begets and the one begotten are one and the same—and the same goes for parent and child— which, in turn, entails the impossibility of the begetter being something other than the begotten, and the Father being something other than the Son.

Again, we have got the one and we have got the other, so that it is clear that there are two of them. Yet, on the other hand, what the one and the other are is one and the same thing, so that it is completely unclear just what there are two of. One is Father and the other Son, and the result is that when I talk of both I seem to be talking of two, while, on the other hand, there is the one thing which both the Father and Son are, and the result is that I am talking of two— but I do not understand what there are two of. For although the Father, on his own, totally is the supreme spirit, and the Son, on his own, totally is the supreme spirit, the Father-Spirit and the Son-Spirit are one and the same thing, but in such a way that they are not two spirits but one spirit.

The individual properties of each do not become plural, because they are not properties of two things. And conversely, that which is common to both is a single unity, even though it belongs wholly to each individual. There are not two Fathers or two Sons, only one Father and one Son. This is because these are individual properties, proper to each. Conversely, there is only one spirit, not two. And this is despite it being true of both the Father, as an individual, and of the Son, as an individual, that they are completely spirit. They are contrasted in terms of their relation such that the one never receives what is proper to the other. They are concordant in terms of their nature such that the essence of one is possessed by the other. What makes one Father and the other Son makes them different, so that the Father is never called Son, or the Son Father. But through their substance they are the same, so that the essence of the Son is always in the Father and that of the Father in the Son. Not differing but the same, not many but one: such is, of both, the essence.

44. *How one is the essence of the other*

Hence also, to say that one is the essence of the other is not to point away from the truth, but to point up the supreme unity and simplicity of their common nature. For this is not what we understand human wisdom to be like. Human beings cannot be wise through themselves; they are wise through wisdom. When, by contrast, we say that the Son's essence is the Father, and the Father's essence the Son, and that thus the Son exists through the Father and the Father through the Son, we do not take this to mean that the existence of one is impossible without the other (for it to exist through). This contrasts with the impossibility of a man's being wise without the wisdom for him to be wise through. Now the supreme wisdom is wise always through itself, and just so, the supreme essence exists always through itself. The Father is wholly the supreme essence, and the Son is wholly the supreme essence. So Father and Son, each exists as a whole through himself, just as each is wise through himself. Now the Son is essence and wisdom born from the Father's essence and wisdom. But this does not mean he is any less wholly essence and wisdom. (He would be less perfectly essence and wisdom, if he did not exist, and be wise, through himself.) The Son exists through himself and has his existence from the Father. This is not a contradiction. For as Father has life (and essence and wisdom) in himself, so has he given the Son to have life (and essence and wisdom) in himself [cf. John 5: 26]. ('In himself': i.e. he exists through his own essence, is wise through his own wisdom, lives through his own life—not through something other than himself. 'Given': i.e. by begetting.) If this were not the case, the being of the Father and Son would not be the same, and the Son would not be equal to the Father. (And just how false this would be, we have already quite clearly seen.)

So then, it is not contradictory for the Son to exist both through himself and from the Father. This is because the Son has, necessarily, his very ability to exist through himself from the Father. Take the case where I am ignorant and some expert teaches me their expertise.[9] It would not be at all illogical to say that it was really their expertise that was teaching me. My expertise owes its being, and its doing what expertise does, to this expertise. But, despite this, it exists, when

---

[9] 'Expertise' here translates *sapientia*, elsewhere translated as 'wisdom'.

it exists, only through its own essence, and it does what expertise does, only through itself. This then is true of the Son—that he exists, is expert, and lives, through himself. And much more so, as the Son is coeternal with the eternal Father, and owes his existence to the Father—but only one essence results, not two. So then the Father is the Son's essence, and the Son is the Father's. Yet this cannot be taken to mean that the one can only exist through the other, and not through himself. Instead this is what it is appropriate and possible to say and understand, with respect to the supreme simple and supremely unique essence that they have in common: each is identical with the other—so much so that each has the other's essence. Now, for both, to have an essence is to be an essence. It is just as true, therefore, that each is the other's essence, i.e. for one to exist is the same as for the other to exist.

45. *The Son is the Father's essence. This is a more appropriate possible claim than that the Father is the Son's essence. Likewise the Son is the Father's strength, wisdom and the like*

It is much more appropriate to call the Son the Father's essence than vice versa, even though both are, as argued above, true. This is because the Father has his essence from nothing but himself. So it is not really adequate to say that he has anything else's essence, but only his own. The Son, on the other hand, has his essence from the Father, as well as having the same essence as the Father. So it is most appropriate to say that he has the Father's essence. Now both have an essence only by being an essence. So to say that the Son is the Father's essence is possible and more suitable than vice versa.

Now, to advance this one claim, is to back its expansion: the Son not only shares one and the same essence with the Father, but also has one and the same essence from the Father. And the result of this: the Son is the Father's essence, i.e. the Son does not differ in essence from the Father's essence, from the Father-Essence. And likewise, then, the Son is the Father's strength, wisdom, truth, justice, and whatever else pertains to the supreme spirit.

46. *Some of these claims can be taken in another way as well*

There would seem to be further, and quite compatible, possible ways of understanding some of these claims. The Son, clearly, is the true

Word. That is, he is the perfect understanding of the whole paternal substance. He understands the very essence of the Father. (And so too, he is perfect cognition, knowledge and wisdom.) To say that the Son is the Father's understanding in this sense, as well as his wisdom, knowledge, cognition—and add comprehension, since he comprehends the Father—does not fall short of the truth at all. And as for truth: the Son can most appropriately be called the Father's truth in another sense as well. First we may take it to mean that the Father's truth is one and the same truth as the Son's truth, as has already been shown. But we may also take it to mean that there is, in the Son, the whole truth of the paternal substance (not some incomplete imitation of it). And the whole truth of the paternal substance is nothing other than what the Father is.

47. *The Son is the understanding of understanding, the truth of truth, and so on*

But if the Father's substance is understanding, knowledge, wisdom and truth it follows logically that, as the Son is the understanding, knowledge, wisdom and truth of the paternal substance, so the Son is the understanding of understanding, the knowledge of knowledge, wisdom of wisdom and the truth of truth.

48. *It makes sense to think of the Father in terms of consciousness and the Son in terms of understanding. And how the Son is the understanding and wisdom of consciousness, the consciousness of the Father and the consciousness of consciousness*

What about consciousness? Is the Son the understanding of consciousness? Is he the consciousness of the Father? Is he the consciousness of consciousness? Well, the supreme wisdom is undeniably conscious of itself. It would be most appropriate, therefore, to understand the Father in terms of consciousness and the son in terms of word. Words, after all, seem to be born from consciousness.

 This can be seen more clearly in the case of the human mind. While the human mind does not always think about itself, it is always conscious of itself. So, at the moment when it does think about itself, its word must be born from its consciousness. And hence were it to be thinking about itself continually, its word would continually be being born from its consciousness. (And, to recapitulate, to think of something that we have consciousness of, is to say it in the mind. And the word for a thing is the very thinking of the thing, consciousness formed into its likeness.)

We can get a very clear perspective on the supreme wisdom from this point. The supreme wisdom is continually saying, and continually conscious of, itself. So then, its coeternal Word is begotten from eternal consciousness. Now it is appropriate to think of a word as a child. Just so then, the most suitable term for consciousness is parent. And if supreme wisdom's child (born from it alone) is the child of its consciousness, it follows that the supreme spirit is the same thing as its own consciousness. It is, indeed, not like human consciousness. Our consciousness is something distinct from what is in it. Objects are in it as one thing in another. By contrast the supreme spirit is self-conscious in such a way that it is its own self-consciousness.

Hence, it follows that as well as being the understanding and wisdom of the Father, the Son is also and likewise the understanding and wisdom of the paternal consciousness. But what the Son is wise about and understands, he also is conscious of. So the Son is the consciousness of the Father and the consciousness of consciousness (i.e. consciousness conscious of the Father—who is consciousness). He is the wisdom of the Father and the wisdom of wisdom (i.e. wisdom wise about the Father—who is wisdom). The Son is consciousness born from consciousness, Wisdom born from Wisdom. The Father, by contrast, is unbegotten consciousness and unbegotten wisdom.

49. *The supreme spirit loves itself*

What delight to gaze upon what is proper to Father and Son and what they have in common! And nothing gives me more delight in contemplation than their mutual love. For the supreme spirit indeed loves itself, just as it is conscious of, and understands, itself. How absurd to deny it! Even a rational mind can love both itself and the supreme spirit. This is demonstrable from the fact that it is conscious of, and understands, itself and the supreme spirit. For consciousness and understanding are utterly sterile and futile without (in rational proportion to the object) love and loathing. Therefore, as it is conscious of, and understands itself, so the supreme spirit loves itself.

50. *One and the same love proceeds equally from Father and Son*

Now it is quite clear to any rational mind that self-consciousness and self-understanding are not due to self-love. But rather self-love happens because of self-consciousness and self-understanding. Self-love is impossible without self-consciousness. It is impossible without self-understanding. Nothing is loved without being the object of consciousness and understanding. And there are plenty of objects of consciousness and understanding that are not loved. Therefore it is clear that the supreme spirit's love proceeds from its being self-conscious and self-understanding. And given that it makes sense to think of the supreme spirit's consciousness as Father, and its understanding as Son, it is evident that the supreme spirit as love proceeds equally from the Father and the Son.

51. *Each loves himself, and the other, with equal intensity*

If the supreme spirit loves itself, then, unquestionably, the Father loves himself, the Son loves himself, and each loves the other. This for two reasons. First the Father, as an individual, is the supreme spirit, and the Son too, as an individual, is the supreme spirit, and also both of them together are one spirit. Secondly, Father and Son each equally is conscious of himself and of the other, and each equally understands himself and the other. And since what loves and what is loved is one and the same thing in Father and in the Son, necessarily, then each loves itself and the other with equal intensity.

52. *This love is as great as the supreme spirit is*

The supreme spirit's love is, thus, common to Father and Son. How big is it? It can only love itself to the extent that it is self-conscious and self-understanding. And its self-consciousness and self-understanding can only be as great as its essence. Granted this, it is obvious that the supreme spirit's love is as great as the supreme spirit.

53. *This Love is the very thing that the supreme spirit is.*
Yet Love plus Father plus Son, makes one spirit

As great as the supreme spirit? But the only thing that can be equal
to the supreme spirit is the supreme spirit. This love, then, is the
supreme spirit. Furthermore, suppose that no creature existed, i.e.
suppose that nothing else had ever existed, other than the supreme
spirit. The Father and the Son would still love themselves and each
other. It follows from this that the Love is nothing other than the
supreme essence (i.e. what the Father and the Son are). But you
cannot have several supreme essences. So it must be the case that
Father, Son and their Love are one supreme essence. What could be
more necessary? This love, therefore, is supreme wisdom, supreme
truth, supreme good—and all the other substance-predicates of the
supreme spirit.

54. *All of it proceeds from the Father, and all of it proceeds from*
the Son, yet there is just one Love

Are there two loves or one? This is a problem which we must take
seriously. Does one proceed from the Father, and another from the
Son? Is there one, proceeding partly from the Father and partly
from the Son? Does one and the same Love proceed as a whole
from each and as a whole from both together? Happily there is an
unproblematically secure resolution. This is based on the fact
that the Love does not proceed from Father and Son being two
separate things. Rather it proceeds from their being one. That is, it
is not in virtue of their being related (as Father and Son—
two things), but in virtue of just their being (their essence, which
cannot be multiple). It is from essence not relatedness that Father
and Son give out this great good. The Father, as an individual, is
the supreme spirit. The Son, as an individual, is the supreme
spirit. But together Father and Son are one spirit (not two). The
structure is parallel: from the Father, as an individual, floods forth
the supreme spirit's whole love. From the Son, as an individual,
floods forth the supreme spirit's whole Love. But from Father and
Son together, floods forth not two whole loves, but one and the same
Love.

55. *Love is not their Son*

Should we not think of their Love as their son—or at least their off-spring? It has its being, after all, from Father and Son. And also, it is entirely similar to them—indeed it is the very same thing that they are.

No. It is true that reason teaches us that it is absolutely the same thing as Father and Son are. However, whereas word immediately and unmistakably declares itself to be the offspring of that for which it is the word, love openly denies it. The word, as soon as one thinks of it, offers an image of its parent. Love, by contrast, offers the thinker no such striking likeness of that from which it derives. (But the thinker can deduce that it proceeds from Father and Son.)

Furthermore, if it is their child, either one of them will be the father and the other the mother, or both are fathers (or both mothers). All of which would seem to be incompatible with the truth. In the first place, this is because it proceeds from the Father in precisely the same way as it proceeds from the Son. And this means that truth forbids us from using different terms for Father and Son here. So one cannot be mother and the other father. In the second place, who ever heard of anything having two mothers or two fathers? Especially when it has completely and indistinguishably the same relationship to both.

So neither Father nor Son are father—or mother—to the Love that floods forth from them. Conclusion: it does not fit the truth, then, that their Love is their son or offspring.

56. *The Father, only, is unbegotten begetter. The Son, only, is begotten. The Love, only, is neither begotten nor unbegotten*

The Love, it seems, cannot be called 'unbegotten'—not in ordinary language. Nor can it be called 'begotten'—not in the proper sense—as used of the Word.

In ordinary [Latin] language 'begotten from' means 'has its existence from'. Thus we say that heat and light are 'begotten from' fire, and effect is 'begotten from' cause. In this sense it is quite impossible to assert that the Love is unbegotten. It flows out, after all, from the supreme spirit.

As for the proper sense of 'begotten', the sense in which the Word is said to be begotten: this cannot be used of the Love. This is because the Word is the utterly authentic offspring, it is the utterly authentic Son. But it is quite clear-cut that the Love is neither son nor offspring.

What we can say—indeed, what we must say—is that the only thing that is unbegotten and begetter is that which the Word is word of. Only this is parent. Only this is Father. And there is no way that it gets its existence from anything else. The Word, alone, is begotten. This is because it alone is son and offspring. And their Love, only, is neither begotten nor unbegotten. And this is because it is neither son, nor offspring. And yet there is no way that it does not get its existence from something else.

57. *Love, like Father and Son, is uncreated Creator. But they do not add up to three uncreated Creators, just one. Love can be called the Spirit of the Father and the Son*

Love, like Father and Son, is, on its own, the supreme essence. And yet Father, Son and their love taken together do not become several supreme essences, but only one. The supreme essence, alone, is uncreated and has created all things through itself and nothing but itself. The consequence of this is that the Father, the Son, and also the Love, are each, as individuals, the uncreated Creator without all three, taken together, making several uncreated Creators, but only one.

Nothing, therefore, creates, causes or begets the Father. As for the Son: the Father, alone, begets, but does not create him. And as for the Love: Father and Son do not create, nor do they beget him. Rather they both equally, somehow 'breathe out' (if it can be put this way) their Love. It is not that the supremely immutable essence breathes in the way we do. But, since love's procession is not so much devolution (into independence) as evolution (into existence), it would seem that this is, perhaps, the only possible way of putting this 'giving out from itself'.

Let us assume that this is a possible way of putting it. Now, the supreme essence's Word is its Son. So in the same way its love could, appropriately enough, be called its Spirit. It is true, of course, that the Love is essentially spirit, and so are the Father and the Son.

However, Father and Son are not thought of as the spirit of anything. In the Father's case, this is because he does not derive from anything else at all. In the Son's case, it is because he is begotten from the Father, not breathed out. The Love, however, is thought of as the Spirit of both Father and Son. This is because it proceeds from both in its own wonderful way. And this inexpressible procession we call 'breathing out', 'expiration'.[9]

And further: love is common to Father and Son. So, if you really feel that its lack of a name that is proper to it is a problem, there would seem to be some grounds for giving it, as a quasi-proper name, that which Father and Son have in common. That is, one would give it the designation 'Spirit', a name that signifies the substance of Father and of Son. The benefit, then, of this name is that it suggests that Love has the same being as Father and Son, and at the same time derives its being from them.

58. *The Spirit is the Father's and the Son's essence, wisdom, and so forth—just as the Son is the Father's essence and wisdom, in the sense that he has the same essence and wisdom as the Father*

The Son is the Father's substance, wisdom and strength, in the sense that he has the same essence, wisdom, and strength as the Father. Likewise, it makes sense to think of the Spirit of Father and Son as their essence, wisdom and strength, on the grounds that it has exactly what they have.

59. *Father, Son, and Spirit exist equally in each other*

Father, Son, and Spirit exist in each other, and with such an equality that none is greater than the others. What a joy it is to behold this! Their equality is demonstrable first in terms of their shared essence, and secondly—and no less—in terms of each individually. For, first, all three together are one supreme essence (even though each, perfectly, is the supreme essence). And the one supreme essence cannot exist without itself, outside itself, or greater or less than itself. And, secondly, the Father, as a complete whole, exists in

[9] 'Breathe out' translates Anselm's verb *spirare*. Hence the link with the name 'spirit' (Latin: *spiritus*). 'Expiration' is the closest English can get to this.

the Son and in their mutual Spirit, the Son in Father and in Spirit, and Spirit in Father and in Son. This is because the supreme essence's consciousness is, as a complete whole, in its understanding and in its love, and its understanding in its consciousness and in its love, and its love in its consciousness and in its understanding. The supreme spirit understands and loves its whole consciousness. It is conscious of and loves its whole understanding. It is conscious of and understands its whole love. By consciousness we understand the Father, by understanding, the Son, and by love, their Spirit. Such, therefore, is the equality of the mutual embrace and the mutual indwelling of Father, Son and Spirit. It demonstrates that none of them is greater than, or can exist without, the others.

60. *None needs another to be conscious, to understand or to love. Because each, on its own, is consciousness, understanding and love (and whatever else belongs necessarily to the supreme essence)*

But I must be careful not to lose sight of what I have become conscious of. The Father is consciousness, the Son understanding, and the Spirit, love. Yes. But it is necessary to understand that the Father does not stand in want of the Son or the Spirit. It is not as if the Father, by and through himself, can only be conscious, and needs the Son in order to understand and the Spirit in order to love. And the same goes, *mutatis mutandis*, for Son and Spirit: none of them needs the others in order to be conscious, understand and love. This is a necessary truth because each of the three is, as an individual, the supreme essence and wisdom, and each is the supreme wisdom and essence so perfectly that the supreme essence and wisdom is conscious, understands and loves, through itself. Each individual is, essentially, consciousness, understanding and love—and whatever else belongs necessarily to the supreme essence.

61. *Not three, but one Father, one Son, one mutual Spirit*

This, I see, invites a question. If the Father is understanding and love, as well as consciousness, how come he is not something's son and something's spirit? If the Son is consciousness and love, in addition to being understanding, why is not he something's father and something's spirit? If the Spirit is consciousness and understanding no less than he is love, for what reason is he not something's father and something's son? This is, after all, how we came to understand the Father as consciousness, the Son as understanding and the Spirit as love.

The solution can easily be found in what I have already rationally worked out: the Father may indeed be understanding and love. But because he is not the understanding that is begotten, he is not a son, and because he is not the love that proceeds from something, he is not another's spirit. He is what he is only as begetter, and only as that from which something else proceeds. The Son, likewise, as far as he himself is concerned, is consciousness and love. However, because he is not the consciousness that begets, he is not a father, and because he is not the love that proceeds from something (he is not like the Spirit), he is not something's spirit. He is what he is only as begetter, and only as that from which something proceeds. He exists only as begotten, and as that from which Spirit proceeds. As for the Spirit—while its consciousness and understanding make it what it is, this does not mean it must be father or son. It is not the consciousness that begets, nor the understanding that is begotten. Whatever it is, it is the only one that proceeds.

In the supreme essence, therefore—and what is there to get in the way of this conclusion?—there is only one Father, only one Son, and only one Spirit; not three Fathers, Sons or Spirits.

62. *How it might seem that many sons are begotten*

But do I not see a contradiction to this? How does it come about that there are not lots of sons? Father, Son and Spirit each speaks itself and the other two. No doubt about it: each understands itself and the others. How come, then, there are not as many Words in the supreme essence as there are speakers and things spoken? If, after all, several people think of the same object, the word for that object is in the thought of each individual. So the number of words is the number of individuals thinking. Again, if one person thinks of several things, there are as many words in their mind as there are things thought.

However, when a person thinks of an object that exists outside their mind, you do not get the word for that object being born from the object itself. This is because the object itself is absent from thought's gaze. Rather, the word is born from an image or likeness of the object. This likeness is either already stored in the thinker's conscious memory, or taken into his mind, there and then, via the bodily senses. By contrast, Father, Son and Spirit are always present to themselves in the supreme essence. (We have already seen that none is less in the others than in himself.) And so that means that not only is it the case that each begets his own word when each says himself, but also, in the same way, when they say each other, each begets his own word when each is said. Each, then, begets his own word both when said by himself, and when said by another. So how can it be the case that the Son and the Spirit do not beget? There is, therefore, a demonstrable number of words begotten from the supreme substance. And, moreover, this number is necessarily (for the reasons given above) the number of sons that it begets, and of spirits that it gives out. So then, according to this argument, there would appear to be, in the supreme essence, many fathers, sons and processors. And indeed not only these but all the other necessary attributes would be many as well.

63. *How in the supreme Spirit there is only one Word for one thing said*

But Father, Son and Spirit are not three speakers. This is certain, although that each one of them really exists is totally certain, and although each of them does speak. Further, although each of them is spoken by itself and by the other two, they are not lots of things spoken.

And this is why. Now, it belongs to the supreme wisdom to know and to understand. And just so, it belongs to the nature of eternal and immutable knowledge and understanding always to have its object present, and always to gaze upon it. For the supreme spirit, to say, is, in this sense, simply to gaze in thought (just as our mental verbalization is simply thinking's visualization). Our arguments have already proved that what belongs to the supreme nature in terms of essence, applies without qualification to Father, Son and Spirit individually, without becoming plural when predicated of all three simultaneously. So then, knowledge and understanding pertain to the essence of the supreme nature, and its knowing and understanding are nothing other than speaking. And its speaking is its gazing on the continually present object of its knowing and understanding. Given all this, the following is necessary: Father, Son, and Spirit, each on its own, as individual, knows and understands—while all three taken together are not three knowers and understanders but just one single knower, one single understander. And in just the same way, each speaks, without all three taken together being three speakers, but only one.

Hence we can also clearly see that there are not lots of things said. For what is said when each of the three is spoken by itself and by the others, but their essence? And since this is just one thing, there is only one thing that is said.

So there is, then, one speaker and one thing spoken; one wisdom in them that speaks, one substance in them that is spoken. From which it follows that there is only one Word there. To conclude: although each says itself, and all say each other, the only possible Word in the supreme essence is that which we have already identified: the Word that can be called true image of, and truly is the Son of— because it is so begotten from—that for which it is the word.

A conclusion which has something of the wonderful and unac- countable about it! For although, clearly, Father, Son and Spirit are each equally said, the one Word that is said cannot be said to be the word for all three, but only the word for one of them. This is because, as we have agreed, this Word is the image and Son of that for which it is the Word. Clearly, the Word cannot appropriately be called the image and Son of itself, nor of the Spirit that proceeds from it. This is because it is not begotten from, nor does it (when it exists) re- semble, either itself, or that which proceeds from it. It does not resemble itself, and it does not derive a likeness to existing-from- itself because you need more than one thing for there to be any resemblance or likeness. It does not resemble the Spirit, nor does it exist in its likeness, because Spirit owes its existence to Son, not vice versa. This leaves as the only option that the one Word is the Word for one thing only: namely, that from which it was born, and hence, to which it owes its existence, and in whose complete likeness it exists. Therefore there are, in the supreme essence, not several Fathers, Sons and proceeding Spirits, but one Father, one Son and one proceeding Spirit.

They are, then, three, but in such a way that Father is not ever either Son or proceeding Spirit, nor Son sometimes either Father or proceeding Spirit, nor the Spirit of Father and Son ever either Father or Son. Each individual, also, is so complete that it stands in need of nothing else. And yet, despite all this, what they are is singular in such a way that it cannot be said in the plural—not of them taken as individuals, and also, likewise, not of all three taken together. Although, in equal measure, each says itself, and all say each other, there is only one Word. And this Word is not the word for them as individuals, nor for all three taken together. It is the Word for only one of them.

64. *Although this is inexplicable, one ought to believe it*

This seems to me to be a sublime mystery, which stretches well beyond the horizon of human understanding. Therefore one ought, I think, to restrain the ambition to explain. When investigating the inexplicable, if it is possible to arrive at an account which is certainly correct, I think one must be content with that even if it is impossible to see how it may be so. There is no argument for disallowing P the certainty of faith where P is asserted as a necessitated and uncontradicted conclusion, but, because of its deep and incomprehensible nature, does not admit of explanation. And what, after all, is as incomprehensible, as ineffable, as that which is above everything else? So then, given that all our assertions so far on the subject of the supreme essence have been made on the basis of necessary reasoning, the fact that understanding cannot fathom so far as to explain them in words does nothing to undermine their certainty. We cannot understand how it is that the supreme wisdom knows what it has created. (Although we do, at least, understand, on the basis of our earlier reasoning that we cannot understand this.) We do, at least, know an awful lot about what it has created—we have to—but nothing, or hardly anything, can be known by humans about the supreme nature itself. Who, then, is going to explain just how it is that the supreme wisdom knows, and says, itself? So (if 'saying itself' is 'generation'): 'who will declare his generation' [Isa. 53: 8]?

65. *How we came to a true conclusion about something ineffable*

But, again, what about the relationship of Father, Son and the Spirit who proceeds? If—no, rather—because such is the rational position to take on ineffability, is it not contrary to our conclusions about this? For if we explained it right, how can the supreme essence be ineffable? If the supreme essence is ineffable, how can the case be as we concluded?

Perhaps it is explicable—and hence our conclusions true—only up to a point; while being incomprehensible, and therefore ineffable, as a whole. But what about our earlier conclusion? Namely, that the supreme essence is above and beyond all other natures. Thus, when we talk about it, the words may be common to both, but not their meanings. But which, then, was the sense in which I have taken all the terms in my thought if not the common and ordinary? So if the ordinary sense of words is inapplicable to the supreme essence, whatever I have thought out is inapplicable as well. How then can I have discovered something true about the supreme essence, if what I did discover is so completely different?

What then? Have I, in some way, brought something to light about something incomprehensible, although, in another way, gained no direct insight into it? We do often speak of lots of things without expressing them properly, i.e. in the way proper to the way they are. What we do, when we cannot, or will not, utter something properly, is to signify it by means of something else—a riddle for example.[10] And often we do not see something properly (i.e. as it is), but we see it by means of some likeness or image—when, for example, we make out someone's face in a mirror. Thus we say and do not say, see and do not see, one and the same thing. For it is through something else that we say it, and we see it. But through what is proper to it, we do not.

This line of reasoning, therefore, allows our conclusions about the supreme nature to be true and the supreme nature itself to remain ineffable. We understand them to be indicating the supreme nature by means of something else, rather than expressing it by means of what is proper to its essence. The names, then, that are apparently predicable of the supreme nature, merely gesture towards it rather than pinpoint it. They signify via some sort of similarity, not through what is proper. For when it comes to thinking of what such words signify, it is much more comfortable for me to form the mental conception of what I experience from the created world, than of what I understand

---

[10] 'Riddle' translates *aenigma*. This, with the 'mirror' of the next sentence will later be picked up by Anselm in a direct reference to 1 Corinthians 13: 12.

about that which transcends all human understanding. And what it is that such words, by their signifying, form in my mind is something far inferior to—worse: far, far removed from—what my mind is trying to understand. And how insubstantial are these signifyings through which my mind has to work! The name 'wisdom' does not suffice to show me that through which all things were made from nothing, and through which all things are preserved from returning to nothing. The name 'essence' cannot express that which is far above (through its unique loftiness) and beyond (through what is proper to its nature) all things. Conclusion: the supreme nature is ineffable, because it simply cannot be made known as it is by means of words. But a claim about the supreme nature, if one can be made that is dictated by reason and is stated indirectly—in a riddle, as it were—is not false.

66. *One comes closest to knowledge of the supreme essence through the rational mind*

It is now clear that one cannot get to see anything about the supreme nature by means of what is proper to it. Rather, one must work through something other than it. And hence, it is certain that what one gets closest to knowledge of it through, is that which most closely resembles it. And the more a creature resembles it, the more excellent its nature must be. So such a thing has a double effect: its close resemblance helps bring the inquiring mind closer to the supreme truth, and the excellence of its created nature teaches the mind what to think about its Creator. And the greater the resemblance and excellence, the more it helps and teaches. Inquire, therefore, into the creative essence through what is closest to it, and the further one will fathom it.

Now our earlier arguments do not allow us to doubt that every essence is similar to the supreme essence in so far as it exists. And we have already recognized the rational mind as that which comes closest to the supreme essence in virtue of its natural essence. So then, the rational mind may be the only created thing that is able to rise to the task of investigating the supreme nature, but it itself is, thereby, that through which it may come closest to finding something out about it. The obvious inference, then, is that the efficacy of the mind's ascent to knowledge of the supreme nature is in direct proportion to the enthusiasm of its intent to learn about itself. And, insofar as it forgets to look to itself, it falls from its reflection on the supreme nature. What could be more obvious?

67. *The mind itself is the image and mirror of the supreme being*

The mind, therefore, might be most appropriately called its own mirror. The mirror in which it sees the reflection of that which, famously, it cannot see 'face to face'. For if the mind, alone of all created things, can love, understand and be conscious of itself, I do not see why one should say that it is not the true image of that essence which, in its love, understanding, and consciousness of itself, constitutes an ineffable threeness. At least the mind is demonstrably an image of the supreme essence, in so far as it can be conscious of, understand, and love it. And the authenticity of the image discerned in the mind is in direct proportion to the greatness and the similarity of the mind to the supreme essence.

The ability to be conscious of, to understand and to love that which, of all things, is greatest and best—no other gift bestowed on rational creation is conceivably as excellent or as similar to the supreme wisdom. No other created trait so betrays the image of its Creator.

68. *Rational creation was made to love the supreme essence*

To strive to give, therefore, expression to this impressed image; to strive to actualize, by an act of will, this, nature's potential: such, above all, is, in consequence, the debt that rational creation owes its Creator. A debt above and beyond the very fact that it exists. To be able to be conscious of, understand and love the supreme good is its most momentous ability. And therefore the most momentous debt that it owes its Creator is to want to be conscious of, understand and love the supreme good. For who would deny that the better something that we can do is, the more we ought to want to do it?

Further, for a rational nature, to be rational is simply to be able to tell the difference between the just and the unjust, the true and the untrue, the good and the not good, and the greater and the lesser good. But this ability by itself, without love and loathing (based on correct principles of judgement), is quite pointless and superfluous. Hence it is clear that since the point of rational existence is to judge,

according to rational principles, between the good, the less good and
the no good, the point is also to love or spurn (with appropriate intensity) the object judged. It is as patently obvious, therefore, as can
be, that the rational creature is made for this purpose: to love the
supreme essence above all other goods (insofar as the supreme
essence is, after all, the good above all other goods). Indeed its
purpose is, in fact, to love the supreme essence and only to love other
things for the sake of the supreme essence. This is because the
supreme essence is good through itself, while everything else is only
good through it. But it cannot love the supreme essence unless it
strives to become conscious of and to understand it. So it is quite
clear, as a result, that what the rational creation ought to do, is to put
all its power and all its will into becoming conscious of, understanding and loving the supreme good. This is what rational creation recognizes that its existence is for.

69. *The soul that loves the supreme essence always will at some point live the truly happy life*

Now the human soul is a rational creature. No doubt about it. Therefore, necessarily, it was created to love the supreme essence. And
therefore, necessarily, it was created either to love it without end, or
at some point to lose this love. (A loss either freely willed, or forcibly
coerced.)

But the latter alternative is blasphemous. It is unthinkable that
supreme wisdom should create the human soul in order for it, at
some point, to turn against so great a good, or lose it against its will.
The former, therefore, is true by elimination. The supreme essence
created the human soul in order that it should love the supreme
essence without ceasing. But it cannot do so unless it lives without
ceasing. So then, it was created in order that it might live always.
Provided, that is, it should always want to do that for which it was
created.

Moreover, for the omnipotent Creator to create something in order
for that something to love him and then, when it truly does love him,
to uncreate it, indeed, to bestow, of his own free will, existence on
what did not love him, in order that it might always love him, and
then to take this existence away (or allow it to be taken away), so that
now it necessarily cannot love him—does this really go with being

supremely good or supremely wise? Especially given the fact—a fact which we ought not to doubt—that he loves everything that truly loves him. It is therefore manifest that the human soul that always strives to love the supreme life never loses its life.

But what sort of life? Long life on its own, after all, is no great thing, not without real immunity from adversity. What is life lived in fear, suffering, or in the illusion of security, but life lived in unhappiness? The happy life is the life that is free of all this. And will the nature that always loves the supremely good and omnipotent, always live an unhappy life? Quite absurd! Clearly, therefore, this is the sort of life that belongs to the human soul: provided that it keeps to the purpose for which it exists, it will, at some time, live the happy life, the life truly immune from death and all distress.

70. *Supreme essence requites its lover with itself*

Superlatively just, superlatively powerful—could the supreme essence ever not requite the soul that steadfastly loves it? Could it ever look as if it did not? It did, after all, give the soul (which, then, did not love) existence that it might have the ability to love. Suppose it does not requite the soul that loves it. In this case it does not distinguish lover from loather. (And it is superlatively just.) Nor does it, then, love the lover. Either that, or its love confers no noticeable benefit—all of which is rather out of tune with the supreme essence. I conclude, therefore, that it does requite each and every steadfast lover.

And what is the requital? It gave rational essence to what was nothing, that it might love. What will it give to what loves unceasingly? If that is love's subsidy, what will be its legacy? If that is the award, what will be the reward? Now, given that the rational creature (which is useless to itself without this love) so excels all other creatures, its reward can only be that which more than excels all other natures. The supreme good demands desire no less than love. For who loves justice, truth, happiness, incorruptibility without also wanting to enjoy them? With what, then, does supreme goodness reward that which loves and desires it if not with itself? Anything else would be gift rather than reward. Anything else would just not requite the love or satisfy the lover. Nothing else would satisfy the desire. (If it wanted to be loved and desired so that it might give something else back, then it would not want to be loved for its own sake, but for the sake of something else. That is, it would not want to be loved. Blasphemous thought!) We may conclude, then, with absolute truth, that every rational soul that strives, as it ought, to love and desire supreme happiness will, at some point, behold and enjoy it. So that what it 'now' sees 'through a glass darkly', as it were, it will then see 'face to face' [1 Cor. 13: 12]. And of course it enjoys supreme happiness without end. It is foolish to doubt it. When it enjoys supreme happiness, no fear can torment it, no false sense of security can deceive it. Having already experienced the lack of such happiness, it cannot not love it. Such happiness will not abandon what loves it. Nor is there anything more powerful that could separate them against their will. So then, once the soul begins to enjoy supreme happiness, it will live the happy life for ever.

71. *Eternal unhappiness for the soul that rejects the supreme essence*

And from this we infer that to reject the supreme good is to rush headlong into eternal unhappiness. Perhaps one might object that it would be more just to punish such contempt with deprivation of one's very existence and life, on the grounds that one had failed to use oneself for the purposes for which one was made. But it is contrary to reason that the punishment for a guilt should be a return to what one was when innocent of any guilt. For, before the soul existed it could not incur guilt or feel punishment. Suppose that the soul that rejects the end it was made for dies and so becomes non-sentient or completely non-existent. Then the guiltiest soul would be in the same state as the most guiltless, and supremely wise justice would be failing to distinguish between that which, being incapable of any good, desires no evil, and that which, while capable of the greatest good, desires the greatest evil. But the contrariness of this is quite clear enough. So then, nothing is more obviously consequent or more firmly to be believed than this conclusion: man's soul is created such that it will suffer eternal unhappiness if it disdains to love the supreme essence. Love will enjoy eternal reward, but disdain will suffer eternal punishment. Love will taste unalterable abundance, but disdain unassuageable indigence.

72. *Every human soul is immortal*

There is eternal happiness, and eternal unhappiness: but not if the soul is mortal. The soul, therefore, (whether it loves or loathes what it was created to love) must necessarily be immortal. But what can we say about souls which neither love nor loathe? The souls of infants would appear to be such. Are they mortal or immortal? Now, all human souls share the same nature. There is no doubt about it. Thus, since we have ascertained that some are immortal, it follows of necessity that all are immortal.

73. *The human soul is either unhappy for ever, or truly happy at some time*

Complete freedom from distress happens to any living thing either never or at some time. True happiness, therefore, happens to any human soul either never or at some time.

74. *No soul is unjustly deprived of the supreme good. The supreme good ought to be the object of our total commitment and exertion*

But how are we to tell unambiguously which souls love and will enjoy what they are created to love, and which souls disdain and will always go without it? And on what principle of desert are souls which appear neither to love or disdain apportioned eternal happiness and unhappiness? Can mortal humans work this out? I do not doubt that, if it is not impossible, it is extremely difficult. But this we must hold on to as absolutely certain: the Creator, supremely just and supremely good, unjustly deprives nothing of that good for which it was made, and every one must exert themself to attain this good by love and desire, with all their heart, all their soul, and all their mind.

75. *One must have hope in the supreme essence*

But the soul could not even attempt such a project, if it thought it could never complete it. Hope, therefore, is as necessary as determination is effectual—the determination to strive, the hope that one will arrive.

76. *One must believe in the supreme essence*

But love and hope are impossible without belief. Believe, then, the Supreme Essence. Believe the things one must believe in order to love it. Such belief paves the human soul's way to the supreme essence; by believing, we progress towards the supreme essence. I can, I think, say the same thing in fewer words if I substitute 'believe in the supreme essence' for 'by believing, progress towards the supreme essence'. Someone who says that they believe in it, reveals two things thereby. First that they are progressing towards the supreme essence by means of the faith they profess. Second, that they believe the things that are relevant to this end. One who believes irrelevant things, or does not progress towards the supreme essence, appears not to believe in it.

Perhaps it makes no difference whether we say 'have an attitude of faith towards' or 'have faith in', just as we can take 'progress towards the supreme essence by faith' and 'progress in the supreme essence by faith' as equivalent? But the fact is that the end of progress towards is not to arrive and remain outside, but to stay inside. A fact that can be put more plainly and naturally by saying that one must make progress in the supreme essence, rather than 'progress towards' it. This is the reason why I think it is possible and more appropriate to say that one must have faith in the supreme essence, rather than 'have an attitude of faith towards' it.

77. *One must have faith in Father, in Son and in their Spirit, equally in each individual and in all three together*

One must, therefore, have faith in Father, in Son and in their Spirit, equally in each individual and in all three together. This is because each individual is the supreme essence, and all three together are one and the same supreme essence. The supreme essence is the only thing that everyone ought to believe. This is because the supreme essence is the only goal at which everyone, in every thought and deed, ought to aim. Hence it is clear that there is no possibility of progress without belief, and no benefit from belief without progress.

78. *Dead faith and live faith*

Therefore, however strong one's faith in this supremely great reality is, unless it lives and thrives by love, it is sterile, and is, as it were, quite dead. Faith accompanied by love is not idle. Given opportunity it produces a whole host of works. This it cannot do without love. This can be proved from the following alone: that which loves supreme justice cannot despise what is just nor allow what is unjust. Now, anything that produces something thereby reveals that there is life in it (without life it would be unable to produce at all). Given this, it is not absurd to say, first, that productive faith is alive, and second, that non-productive faith is dead. The former on the grounds that it has, the latter on the grounds that it lacks, the life of love, without which it could not produce its works. We can use the term 'blind' of that which is not able, but ought to be able, to see, and not just of that which has lost its eyesight. Why cannot we similarly call faith without love 'dead' on the grounds that it does not have what it ought always to have, and not just because it has lost its life (which is love)? So then we recognize the faith that works through love to be alive [cf. Jas. 2: 20, 26; Gal. 5: 6]. And just so we can diagnose that the faith that, through contempt, shirks, is dead.

It is, therefore, possible and suitable enough to say that, while the faith that merely believes what it ought to believe is dead the faith that believes in what it ought to believe in is alive.

79. *What the three are: possible terminology*

So now, it is clear that it is to man's advantage to believe in this ineffable triple singularity and singular triplicity. One and a unity by virtue of the one essence, three and a Trinity by virtue of the three— three I-do-not-know-whats. I can say that it is a Trinity in virtue of Father, Son and Spirit. Father, Son and Spirit are three. I cannot, however, offer one name for that in virtue of which these three are three, as I might, for instance, say three persons, and one substance. For they must not be thought of as three persons. This is because a person is an independently existing thing. A number of persons always subsist as individuals independently of each other. Thus the number of persons is the number of substances. This is recognizably the case with a group of human beings: there are as many individual substances as there are persons. Hence, since there are not several substances in the supreme essence, there are not several persons.

But suppose we just want to talk about this subject with someone else, what word can we use to refer to what the three, Father, Son and Spirit, are? The only move we can make is a move forced by the lack of a proper name. This is to choose a name that cannot be predicated, in the plural, of the supreme essence, and to use it to flag what cannot be predicated by an appropriate name. Thus one might say that the wonderful Trinity is one essence, or nature, and three persons, or substances. The last two names seem more suitable as signposts for plurality: 'person' is only used of an individual rational nature, 'substance' is mainly used of individuals which, in particular, consist of several components. For it is individual things, in particular, that exist as the subjects of accidents—and hence are more properly called substances. (This is the reason that was given earlier for substance not being the proper term for the supreme essence: supreme essence is not subject to accidents. Substance, however, might, as we said, stand for essence.)

On the grounds, therefore, of linguistic necessity, it is possible to refer with a clear conscience to the unitary Trinity and trinitary unity as one essence and three persons or substances.

80. *The supreme essence rules and regulates all things. It alone is God*

It appears, therefore—no, rather it is patently obvious—that what we call God is not nothing. It is to the supreme essence alone that we properly give the name God. For if you say that God exists, irrespective of whether you say that one or many Gods exist, this is an idea that you cannot make sense of unless you think of God as that substance which is superior to every nature that is not God. This is the kind of substance that is so pre-eminently valuable that people have to worship it; the kind of substance that one ought to pray to for help against the forces that threaten. And what is so valuable as to be worshipped, what is to be prayed to—for anything—so much as the supremely good and supremely powerful spirit that dominates and regulates all things? We have established that all things were created and are supported through the supremely good and supremely wise omnipotence of this spirit. And so it would be extremely contrary to claim that it does not dominate what it has created, that either something else, less powerful, wise and good, or nothing at all—just the entirely irrational, unstructured chaos of chance—controls what it has created. For the supreme essence alone is that through which anything good is good, without which nothing is good, and out of, through and in which all things exist. So then, since it, alone, is not just a good Creator, but is also the superlatively powerful master and the superlatively wise controller of all things, it is superlatively clear that this is the only thing that all other natures ought, with all their might, to love and worship. It is the only thing from which benefits are to be hoped for. It alone is that towards which one must fly from adversity. It alone is that to which one must address one's supplications for anything whatsoever. Truly, therefore, not only is the supreme spirit God, but, it alone is God ineffably three and one.

PROSLOGION

PREFACE

After I had published, at the pressing entreaties of several of my brethren, a certain short tract [the *Monologion*] as an example of meditation on the meaning of faith from the point of view of one seeking, through silent reasoning within himself, things he knows not—reflecting that this was made up of a connected chain of many arguments, I began to wonder if perhaps it might be possible to find one single argument that for its proof required no other save itself, and that by itself would suffice to prove that God really exists, that He is the supreme good needing no other and is He whom all things have need of for their being and well-being, and also to prove whatever we believe about the Divine Being. But as often and as diligently as I turned my thoughts to this, sometimes it seemed to me that I had almost reached what I was seeking, sometimes it eluded my acutest thinking completely, so that finally, in desperation, I was about to give up what I was looking for as something impossible to find. However, when I had decided to put aside this idea altogether, lest by uselessly occupying my mind it might prevent other ideas with which I could make some progress, then, in spite of my unwillingness and my resistance to it, it began to force itself upon me more and more pressingly. So it was that one day when I was quite worn out with resisting its importunacy, there came to me, in the very conflict of my thoughts, what I had despaired of finding, so that I eagerly grasped the notion which in my distraction I had been rejecting.

Judging, then, that what had given me such joy to discover would

---

* Several minor liberties have been taken in the translation. The formula 'that-than-which-nothing-greater-can-be-thought' and its variants have been hyphenated for the sake of convenience; the Fool of the Psalmist has been given a capital letter; italics have been added in a few passages to make the meaning clearer; and some supplementary words and phrases (enclosed in square brackets) have also been interpolated for the same purpose. Biblical quotations have been translated directly from St Anselm's text which differs slightly from that of the Latin Vulgate version. References to the Psalms follow the Vulgate numbering which differs from that of the Hebrew texts followed by most other versions.

afford pleasure, if it were written down, to anyone who might read it, I have written the following short tract dealing with this question as well as several others, from the point of view of one trying to raise his mind to contemplate God and seeking to understand what he believes. In my opinion, neither this tract nor the other I mentioned before deserves to be called a book or to carry its author's name, and yet I did not think they should be sent forth without some title (by which, so to speak, they might invite those into whose hands they should come, to read them); so I have given to each its title, the first being called *An Example of Meditation on the Meaning of Faith*, and the sequel *Faith in Quest of Understanding*.

However, as both of them, under these titles, had already been copied out by several readers, a number of people (above all the reverend Archbishop of Lyons, Hugh, apostolic delegate to Gaul, who commanded me by his apostolic authority) have urged me to put my name to them. For the sake of greater convenience I have named the first book *Monologion*, that is, a soliloquy; and the other *Proslogion*, that is, an allocution.

Chapters

1. A rousing of the mind to the contemplation of God

2. That God truly exists

3. That God cannot be thought not to exist

4. How 'the Fool said in his heart' what cannot be thought

5. That God is whatever it is better to be than not to be, and that existing through Himself alone He makes all other beings from nothing

6. How He is perceptive although He is not a body

7. How He is omnipotent although He cannot do many things

8. How He is both merciful and impassible

9. How the all-just and supremely just One spares the wicked and justly has mercy on the wicked

10. How He justly punishes and justly spares the wicked

11. How 'all the ways of the Lord are mercy and truth', and yet how 'the Lord is just in all His ways'

1. *A rousing of the mind to the contemplation of God*

Come now, insignificant man, fly for a moment from your affairs, escape for a little while from the tumult of your thoughts. Put aside now your weighty cares and leave your wearisome toils. Abandon yourself for a little to God and rest for a little in Him. Enter into the inner chamber of your soul, shut out everything save God and what can be of help in your quest for Him and having locked the door seek Him out [Matt. 6: 6]. Speak now, my whole heart, speak now to God: 'I seek Your countenance, O Lord, Your countenance I seek' [Ps. 26: 8].

Come then, Lord my God, teach my heart where and how to seek

You, where and how to find You. Lord, if You are not present here, where, since You are absent, shall I look for You? On the other hand, if You are everywhere why then, since You are present, do I not see You? But surely You dwell in 'light inaccessible' [1 Tim. 6: 16]. And where is this inaccessible light, or how can I approach the inaccessible light? Or who shall lead me and take me into it that I may see You in it? Again, by what signs, under what aspect, shall I seek You? Never have I seen You, Lord my God, I do not know Your face. What shall he do, most high Lord, what shall this exile do, far away from You as he is? What shall Your servant do, tormented by love of You and yet cast off 'far from Your face' [Ps. 31: 22]? He yearns to see You and Your countenance is too far away from him. He desires to come close to You, and Your dwelling place is inaccessible; he longs to find You and does not know where You are; he is eager to seek You out and he does not know Your countenance. Lord, You are my God and my Lord, and never have I seen You. You have created me and re-created me and You have given me all the good things I possess, and still I do not know You. In fine, I was made in order to see You, and I have not yet accomplished what I was made for.

How wretched man's lot is when he has lost that for which he was made! Oh how hard and cruel was that Fall! Alas, what has man lost and what has he found? What did he lose and what remains to him? He lost the blessedness for which he was made, and he found the misery for which he was not made. That without which nothing is happy has gone from him and that which by itself is nothing but misery remains to him. Once 'man ate the bread of angels' [Ps. 77: 25], for which now he hungers; now he eats 'the bread of sorrow' [Ps. 126: 2], which then he knew nothing of. Alas the common grief of mankind, alas the universal lamentation of the children of Adam! He groaned with fullness; we sigh with hunger. He was prosperous; we go begging. He in his happiness had possessions and in his misery abandoned them; we in our unhappiness go without and miserably do we yearn and, alas, we remain empty. Why, since it was easy for him, did he not keep for us that which we lack so much? Why did he deprive us of light and surround us with darkness? Why did he take life away from us and inflict death upon us? Poor wretches that we are, whence have we been expelled and whither are we driven? Whence have we been cast down and whither buried? From our homeland into exile; from the vision of God into our present blindness; from the joy of immortality into the bitterness and horror of death. Oh wretched change from so great a good to so great an evil! What a grievous loss, a grievous sorrow, utterly grievous!

Alas, unfortunate that I am, one of the miserable children of Eve, separated from God. What have I undertaken? What have I actually done? Where was I going? Where have I come to? To what was I aspiring? For what do I yearn? 'I sought goodness' [Ps. 121: 9] and, lo, 'there is confusion' [Jer. 14: 19]. I yearned for God, and I was in my own way. I sought peace within myself and 'I have found tribulation and sadness' in my heart of hearts [Ps. 114: 3]. I wished to laugh from out the happiness of my soul, and 'the sobbing of my heart' [Ps. 37: 9] makes me cry out. I hoped for gladness and, lo, my sighs come thick and fast.

And You, 'O Lord, how long' [Ps. 6: 4]? How long, Lord, will You be unmindful of us? 'How long will You turn Your countenance' from us [Ps. 12: 1]? When will You look upon us and hear us [Ps. 12: 4]? When will You enlighten our eyes and show 'Your countenance' to us [Ps. 79: 4]? When will You give Yourself again to us? Look upon us, Lord; hear us, enlighten us, show Yourself to us. Give Yourself to us that it may be well with us, for without You it goes so ill for us. Have pity upon our efforts and our strivings towards You, for we can avail nothing without You. You call to us, 'so help us' [Ps. 78: 9]. I beseech You, Lord, let me not go sighing hopelessly, but make me breathe hopefully again. My heart is made bitter by its desolation; I beseech You, Lord, sweeten it by Your consolation. I set out hungry to look for You; I beseech You, Lord, do not let me depart from You fasting. I came to You as one famished; do not let me go without food. Poor, I have come to one who is rich. Unfortunate, I have come to one who is merciful. Do not let me return scorned and empty-handed. And if now I sigh before I eat [Job 3: 4], give me to eat after my sighs. Lord, bowed down as I am, I can only look downwards; raise me up that I may look upwards. 'My sins are heaped up over my head'; they cover me over and 'like a heavy load' crush me down [Ps. 37: 5]. Save me, disburden me, 'lest their pit close its mouth over me' [Ps. 68: 16]. Let me discern Your light whether it be from afar or from the depths. Teach me to seek You, and reveal Yourself to me as I seek, because I can neither seek You if You do not teach me how, nor find You unless You reveal Yourself. Let me seek You in desiring You; let me desire You in seeking You; let me find You in loving You; let me love You in finding You.

I acknowledge, Lord, and I give thanks that You have created Your image in me, so that I may remember You, think of You, love You. But this image is so effaced and worn away by vice, so darkened by the smoke of sin, that it cannot do what it was made to do unless You renew it and reform it. I do not try, Lord, to attain Your lofty heights, because my understanding is in no way equal to it. But I do desire to understand Your truth a little, that truth that my heart believes and loves. For I do not seek to understand so that I may believe; but I believe so that I may understand. For I believe this also, that 'unless I believe, I shall not understand' [Isa. 7: 9].

2. *That God truly exists*

Well then, Lord, You who give understanding to faith, grant me that I may understand, as much as You see fit, that You exist as we believe You to exist, and that You are what we believe You to be. Now we believe that You are something than which nothing greater can be thought. Or can it be that a thing of such a nature does not exist, since 'the Fool has said in his heart, there is no God' [Ps. 13: 1; 52: 1]? But surely, when this same Fool hears what I am speaking about, namely, 'something-than-which-nothing-greater-can-be-thought', he understands what he hears, and what he understands is in his mind, even if he does not understand that it actually exists. For it is one thing for an object to exist in the mind, and another thing to understand that an object actually exists. Thus, when a painter plans beforehand what he is going to execute, he has [the picture] in his mind, but he does not yet think that it actually exists because he has not yet executed it. However, when he has actually painted it, then he both has it in his mind and understands that it exists because he has now made it. Even the Fool, then, is forced to agree that something-than-which-nothing-greater-can-be-thought exists in the mind, since he understands this when he hears it, and whatever is understood is in the mind. And surely that-than-which-a-greater-cannot-be-thought cannot exist in the mind alone. For if it exists solely in the mind, it can be thought to exist in reality also, which is greater. If then that-than-which-a-greater-cannot-be-thought exists in the mind alone, this same that-than-which-a-greater-*cannot*-be-thought is that-than-which-a-greater-*can*-be-thought. But this is obviously impossible. Therefore there is absolutely no doubt that something-than-which-a-greater-cannot-be-thought exists both in the mind and in reality.

3. *That God cannot be thought not to exist*

And certainly this being so truly exists that it cannot be even thought not to exist. For something can be thought to exist that cannot be thought not to exist, and this is greater than that which can be thought not to exist. Hence, if that-than-which-a-greater-cannot-be-thought can be thought not to exist, then that-than-which-a-greater-cannot-be-thought is not the same as that-than-which-a-greater-cannot-be-thought, which is absurd. Something-than-which-a-greater-cannot-be-thought exists so truly then, that it cannot be even thought not to exist.

And You, Lord our God, are this being. You exist so truly, Lord my God, that You cannot even be thought not to exist. And this is as it should be, for if some intelligence could think of something better than You, the creature would be above its Creator and would judge its Creator—and that is completely absurd. In fact, everything else there is, except You alone, can be thought of as not existing. You alone, then, of all things most truly exist and therefore of all things possess existence to the highest degree; for anything else does not exist as truly, and so possesses existence to a lesser degree. Why then did 'the Fool say in his heart, there is no God' [Ps. 13: 1; 52: 1] when it is so evident to any rational mind that You of all things exist to the highest degree? Why indeed, unless because he was stupid and a fool?

4. *How 'the Fool said in his heart' what cannot be thought*

How indeed has he 'said in his heart' what he could not think; or how could he not think what he 'said in his heart', since to 'say in one's heart' and to 'think' are the same? But if he really (indeed, since he really) both thought because he 'said in his heart' and did not 'say in his heart' because he could not think, there is not only one sense in which something is 'said in one's heart' or thought. For in one sense a thing is thought when the word signifying it is thought; in another sense when the very object which the thing is is understood. In the first sense, then, God can be thought not to exist, but not at all in the second sense. No one, indeed, understanding what God is can think that God does not exist, even though he may say these words in his heart either without any [objective] signification or with some peculiar signification. For God is that-than-which-nothing-greater-can-be-thought. Whoever really understands this understands clearly that this same being so exists that not even in thought can it not exist. Thus whoever understands that God exists in such a way cannot think of Him as not existing.

I give thanks, good Lord, I give thanks to You, since what I believed before through Your free gift I now so understand through Your illumination, that if I did not want to *believe* that You existed, I should nevertheless be unable not to *understand* it.

5. *That God is whatever it is better to be than not to be and that, existing through Himself alone, He makes all other beings from nothing*

What then are You, Lord God, You than whom nothing greater can be thought? But what are You save that supreme being, existing through Yourself alone, who made everything else from nothing? For whatever is not this is less than that which can be thought of; but this cannot be thought about You. What goodness, then, could be wanting to the supreme good, through which every good exists? Thus You are just, truthful, happy, and whatever it is better to be than not to be—for it is better to be just rather than unjust, and happy rather than unhappy.

6. *How He is perceptive although He is not a body*

But since it is better to be perceptive, omnipotent, merciful, impassible, than not to be so, how are You able to perceive if You are not a body; or how are You omnipotent if You are not able to do everything; or how are You merciful and impassible at the same time? For if only corporeal things are capable of perception, since the senses are involved with the body and in the body, how are You perceptive, since You are not a body but the supreme spirit who is better than any body? But if to perceive is nothing else than to know, or if it is directed to knowing (for he who perceives knows according to the appropriate sense, as, for example, colours are known by sight and flavours through taste), one can say not inappropriately that whatever in any way knows also in some way perceives. So it is, Lord, that although You are not a body You are supremely perceptive, in the sense that You know supremely all things and not in the sense in which an animal knows through a bodily sense-faculty.

7. *How He is omnipotent although He cannot do many things*

Again, how are You omnipotent if You cannot do all things? But, how can You do all things if You cannot be corrupted, or tell lies, or make the true into the false (such as to undo what has been done), and many similar things? Or is the ability to do these things not power but impotence? For he who can do these things can do what is not good for himself and what he ought not to do. And the more he can do these things, the more power adversity and perversity have over him and the less he has against them. He, therefore, who can do these things can do them not by power but by impotence. It is said, then, that he 'can', not because he himself can do them but because his impotence gives another power against him. Or it is said in some other manner of speaking, in the sense in which many words are used improperly, as, for example, when we use 'to be' for 'not to be', and 'to do' for 'not to do' or for 'to do nothing'. Thus we often say to someone who denies that some thing exists: 'It *is* as you say it *is*', although it would seem much more proper to say, 'It *is not* as you say it *is not*'. Again, we say 'This man is sitting', just as we say 'That man is doing [something]'; or we say 'This man is resting', just as we say 'That man is doing [something]'. But 'to sit' is *not* to do something, and 'to rest' is to do *nothing*. In the same way, then, when someone is said to have the 'power' of doing or suffering something which is not to his advantage or which he ought not to do, then by 'power' here we mean 'impotence', for the more he has this 'power', the more adversity and perversity have power over him and the more is he powerless against them. Therefore, Lord God, You are the more truly omnipotent since You can do nothing through impotence and nothing can have power against You.

8. *How He is both merciful and impassible*

But how are You at once both merciful and impassible? For if You are impassible You do not have any compassion; and if You have no compassion Your heart is not sorrowful from compassion with the sorrowful, which is what being merciful is. But if You are not merciful whence comes so much consolation for the sorrowful?

How, then, are You merciful and not merciful, O Lord, unless it be that You are merciful in relation to us and not in relation to Yourself? In fact, You are [merciful] according to our way of looking at things and not according to Your way. For when You look upon us in our misery it is we who feel the effect of Your mercy, but You do not experience the feeling. Therefore You are both merciful because You save the sorrowful and pardon sinners against You; and You are not merciful because You do not experience any feeling of compassion for misery.

9. *How the all-just and supremely just One spares the wicked and justly has mercy on the wicked*

But how do You spare the wicked if You are all-just and supremely just? For how does the all-just and supremely just One do something that is unjust? Or what kind of justice is it to give everlasting life to him who merits eternal death? How then, O good God, good to the good and to the wicked, how do You save the wicked if this is not just and You do not do anything which is not just? Or, since Your goodness is beyond comprehension, is this hidden in the inaccessible light in which You dwell? Truly in the deepest and most secret place of Your goodness is hidden the source whence the stream of Your mercy flows. For though You are all-just and supremely just You are, however—precisely because You are all-just and supremely just— also beneficent even to the wicked. You would, in fact, be less good if You were not beneficent to any wicked man. For he who is good to both good and wicked is better than he who is good only to the good. And he who is good to the wicked by both punishing and sparing them is better than he who is good to the wicked only by punishing them. You are merciful, then, because You are all-good and supremely good. And though perhaps it is apparent why You should reward the good with good and the bad with bad, what is indeed to be wondered at is why You, the all-just One who wants for nothing, should bestow good things on Your wicked and guilty creatures.

O God, how profound is Your goodness! It is apparent whence Your mercy comes, and yet it is not clearly seen. Whence the stream flows is obvious, and yet the source where it rises is not seen directly. For on the one hand it is from plenitude of goodness that You are gentle with those who sin against You; and on the other hand the reason why You are thus is hidden in the depths of Your goodness. For although from Your goodness You reward the good with good and the bad with bad, yet it seems that the very definition of justice demands this. But when You give good things to the wicked, one both understands that the supreme Good has willed to do this and one wonders why the supremely just One could have willed it.

O mercy, from what abundant sweetness and sweet abundance do you flow forth for us! O boundless goodness of God, with what feeling should You be loved by sinners! For You save the just whom justice commends, but You free sinners whom justice condemns. The former [are saved] by the aid of their merits; the latter despite their merits. The former [are saved] by regarding the good things You have given; the latter by disregarding the bad things which You hate. O boundless goodness which so surpasses all understanding, let that mercy come upon me which proceeds from Your so great abundance! Let that which flows forth from You flow into me! Forbear through mercy lest You be avenged through justice! For even if it be difficult to understand how Your mercy is not apart from Your justice, it is, however, necessary to believe that it is not in any way opposed to justice, for it derives from goodness which is naught apart from justice, which indeed really coincides with justice. Truly, if You are merciful because You are supremely good, and if You are supremely good only in so far as You are supremely just, truly then You are merciful precisely because You are supremely just. Help me, just and merciful God, whose light I seek, help me so that I may understand what I am saying. Truly, then, you are merciful because You are just.

Is Your mercy not then derived from Your justice? Do You not then spare the wicked because of justice? If it is so, Lord, if it is so, teach me how it is so. Is it because it is just that You are so good that You cannot be conceived to be better, and that You act with so much power that You cannot be thought to be more powerful? For what is more just than this? This, however, would not be the case if You were good only by way of retribution and not by way of forgiveness, and if You made to be good only those not yet good, and not also the wicked. In this way, then, it is just that You spare the wicked and make good men from bad. Finally, what is done unjustly ought not to be done; and what ought not to be done is done unjustly. If, then, it is unjust that You should have mercy on the wicked, You ought not to be merciful; and if You ought not to be merciful it is unjust of You to be merciful. But if it is improper to say this, then it is proper to believe that it is just of You to have mercy on the wicked.

10. *How He justly punishes and justly spares the wicked*

But it is also just that You punish the wicked. For what is more just than that the good should receive good things and the bad receive bad things? How then is it just both that You punish the wicked and that You spare the wicked?

Or do You with justice in one way punish the wicked and with justice in another way spare the wicked? For when You punish the wicked it is just, since it agrees with their merits; however, when You spare the wicked it is just, not because of their merits but because it is befitting to Your goodness. For in sparing the wicked You are just in relation to Yourself and not in relation to us, even as You are merciful in relation to us and not in relation to Yourself. Thus it is, as You are merciful (in saving us whom You might with justice lose) not because You experience any feeling, but because we experience the effect of Your mercy, so You are just not because You give us our due, but because You do what befits You as the supreme good. Thus, then, without inconsistency justly do You punish and justly do You pardon.

11. *How 'all the ways of the Lord are mercy and truth', and yet how 'the Lord is just in all His ways'*

But is it not also just in relation to Yourself, Lord, that You should punish the wicked? It is just inasmuch as You are so just that You cannot be thought to be more just. But You would in no wise be so if You only returned good to the good and did not return bad to the bad. For he is more just who rewards the merits of both good and bad than he who rewards the merits of the good alone. Therefore it is just in relation to You, O just and benevolent God, both when You punish and when You pardon. Truly, then, 'all the ways of the Lord are mercy and truth' [Ps. 24: 10] and yet 'the Lord is just in all His ways' [Ps. 144: 17]. And [this is so] without any inconsistency at all, since it is not just for those to be saved whom You will to punish, and it is not just for those to be damned whom You will to pardon. For that alone is just which You will, and that is not just which You do not will. Thus, then, Your mercy is derived from Your justice since it is just that You are so good that You are good even in forgiving. And perhaps this is why one who is supremely just can will good for the wicked. But if it can in some way be grasped why You can will to save the wicked, it certainly cannot be understood by any reason why from those who are alike in wickedness You save some rather than others through Your supreme goodness, and damn some rather than others through Your supreme justice.

Thus, then, truly are You perceptive, omnipotent, merciful, and impassible, just as You are living, wise, good, blessed, eternal, and whatever it is better to be rather than not to be.

12. *That God is the very life by which He lives and that the same holds for like attributes*

But clearly, whatever You are, You are not that through another but through Your very self. You are therefore the very life by which You live, the wisdom by which You are wise, the very goodness by which You are good to both good men and wicked, and the same holds for like attributes.

13. *How He alone is limitless and eternal, although other spirits are also limitless and eternal*

All that which is enclosed in any way by place or time is less than that which no law of place or time constrains. Since, then, nothing is greater than You, no place or time confines You but You exist everywhere and always. And because this can be said of You alone, You alone are unlimited and eternal. How then are other spirits also said to be unlimited and eternal?

Now, You alone are said to be eternal because, alone of all beings, You will not cease to exist just as You have not begun to exist. But how are You alone unlimited? Is it that compared with You the created spirit is limited, but unlimited with respect to a body? Certainly that is absolutely limited which, when it is wholly in one place, cannot at the same time be somewhere else. This is seen in the case of bodies alone. But that is unlimited which is wholly everywhere at once; and this is true only of You alone. That, however, is limited and unlimited at the same time which, while wholly in one place, can at the same time be wholly somewhere else but not everywhere; and this is true of created spirits. For if the soul were not wholly in each of the parts of its body it would not sense wholly in each of them. You then, O Lord, are unlimited and eternal in a unique way and yet other spirits are also unlimited and eternal.

14. *How and why God is both seen and not seen by those*
    seeking Him

Have you found, O my soul, what you were seeking? You were seeking God, and you found Him to be something which is the highest of all, than which a better cannot be thought, and to be life itself, light, wisdom, goodness, eternal blessedness and blessed eternity, and to exist everywhere and always. If you have not found your God, how is He this which you have found, and which you have understood with such certain truth and true certitude? But if you have found [Him], why is it that you do not experience what you have found? Why, O Lord God, does my soul not experience You if it has found You?

Or has it not found that which it has found to be the light and the truth? But then, how did it understand this save by seeing the light and the truth? Could it understand anything at all about You save through 'Your light and Your truth' [Ps. 42: 3]? If, then, it saw the light and the truth, it saw You. If it did not see You then it did not see the light or the truth. Or is it that it saw both the truth and the light, and yet it did not see You because it saw You only partially but did not see You as You are?

Lord my God, You who have formed and reformed me, tell my desiring soul what You are besides what it has seen so that it may see clearly that which it desires. It strives so that it may see more, and it sees nothing beyond what it has seen save darkness. Or rather it does not see darkness, which is not in You in any way; but it sees that it cannot see more because of its own darkness. Why is this, Lord, why is this? Is its eye darkened by its weakness, or is it dazzled by Your splendour? In truth it is both darkened in itself and dazzled by You. It is indeed both darkened by its own littleness and overwhelmed by Your immensity. It is, in fact, both restricted by its own limitedness and overcome by Your fullness. For how great is that light from which shines every truth that gives light to the understanding! How complete is that truth in which is everything that is true and outside of which nothing exists save nothingness and falsity! How boundless is that which in one glance sees everything that has been made, and by whom and through whom and in what manner it was made from nothing! What purity, what simplicity, what certitude and splendour is there! Truly it is more than can be understood by any creature.

15. *How He is greater than can be thought*

Therefore, Lord, not only are You that than which a greater cannot be thought, but You are also something greater than can be thought. For since it is possible to think that there is such a one, then, if You are not this same being something greater than You could be thought—which cannot be.

16. *That this is the 'inaccessible light' in which He 'dwells'*

Truly, Lord, this is the inaccessible light in which You dwell. For truly there is nothing else which can penetrate through it so that it might discover You there. Truly I do not see this light since it is too much for me; and yet whatever I see I see through it, just as an eye that is weak sees what it sees by the light of the sun which it cannot look at in the sun itself. My understanding is not able [to attain] to that [light]. It shines too much and [my understanding] does not grasp it nor does the eye of my soul allow itself to be turned towards it for too long. It is dazzled by its splendour, overcome by its fullness, overwhelmed by its immensity, confused by its extent. O supreme and inaccessible light; O whole and blessed truth, how far You are from me who am so close to You! How distant You are from my sight while I am so present to Your sight! You are wholly present everywhere and I do not see You. In You I move and in You I have my being and I cannot come near to You. You are within me and around me and I do not have any experience of You.

17. *That harmony, fragrance, sweetness, softness, and beauty are in God according to His own ineffable manner*

Still You hide away, Lord, from my soul in Your light and blessedness, and so it still dwells in its darkness and misery. For it looks all about, and does not see Your beauty. It listens, and does not hear Your harmony. It smells, and does not sense Your fragrance. It tastes, and does not recognize Your savour. It feels, and does not sense Your softness. For You have in Yourself, Lord, in Your own ineffable manner, those [qualities] You have given to the things created by You according to their own sensible manner. But the senses of my soul, because of the ancient weakness of sin, have become hardened and dulled and obstructed.

18. *That there are no parts in God or in His eternity which He is*

Behold, once more confusion, once more sorrow and grief stand in my way as I seek joy and happiness! Even now my soul hoped for fulfilment, and, lo, once again it is overwhelmed by neediness! Even now I sought to have my fill, and, lo, I hunger the more! I strove to ascend to God's light and I have fallen back into my own darkness. Indeed, not only have I fallen back into it, but I feel myself enclosed within it. I fell before 'my mother conceived me' [Ps. 50: 7]. In that darkness indeed 'I was conceived' [ibid.] and I was born under its shadow. We all, in fact, at one time fell in him 'in whom all of us' sinned [Rom. 5: 12]. In him (who easily possessed and wickedly lost it for himself and for us), we all lost that which, when we wish to look for it, we do not know; that which, when we look for it, we do not find; that which, when we find it, is not what we are looking for. Help me 'because of Your goodness, Lord' [Ps. 24: 7]. 'I sought Your countenance, Your countenance I will seek, O Lord; do not turn Your face away from me' [Ps. 26: 8]. Raise me up from my own self to You. Purify, heal, make sharp, 'illumine' the eye of my soul so that it may see You [Ps. 12: 4]. Let my soul gather its strength again and with all its understanding strive once more towards You, Lord.

What are You, Lord, what are You; what shall my heart understand You to be? You are, assuredly, life, You are wisdom, You are truth, You are goodness, You are blessedness, You are eternity, and You are every true good. These are many things, and my limited understanding cannot see them all in one single glance so as to delight in all at once. How then, Lord, are You all these things? Are they parts of You, or rather, is each one of these wholly what You are? For whatever is made up of parts is not absolutely one, but in a sense many and other than itself, and it can be broken up either actually or by the mind—all of which things are foreign to You, than whom nothing better can be thought. Therefore there are no parts in You, Lord; neither are You many, but You are so much one and the same with Yourself that in nothing are You dissimilar with Yourself. Indeed You are unity itself not divisible by any mind. Life and wisdom and the other [attributes], then, are not parts of You, but all are one and each one of them is wholly what You are and what all the others are. Since, then, neither You nor Your eternity which You are have parts, no part of You or of Your eternity is anywhere or at any time, but You exist as a whole everywhere and Your eternity exists as a whole always.

19. *That He is not in place or time but all things are in Him*

But if through Your eternity You have been and are and will be, and if to have been is not to be in the future, and to be present is not to have been or to be in the future—how does Your eternity exist as a whole always?

Or is there nothing past in Your eternity, so that it is now no longer; nor anything future, as though it were not already? You were not, therefore, yesterday, nor will You be tomorrow, but yesterday and today and tomorrow You *are*. Indeed You exist neither yesterday nor today nor tomorrow but are absolutely outside all time. For yesterday and today and tomorrow are completely in time; however, You, though nothing can be without You, are nevertheless not in place or time but all things are in You. For nothing contains You, but You contain all things.

20. *That He is before and beyond even all eternal things*

You therefore permeate and embrace all things; You are before and beyond all things. You are before all things of course since, before they came to be, You already *are*. But how are You beyond all things? For in what way are You beyond those things that will never have an end?

Is it because these things can in no way exist without You, though You do not exist any the less even if they return to nothingness? For in this way, in a sense, You are beyond them. Or is it also that they can be thought to have an end while You cannot in any way? For in this way, in a sense, they do indeed have an end, but You do not in any sense. And assuredly that which does not have an end in any way at all is beyond that which does come to an end in some way. Is it also in this way that You surpass even all eternal things, since Your eternity and theirs is wholly present to You, though they do not have the part of their eternity which is yet to come just as they do not now have what is past? In this way, indeed, are You always beyond those things, because You are always present at that point (or because it is always present to You) which they have not yet reached.

21. *Whether this is the 'age of the age' or the 'ages of the ages'*

Is this, then, the 'age of the age' or the 'ages of the ages'? For just as an age of time contains all temporal things, so Your eternity contains also the very ages of time. Indeed this [eternity] is an 'age' because of its indivisible unity, but 'ages' because of its immensity without limit. And although You are so great, Lord, that all things are filled with You and are in You, yet You exist without any spatial extension so that there is neither a middle nor half nor any part in You.

22. *That He alone is what He is and who He is*

You alone then, Lord, are what You are and You are who You are. For what is one thing as a whole and another as to its parts, and has in it something mutable, is not altogether what it is. And what began [to exist] from non-existence, and can be thought not to exist, and returns to non-existence unless it subsists through some other; and what has had a past existence but does not now exist, and a future existence but does not yet exist—such a thing does not exist in a strict and absolute sense. But You are what You are, for whatever You are at any time or in any way this You are wholly and forever.

And You are the being who exists in a strict and absolute sense because You have neither past nor future existence but only present existence; nor can You be thought not to exist at any time. And You are life and light and wisdom and blessedness and eternity and many suchlike good things; and yet You are nothing save the one and supreme good, You who are completely sufficient unto Yourself, needing nothing, but rather He whom all things need in order that they may have being and well-being.

23. *That this good is equally Father and Son and Holy Spirit; and that this is the one necessary being which is altogether and wholly and solely good*

You are this good, O God the Father; this is Your Word, that is to say, Your Son. For there cannot be any other than what You are, or any thing greater or lesser than You, in the Word by which You utter Yourself. For Your Word is as true as You are truthful and is therefore the very truth that You are and that is not other than You. And You are so simple that there cannot be born of You any other than what You are. This itself is the Love, one and common to You and to Your Son, that is the Holy Spirit proceeding from both. For this same Love is not unequal to You or to Your Son since Your love for Yourself and Him, and His love for You and Himself, are as great as You and He are. Nor is that other than You and than Him which is not different from You and Him; nor can there proceed from Your supreme simplicity what is other than that from which it proceeds. Thus, whatever each is singly, that the whole Trinity is altogether, Father, Son, and Holy Spirit; since each singly is not other than the supremely simple unity and the supremely unified simplicity which can be neither multiplied nor differentiated.

'Moreover, one thing is necessary' [Luke 10: 42]. This is, moreover, that one thing necessary in which is every good, or rather, which is wholly and uniquely and completely and solely good.

24. *A speculation as to what kind and how great this good is*

Now, my soul, rouse and lift up your whole understanding and think as much as you can on what kind and how great this good is. For if particular goods are enjoyable, consider carefully how enjoyable is that good which contains the joyfulness of all goods; not [a joy] such as we have experienced in created things, but as different from this as the Creator differs from the creature. For if life that is created is good, how good is the Life that creates? If the salvation that has been brought about is joyful, how joyful is the Salvation that brings about all salvation? If wisdom in the knowledge of things that have been brought into being is lovable, how lovable is the Wisdom that has brought all things into being out of nothing? Finally, if there are many great delights in delightful things, of what kind and how great is the delight in Him who made these same delightful things?

25. *Which goods belong to those who enjoy this good, and how great they are*

Oh he who will enjoy this good, what will be his and what will not be his! Whatever he wishes will certainly be his and whatever he does not wish will not be his. In fact, all the goods of body and soul will be there such that 'neither eye has seen, nor ear heard, nor the heart of man conceived' [1 Cor. 2: 9]. Why, then, do you wander about so much, O insignificant man, seeking the goods of your soul and body? Love the one good in which all good things are, and that is sufficient. Desire the simple good which contains every good, and that is enough. For what do you love, O my flesh, what do you desire, O my soul? There it is, there it is, whatever you love, whatever you desire. If beauty delights you, 'the just will shine as the sun' [Matt. 13: 43]. If the swiftness or strength or freedom of the body that nothing can withstand [delights you], 'they will be like the angels of God' [Matt. 22: 30]; for it is 'sown as a natural body and shall rise as a spiritual body' [1 Cor. 15: 44] by a supernatural power. If it is a long and healthy life, a healthy eternity and an eternal health is there since 'the just will live forever' [Wis. 5: 16] and 'the salvation of the just is from the Lord' [Ps. 36: 39]. If it is satisfaction, they will be satisfied 'when the glory of God will appear' [Ps. 16: 15]. If it is quenching of thirst, 'they will be inebriated with the abundance of the house of God' [Ps.

35: 9]. If it is melody, there the choirs of angels play unceasingly to God. If it is pleasure of any kind, not impure but pure, God 'will make them drink from the torrent of His pleasure' [Ps. 35: 9]. If it is wisdom, the very Wisdom of God will show itself to them. If it is friendship, they will love God more than themselves and one another as themselves, and God will love them more than they love themselves because it is through Him that they love Him and themselves and one another, and He loves Himself and them through Himself. If it is peace, for all of them there will be one will, since they will have none save the will of God. If it is power, they will be all-powerful with regard to their wills, as God is with His. For just as God will be able to do what He wills through Himself, so through Him they will be able to do what they will; because, just as they will not will anything save what He wills, so He will will whatever they will, and what He intends to will cannot not be. If it is honours and riches, God will set His good and faithful servants over many things [Matt. 25: 21, 23]; indeed, they will be called 'sons of God' and 'Gods' [Matt. 5: 9] and will in fact be so; and where the Son will be there also they will be, 'heirs indeed of God and co-heirs of Christ' [Rom. 8: 17]. If it is real security, they will indeed be as assured that this same [security], or rather this same good, will never in any way fail them, as they will be assured that they will not lose it of their own accord, nor that the loving God will take it away against their will from those who love Him, nor that anything more powerful than God will separate God and them against their will.

What joy there is indeed and how great it is where there exists so great a good! O human heart, O needy heart, O heart experienced in suffering, indeed overwhelmed by suffering, how greatly would you rejoice if you abounded in all these things! Ask your heart whether it could comprehend its joy in its so great blessedness? But surely if someone else whom you loved in every respect as yourself possessed that same blessedness, your joy would be doubled for you would rejoice as much for him as for yourself. If, then, two or three or many more possessed it you would rejoice just as much for each one as for yourself, if you loved each one as yourself. Therefore in that perfect and pure love of the countless holy angels and holy men where no one will love another less than himself, each will rejoice for every other as for himself. If, then, the heart of man will scarcely be able to comprehend the joy that will belong to it from so great a good, how will it comprehend so many and such great joys? Indeed, to the degree that each one loves some other, so he will rejoice in the good of that other; therefore, just as each one in that perfect happiness will love God incomparably more than himself and all others with him, so he will rejoice immeasurably more over the happiness of God than over his own happiness and that of all the others with him. But if they love God with their whole heart, their whole mind, their whole soul, while yet their whole heart, their whole mind, their whole soul, is not equal to the grandeur of this love, they will assuredly so rejoice with their whole heart, their whole mind, and their whole soul, that their whole heart, their whole mind, their whole soul will not be equal to the fullness of their joy.

26. *Whether this is the 'fullness of joy' which the Lord promises?*

My God and my Lord, my hope and the joy of my heart, tell my soul if this is the joy of which You speak through Your Son: 'Ask and you will receive, that your joy may be complete' [John 16: 24]. For I have discovered a joy that is complete and more than complete. Indeed, when the heart is filled with that joy, the mind is filled with it, the soul is filled with it, the whole man is filled with it, yet joy beyond measure will remain. The whole of that joy, then, will not enter into those who rejoice, but those who rejoice will enter wholly into that joy. Speak, Lord, tell Your servant within his heart if this is the joy into which Your servants will enter who enter 'into the joy of the Lord' [Matt. 25: 21]. But surely that joy in which Your chosen ones will rejoice is that which 'neither eye has seen, nor ear heard, nor has it entered into the heart of man' [1 Cor. 2: 9]. I have not yet said or thought, then, Lord, how greatly your blessed will rejoice. They will, no doubt, rejoice as much as they love, and they will love as much as they know. How much will they know You, then, Lord, and how much will they love You? In very truth, 'neither eye has seen, nor ear heard, nor has it entered into the heart of man' [ibid.] in this life how much they will know You and love You in that life.

I pray, O God, that I may know You and love You, so that I may rejoice in You. And if I cannot do so fully in this life may I progress gradually until it comes to fullness. Let the knowledge of You grow in me here, and there [in heaven] be made complete; let Your love grow in me here and there be made complete, so that here my joy may be great in hope, and there be complete in reality. Lord, by Your Son You command, or rather, counsel us to ask and you promise that we shall receive so that our 'joy may be complete' [John 16: 24]. I ask, Lord, as You counsel through our admirable counsellor. May I receive what You promise through Your truth so that my 'joy may be complete' [ibid.]. God of truth, I ask that I may receive so that my 'joy may be complete' [ibid.]. Until then let my mind meditate on it, let my tongue speak of it, let my heart love it, let my mouth preach it. Let my soul hunger for it, let my flesh thirst for it, my whole being desire it, until I enter into the 'joy of the Lord' [Matt. 25: 21], who is God, Three in One, 'blessed forever. Amen' [1 Rom. 1: 25].

PRO INSIPIENTE

(ON BEHALF OF THE FOOL)
BY GAUNILO OF MARMOUTIERS

I

To one doubting whether there is, or denying that there is, something of such a nature than which nothing greater can be thought, it is said here [in the *Proslogion*] that its existence is proved, first because the very one who denies or doubts it already has it in his mind, since when he hears it spoken of he understands what is said; and further, because what he understands is necessarily such that it exists not only in the mind but also in reality. And this is proved by the fact that it is greater to exist both in the mind and in reality than in the mind alone. For if this same being exists in the mind alone, anything that existed also in reality would be greater than this being, and thus that which is greater than everything would be less than some thing and would not be greater than everything, which is obviously contradictory. Therefore, it is necessarily the case that that which is greater than everything, being already proved to exist in the mind, should exist not only in the mind but also in reality, since otherwise it would not be greater than everything.

2

But he [the Fool] can perhaps reply that this thing is said already to exist in the mind only in the sense that I understand what is said. For could I not say that all kinds of unreal things, not existing in themselves in any way at all, are equally in the mind since if anyone speaks about them I understand whatever he says? Unless perhaps it is manifest that this being is such that it can be entertained in the mind in a different way from unreal or doubtfully real things, so that I am not said to think of or have in thought what is heard, but to understand and have it in mind, in that I cannot really think of this being in any other way save by understanding it, that is to say, by grasping by certain knowledge that the thing itself actually exists. But if this is the case, first, there will be no difference between having an object in mind (taken as preceding in time), and understanding that the object actually exists (taken as following in time), as in the case of the picture which exists first in the mind of the painter and then in the completed work. And thus it would be scarcely conceivable that, when this object had been spoken of and heard, it could not be thought not to exist in the same way in which God can [be thought] not to exist. For if He cannot, why put forward this whole argument against anyone denying or doubting that there is something of this kind? Finally, that it is such a thing that, as soon as it is thought of, it cannot but be certainly perceived by the mind as indubitably existing, must be proved to me by some indisputable argument and not by that proposed, namely, that it must already be in my mind when I understand what I hear. For this is in my view like [arguing that] any things doubtfully real or even unreal are capable of existing if these things are mentioned by someone whose spoken words I might understand, and, even more, that [they exist] if, though deceived about them as often happens, I should believe them [to exist]—which argument I still do not believe!

3

Hence, the example of the painter having the picture he is about to make already in his mind cannot support this argument. For this picture, before it is actually made, is contained in the very art of the painter and such a thing in the art of any artist is nothing but a certain part of his very understanding, since as St Augustine says [*In Iohannem*, tract. 1, n. 16], 'when the artisan is about actually to make a box he has it beforehand in his art. The box which is actually made is not a living thing, but the box which is in his art is a living thing since the soul of the artist, in which these things exist before their actual realization, is a living thing.' Now how are these things living in the living soul of the artist unless they are identical with the knowledge or understanding of the soul itself? But, apart from those things which are known to belong to the very nature of the mind itself, in the case of any truth perceived by the mind by being either heard or understood, then it cannot be doubted that this truth is one thing and that the understanding which grasps it is another. Therefore even if it were true that there was something than which nothing greater could be thought, this thing, heard and understood, would not, however, be the same as the not-yet-made picture is in the mind of the painter.

4

To this we may add something that has already been mentioned, namely, that upon hearing it spoken of I can so little think of or entertain in my mind this being (that which is greater than all those others that are able to be thought of, and which it is said can be none other than God Himself) in terms of an object known to me either by species or genus, as I can think of God Himself, whom indeed for this very reason I can even think does not exist. For neither do I know the reality itself, nor can I form an idea from some other things like it since, as you say yourself, it is such that nothing could be like it. For if I heard something said about a man who was completely unknown to me so that I did not even know whether he existed, I could nevertheless think about him in his very reality as a man by means of that specific or generic notion by which I know what a man is or men are. However, it could happen that, because of a falsehood on the part of the speaker, the man I thought of did not actually exist, although I thought of him nevertheless as a truly existing object—not this particular man but any man in general. It is not, then, in the way that I have this unreal thing in thought or in mind that I can have that object in my mind when I hear 'God' or 'something greater than everything' spoken of. For while I was able to think of the former in terms of a truly existing thing which was known to me, I know nothing at all of the latter save for the verbal formula, and on the basis of this alone one can scarcely or never think of any truth. For when one thinks in this way, one thinks not so much of the word itself, which is indeed a real thing (that is to say, the sound of the letters or syllables), as of the meaning of the word which is heard. However, it [that which is greater than everything] is not thought of in the way of one who knows what is meant by that expression— thought of, that is, in terms of the thing [signified] or as true in thought alone. It is rather in the way of one who does not really know this object but thinks of it in terms of an affection of his mind produced by hearing the spoken words, and who tries to imagine what the words he has heard might mean. However, it would be astonishing if he could ever [attain to] the truth of the thing. Therefore, when I hear and understand someone saying that there is something greater than everything that can be thought of, it is agreed that it is in this latter sense that it is in my mind and not in any other sense. So much for the claim that that supreme nature exists already in my mind.

5

That, however, [this nature] necessarily exists in reality is demonstrated to me from the fact that, unless it existed, whatever exists in reality would be greater than it and consequently it would not be that which is greater than everything that undoubtedly had already been proved to exist in the mind. To this I reply as follows: if something that cannot even be thought in the true and real sense must be said to exist in the mind, then I do not deny that this also exists in my mind in the same way. But since from this one cannot in any way conclude that it exists also in reality, I certainly do not yet concede that it actually exists, until this is proved to me by an indubitable argument. For he who claims that it actually exists because otherwise it would not be that which is greater than everything does not consider carefully enough whom he is addressing. For I certainly do not yet admit this greater [than everything] to be any truly existing thing; indeed I doubt or even deny it. And I do not concede that it exists in a different way from that—if one ought to speak of 'existence' here—when the mind tries to imagine a completely unknown thing on the basis of the spoken words alone. How then can it be proved to me on that basis that that which is greater than everything truly exists in reality (because it is evident that it is greater than all others) if I keep on denying and also doubting that this is evident and do not admit that this greater [than everything] is either in my mind or thought, not even in the sense in which many doubtfully real and unreal things are? It must first of all be proved to me then that this same greater than everything truly exists in reality somewhere, and then only will the fact that it is greater than everything make it clear that it also subsists in itself.

6

For example: they say that there is in the ocean somewhere an island which, because of the difficulty (or rather the impossibility) of finding that which does not exist, some have called the 'Lost Island'. And the story goes that it is blessed with all manner of priceless riches and delights in abundance, much more even than the Happy Isles, and, having no owner or inhabitant, it is superior everywhere in abundance of riches to all those other lands that men inhabit. Now, if anyone tell me that it is like this, I shall easily understand what is said, since nothing is difficult about it. But if he should then go on to say, as though it were a logical consequence of this: You cannot any more doubt that this island that is more excellent than all other lands truly exists somewhere in reality than you can doubt that it is in your mind; and since it is more excellent to exist not only in the mind alone but also in reality, therefore it must needs be that it exists. For if it did not exist, any other land existing in reality would be more excellent than it, and so this island, already conceived by you to be more excellent than others, will not be more excellent. If, I say, someone wishes thus to persuade me that this island really exists beyond all doubt, I should either think that he was joking, or I should find it hard to decide which of us I ought to judge the bigger fool— I, if I agreed with him, or he, if he thought that he had proved the existence of this island with any certainty, unless he had first convinced me that its very excellence exists in my mind precisely as a thing existing truly and indubitably and not just as something unreal or doubtfully real.

7

Thus first of all might the Fool reply to objections. And if then someone should assert that this greater [than everything] is such that it cannot be thought not to exist (again without any other proof than that otherwise it would not be greater than everything), then he could make this same reply and say: When have I said that there truly existed some being that is 'greater than everything', such that from this it could be proved to me that this same being really existed to such a degree that it could not be thought not to exist? That is why it must first be conclusively proved by argument that there is some higher nature, namely that which is greater and better than all the things that are, so that from this we can also infer everything else which necessarily cannot be wanting to what is greater and better than everything. When, however, it is said that this supreme being cannot be *thought* not to exist, it would perhaps be better to say that it cannot be *understood* not to exist nor even to be able not to exist. For, strictly speaking, unreal things cannot be *understood*, though certainly they can be *thought* of in the same way as the Fool *thought* that God does not exist. I know with complete certainty that I exist, but I also know at the same time nevertheless that I can not-exist. And I *understand* without any doubt that that which exists to the highest degree, namely God, both exists and cannot not exist. I do not know, however, whether I can *think* of myself as not existing while I know with absolute certainty that I do exist; but if I can, why cannot [I do the same] with regard to anything else I know with the same certainty? If however I cannot, this will not be the distinguishing characteristic of God [namely, to be such that He cannot be thought not to exist].

8

The other parts of this tract are argued so truly, so brilliantly and so splendidly, and are also of so much worth and instinct with so fragrant a perfume of devout and holy feeling, that in no way should they be rejected because of those things at the beginning (rightly intuited, but less surely argued out). Rather the latter should be demonstrated more firmly and so everything received with very great respect and praise.

REPLY TO GAUNILO

Since it is not the Fool, against whom I spoke in my tract, who takes me up, but one who, though speaking on the Fool's behalf, is an orthodox Christian and no fool, it will suffice if I reply to the Christian.

I

You say then—you, whoever you are, who claim that the Fool can say these things—that the being than-which-a-greater-cannot-be-thought is not in the mind except as what cannot be thought of, in the true sense, at all. And [you claim], moreover, that what I say does not follow, namely, that 'that-than-which-a-greater-cannot-be-thought' exists in reality from the fact that it exists in the mind, any more than that the Lost Island most certainly exists from the fact that, when it is described in words, he who hears it described has no doubt that it exists in his mind. I reply as follows: If 'that-than-which-a-greater-cannot-be-thought' is neither understood nor thought of, and is neither in the mind nor in thought, then it is evident that *either* God is not that-than-which-a-greater-cannot-be-thought *or* is not understood nor thought of, and is not in the mind nor in thought. Now my strongest argument that this is false is to appeal to your faith and to your conscience. Therefore 'that-than-which-a-greater-cannot-be-thought' is truly understood and thought and is in the mind and in thought. For this reason, [the arguments] by which you attempt to prove the contrary are either not true, or what you believe follows from them does not in fact follow.

Moreover, you maintain that, from the fact that that-than-which-a-greater-cannot-be-thought is understood, it does not follow that it is in the mind, nor that, if it is in the mind, it therefore exists in reality. I insist, however, that simply if it can be thought it is necessary that it exists. For 'that-than-which-a-greater-cannot-be-thought' cannot be thought save as being without a beginning. But whatever can be thought as existing and does not actually exist can be thought as having a beginning of its existence. Consequently, 'that-than-which-a-greater-cannot-be-thought' cannot be thought as existing and yet not actually exist. If, therefore, it can be thought as existing, it exists of necessity.

Further: even if it can be thought of, then certainly it necessarily exists. For no one who denies or doubts that there is something-than-which-a-greater-cannot-be-thought, denies or doubts that, if this being were to exist, it would not be capable of not-existing either actually or in the mind—otherwise it would not be that-than-which-a-greater-cannot-be-thought. But, whatever can be thought as existing and does not actually exist, could, if it were to exist, possibly not exist either actually or in the mind. For this reason, if it can merely be thought, 'that-than-which-a-greater-cannot-be-thought' cannot not exist. However, let us suppose that it does not exist even though it can be thought. Now, whatever can be thought and does not actually exist would not be, if it should exist, 'that-than-which-a-greater-cannot-be-thought'. If, therefore, it were 'that-than-which-a-greater-cannot-be-thought' it would not be that-than-which-a-greater-cannot-be-thought, which is completely absurd. It is, then, false that something-than-which-a-greater-cannot-be-thought does not exist if it can merely be thought; and it is all the more false if it can be understood and be in the mind.

I will go further: It cannot be doubted that whatever does not exist in any one place or at any one time, even though it does exist in some place or at some time, can however be thought to exist at no place and at no time, just as it does not exist in some place or at some time. For what did not exist yesterday and today exists can thus, as it is understood not to have existed yesterday, be supposed not to exist at any time. And that which does not exist here in this place, and does exist elsewhere can, in the same way as it does not exist here, be thought not to exist anywhere. Similarly with a thing some of whose particular parts do not exist in the place and at the time its other parts exist—all of its parts, and therefore the whole thing itself, can be thought to exist at no time and in no place. For even if it be said that time always exists and that the world is everywhere, the former does not, however, always exist as a whole, nor is the other as a whole everywhere; and as certain particular parts of time do not exist when other parts do exist, therefore they can be even thought not to exist at any time. Again, as certain particular parts of the world do not exist in the same place where other parts do exist, they can thus be supposed not to exist anywhere. Moreover, what is made up of parts can be broken up in thought and can possibly not exist. Thus it is that whatever does not exist as a whole at a certain place and time can be thought not to exist, even if it does actually exist. But 'that-than-which-a-greater-cannot-be-thought' cannot be thought not to exist if it does actually exist; otherwise, if it exists it is not that-than-which-a-greater-cannot-be-thought, which is absurd. In no way, then, does this being not exist as a whole in any particular place or at any particular time; but it exists as a whole at every time and in every place.

Do you not consider then that that about which we understand these things can to some extent be thought or understood, or can exist in thought or in the mind? For if it cannot, we could not understand these things about it. And if you say that, because it is not completely understood, it cannot be understood at all and cannot be in the mind, then you must say [equally] that one who cannot see the purest light of the sun directly does not see daylight, which is the same thing as the light of the sun. Surely then 'that-than-which-a-greater-cannot-be-thought' is understood and is in the mind to the extent that we understand these things about it.

2

I said, then, in the argument that you criticize, that when the Fool hears 'that-than-which-a-greater-cannot-be-thought' spoken of he understands what he hears. Obviously if it is spoken of in a known language and he does not understand it, then either he has no intelligence at all, or a completely obtuse one.

Next I said that, if it is understood it is in the mind; or does what has been proved to exist necessarily in actual reality not exist in any mind? But you will say that, even if it is in the mind, yet it does not follow that it is understood. Observe then that, from the fact that it is understood, it does follow that it is in the mind. For, just as what is thought is thought by means of a thought, and what is thought by a thought is thus, as thought, *in* thought, so also, what is understood is understood by the mind, and what is understood by the mind is thus, as understood, *in* the mind. What could be more obvious than this?

I said further that if a thing exists even in the mind alone, it can be thought to exist also in reality, which is greater. If, then, it (namely, 'that-than-which-a-greater-cannot-be-thought') exists in the mind alone, it is something than which a greater *can* be thought. What, I ask you, could be more logical? For if it exists even in the mind alone, cannot it be thought to exist also in reality? And if it can [be so thought], is it not the case that he who thinks this thinks of something greater than it, if it exists in the mind alone? What, then, could follow more logically than that, if 'that-than-which-a-greater-*cannot*-be-thought' exists in the mind alone, it is the same as that-than-which-a-greater-*can*-be-thought? But surely 'that-than-which-a-greater-*can*-be-thought' is not for any mind [the same as] 'that-than-which-a-greater-*cannot*-be-thought'. Does it not follow, then, that 'that-than-which-a-greater-*cannot*-be-thought', if it exists in anyone's mind, does not exist in the mind alone? For if it exists in the mind alone, it is that-than-which-a-greater-*can*-be-thought, which is absurd.

3

You claim, however, that this is as though someone asserted that it cannot be doubted that a certain island in the ocean (which is more fertile than all other lands and which, because of the difficulty or even the impossibility of discovering what does not exist, is called the 'Lost Island') truly exists in reality since anyone easily understands it when it is described in words. Now, I truly promise that if anyone should discover for me something existing either in reality or in the mind alone—except 'that-than-which-a-greater-cannot-be-thought'—to which the logic of my argument would apply, then I shall find that Lost Island and give it, never more to be lost, to that person. It has already been clearly seen, however, that 'that-than-which-a-greater-cannot-be-thought' cannot be thought not to exist, because it exists as a matter of such certain truth. Otherwise it would not exist at all. In short, if anyone says that he thinks that this being does not exist, I reply that, when he thinks of this, either he thinks of something than which a greater cannot be thought, or he does not think of it. If he does not think of it, then he does not think that what he does not think of does not exist. If, however, he does think of it, then indeed he thinks of something which cannot be even thought not to exist. For if it could be thought not to exist, it could be thought to have a beginning and an end—but this cannot be. Thus, he who thinks of it thinks of something that cannot be thought not to exist; indeed, he who thinks of this does not think of it as not existing, otherwise he would think what cannot be thought. Therefore 'that-than-which-a-greater-cannot-be-thought' cannot be thought not to exist.

4

You say, moreover, that when it is said that this supreme reality cannot be *thought* not to exist, it would perhaps be better to say that it cannot be *understood* not to exist or even to be able not to exist. However, it must rather be said that it cannot be *thought*. For if I had said that the thing in question could not be *understood* not to exist, perhaps you yourself (who claim that we cannot understand—if this word is to be taken strictly—things that are unreal) would object that nothing that exists can be understood not to exist. For it is false [to say that] what exists does not exist, so that it is not the distinguishing characteristic of God not to be able to be understood not to exist. But, if any of those things which exist with absolute certainty can be understood not to exist, in the same way other things that certainly exist can be understood not to exist. But, if the matter is carefully considered, this objection cannot be made apropos [the term] 'thought'. For even if none of those things that exist can be *understood* not to exist, all however can be *thought* as not existing, save that which exists to a supreme degree. For in fact all those things (and they alone) that have a beginning or end or are made up of parts and, as I have already said, all those things that do not exist as a whole in a particular place or at a particular time can be thought as not existing. Only that being in which there is neither beginning nor end nor conjunction of parts, and that thought does not discern save as a whole in every place and at every time, cannot be thought as not existing.

Know then that you can think of yourself as not existing while yet you are absolutely sure that you exist. I am astonished that you have said that you do not know this. For we think of many things that we know to exist, as not existing; and [we think of] many things that we know not to exist, as existing—not judging that it is really as we think but imagining it to be so. We *can*, in fact, think of something as not existing while knowing that it does exist, since we can [think of] the one and know the other at the same time. And we *cannot* think of something as not existing if yet we know that it does exist, since we cannot think of it as existing and not existing at the same time. He, therefore, who distinguishes these two senses of this assertion will understand that [in one sense] nothing can be thought as not existing while yet it is known to exist, and that [in another sense] whatever exists, save that-than-which-a-greater-cannot-be-thought, can be thought of as not existing even when we know that it does exist. Thus it is that, on the one hand, it is the distinguishing characteristic of God that He cannot be thought of as not existing, and that, on the other hand, many things, the while they do exist, cannot be thought of as not existing. In what sense, however, one can say that God can be thought of as not existing I think I have adequately explained in my tract.

5

As for the other objections you make against me on behalf of the Fool, it is quite easy to meet them, even for one weak in the head, and so I considered it a waste of time to show this. But since I hear that they appear to certain readers to have some force against me, I will deal briefly with them.

First, you often reiterate that I say that that which is greater than everything exists in the mind, and that if it is in the mind, it exists also in reality, for otherwise that which is greater than everything would not be that which is greater than everything. However, nowhere in all that I have said will you find such an argument. For 'that which is greater than everything' and 'that-than-which-a-greater-cannot-be-thought' are not equivalent for the purpose of proving the real existence of the thing spoken of. Thus, if anyone should say that 'that-than-which-a-greater-cannot-be-thought' is not something that actually exists, or that it can possibly not exist, or even can be thought of as not existing, he can easily be refuted. For what does not exist can possibly not exist, and what can not exist can be thought of as not existing. However, whatever can be thought of as not existing, if it actually exists, is not that-than-which-a-greater-cannot-be-thought. But if it does not exist, indeed even if it should exist, it would not be that-than-which-a-greater-cannot-be-thought. But it cannot be asserted that 'that-than-which-a-greater-cannot-be-thought' is not, if it exists, that-than-which-a-greater-cannot-be-thought, or that, if it should exist, it would not be that-than-which-a-greater-cannot-be-thought. It is evident, then, that it neither does not exist nor can not exist or be thought of as not existing. For if it does exist in another way it is not what it is said to be, and if it should exist [in another way] it would not be [what it was said to be].

However it seems that it is not as easy to prove this in respect of what is said to be greater than everything. For it is not as evident that that which can be thought of as not existing is not that which is greater than everything, as that it is not that-than-which-a-greater-cannot-be-thought. And, in the same way, neither is it indubitable that, if there is something which is 'greater than everything', it is identical with 'that-than-which-a-greater-cannot-be-thought'; nor, if there were [such a being], that no other like it might exist—as this is certain in respect of what is said to be 'that-than-which-a-greater-cannot-be-thought'. For what if someone should say that something that is greater than everything actually exists, and yet that this same being can be thought of as not existing, and that something greater than it can be thought, even if this does not exist? In this case can it be inferred as evidently that [this being] is therefore not that which is greater than everything, as it would quite evidently be said in the other case that it is therefore not that-than-which-a-greater-cannot-be-thought? The former [inference] needs, in fact, a premiss in addition to this which is said to be 'greater than everything'; but the latter needs nothing save this utterance itself, namely, 'that-than-which-a-greater-cannot-be-thought'. Therefore, if what 'that-than-which-a-greater-cannot-be-thought' of itself proves concerning itself cannot be proved in the same way in respect of what is said to be 'greater than everything', you criticize me unjustly for having said what I did not say, since it differs so much from what I did say.

If, however, it can [be proved] by means of another argument, you should not have criticized me for having asserted what can be proved. Whether it can [be proved], however, is easily appreciated by one who understands that it can [in respect of] 'that-than-which-a-greater-cannot-be-thought'. For one cannot in any way understand 'that-than-which-a-greater-cannot-be-thought' without [understanding that it is] that which alone is greater than everything. As, therefore, 'that-than-which-a-greater-cannot-be-thought' is understood and is in the mind, and is consequently judged to exist in true reality, so also that which is greater than everything is said to be understood and to exist in the mind, and so is necessarily inferred to exist in reality itself. You see, then, how right you were to compare me with that stupid person who wished to maintain that the Lost Island existed from the sole fact that being described it was understood.

<h1 style="text-align:center">6</h1>

You object, moreover, that any unreal or doubtfully real things at all can equally be understood and exist in the mind in the same way as the being I was speaking of. I am astonished that you urge this [objection] against me, for I was concerned to prove something which was in doubt, and for me it was sufficient that I should first show that it was understood and existed in the mind *in some way or other*, leaving it to be determined subsequently whether it was in the mind alone as unreal things are, or in reality also as true things are. For, if unreal or doubtfully real things are understood and exist in the mind in the sense that, when they are spoken of, he who hears them understands what the speaker means, nothing prevents what I have spoken of being understood and existing in the mind. But how are these [assertions] consistent, that is, when you assert that if someone speaks of unreal things you would understand whatever he says, and that, in the case of a thing which is not entertained in thought in the same way as even unreal things are, you do not say that you think of it or have it in thought upon hearing it spoken of, but rather that you understand it and have it in mind since, precisely, you cannot think of it save by understanding it, that is, knowing certainly that the thing exists in reality itself? How, I say, are both [assertions] consistent, namely that unreal things are understood, and that 'to understand' means knowing with certainty that something actually exists? You should have seen that nothing [of this applies] to me. But if unreal things are, in a sense, understood (this definition applying not to every kind of understanding but to a certain kind) then I ought not to be criticized for having said that 'that-than-which-a-greater-cannot-be-thought' is understood and is in the mind, even before it was certain that it existed in reality itself.

7

Next, you say that it can hardly be believed that when this [that-than-which-a-greater-cannot-be-thought] has been spoken of and heard, it cannot be thought not to exist, as even it can be thought that God does not exist. Now those who have attained even a little expertise in disputation and argument could reply to that on my behalf. For is it reasonable that someone should therefore deny what he understands because it is said to be [the same as] that which he denies since he does not understand it? Or if that is denied [to exist] which is understood only to some extent and is the same as what is not understood at all, is not what is in doubt more easily proved from the fact that it is in some mind than from the fact that it is in no mind at all? For this reason it cannot be believed that anyone should deny 'that-than-which-a-greater-cannot-be-thought' (which, being heard, he understands to some extent), on the ground that he denies God whose meaning he does not think of in any way at all. On the other hand, if it is denied on the ground that it is not understood completely, even so is not that which is understood in some way easier to prove than that which is not understood in any way? It was therefore not wholly without reason that, to prove against the Fool that God exists, I proposed 'that-than-which-a-greater-cannot-be-thought', since he would understand this in some way, [whereas] he would understand the former [God] in no way at all.

8

In fact, your painstaking argument that 'that-than-which-a-greater-cannot-be-thought' is not like the not-yet-realized painting in the mind of the painter is beside the point. For I did not propose [the example] of the foreknown picture because I wanted to assert that what was at issue was in the same case, but rather that so I could show that something not understood as existing exists in the mind.

Again, you say that upon hearing of 'that-than-which-a-greater-cannot-be-thought' you cannot think of it as a real object known either generically or specifically or have it in your mind, on the grounds that you neither know the thing itself nor can you form an idea of it from other things similar to it. But obviously this is not so.

For since everything that is less good is similar in so far as it is good to that which is more good, it is evident to every rational mind that, mounting from the less good to the more good we can from those things than which something greater can be thought conjecture a great deal about that-than-which-a-greater-cannot-be-thought. Who, for example, cannot think of this (even if he does not believe that what he thinks of actually exists) namely, that if something that has a beginning and end is good, that which, although it has had a beginning, does not, however, have an end, is much better? And just as this latter is better than the former, so also that which has neither beginning nor end is better again than this, even if it passes always from the past through the present to the future. Again, whether something of this kind actually exists or not, that which does not lack anything at all, nor is forced to change or move, is very much better still. Cannot this be thought? Or can we think of something greater than this? Or is not this precisely to form an idea of that-than-which-a-greater-cannot-be-thought from those things than which a greater can be thought? There is, then, a way by which one can form an idea of 'that-than-which-a-greater-cannot-be-thought'. In this way, therefore, the Fool who does not accept the sacred authority [of Revelation] can easily be refuted if he denies that he can form an idea from other things of 'that-than-which-a-greater-cannot-be-thought'. But if any orthodox Christian should deny this let him remember that 'the invisible things of God from the creation of the world are clearly seen through the things that have been made, even his eternal power and Godhead' [Rom. 1: 20].

9

But even if it were true that [the object] that-than-which-a-greater-cannot-be-thought cannot be thought of nor understood, it would not, however, be false that [the formula] 'that-than-which-a-greater-cannot-be-thought' could be thought of and understood. For just as nothing prevents one from saying 'ineffable' although one cannot specify what is said to be ineffable; and just as one can think of the inconceivable—although one cannot think of what 'inconceivable' applies to—so also, when 'that-than-which-a-greater-cannot-be-thought' is spoken of, there is no doubt at all that what is heard can be thought of and understood even if the thing itself cannot be thought of and understood. For if someone is so witless as to say that there is not something than-which-a-greater-cannot-be-thought, yet he will not be so shameless as to say that he is not able to understand and think of what he was speaking about. Or if such a one is to be found, not only should his assertion be condemned, but he himself condemned. Whoever, then, denies that there is something than-which-a-greater-cannot-be-thought, at any rate understands and thinks of the denial he makes, and this denial cannot be understood and thought about apart from its elements. Now, one element [of the denial] is 'that-than-which-a-greater-cannot-be-thought'. Whoever, therefore, denies this understands and thinks of 'that-than-which-a-greater-cannot-be-thought'. It is evident, moreover, that in the same way one can think of and understand that which cannot not exist. And one who thinks of this thinks of something greater than one who thinks of what can not exist. When, therefore, one thinks of that-than-which-a-greater-cannot-be-thought, if one thinks of what can not exist, one does not think of that-than-which-a-greater-cannot-be-thought. Now the same thing cannot at the same time be thought of and not thought of. For this reason he who thinks of that-than-which-a-greater-cannot-be-thought does not think of something that can not exist but something that cannot not exist. Therefore what he thinks of exists necessarily, since whatever can not exist is not what he thinks of.

10

I think now that I have shown that I have proved in the above tract, not by a weak argumentation but by a sufficiently necessary one, that something-than-which-a-greater-cannot-be-thought exists in reality itself, and that this proof has not been weakened by the force of any objection. For the import of this proof is in itself of such force that what is spoken of is proved (as a necessary consequence of the fact that it is understood or thought of) both to exist in actual reality and to be itself whatever must be believed about the Divine Being. For we believe of the Divine Being whatever it can, absolutely speaking, be thought better to be than not to be. For example, it is better to be eternal than not eternal, good than not good, indeed goodness-itself than not goodness-itself. However, nothing of this kind cannot but be that-than-which-a-greater-cannot-be-thought. It is, then, necessary that 'that-than-which-a-greater-cannot-be-thought' should be whatever must be believed about the Divine Nature.

I thank you for your kindness both in criticizing and praising my tract. For since you praised so fulsomely those parts that appeared to you to be worthy of acceptance, it is quite clear that you have criticized those parts that seemed to you to be weak, not from any malice but from good will.

DE GRAMMATICO

(DIALOGUE ON LITERACY AND THE LITERATE)

In order to make reasonable sense of what is going on in this dialogue, some minimal knowledge of its historical antecedents is essential. These may be summarized as follows:

A proposition containing an adjectival predicate has customarily been described as one which predicates some quality of its subject; thus 'William is white' is said to predicate whiteness of William, or to attribute whiteness to William. The concrete adjectival form used in such a situation was sometimes said (e.g. by Boethius) to be derived from the corresponding abstract form (as 'white' from 'whiteness', 'just' from 'justice', and so on), thus enabling the subject in question (e.g. William) to be 'denominated' from the abstract by means of the concrete form. The quality in question (e.g. whiteness) is then said to be predicated of its subject in a denominative or paronymous fashion. All this involves the shaky assumption that such adjectives may indeed be distinguished from substantives (e.g. 'dog') on the basis of the former's correlation with available abstract forms which the latter lack; e.g. although the adjective 'white' is correlated with the abstract 'whiteness', the substantive 'dog' is not ordinarily correlated with an abstract 'dogness'.

It was against some such background that Latin Western philosophers inherited Boethius's translation of Aristotle's list of categories (substance, quantity, quality, etc.) in which *white* and *literate* were given as examples of the category of quality (in the original Latin: *Qualitas, ut album, grammaticum*). This brief characterization occasioned much medieval commentary, since it is immediately evident that it goes contrary to the conventions outlined above. Usage would surely prefer 'Quality, such as whiteness, literacy', as the appropriate itemization, so as to avoid the 'Literate is a quality, namely literacy' which is presumably entailed by Aristotle's technical text as it stands. Certainly 'Literacy is a quality' would seem to be more exact. The situation becomes even more troublesome in the original Latin, which has no difficulty at all in sometimes allowing *grammaticus* (literate) to have the sense of '[a] literate [being]', so that Aristotle's itemization could authorize the apparent nonsense that a literate (e.g. a man) is a quality, namely literacy. Even worse, this example, thus interpreted, makes the categorization itself suspect, since '[A] literate [being, e.g. a man] is a substance' now appears to be more acceptable.

Such, therefore, are samples of the multiple historical linguistic threads lying behind the opening sentence of the dialogue; knowledge of those threads serves to make that opening quite intelligible.

The denominatives 'literate' and 'white' have been italicized throughout the translation, since the problematical grammatical status of such adjectives is, in effect, one of the dialogue's main topics. Until clarification is achieved, it is doubtful whether, in their various contexts of occurrence, they are names, names of names (nowadays shown by quotation marks), name-forming incompletenesses, or even words which are participial in sense. The italics thus serve to signal this dubious situation.

The numerical references have been added by the translator as aids in cross-referring, which otherwise becomes a most tedious task, productive only of dubious outcomes.

I

1.000　　　　*Student* I would like you to clear up for me the question as to whether *literate* is substance or quality, so that when I have appreciated this case, I will know how I ought to view other items which are likewise predicated paronymously.

Teacher First tell me why you are undecided.

S. Because it looks as though cogent reasons are available which both prove and disprove either alternative.

T. So prove this.

S. As long as you are not too hasty in disagreeing with everything I have to say; just let me finish my piece before you concur or correct.

T. As you will.

1.100, 1.101　　*S.* To prove that *literate* is substance one only needs the following premisses:

1.11　　　　Every *literate* is a man;

1.12　　　　Every man is a substance.

1.13　　　　For a *literate* has that from which his substantiality ensues, whatever that may be, only on account of his being a man: so granted that a *literate* is a man, the same things may be inferred from *literate* as from *man*.

1.20, 1.201　　On the other hand, that *literate* is quality is obviously believed by those philosophers who have written about this matter, and it is impudent to disregard their authority on these subjects.

1.21　　　　Again, *literate* must be substance or quality in such a fashion that if it is the one of these then it is not the other, and if it is not the one of these then it must be the other;

hence correspondingly, whatever serves to establish one alternative refutes the other, and whatever weakens the one strengthens the other. Now as only one of the two can hold, I would like you to make clear where the falsehood lies, so as thus to lay bare the truth for me.

2

2.00   *T.* The points you urge in favour of both alternatives involve cogency, but not your assertion that if the one holds the other cannot. So you should not ask me to show the falsity of one or the other of the two—this just cannot be done—but rather, if I can manage it, I will make clear how they can be compatible. However, first of all I would like to hear what you think might constitute objections to the arguments which you advanced.

S. You are asking me to take on exactly the task that I was keen that you should perform; but as you assert that the arguments in question are in order, it is up to me, as the doubter, to disclose the qualms I feel about those alternatives, and then your job will be to establish the validity and compatibility of each of them.

T. Confide your qualms, then, and I will try to do as you ask.

3.00   *S.* Well, it seems to me that the premiss [1.11] to the effect that a *literate* is a man could be disproved thus:

3.101   No *literate* can be understood [as being] without literacy;

3.102   Every man can be understood [as being] without literacy.

3.110   Again,

3.111   Every *literate* is susceptible of degree;
3.112   No man is susceptible of degree.

From either of these two sets of premisses an identical conclusion can be drawn, namely:

3.113   No *literate* is a man.

3

3.20   *T.* It does not follow.
        S. But why not?

3.21   *T.* Does the name 'animal' appear to you to signify anything other than *animated sensitive substance*?

    S. To be sure, *animal* is just *animated sensitive substance*, and *animated sensitive substance* is just *animal*.

    T. Quite so. And now tell me: is it not the case that every being that is just animated sensitive substance can be understood to be without rationality, and that such a being is not necessarily rational?

    S. I cannot deny that.

    T. Hence every animal can be understood [to be] without rationality, and no animal is necessarily rational.

    S. There is no knowing where my admissions may not lead, but I have a shrewd notion of what you are aiming for.

    T. On the other hand, no man can be understood [to be] without rationality, and every man must necessarily be rational.

    S. Now I am hemmed in on both flanks. For if I admit your last assertion, then you can infer that no man is animal; if, on the other hand, I deny it, you will say that I am not merely understandable as being without rationality, but that I am in fact completely devoid of it.

    T. Do not worry! The consequences are not what you think they are.

    S. If that is a promise, then I freely grant any of your suggestions; otherwise I am rather reluctant.

    T. Then construct for yourself two syllogisms based on these four premisses of mine.

    S. They can certainly be laid out as follows:

3.221   Every animal can be understood [to be] without rationality;

3.222   No man can be understood [to be] without rationality.

Again:

3.231   No animal is necessarily rational;
3.232   Every man is necessarily rational.

From this arrangement of the two sets of premisses it seems to follow in either case that

3.233   No man is animal.

But this is altogether false, even though there does not seem to be anything shaky in any of the foregoing premisses.

3.234   The two which have 'man' as their subject term [3.222, 3.232] are so self-evident that it would be silly to try to prove

them, while the two which involve 'animal' as subject term
[3.221, 3.231] are apparently so sound that to deny them
would be just brash. However, I notice that the structure
of these two syllogisms is wholly similar to that of those
two which I advanced a few moments ago [3.10, 3.11].
This makes me suspect that your only motive for producing them is to allow me to sort out the reasons for their
obviously false conclusions, so that I may then realize that
the same reasons apply to the similar ones which I framed
myself.

T. That is so.

S. Then show me how in both cases there can be a mistake
so serious that although the premisses are true, and seem to
be arranged in conformity with the rules of the syllogism, not
the least scrap of truth is preserved in their conclusions.

4

3.30   *T.* I will do this for your syllogisms, and then you can
analyse mine if you like.

S. Do as you think fit.

3.310   *T.* Recall and reconstruct the syllogisms you produced
earlier.

3.311   *S.* 'Every man can be understood without literacy'
[3.102].

T. What is it that you here assert to be man and to be
understandable without literacy?

S. Man.

T. Now include that which you thus understand within the
major premiss itself.

S. Every man can be understood to be a man without
literacy.

T. Agreed: now state the minor.

3.312   *S.* 'No *literate* can be understood without literacy' [3.101].

T. What is it that cannot be understood to be *literate*
without literacy?

S. A *literate*.

T. Then state in full what it is that you understand.

S. No *literate* can be understood to be *literate* without
literacy.

3.3121   *T.* Now combine, as you did before, these two reformu-
lated premisses.

S. Every man can be understood to be a man without literacy [3.311];

No *literate* can be understood to be *literate* without literacy [3.312].

T. So now check whether they happen to have a term in common; without that they have no inferential efficacy.

S. I observe that they involve no common term, so that nothing follows from them.

T. Now reconstruct your other syllogism [3.11].

3.320 *S.* There is now no point in your going to the trouble of analysing it, for I now see the fallacy which it involves. I was understanding those premisses in a way which allowed them to assert:

3.321 No man is susceptible of degree as man [3.112];

3.322 Every *literate* is susceptible of degree as *literate* [3.111].

3.3221 And as these two premisses have no common term, they prove nothing.

T. So it seems to you that nothing can be inferred from your combination of premisses?

S. That was my impression: but your question makes me suspect that perhaps they still possess some concealed cogency. Yet how can they be used to prove something if they have no common term?

3.33 *T.* The common term of a syllogism consists not so much in the manner of its being set forth as in its meaning; for on the same grounds as those according to which no proof emerges from a merely verbal identity of terms without identical sense, there is nothing wrong with an identity which is understood but not overtly set forth. The meaning of the words is what really binds the syllogism together, and not just the words themselves.

5

3.40 *S.* Now I am looking forward to your restoration of cogency to my premisses.

T. You can certainly prove something from them, but not what you think you are going to get.

S. I will be grateful for anything, whatever it may be.

T. When it is asserted that

Every man can be understood to be man without literacy [3.102, 3.311],

and

No *literate* can be understood to be *literate* without literacy [3.101, 3.312],

does this not mean that

3.41 Being a man does not require literacy,

and

3.42 Being a *literate* requires literacy?

S. Quite so.

3.430 T. And have these two premisses [3.41, 3.42] which I have just asserted as being implied by the other two [3.311, 3.312] a term in common?

S. They have.

3.431, 3.44 T. It thence emerges, therefore, that being a *literate* is not being a man in the sense that *literate* and man are not identically defined [cf. 3.800].

S. This is indubitably the case, as well as being logically sound.

3.450, 3.451, 3.452 T. But it does not hence follow that A *literate* is not a man [3.103, 3.113] as you were thinking. If, however, you interpret 'A *literate* is not a man' as asserting that a *literate* is not the same as a man in the sense that they are not identically defined, then your conclusion is a true one.

6

3.500 S. I understand your point.

T. So, if you have fully grasped what I have been saying, tell me how you would refute a syllogism put together as follows:

3.501 Every *literate* is asserted [so to be] in respect of quality;

3.502 No man is asserted [to be such] in respect of quality.

3.503 Hence:

No man is *literate*.

3.510 S. This seems to me to resemble the assertion of

3.511 Every rational being is asserted [to be so] in respect of quality;

3.512   No man is asserted [to be such] in respect of quality.

3.513   Hence:

          No man is rational.

3.520   But this is not capable of constituting a valid proof that
          rational is predicable of no man. Likewise that syllogism
          which you put forward just now [3.500] does not necessarily
          prove that *literate* is not predicable of man, for if we inter-
          pret its premises in such a way that their truth is preserved,
          we see that they amount to the following assertions:

3.521   Every *literate* is asserted [to be] *literate* in respect of
          quality [3.501];

3.5220   No man is asserted [to be] man in respect of quality
          [3.503].

3.5221,   But from these two propositions it by no means follows
3.530,   that *literate* is predicated of no man, for it is not the same
3.531,   term which is affirmed of *literate* and denied of *man*.
3.532,   Of course, they would have a common term and be
3.5330,   necessarily conclusive if either the major remaining as it is
3.5331,   [3.521] the following minor were to be the case: No man is
3.5332,   asserted [to be] *literate* in respect of quality or the minor
3.5333   remaining as before [3.5220] the major could indeed become:
          Every *literate* is asserted [to be] man in respect of quality, for
          then both these combinations [3.531, 3.532; 3.5331, 3.5332]
          would produce the conclusion that *literate* is not predicable
          of any man.

3.540, 3.541,   For if one understands the assertion, 'A man is not a
3.542, 3.543   *literate*' in a sense similar to that found in the assertion,
          'Either the lightning is the flash or else the lightning is not
          the flash'—that is to say, 'The lightning either is or else is
          not identical with the flash'—if, I say, one interprets the
          assertion 'A man is not a *literate*' in this sense, then it follows
          from the premises in question, on a careful scrutiny of their
          import, that no man is *literate*. This is because insofar as we
          are concerned to prove that the essence of *man* is not the
          essence of *literate* their meaning does involve a common
          term.

7

3.60   *T.* You have understood what I said correctly, but perhaps
          you have not scrutinized it properly.

S. But how could I have understood it fully, and yet not have scrutinized it properly?

T. Tell me now: what would follow from these assertions, should someone propound them:

3.611   No man can be understood [to be] without rationality;

3.612   Every stone can be understood [to be] without rationality?

S. What could follow other than

3.6121   No stone is a man?

3.620, 3.621,   T. And how do you interpret this? Does it mean that a
3.622   stone is in no sense a man? Or does it mean that a stone is not the same as a man?

S. It means that a stone is in no sense a man.

3.630   T. Tell me then: how does this last syllogism [3.61] differ from that earlier one [3.10] of yours, in which you held that a *literate* cannot be understood without literacy, but a man can, and hence a *literate* is not a man?

3.631   S. As far as logical cogency is concerned, I fail to see any difference at all between the latter and the former; we saw how the former [3.10] is to be understood as asserting that a *literate* cannot be understood to be a *literate* without literacy [3.312], and that a man can be understood to be a man without literacy [3.311], so that the latter [3.61] may likewise be understood to assert:

3.6311   A man cannot be understood to be a man without rationality,

and

3.6312   A stone can be understood to be a stone without rationality.

3.6313   Now the conclusion of the syllogism here in question [3.612] is securely established, since no stone is in any sense a man [cf. 3.62]; hence it looks to me as though your skill in analysis overwhelms the conclusion of that exactly similar syllogisms [3.10] of mine. So now I understand your saying that I had understood what you said, but without scrutinizing it properly: I understood well enough what you might mean verbally, but I did not concentrate adequately on the exact point of what you were meaning, since I had no idea how that syllogism might mislead me.

3.6320   T. You certainly did not concentrate adequately; what you

did not realise was the way in which you might not have been
misled by it.

S. And in which way is that?

T. It is true that if this syllogism which I put forward just
now [3.61] is expressed in the same way as in the analysis
[3.631] of your own [3.101, 3.102] which I gave, so that it
asserts that no man can be understood to be a man without
rationality [3.6311], and that every stone can be understood
to be a stone without rationality [3.6312], then it will be no
more capable of producing a conclusion than I asserted yours
[3.101, 3.102] to be. Yet because the present one [3.61] can
be analysed in another way—a way which is inapplicable to
yours—it does produce the conclusion that a stone can in no
sense be a man [3.621]. For when I assert that no man can be
understood without rationality [3.611] and every stone can be
understood without rationality [3.612], then these propositions can, and indeed ought, to be taken to assert:

3.6321   No man is in some sense understandable without
              rationality,
              and

3.6322   Every stone is in any sense understandable without
              rationality.

Whence it follows:

3.63221   No stone is in some sense a man.

3.6330,   In contrast, your own premisses [3.10] are such that the
3.6331,   truth is not in the least susceptible of being likewise
3.6332,   conveyed by them, for one cannot assert that no *literate* is
3.6333,   in some sense understandable without literacy [cf. 3.6321]
3.6334,   or that every man is in any sense understandable without
3.6340,   literacy [cf. 3.6322], because not only is it the case that
3.6341   everything which is *literate* can be understood to be a man
              without literacy [cf. 3.6331], but also that no man can be
              understood to be a *literate* without literacy [cf. 3.6332]. On
              this account your premisses cannot produce the conclusion
              that a *literate* is in no sense a man.

8

3.700   *S.* I have no objections to raise against your verdict; but
              since you guide me surreptitiously, so that I do not rest
              content with understanding what you assert, but concentrate
              on exactly what it is that you are asserting, it now occurs to

me that we should scrutinize the conclusion which you
showed to follow from my syllogism [3.1], namely: Being a
literate is not being a man [3.431].

3.701, 3.71,   If this [3.431] is granted, then whatever is essentially
3.711,   *literate* need not therefore be essentially man, but if
3.7111,   *man* follows from *literate*, then the essence of man follows
3.72,   from the essence of *literate*. But the second of these two
3.721,   sequences does not hold [cf. 3.701], hence neither does the
3.7211   first, so that not every *literate* is a man. Further, every *liter-
                ate* has some single feature which makes him susceptible of
                being a man, so that either every *literate* is a man or none are.
                But it has been shown [3.7111] that not every *literate* is a
                man. Therefore, no *literate* is a man. So now it looks as
                though you have even more ingeniously yielded up for the
                taking that very conclusion which you so cunningly removed
                from my syllogism [3.10].

3.800   *T.* Although I do indeed surreptitiously lead you to con-
                centrate on what you hear, it is not my aim to endow the
                process with an air of complete futility. And now that you
                have gone and proved sophistically that no *literate* is a man
                [3.7211] by making use of the fact that being a *literate* is not
                being a man [3.431], it will nevertheless still be a handy exer-
                cise if you can get to the bottom of the fallacy which persists
                in muddling you with its apparent logicality.

                S. Then show me just how and where this proof [3.7]
                involving *literate* which I put together just now is muddling
                me.

                T. Let us go back to the cases of *animal* and *man*; these are
                cases in which, as it were, we so sense the truth that we can-
                not be taken in by any spurious proof which might force us
                into a false opinion.

                Tell me whether it is the case that the being of each and
                every thing is circumscribed by its definition.

                S. It is the case.

                T. Is the definition of man also the definition of animal?

3.8010,   *S.* Not at all; for if *rational mortal animal*, the definition
3.8011   of *man*, were likewise the definition of *animal*, then to what-
                soever 'animal' was applicable, 'rational mortal' would also
                apply; but this is not so.

3.8012   *T.* Hence, being a man is not being an animal.

                S. So it follows.

3.810   *T.* Now from this conclusion, by using the same form of

reasoning [3.7] as that whereby a moment ago you concluded
that no *literate* is a man [3.7211], you can go on to show that

3.811   no man is an animal.

So if it is clear to you in this instance that your form of
reasoning leads to untruth, you can have no confidence in the
supposed truth [3.7211] which emerged from your earlier
playing about with the same form.

3.900, 3.901   *S.* You have shown that it misled me: now show me just
where it did so.

T. Do you not recall that a short while ago [3.4] I asserted,
and you agreed, that being a *literate* is not being a man [3.431]
means the same as the statement that the definition of *literate* is not the definition of *man* [3.44]? This amounted to
saying that a *literate* and a man are not altogether identical
[cf. 3.452], for just as *man* should not be defined as possessing literacy, so also *literate* is not definable without literacy
[cf. 3.41, 3.42].

3.910,   Consequently, that contention of yours [3.701] should
3.911,   be understood as follows: if being *literate* is not being man
3.920,   and only man, then whatsoever is essentially *literate* need
3.921,   not on that account be essentially man and only man
3.922,   [cf. 3.701]. Likewise we are to understand that it is false that
3.930,   from *literate* one can infer *man* and only *man* [cf. 3.71, 3.711],
3.931   that is to say: if something is *literate*, then it does not follow
that it is a man and only a man. So that really the only conclusion is: No *literate* is a man and only a man.

S. Nothing could be more obvious.

9

3.940,   *T.* Were it to be proved true, as I believe could quite
3.9410,   easily be done, that being a *literate* is not being a man
3.9411,   is like being a *white* is not being a man (for a man can
3.9412,   be without *white*, and *white* can be without a man), then from
3.9420,   this one could indeed draw the consequence that some *lit-
3.9421   erate* can be other than a man [cf. 4.24120].

S. So why do we take all this trouble, if this can be proved?
Prove it, and the question at issue will be settled.

3.9430,   *T.* That is an improper demand at this point, for in the
3.9431   present investigation we are not trying to find out whether it
is possible for there to be some non-human *literate*, but
whether there is some non-human *literate*. And this, as you
realize, cannot be shown.

4.100   *S.* It is not yet obvious to me, for I still want to raise a point to the contrary.

        T. Carry on.

        S. Aristotle showed that

4.101   A *literate* is one of those things which are incidental to a subject,

but

4.102   No man is incidental to a subject,

hence

4.103   No *literate* is a man [cf. 1.11].

4.110   *T.* Aristotle did not want this consequence to be drawn from what he said, for this same text of his uses *literate* not only of such and such a man, but also of *man* and *animal*.

        S. How then can this syllogism of mine be refuted?

4.1101   *T.* Tell me now: when you speak to me about a *literate*, whereof may I understand you to be speaking—of the name, or of the things signified by the name?

        S. Of the things signified.

        T. What things does it signify then?

        S. Man and literacy.

4.1102,   *T.* On hearing this name, then, I may understand a man or
4.1103   literacy, and when I speak of a *literate*, my speech may concern a man or literacy.

        S. That must be the case.

4.1104   *T.* So tell me: is a man a substance, or is he incidental to a subject?

        S. A substance, and not incidental to a subject.

4.1105   *T.* Is literacy a quality and incidental to a subject?

        S. It is both.

4.111,   *T.* Well then, nothing extraordinary is being asserted if
4.112   one says that insofar as the man is concerned, the *literate* is a substance and not incidental to a subject, whereas insofar as literacy is concerned, *literate* is a quality and is incidental to a subject.

10

4.1200   *S.* I cannot deny all this, but I might mention one more reason why *literate* is not a substance:

4.1201   Every substance is either primary or secondary, whereas *literate* is neither primary nor secondary substance.

        T. Call to mind that assertion of Aristotle's which I

mentioned a little while ago [4.1100] according to which *lit-erate* is both primary and secondary substance, since he invokes the fact that *literate* is used not only of such and such a man, but also of *man* and *animal*. On what grounds, there-fore, can you show *literate* to be neither a primary nor a sec-ondary substance?

4.121   *S.* Because unlike any substance, it is incidental to a subject; also it is asserted of many things, and this is not a mark of primary substance.

4.122   Further, it is neither genus nor species, nor is it predicated in respect of quiddity, as are secondary substances.

4.130   *T.* None of your points, if you bear in mind what has been said, deprives *literate* of its substantial aspect.

4.131   For insofar as something *literate* is not incidental to a subject, not only is it both genus and species, but it is also predicated in respect of quiddity; this is because such a being is both a man, i.e. a species, and an animal, i.e. a genus, and these are predicated in respect of quiddity [cf. 4.122].

4.132   But it also occurs individually, as in the cases of a man or an animal, for a given *literate* is individual in the same way as are a given man and a given animal. For instance, Socrates is not only an animal and a man, but also a *literate*.

S. There is no denying what you say.

I I

4.14   *T.* If you have no other grounds on which to base a proof that *literate* is not *man*, now prove that it is not literacy.

S. I could manage to do that more easily by pointing rather than by argument, now that you have shattered all my con-tentions by showing the various senses of *literate*, and how speech and understanding involving *literate* should corre-spond to those senses [cf. 4.11]. Yet although perhaps I cannot deny all this, my mind is nevertheless not satisfied in such a way that it can settle down, so to speak, having discovered the required solution. Indeed, it looks to me as though you are concerned not so much with my enlightenment, as with the refutation of my points. But in fact my job was only to make explicit those factors which perplexed me when either of the alternatives in question [cf. 1.1, 1.2] was adopted; yours was either to refute one of those alternatives, or to show how both are mutually compatible.

T. Why, in your view, does not the fact that *literate* can be properly spoken of and understood sometimes in respect of man and sometimes in respect of literacy [cf. 4.11] sufficiently bring out the complete absence of incompatibility between the assertions that *literate* is a substance and *literate* is a quality?

4.20   *S.* Because while it is quite true that no one who understands the name *literate* is unaware that it signifies literacy as well as *man*, yet if, on the strength of this, I were to assert at some gathering, 'A *literate* is a useful form of knowledge', or 'That man has a thorough knowledge of a *literate*', then not only would this immensely irritate the literates, but even the ignorant would guffaw.

4.210   So I just find it impossible to credit that authors of logical works can have no further grounds for so frequently and seriously committing themselves, when writing in their books, to positions that they would be ashamed to exemplify in conversation.

4.211   After all, when in their logical discussions they want to show a quality or an accident, they most usually add 'such as *literate* and the like'.

4.212   Yet everyone's spoken usage vouches for the fact that *literate* is a substance rather than a quality or an accident. But when the authors want to make a point about substance, they never come out with 'such as *literate* or something of that sort'.

4.22   The question boils down to this: if *literate*, because it signifies man and literacy, must therefore be said to be quality as well as substance, why is not man likewise quality as well as substance? After all, *man* signifies a substance along with all the characteristics of *man*, such as sensibility and mortality, yet when something is propounded in a written work concerning some quality or other, we never find *man* produced as an example.

12

4.230   *T.* You reject my argument in favour of regarding *literate* as both substance and quality because it is not equally applicable in the case of the name 'man'. You do this, I suspect, because you do not realize the vast difference between the way in which the name 'man' can signify man's make-up, and the way in which the name *literate* can signify man and literacy.

4.231   For in truth the name *man* signifies precisively and as a single whole the complete make-up of man. Of this, substance is the chief feature, it being the ground and possessor of the others, and this not in the sense that it is incomplete without them, but rather that they are incomplete without it. After all, there is no characteristic of substance in the absence of which substance is also absent, whereas in the absence of substance no characteristics can exist. So that although all those characteristics, at the same time, form as it were a single whole covered by a single meaning, and receive as their appellation the single name 'man', nevertheless this name both principally signifies and is appellative of substance. Thus it would be correct to assert 'The substance is *man*' and '*Man* is a substance', whereas no-one would say 'The rationality is *man*' or 'Man is rationality'; rather, *man* is said to participate in rationality.

4.232   In contrast, *literate* does not signify *man* and literacy as a single whole; rather it signifies precisely just literacy, while obliquely signifying *man*.

4.233   Indeed, although the name *literate* is appellative of *man*, it nevertheless may not properly be said to signify *man*.

4.234   Further, even though *literate* signifies literacy, it is not, however, appellative of literacy.

4.2341   For at this point I want to stipulate that the name of a thing is appellative of that thing when it is the name by which that very thing is itself called in the customary course of utterance. Thus assertions such as, 'Literacy is *literate*', or, '*Literate* is literacy' run counter to such customary usage; we say rather, 'The man is *literate*', or 'The *literate* is a man' [cf. 4.21].

13

4.240   *S.* I do not see the point of your saying that *literate* signifies literacy precisively and *man* obliquely, and yet that it only signifies literacy. For just as *man* comprises *animal* along with rationality and mortality, so that *man* signifies all these three, so also, since *literate* comprises *man* and literacy, the name *literate* must signify both of these; after all, neither a man without literacy, nor literacy apart from a man, are ever asserted to be *literate*.

4.2410   *T.* Then if you are correct, 'A man having the learning constituting literacy', would define and state what is involved in being a *literate*.

S. It cannot be otherwise.

4.2411   *T.* Therefore as literacy distinguishes the *literate* man from the illiterate, it is the *literate*'s link with being—the constitutive part of that which is its being—so that any alternation in its presence or absence can only result in the *literate*'s perishing.

S. And so what?

T. It would follow, therefore, that literacy is not something incidental, but rather a constitutive characteristic, with man as the genus, and *literate* as the species. And the same would apply to the cases of whiteness and similar accidents. But the treatise on how to deal with wholes shows that this is not the case.

S. Though I cannot deny your contentions, I am still not convinced that *literate* may not signify *man*.

4.24120   *T.* Let it be supposed that there is some rational animal—other than man—which has the learning constituting literacy in the same way as does man.

S. That is easily supposed [cf. 3.9421].

T. There is thus some non-man having the learning constituting literacy.

S. So it follows.

T. And every haver of the learning constituting literacy is *literate*.

S. Granted.

T. There is therefore some *literate* non-man.

S. So it follows.

T. But you persist in asserting that *literate*, according to your understanding, comprises *man*.

S. I do.

T. So that some non-man is man, and this is false.

S. This is the outcome of the inference.

4.24121   *T.* So do you not see that *literate* no more signifies *man* than *white* does? It just happens to be the case that man alone has the learning constituting literacy, whereas whiteness is found in beings other than men.

S. That is what follows from the supposition adopted, but

I would rather you produced a proof which does not depend upon such suppositious cases.

4.2413   *T.* In the same way as *animal* is not predicated along with *man*, since it is comprised in *man*, so also, if *man* is comprised in *literate*, the former is not simultaneously predicated along with the latter of some subject. For example, it is inappropriate to say that Socrates is an animal man.

S. That cannot be denied.

T. But it is proper to say that Socrates is a *literate* man.

S. It is proper.

T. Therefore *man* is not comprised in *literate*.

S. I grasp that it does so follow.

4.2414   *T.* Again, if *literate* is *man having the learning constituting literacy*, then wherever *literate* appears, the words 'man having the learning constituting literacy' may be correctly substituted for it.

S. That is right.

T. Hence, if it is appropriate to say 'Socrates is a *literate* man', it is equally appropriate to say, 'Socrates is a man having the learning constituting literacy man'.

S. So it follows.

T. But every man having the learning constituting literacy is a *literate* man.

S. Yes.

T. Thus Socrates, who is a man having the learning constituting literacy man, is a *literate* man man, and since a literate is a man having the learning constituting literacy, it follows that Socrates is a man having the learning constituting literacy man man, and so on to infinity.

S. I cannot gainsay such obvious inferences.

4.2415   *T.* Again, if by *literate* we are to understand *man* as well as literacy, then in all cases of paronymous meaning we must understand that which is named paronymously along with that from which it derives its name.

S. That was my idea.

T. So that *today's* must signify both that which is called today's, and, in addition, it must signify today.

S. And so what?

T. Thus *today's* signifies something along with a temporal import.

S. It must be so.

T. Under such conditions, then, since *today's* is an incomplex expression having a temporal side-import, it must be a verb rather than a name.

14

4.30   *S.* You have proved to my satisfaction that *literate* does not signify *man*.

     T. You see the point, then, of what I said about *literate* not signifying *man*? [4.233]

     S. I do see it, and now I am waiting for you to show that *literate* signifies literacy.

4.31   *T.* Did you not assert a few moments ago [4.2410] that *literate* signifies *man having the learning constituting literacy*?

     S. That was my opinion.

     T. But now it has been sufficiently proved that *literate* does not signify man?

     S. Quite sufficiently.

     T. What then is left?

     S. . . . having the learning constituting literacy is all that it can signify.

     T. It signifies literacy then.

4.40, 4.411,   *S.* It has been amply proved that *literate* is appellative of
4.412   man [4.233] and not of literacy [4.234], and that *literate* signifies literacy [4.232], but not *man* [4.233].

4.413, 4.414,   However, since you asserted that *literate* signifies lit-
4.415   eracy precisively and man obliquely [4.232], I would like you to clarify the distinction between these two types of meaning so that I can understand how *literate* does not signify [4.412] that which it in some sense does signify [4.413], and how *literate* can be an appellative [4.411] of that which it does not signify [4.412].

4.4210   *T.* Suppose that, unknown to you, a *white* horse were to be enclosed within some dwelling or other, and someone told you, 'There's a *white* in this building'; would that inform you that the horse is inside?

     S. No; for whether they speak of a *white*, or of whiteness, or of that within which the whiteness is enclosed, no definite thing is brought to my mind apart from the essence of this colour.

     T. Even though you did happen to understand something over and above the colour, it is at least definite that the name in question conveys to you nothing as to exactly what that object is which is informed by that colour.

S. That is quite definitely so. True, that name brings to mind a body or a surface, but this is simply because experience has shown me that whiteness is usually found in such things. However, of itself the name *white* signifies neither of these, as was shown in the case of *literate*. And now I am waiting for you to show me what it does in fact signify.

4.422   *T.* Suppose you were confronted with a *white* horse and a black bull standing together, and someone issued the order, 'Give it a thwack!', thereby meaning the horse, but without giving any indication as to which he intended; would you then know that he was referring to the horse?

S. No.

T. But suppose, while still in ignorance, you were to ask 'Which?', and they were to reply, 'The *white*!', would you then gather his reference?

S. I would gather from the name *white* that he meant the horse.

T. Thus for you the name *white* would signify the horse.

S. It certainly would.

T. And do you notice that this would be in a fashion other than that proper to the name 'horse'?

4.4231   *S.* I quite see that. I notice that even before I know the horse to be *white*, the name 'horse' signifies to me the substance of horse precisively, not obliquely.

4.4232   On the other hand, the name *white* signifies the substance horse not precisively, but only obliquely, that is, thanks to my being aware that the horse is *white*.

4.4233   Now the name *white* is equisignificant with the phrase '. . . having whiteness'; similarly, the precise effect of this phrase is to bring to my mind the understanding of whiteness, but not of the thing which has the whiteness, so that the name *white* has the same effect.

4.4234   However, because I know, otherwise than by means of the name *white*—by sight, for example—that the whiteness is in the horse, then when whiteness has been thus conveyed by means of that name, I also gather the reference to the horse, because I know that the whiteness is in the horse. Nevertheless, this is otherwise than by means of the name *white*, even though that word is an appellative of the horse.

15

4.424   *T.* So now you grasp how *white* does not signify what it does in some way signify [4.414] and how it is appellative of what it does not signify [4.415].

    S. I now see this further point: *white* signifies yet does not signify the horse.

4.4241   It signifies the horse obliquely, and not precisively, and nevertheless *white* is appellative of the horse.

4.4242   Further, I realize that what I now discern in the case of *white* is applicable to *literate* and all like paronyms.

4.4243   On these grounds it appears to me that the signification of both names and verbs can be diversely classified: one sort is precisive signification, and the other is oblique.

4.430   *T.* Note also that while the precisive type of signification pertains essentially to significant utterances as such, the other type is only incidental to such utterances.

4.431   Thus, when a name or a verb is defined as a significant utterance, the signification in question is to be understood only as being of the precisive sort. Were the oblique sense of signification to be understood in the definition of a name or a verb, then *today's* would be a verb, and not a name, for it signifies some time or other because of its signifying something with a temporal side-import, and this, as I remarked before [4.2415], is proper to a verb and not to a name.

16

4.500,   *S.* Obviously it is as you say. Still, it is awkward to think
4.501,   of *literate*, although it does signify literacy, as being a
4.5020,   quality, or to think of man alone, that is, without literacy, as
4.5021,   being *literate*; for since man can only be *literate* alone or with
4.5022   literacy, that man alone is *literate* follows as a consequence of the proof [4.24] that man along with literacy is not *literate*. For although the name *literate* signifies literacy, nevertheless the correct answer to the question 'What is *literate*?' could scarcely be '*Literate* is literacy' or '*Literate* is a quality'.

4.503   And again, since a *literate* must participate in literacy, it follows that a man can only be a *literate* in conjunction with literacy.

4.510   *T.* The assertion that man alone, in the sense of man without literacy, is *literate*, can be interpreted in two fashions,

one correct and the other incorrect, and this is enough to
solve your problem.

4.511,   For on the one hand, man alone, without literacy, is indeed
4.5120, *literate*, in the sense that he alone ever participates in
4.5121, literacy; for literacy itself does not participate in literacy,
4.5122   either alone or along with man. On the other hand, man
alone, i.e. deprived of literacy, is not *literate*, for in the
absence of literacy no one can be *literate*. The first case is like
that of someone preceding, leading someone else, and alone
being the one who precedes, for that which follows is not a
precedent, either separately or in such a way that the two
form a single precedent. In the second case, one who is alone
is not one who precedes, for unless there is a follower, it is
impossible for there to be a precedent. And of course, when
it is asserted that *literate* is a quality, this assertion is only
correct if made in the sense which occurs in Aristotle's treatise *On the Categories*.

17

4.513   *S.* But does not that treatise make the point, 'Everything
which is, is one or other of either substance or quantity or
quality', and so on? So, if man alone is *literate*, a substance
alone is *literate*. Then how comes it that that treatise accounts
literate a quality rather than a substance?

4.5141, *T.* Although the text in question might be interpreted
4.5142, in the way you claim, since everything which is is some one
4.5143, or other of the items to which you allude, nevertheless Aris-
4.5144   totle's main intention in that book was not to show this, but
rather to show how every name or verb signifies one or other
of them. It was not his aim to show the nature of particular
sorts of things, nor yet of what things particular types of
words can be appellative; rather, he wished to show what
things they signify. However, since words can only signify
things, he had, in order to indicate what it is that words
signify, to indicate what those things could be. For, without
going into further detail, the classification which he under-
took at the opening of his work *On the Categories* is enough
to bear out what I assert. He does not say, 'Each item of whatever is, is either a substance or a quantity', and so on, nor yet
'Each item of whatever is expressed independently of context
has "substance" or "quantity" as its appellation', but rather,

'Each item of whatever is expressed independently of context signifies a substance or a quantity'.

S. Your point is persuasive.

4.515   *T.* Now when Aristotle says, 'Each item of whatever is expressed independently of context signifies a substance or a quantity', and so on, to which type of signification does it appear to you that he is referring? Is it to that whereby the utterances as such signify precisively, and which settles their theoretical situation, or is it to that other type which is oblique, and only incidental to the utterances?

S. He can only be referring to that sort of signification whereby they signify precisively, and which he himself imputes to such utterances when defining the name and the verb.

T. And do you consider that anywhere in his work he treated the matter otherwise than he did in this classification, or that any of his followers wished to adopt an attitude differing from his own on this topic, when writing on logic?

S. Their writings contain no grounds whatever for such an opinion, for at no point does one find any of them proffering an utterance to show something it can signify obliquely; they always proffer an utterance to show what it signifies precisively. Thus, when they want to show a substance, none of them proffers *white* or *literate*; however, *white* and *literate* and so on are advanced as examples when they are dealing with quality.

18

4.600   *T.* So that if, given the aforementioned classification, I were to ask you what *literate* is in terms of that classification, and in keeping with the opinions of those whose logical writings make appeal to it, what kind of question would I be asking, and what kind of a reply would you give?

4.601, 4.602,   *S.* This question must indubitably concern either the word
4.603   or the thing it signifies. Hence since it is agreed that in terms of this classification *literate* signifies literacy and not *man*, I would forthwith reply: if your question concerns the word, then it is a word signifying quality; if, however, your question is about the thing, then it is a quality.

4.604   *T.* You realize, do you not, that in this same work Aristotle refers to words by the names of the things which those words signify, and not by the names of those of which they are merely appellative? Thus when he says, 'Every substance would appear to signify this particular thing', then what he means is, 'Every word signifying a substance'. It is in this way that he names, or rather shows things (as you reminded us just now) by recourse to utterances which only signify them, and which frequently are not appellative of them at all.

4.610, 4.611   *S.* I cannot help realizing this. Hence, whether the question is posed in respect of the word or in respect of the thing, when one asks what *literate* is according to Aristotle's treatise, and according to his followers, the correct answer is: a quality. However, from the point of view of appellation it certainly is a substance.

4.620, 4.621   *T.* Quite so: we must not be disturbed by the fact that logicians make written assertions about words insofar as they signify, and yet, in speaking, and given the appellative functions of those words, they use them in a fashion which is at variance with those assertions: for the grammarians also assert one thing about a word considered as an exemplar, but quite another when it is considered in relation to the constitution of things. After all, they tell us that 'stone' is masculine in gender, 'rock' feminine, but 'slave' neuter, and that 'to fear' is an active verb, whereas 'to be feared' is passive; yet no one asserts that a stone is male, a rock female, or a slave neither male nor female, nor that to fear is to perform an activity, whereas to be feared is to undergo an action.

19

4.700   *S.* Clearly it would be unreasonable on my part to question what you have laid down, but there is still another point in connection with this problem which I would like you to clear up for me. Thus if *literate* is a quality because it signifies a quality, I fail to see why *armed* is not a substance because it signifies a substance. At the same time, if *armed* is categorized as a 'having' on account of its signifying a having, I do not see why *literate* is not similarly categorized because it too signifies a having. For in exactly the same way as *literate* is proved to signify a quality because it signifies the having of a quality, so also *armed* signifies a substance because it signifies the having of a substance, namely, arms. Again, since *armed* quite obviously signifies having (for it signifies having arms), *literate* must also signify having because it signifies having the learning.

T. If we are to take these points into account I just cannot deny that *armed* is a substance or *literate* a having.

S. Can a single item be assigned to different categories then? I would like you to settle this for me.

4.710   *T.* I do not think that any one and the same item can properly be assigned to several categories, although in certain cases this may be a matter of opinion; in my view this calls for a rather more lengthy and technical argument than we can undertake in our present brief discussion. However, I do not see why one word which signifies several items, but not as a single whole, should not at times be variously categorized, e.g. if *white* were said to be both a quality and a having. In this instance *white* does not signify quality and having as a single whole in the same way as *man* does signify as a single whole both the substance and the qualities which constitute man. This is so because that which receives the appellation 'man' is a unitary object constituted in the way I mentioned, whereas the object which receives the appellation *white* is not just some one object made up of a having and a quality, for only the thing that has whiteness receives the appellation *white*, and such a thing is certainly not composed of a having and a quality.

4.711, 4.712   In contrast, should it be asserted that *man* is a substance and *man* is a quality, then one and the same thing which this name signifies, and of which it is appellative, would be asserted to be both a substance and a quality, and this seems unacceptable. When, however, we say that *white* is both a quality and a having, we are not asserting that that of which this name is appellative is both a quality and a having, but that this name signifies both, so that nothing improper follows.

4.713   *S.* But then why is not *man* a substance and a quality in terms of Aristotle's classification, on account of its signifying both, in the same way that *white* is a quality and a having on account of its signifying both?

4.714   *T.* I think that what I have already said should be enough to settle your query: *man* predominantly signifies a substance, something qualified, rather than a quality. On the other hand *white* has no dominant signification but relates equally to quality and having, nor does any kind of unity result from *white*'s predominantly signifying one or other of them.

20

4.72   S. I would like you to explain to me more fully how it comes about that something forming a single whole does not result from the things signified by *white*.

T. If something is composed of them, then it is either a substance or something in one or other of the categories.

S. It must be so.

T. But no category comprises both having and whiteness.

S. I cannot deny that.

T. Again, a single whole can only be made up out of a multiplicity either by the composition of parts which are of the same category, in the way that animal is made up of body and soul, or by the assemblage of a genus and one or more characteristics, as in the cases of body and man, or by the species and collection of properties, as with Plato. Now the things that *white* signifies do not belong to any one category only, neither is one of them related to the other as genus to constitutive characteristic or as species to collection of properties, nor yet again are they characteristics pertaining to one genus: they are in fact accidents of the same subject. Yet *white* does not signify that subject: it signifies only a having and a quality. Therefore no unity results from the things that *white* signifies.

4.800   S. Your assertion seems to me to be perfectly reasonable. Still, I would like to hear what you would reply should someone object as follows to what you said about *white*'s signifying only a having and a quality.

4.801,   As *white* is equivalent to *having whiteness* it does not deter-
4.8020,   minately signify this or that object having whiteness, such as
4.8021   a body; rather it signifies indeterminately some object having whiteness. This is because a *white* is either that which has whiteness or that which has not whiteness; but that which has not whiteness is not *white*, so that a *white* is that which has whiteness. Further, since everything which has whiteness must needs be something, a *white* must be something which has whiteness, or something having whiteness. Finally, *white* signifies either something having whiteness or nothing; but nothing cannot be conceived as having whiteness; hence *white* must signify something having whiteness.

4.810   T. The question at issue is not whether everything which is *white* is something, or whether it is that which has, but whether the word *white* contains in its signification the expression *something* or *that which has*, and this in the same way as that in which *man* contains *animal*, with the consequence that in the same way as *man* is *rational mortal animal*, so also *white* is *something having whiteness* or *that which has whiteness*.

4.811,   Now many things are necessary to the being of anything
4.8120   you care to mention, and yet they are not signified by the name of the thing in question. For example, every animal must be coloured, as well as being either rational or irrational, yet the name animal signifies none of these things. Hence, although there is no *white* which is not something having whiteness or which is not that which has whiteness, nevertheless *white* need not signify these facts. Nevertheless, let us suppose that *white* can signify *something having whiteness*. Now *something having whiteness* is the same as *something white*.

S. It must be so.

T. *White* therefore always signifies *something white*.

S. Quite so.

T. So that wherever *white* appears, it is always correct to substitute *something white* for *white*.

S. That follows.

T. Hence when *something white* is used, the double expression *something something white* is also correct; when the double is correct, so also is the triple, and so on to infinity.

S. This is both derivable and absurd.

4.8121   T. Again, let *white* be also identical with *that which has whiteness*. Now 'has . . .' is the same as 'is a haver of . . .'.

S. It cannot be otherwise.

T. Therefore *white* is the same as *that which is a haver of whiteness*.

S. Exactly.

T. But when *a haver of whiteness* is used, this phrase is equisignificant with *white*.

S. That is so.

T. Hence *white* is the same as *that which is white*.

S. So it follows.

T. Wherever, therefore, *white* appears, *that which is white* may properly be substituted for it.

S. That I cannot deny.

T. Then if *white* is the same as *that which is white*, it is also the same as *that which is that which is white*; if it is this, so also is it *that which is that which is that which is white*, and so on to infinity.

S. This is just as logical and just as absurd as the case in which the repetition of *something something . . .* results.

T. And now, when it is asserted [4.8021] that *white* signifies either something having whiteness or nothing, and this is interpreted as asserting that *white* signifies either *something having* or *not-something having*, then as *not-something* is a negative name, this disjunction is neither exhaustive nor true, and hence proves nothing. It's like someone asserting, 'The blind man either sees something or he sees not-something'. If, in contrast, the assertion is interpreted as meaning that the word either signifies or does not signify *something having*, the disjunction is exhaustive and true, and is not incompatible with what has been laid down previously.

4.82

S. It is now adequately evident that *white* signifies neither *something having whiteness* nor *that which has whiteness*, but only . . . *having whiteness*, that is, a quality and a having, and as these alone do not constitute one thing, *white* is both of them, since it signifies them both equally. I see that this reasoning is valid in relation to whatever is expressed independently of context, and which likewise signifies some multiplicity which is of such a kind as does not form a single whole. It also seems to me that no valid objection can be made to the theses you have advanced in the course of this discussion.

T. So it seems to me at the moment. You are well aware, however, of the degree to which contemporary logicians are at loggerheads about this problem of yours, so I do not want you to stick to our findings to the extent of stubbornly hanging on to them should someone manage, by dint of better opposing arguments, to demolish our results and establish different ones. Should this occur, at least you cannot deny that all this has been handy as an exercise in the art of disputation.

ON TRUTH

Preface

Over a period of time I have written three treatises which pertain to the study of Sacred Scripture; they are alike in employing the style of question and answer, the person asking being designated the Student and the one responding the Teacher. I wrote a fourth in this same mode, not without its utility, I think, as an introduction to dialectic, called *De Grammatico* (*On the Grammarian*), but since it pertains to a different inquiry than the three just mentioned, I do not number it among them.

One of the three is *On Truth*, what it is and in what things it is customarily said to be found; and what is justice. The second is *On Free Will*, what it is, and whether a man always has it, and how many different ways there are of having and not having rectitude of will, the preserving of which is the task of the rational creature. In it I showed how great the natural strength of the will is for preserving rectitude once acquired, not how necessary grace might be for it. The third asks how the devil sinned, because 'he has not stood in the truth' [John 8: 44], since God did not grant him perseverance, which cannot be had if he does not give it; yet if God had given it, he had it, just as the good angels did, because God gave it to them. Although I treat in it of the confirmation of the good angels, I gave it the title *On the Fall of the Devil*, since it just happened that I spoke of the good angels in writing of the bad, which was the intent of the question.

Although these treatises do not cohere by any continuity of dictation, their matter and similarity of style demanded that they be written in the order that I have listed them. Therefore although they were transcribed by certain hasty souls in another order, before they were completed, I wish them to be arranged as I now have stated.

Chapters

1. *That truth has neither beginning nor end*

Student. Since we believe that God is truth and we say that truth is in many other things, I wish to know whether whenever truth is spoken of we ought to be saying that it is God of whom we speak. For you yourself in the *Monologion* prove from the truth of speech that the highest truth has neither beginning nor end, saying: 'Let him who thinks so state when this truth began or when it was not, namely, that something was going to be. Or when it will cease to be true and will no longer be true that something has been. But if neither of these can be thought, and both truths can only be such if there is truth, it is impossible to think that truth should have a beginning or an end. Finally if truth had a beginning and will have an end, before it came to be it was then true that truth was not. But the true cannot be without truth. Therefore there was a truth before truth existed, and there will be truth after truth has ceased to be, which is absurd. Therefore whether truth should be said to have, or is understood not to have, a beginning or end, truth cannot be confined by beginning or end.'

That is what you say in the *Monologion*. Consequently I await a definition of truth from you.

Teacher. I do not remember that I ever found a definition of truth, but if you like we can seek it by looking at the different things in which we say truth exists.

S. If I can help you in no other way it will be in listening.

2. *On the signification of truth and of the two truths of
   statements*

T. We will first seek, then, what truth there might be in speech,
since we often say that is true or false.

S. You seek and I will keep whatever you find.

T. When is a statement true?

S. When what is stated, either by affirming or denying, exists. For
I say that a person states something even when he denies that what
is not is, since he thus states the way things are.

T. Does it then seem to you that the thing stated is the truth of
the statement?

S. No.

T. Why?

S. Because something is true only by participating in the truth,
and therefore the truth of the true is in the true itself, but the thing
stated is not in the true statement. Hence it should not be called its
truth, but the cause of its truth. That is why it seems to me that its
truth must be looked for in speech itself.

T. Let us see then whether speech itself or its signification or
some one of the things which is put into the definition of a statement might be what you are looking for.

S. I do not think so.

T. Why?

S. Because if it were, it would always be true, since all the things
that are in the definition of a statement remain the same whether or
not what is stated is or is not. There is the same statement and the
same meaning and so too with the other things.

T. What then seems to you to be the truth there?

S. I only know that when it signifies that what is is, then truth is
in it and it is true.

T. What is the purpose of an affirmation?

S. To signify that what is is.

T. It ought to do that.

S. Certainly.

T. Therefore when it signifies that what is is, it signifies what it
should.

S. Clearly.

T. And when it signifies what it ought it signifies correctly.

S. Yes.

T. But when it signifies correctly, its signification is correct.

S. No doubt.

T. Therefore when it signifies that what is is, there is correct signification.

S. That follows.

T. And again when it signifies that what is is, it is true signification.

S. It is indeed correct and true when it signifies that what is is.

T. So it is the same thing for it to be correct and to be true, that is, to signify that what is is.

S. They are indeed the same.

T. So for it truth is no different from rectitude.

S. I clearly see now that its truth is rectitude.

T. And it is similar when a statement signifies that what is not is not.

S. I see what you are saying. But show me how I can answer, if someone should say that, even when a statement signifies that what is not is, it signifies what it should. He seems to take signifying to apply equally to what is and to what is not, for if it were not taken to signify even what is not, it would not signify. Therefore even when it signifies that what is not is, it signifies what it ought. But if by signifying as it should it is correct and true, as you have shown, a statement is true even when it states that what is not is.

T. But although it is not customary to say that it is true when it signifies that what is not is, still it has truth and rectitude insofar as it is a well-formed sentence. But when it says that what is is, it doubly does what it ought to, since it signifies both what it undertakes to signify and is a well-formed sentence. When it signifies that what is is, by right and true use it is called a statement because of that rectitude and truth, but not when it signifies that what is not is. The standard case is had when it fulfils its function rather than when it does not. Indeed, its ability to signify that a thing is when it is not is parasitic on its standardly signifying that what is is and what is not is not.

A statement then is right and true either because it is correctly formed or because it fulfils its function of signifying correctly. The former belongs immutably to it, the latter is mutable. The former it always has, the latter not always. The former it naturally has, the latter accidentally and according to use. For when I say, 'It is day', in order to signify what is is, I correctly use what the utterance means, because this is why it was fashioned, and therefore it then is correctly said to signify. But when by the same utterance I signify that what is not is, I do not use it correctly, because it was not fashioned for this purpose, and its signification is not then called correct. These two rectitudes or truths are inseparable in some utterances, as when we say, 'Man is an animal', or 'Man is not a stone'. That affirmation always signifies that what is is and that negation that what is not is not, nor can we use the former to signify that what is not is—for man is always an animal—nor the latter to signify that what is is not, because man is never a stone.

We have begun to ask about the truth an utterance has insofar as someone uses it correctly, since it is on this basis that common usage judges it to be true. Of that truth which it cannot not have, we will speak later.[1]

S. Go back then to where you began, since it seems to me that you have sufficiently distinguished between the two truths of an utterance. Since it has some truth when it lies, as you say.

T. On the truth of signification, concerning which we began, these things will suffice for now. For the same notion of truth that we perceive in the voiced statement should be found in all signs fashioned to signify that something is or is not, such as script and sign language.

S. Then let us go on to the other things.

3. *On the truth of opinion*

T. We also say that thought is true when what we think by reason or some other mode is, and false, when it is not.

S. So we do.

T. What then does truth in thought seem to you to be?

S. According to our reasoning in the case of the proposition, the truth of thought could not correctly be called anything other than its rectitude. The reason the ability to think that something is or is

---

[1] Anselm's examples suggest that he is distinguishing between contingent and necessary truths, but also involved is the distinction between being truly a statement and being a true statement.

not has been given us is that we might think that what is is, and what is not is not. So he who thinks that what is is thinks as he ought, and his thought is therefore correct. If then thought is only true and correct because we think that what is is or that what is not is not, its truth is nothing other than its correctness.

T. You are thinking correctly.

4. *On the truth of the will*

T. But Truth itself tells us that truth is in the will, when he says of the devil, 'He did not stand in the truth' [John 8: 44]. For it was only due to will that he was not in the truth or deserted the truth.

S. So I believe. For if he always willed what he ought, he would never have sinned, since it was only by sinning that he deserted the truth.

T. Say what you think truth is in that case.

S. Nothing but rectitude. For if, so long as he wills what he ought, which is why he was given a will, he was in rectitude and in truth, and when he willed what he ought not, he deserted rectitude and truth, such truth can only be understood as rectitude since both truth and rectitude of will were nothing other than to will what he ought.

T. You have understood well.

5. *On the truth of natural and non-natural action*

T. Truth must also be recognized in action, as the Lord says, 'he who does evil hates the light' [John 3: 20] and 'who does the truth, comes into the light' [John 3: 21].

S. I see what you are saying.

T. Consider what truth might be in this case, if you can.

S. Unless I am mistaken, we should use the same argument about action that we used earlier when we identified truth in the other things.

T. Yes. But if to act badly and to do the truth are opposites, as the Lord shows, when he says 'he who acts badly hates the light' and 'he who does the truth comes into the light', to do the truth and to act well are the same thing. For acting well is contrary to acting badly. Therefore if doing the truth and acting well are contrary to the same thing, they are not different in signification. But it is everyone's opinion that he who does what he ought acts well and with rectitude. Hence it follows that to bring about rectitude and to do the truth are the same. For it is clear that to do the truth is to act well, and to act well is to bring about rectitude. What could be more obvious then than that the truth of action is rectitude.

S. I can find no fault in your thinking.

T. Consider whether every action that does what it ought is fittingly said to do the truth. For there is rational action, such as giving alms, and irrational action, such as the action of the fire that heats. Do you think we would fittingly say that fire does the truth?

S. If fire receives the ability to heat from the one that makes it exist, then when it heats, it does what it ought. So I do not see where the unfittingness would be in saying that fire exhibits truth and rectitude when it does what it ought.

T. I think no differently myself. Hence it can be noted that rectitude or truth of action is sometimes necessary and sometimes not. For fire necessarily exhibits rectitude and truth when it heats, but a man when he acts well does not necessarily act rightly and truly.

When the Lord said 'he who does the truth, comes into the light' [John 3: 21], he is not using 'to do' (*facere*) only for that which is properly called doing, but for every verb. For he does not separate from this truth or light one who suffers persecution 'for justice's sake' [Matt. 5: 10], or what is when and where it ought to be, or that stands or sits, when it ought, and so on. No one says that these are not instances of *doing* well. And when the Apostle says that everyone receives 'what he has won' [2 Cor. 5: 10], this should there be understood of whatever we are accustomed to call doing well or doing badly.

S. The ordinary use of this locution is such that to suffer and many other things are called doings which we do not *do*. For this reason, if I am not mistaken, we can also number correct willing, whose truth we discussed earlier before the truth of action, among right actions.

T. You are not mistaken. For one who wills what he ought, is said to act rightly and well, nor is he excluded from those 'who do the truth'. But since we say this in the course of investigating truth, and the Lord seems to make special mention of that truth which is in the will when he says of the devil 'that he does not stand in the truth', I wanted to consider separately what truth in the will is.

S. I am pleased that you did.

T. Since it is clear that the truth of natural action is one thing and that of non-natural action another, the truth of speech, which we saw above cannot be separated from it, should be placed under natural action. For just as fire when it heats exhibits the truth because it receives this from the one from whom it has existence, so too this utterance, namely 'It is day,' exhibits the truth because it signifies that day is, whether or not it is day, since it naturally is fashioned to do so.[2]

S. Now I see for the first time the truth in false utterance.

6. *On the truth of the senses*

T. Do you think that we have located all senses of the truth apart from the highest truth?

S. I am remembering a truth that I do not find in the things you have treated.

T. And what is that?

S. There is truth in the body's senses, though not always. For sometimes they deceive us. Sometimes when I look through the medium of glass, sight deceives me because it reports to me that a body I see beyond the glass is of the same colour as the glass, although it is actually of a different colour. And sometimes it causes me to think that the glass has the colour of the thing that I see beyond, although it does not. And there are many other instances in which sight and the other senses mislead.

T. This truth or falsity seems to me to be in opinion rather than in the senses. For if the inner sense is deceived, the exterior does not lie to it. This is sometimes easily known, sometimes with difficulty. For when a child fears the sculpted dragon with its mouth open, it is easily seen that sight does not do this, since it reports nothing to the child that it does not to adults, but the child's interior sense does not yet know how to tell the difference between a thing and its likeness. This is the case when someone similar to someone else is thought to be him, or when hearing something other than a human voice we think it to be a human voice. But it is the interior sense that does this.

---

[2] The natural end of speech is to state the truth, and this remains true even when we lie or state what is false.

As to what you say of the glass, this is so because when sight travels through some body of the colour of air it is not prevented from receiving the likeness of colour that it sees beyond any more than when it passes through air—this only happens when what the body passed through is thicker and darker than air. For example, when it passes through a window of its own colour, that is, in which no other colour is mixed, or through the purest water or crystal or something else of similar colour. But when the same seeing passes through another colour, as through glass not of its own colour, but to which another colour is added, it receives the first colour it encounters. Thus, after one colour is received, by which it is affected, another is either not received at all or less completely and it reports the one it first receives, either alone or with another. For if sight, insofar as it is capable of colour, is affected only by the first colour, it cannot at the same time sense another colour. But if it can sense the first colour that it is affected by less, it can sense another. If it travels through some body, such as glass, which is so completely red that sight is completely affected by its redness, it cannot at the same time be affected by another colour. But if it does not perfectly receive the redness that first occurs, that is, to the full degree of which it is capable, then it can receive another colour insofar as its capacity is not fulfilled by the first colour. One who does not know this thinks that sight reports that everything that it senses after the first colour received is entirely or to some extent of the same colour. So it happens that the interior sense imputes its mistake to the exterior sense.

So too when a stick, part of which is under water and part not, is thought to be crooked, or when we think that sight finds our faces in a mirror, and when many other things seem otherwise to us, sight and the other senses report what is, for it is no fault of the senses that report what they can, as they can receive it, but it should be imputed to the judgement of the soul which does not discern well what the senses can do or what they ought to do.

I do not think we should use up our time to show this since it is more laborious that fruitful for our purposes. Suffice it to say that the senses, whatever they seem to report, whether they do this from their own nature or from some other cause, do what they ought to do and therefore exhibit rectitude and truth. This truth is contained under the truth that is in action.

S. Your reply has satisfied me and I do not want you to delay longer on this question of the senses.

7. *On the truth of the essence of things*

T. Consider now whether, apart from the highest truth, truth might be understood to be in anything besides what we have already looked into.

S. What could it be?

T. Do you think that anything could be at any time or at any place that was not in the highest truth and that did not receive what it is, insofar as it is, or that it could be something else than what it now is?

S. That is unthinkable.

T. Therefore whatever is, truly is, insofar as it is such as it is.

S. You can conclude absolutely that everything that is, truly is, since it is not other than what it then is.

T. Therefore there is truth in the essence of all things, because it is by being in the highest truth that they exist.

S. I see that the truth is such that there can be no falsity there, since what is false is not.

T. Well said. But tell me if anything ought to be otherwise than it is in the highest truth.

S. No.

T. Therefore if all things are what they are there, they are without doubt what they ought to be.

S. They are truly what they ought to be.

T. And whatever is what it ought to be, exists rightly.

S. It cannot be otherwise.

T. Therefore, whatever is, exists rightly.

S. Nothing is more obvious.

T. Therefore if truth and rectitude are in the essence of things because they are that which they are in the highest truth, it is certain that the truth of things is rectitude.

S. Nothing is plainer than the consequence of the argument.

8. *On the different concepts 'ought' and 'ought not' and 'can' and 'cannot'*

S. But, as to the truth of the matter, how can we say that whatever is ought to be, since there are many evil deeds which certainly ought not to be.

T. Why do you wonder that the same thing both ought to be and ought not to be?

S. How could that be the case?

T. Surely you do not think that anything could exist in any way if God did not either make it or permit it.

S. I certainly do not.

T. Would you dare deny that God always does or permits a thing wisely and well?

S. I would assert that he does nothing except wisely and well.

T. Would you think that anything such Goodness and Wisdom does or permits ought not to be?

S. Could anyone of intelligence dare to think so?

T. Well then, whatever God does or whatever, God permitting, comes about ought equally to be?

S. What you say is self-evident.

T. Tell me then whether you think that the effect of an evil will ought to exist.

S. That is tantamount to asking whether some bad deed ought to be, which no one in his sense would concede.

T. But God permits some to do badly what they badly will.

S. Would that he did not permit it so often.

T. Therefore the same thing ought to be and ought not to be. For it ought to be, insofar as it could only be if he wisely and well permits it to be; and it ought not to be insofar as it is conceived by an evil will. In this way, the Lord Jesus, who alone was innocent, ought not to suffer death, nor ought anyone to have inflicted it on him, and yet he ought to have suffered it, because he wisely and benignly and usefully wished to suffer it. There are many ways in which the same thing receives contrary appraisals from different considerations. This often happens in action, for example, striking. Striking involves an agent and a patient so it can be called both an action and being acted upon. As words, 'action' or 'striking', and other things which are signified actively but from what is acted on, seem to refer to the thing acted upon rather than to the agent. Indeed that which acts is more properly called an agent or striker, and that which is the recipient, action or striking. For agents and strikers are named from the doer and striker, as providence is from the one who provides, and continence from the one containing, and these, agent, striker, provider, container, are active; action and striking are derived from what is done or struck, and are passive.

But since—that I might say of one case what you will understand in others—just as the striker is not without the struck, nor the struck without the striker, so strikers and striking can only be understood with one another, indeed it is one and the same thing which is signified by different names according to different parts, and therefore a blow is said to be of both the striker and the struck.

Wherefore insofar as the agent and the thing acted upon are subject to the same or to contrary judgement, the action itself is judged to be the same or contrary. When therefore the one who strikes rightly strikes, and the one who is struck is rightly struck, as when a sinner is corrected by one who has the right to do so, there is right on both sides, because on both sides the blow ought to be struck. It is the opposite when the just man is struck by a bad man, since the one ought not to strike and the other ought not to be struck, so on both sides it is not right since on neither side ought the blow to be struck. But when the sinner is struck by someone who has not the right to do so, then the one ought to be struck but the other ought not to strike, and the blow both ought to be and ought not to be. Thus it cannot be denied that it is both right and not right. But if we think of the judgement of the supreme Wisdom and Goodness that the blow ought not to be struck, whether from one alone or from both sides, namely of the agent and of the one being acted upon, who would dare deny that what is permitted by such Wisdom and Goodness ought to be?

S. Let him who dares deny it; I certainly do not dare.

T. What then, if you consider the nature of things, as when iron nails were driven into the body of the Lord, would you say that the fragile flesh ought not to be penetrated or that when penetrated by the sharp steel it ought not to feel pain?

S. I would speak against nature.

T. Therefore it can happen that an action or passion ought to be according to nature which ought not to be with respect to the agent or the one acted upon, since the former ought not to act and the latter ought not to suffer it.

S. I cannot deny that.

T. So you see that it can very often come about that the same action both ought to be and ought not to be under different conditions?

S. You have made it so clear that I could hardly not see.

T. Indeed among the things I want you to know is that 'ought to be' and 'ought not to be' are sometimes used improperly, as when I say, that I ought to be loved by you. For if I truly ought, I ought to render what I owe and am at fault if I am not loved by you.

S. That seems to follow.

T. But that I ought to be loved by you is demanded not of me but of you.

S. I have to agree.

T. Therefore when I say that I ought to be loved by you, this does not mean that I owe something, but rather that you owe love to me. Similarly when I say that I ought not to be loved by you, this should be understood to mean that you do not owe love to me.

This mode of speaking is also in play with being able and being unable. As when it is said that Hector can be conquered by Achilles, and that Achilles cannot be conquered by Hector. For there is no power in the one who can be conquered but in the one who can conquer, nor the inability in the one who cannot be conquered, but in the one who cannot conquer.

S. What you say pleases me. Indeed I think it is useful to know this.

T. You think rightly.

9. *That every action signifies the true or false*

T. But let us return to the truth of signification with which I began in order that I might lead you from the more known to the less known. For all speak of the truth of signification, but few consider the truth that is in the essence of things.

S. It was to my profit that you led me in the order you did.

T. Let us see, therefore, how broad is the truth of signification. It is not only in those things which we are accustomed to call signs, but in all other things of which we say there is true or false signification. Since one ought to do only what he ought to do, by the very fact that someone does something, he says and signifies that he ought to do it. And if he ought to do what he does, he calls it true. But if he ought not, he lies.

S. Although it seems to me that I understand, because I never heard this before, show more clearly what you are saying.

T. If you were in a place where you knew that there were both healthy and poisonous herbs, though you did not know how to distinguish between them, but there was someone else there whom you did not doubt knew how to distinguish them, and when you asked him he told you which were healthy and which poisonous, and he told you that some were healthy yet he himself ate others, which would you believe, his word or his deed?

S. I would not believe the word but the deed.

T. Therefore he told you more by deed than by word which ones were healthy.

S. Just so.

T. Therefore, if you did not know that one ought not to lie and someone lies to you, even if he told you that he ought not to lie, he would rather tell you by his deed that he ought to lie than by his word that he ought not. Similarly when someone thinks or wills something, if you did not know whether he ought to do or will it, if you could see his will and thought, they would signify to you by the deed that he ought to think or will this. Which if so he ought, he would convey to you what is true. If not, he would lie. There is true and false signification in the existence of things too, since by the fact that a thing is, it says that it ought to be.

S. I see now what before I did not.

T. Then let us go on to what remains.

S. You lead and I will follow.

10. *The highest truth*

T. You will not deny that the highest truth is rectitude.

S. There is nothing else that I can say it is.

T. Consider that, since all the foregoing rectitudes are such because they are in things which are or do what they ought, but the highest truth is not rectitude because it owes anything. All other things owe him but he owes nothing to another, nor is there any other reason why he is than that he is.

S. I understand.

T. You will also see how this rectitude is the cause of all other truth and rectitude but nothing is the cause of it?

S. I see and I note in others that some are only effects whereas some are both causes and effects—as when the truth that is in the things that exist is the effect of the highest truth, but it is also the cause of the truth which is in knowledge and of that which is in the statement, but these two truths are not the cause of any other truth.

T. Well done. Hence you can now understand how in my *Monologion* I proved that the highest truth has neither beginning nor end by the truth of speech. For when I said, 'that it was not true that something was to be', I did not mean that this utterance had no beginning, or that this truth would be God, but that it could not be understood that truth would be lacking to it, if the utterance were true. By the fact that it is not understood when this truth could not be, if there were an utterance in which it could be, this truth is understood to have been without beginning and is the first cause of this truth. Indeed the truth of the utterance could not always be if its cause were not always. Nor is the utterance that something will be true unless that thing will be, nor is anything future if it is not in the highest truth.

The utterance that something has been should be understood similarly. For if no intellect could fail to see the truth of this utterance if it were made, it is necessary that no end can be understood of the truth that is its highest cause. Therefore something is truly said to have been because it is so in reality, and therefore there is something past because so it is in the highest truth.

Wherefore if it could never be true that something will be and it could never not be true that something had been, it is impossible that there was a beginning of the highest truth or that there will be an end of it.

S. I see nothing to object to in your argument.

11. *The definition of truth*

T. Let us return to the investigation of truth where we began.

S. All this pertains to the investigation of truth, but I will return where you like.

T. Then tell me whether it seems to you that there is any rectitude other than those we have discussed.

S. There is none besides them, unless that which is in bodily things, which is quite foreign to these, for example, the straightness of a branch.

T. How do you think that differs from the others?

S. Because it can be known by bodily sight, but the pondering of reason grasps the others.

T. But is not that rectitude of bodies understood by reason and thought of without its subject? Or if you should doubt of some absent body whether its lines were straight and it can be shown that in no part do they bend, is it not inferred by reason that it must be straight?

S. Yes. But the same thing which is thus understood by reason is sensed by sight in the subject. But the others can only be grasped by the mind.

T. Therefore we can, unless I am mistaken, define truth as a rectitude perceptible by mind alone.

S. I cannot see how in saying this you could possibly be wrong. Indeed this definition of truth contains no more and no less than is needed, since the name of rectitude distinguishes it from everything which is not called rectitude, and by saying it is grasped by mind alone, it is distinguished from visible rectitude.

12. *On the definition of justice*

S. Since you have taught me that all truth is rectitude, and it seems to me that rectitude and justice are the same, teach me what to understand about justice as well. It seems that whatever is right is also just and, conversely, whatever is just is right. For it seems right and just that fire should be hot and that each man should love those who love him. Thus whatever ought to be is right and just, nor is a thing right and just unless it ought to be, or so I think, and justice does not differ from rectitude. Doubtless rectitude and justice are the same in the highest and simplest nature, although it is not just and right because it ought to do something.

T. If justice does not differ from rectitude you already have a definition of justice. And since we are speaking of the rectitude that is perceptible by mind alone, truth and rectitude and justice mutually define one another. He who knows one of them knows the others and can from the known go on to knowledge of the unknown. Indeed he who knows one cannot be in ignorance of the others.

S. What then? Should we call a stone just, because it seeks to be below when it is above and thus does what it ought in the same way that we say a man is just when he does what he should?

T. We are not accustomed to calling someone just because of justice in that sense.

S. Why should a man be more just than a stone if both act justly?

T. Do you not yourself think that what a man does and what a stone does differ in some way?

S. I know the man acts willingly but the stone acts naturally and not by willing.

T. The stone is not called just on that account, because only that which does what it ought to do willingly is just.

S. Will we then call a horse just when he wishes to go to the pasture since he willingly does what he does?

T. I did not say that whatever does willingly what it ought is just; I said that it is not just if it does not willingly do what it does.

S. Tell me then who is just.

T. I see that you seek a definition of justice as that which merits praise and of its contrary, injustice, as that to which blame is due.

S. That is what I seek.

T. Notice that justice is not in any nature that does not know rectitude. Therefore whatever does not will rectitude, even if it has it, does not merit praise for its rectitude. One who does not know it cannot will it.

S. That is true.

T. Therefore the rectitude that earns praise for the one having it is found only in the rational nature, which alone perceives the rectitude of which we speak.

S. That follows.

T. Therefore since all justice is rectitude, the justice that makes the one having it praiseworthy is found only in rational beings.

S. It cannot be otherwise.

T. Where then does it seem to you that this justice is in man who is rational?

S. It can only be in will or in knowledge or in deed.

T. What if someone understands rightly or acts rightly but does not will rightly: should such a one be praised for justice?

S. No.

T. Therefore justice is not rectitude of knowledge or action, but of will.

S. Either that or nothing.

T. Do you think the justice that we seek is sufficiently defined?

S. You decide.

T. Do you think that whoever wills what he ought wills rightly and has rectitude of will?

S. If anyone unknowingly does what he ought to, for example, if he unwittingly locks out someone who wants to kill another person in the house—well, whether or not he has some rectitude of will, he does not have that which we are seeking.

T. What do you say of him who knows he ought to will what he wills?

S. It can happen that someone knowingly wills what he ought yet does not will it because he ought to. For when the thief is forced to return the money he has taken, it is clear that he does not want to have to, and therefore is forced to want to return it because he should. But he is in no way praised for his rectitude.

T. One who feeds the poor out of vainglory wills what he ought to will. Is he on that account praised for willing to do what he ought? What do you make of him?

S. Such rectitude ought not to be praised and therefore does not suffice for the justice we are seeking. But show me now what would suffice.

T. Every will wills both something and for the sake of something. As we must consider what it wills, similarly we should look into why it wills. What is willed should not count more for rectitude than that for the sake of which it is willed.

Accordingly, every will has a what and a why. For there is no way we can will anything without there also being a reason why we will it.

S. We all know this within ourselves.

T. Why do you think that anyone should will what he wills in order that he might have a praiseworthy will? What ought to be willed is clear enough, since he who does not will what he ought is not just.

S. It seems to me no less clear that just as everyone ought to will what he ought, he ought so to will it that his will is just.

T. You well understand then that these two are necessary for justice in the will, namely, to will what it ought and for the reason it ought to. But tell me if these suffice.

S. Why not?

T. When someone wills what he ought to because he is forced, does he not in some way will what he ought to because he ought to?

S. Maybe so, but he wills it in one way and the just man in another.

T. Distinguish these two ways.

S. When the just man wills what he ought, he preserves rectitude of will for no other reason than to preserve it. But one who wills what he ought to only when forced or persuaded by extraneous reward can be said to preserve rectitude, not for its own sake, but for the sake of something else.

T. Therefore the will is just when it preserves its rectitude for the sake of rectitude itself.

S. Either that or no will is just.

T. Therefore justice is rectitude of will preserved for its own sake.

S. Truly this is the definition of justice that I sought.

T. Do you see anything in it that needs to be corrected?

S. I see nothing in it that ought to be corrected.

T. Nor do I. Therefore there is no justice that is not rectitude, nor is justice as such anything other than the rectitude of will. The rectitude of action is called justice, but only when action comes about with a just will. Rectitude of will, even if it is impossible that what we rightly will come about, does not lose the name of justice.

Perhaps someone will explain what 'preserved' means in the following way. If there is only justice of the will when rectitude is preserved, then justice is not yet had, nor do we acquire justice when we acquire it, but we cause it to be justice by preserving it. For we must receive and have it before we can preserve it. Therefore we do not receive it nor first have it because we preserve it, but we begin to preserve it because we have acquired and possessed it.

But in response we can say that we receive, will and have it simultaneously. For we only have it by willing, and, if we will it, by this very fact we have it. But just as we have and will it simultaneously, so at the same time we will and preserve it, since just as we do not preserve it unless we will it, it is not when we will it but do not preserve it; rather, as long as we will it, we preserve it, and as long as we preserve it, we will it. Therefore since it happens that we will and have it at the same time, and do not will and preserve it in ourselves at a different time, we necessarily preserve it as long as we have it, and as long as we have it, we preserve it, nor is there anything absurd about this explanation.

Indeed, just as the acquisition of this rectitude is naturally prior to having or willing it—since having or willing are not the cause of the acquisition, but the acquisition causes willing and having—still, receiving and willing and having are simultaneous, and as soon as it is acquired it is had and we will it—so to have or to will it, although they are naturally prior to preserving it, are simultaneous. Wherefore that from which we simultaneously acquire and have and will and preserve rectitude of will is that from which we receive justice, and as soon as we have and will that same rectitude of will, it ought to be called justice.

That we add 'for its own sake' is necessary in order that this rectitude is justice only insofar as it is preserved for its own sake.

S. I can think nothing contrary.

T. Does it seem to you that this definition can be adapted to the highest justice, insofar as we can speak of it, of which nothing or little can be properly said?

S. Although his will and rectitude do not differ, yet just as we say 'the power of divinity' or 'the divine power' or 'divinity is able', since in divinity there is no difference between power and divinity, so not unfittingly do we speak here of the rectitude of will or voluntary rectitude or right will. But if we say that rectitude ought to be preserved for its own sake, it seems that this could not be said more properly of any other rectitude. For just as it does not preserve something else but itself, and not by something else but by itself, so not for the sake of something else but for the sake of itself.

T. Indubitably then we can say that justice is rectitude of will, which rectitude is preserved for its own sake. And since there is no present passive participle of the verb 'preserve' we can here use its past passive participle.

S. It is common to use past passive participles for present when Latin does not have them, just as it does not have past participles of active and neuter verbs; and we use the present for the past that is not available, as when I say of someone: what some one learns by studying and reading, he will teach only if forced. That is, that while he studies and reads he learns, and will teach only when he is forced to.

T. So we rightly said that justice is rectitude of the will that is preserved for its own sake. That is why the just are sometimes said to be 'right of heart [*recti corde*]', that is, right in will, and sometimes simply right, without mention of heart, because no one who does not have a right will is understood to be right. Thus in Psalm 31: 11, 'Be glad in the Lord and rejoice, you just, and exult, all you upright of heart!' and in Psalm 106: 42, 'The just see and rejoice . . .'

S. You have satisfied even children concerning the definition of justice; let us go on to other things.

13. *That there is one truth in all true things*

T. Let us go back to 'rectitude' or 'truth'. When we use these words to speak of the rectitude perceptible by mind alone, we mean one thing and that the genus of justice. We ask then whether there is only one truth in all the things in which we say truth is, or as many truths as there are things called true.

S. That is something I would much like to know.

T. It is clear that whatever truth is it is nothing other than rectitude.

S. I do not doubt that.

T. So if there are many truths in many things there must also be many rectitudes.

S. That is no less certain.

T. If there must be as many different rectitudes as there are things, their existence would depend on those things; and rectitudes would necessarily differ as their subjects vary.

S. Show this in one case so that I might see it in all.

T. Well, if the rectitude of signification differs from that of will because the one is in will and the other in signification, rectitude would exist because of signification and change as it does.

S. Just so. For signification is correct when what is is said to be or when what is not is said not to be. Clearly there is a rectitude without which the signification could not be correct. If however what is not is said to be or what is is said not to be, or if absolutely nothing at all were signified, the rectitude peculiar to signification will not be had. So such rectitude exists only in signification and changes when signification does, just as colour has existence and non-existence in body. If the body exists, its colour necessarily is, and when the body is destroyed its colour cannot remain.

T. But colour does not relate to body as rectitude does to signification.

S. Show me the difference.

T. If no one wishes to signify what a sign ought to mean, will the sign have any signification?

S. None.

T. How then can it be correct in order to signify what it ought to?

S. Rectitude will not on this account be less, nor need this any less.

T. Therefore, when it does not mean it does not lose the rectitude by which it exists and which requires it to signify what it ought to.

S. If it were destroyed this correct thing would not exist nor need to do this.

T. Do you think that, when what ought to be signified is signified, the signification is correct on account of and according to this rectitude?

S. I can hardly think otherwise. For if signification were correct by some other rectitude and this one were destroyed, nothing would prevent the signification from being correct. But there is no correct signification which signifies what is not correct and that rectitude requires.

T. Therefore no signification is correct by any rectitude other than that which remains when signification perishes.

S. That is clear.

T. Do you not then see that there is no rectitude in signification which comes into existence when what is is said to be or what is not is said not to be, but that signification then comes to be according to a rectitude which always is, and when it means what it should not or nothing at all, it then falls away from a never failing rectitude?

S. I see that I am unable not to see this.

T. Therefore the rectitude whereby signification is called correct does not exist or change through signification, however signification itself might change.

S. Nothing is now clearer to me.

T. Can you prove that colour relates to body in the same way that rectitude does to signification?

S. I am now more ready to prove that they are completely dissimilar.

T. I think you know now what should be thought of will and its rectitude and of the other things that ought to have rectitude.

S. I see that by this argument is also proved completely that, however it be with these, rectitude remains immutable.

T. So what do you think follows from the other rectitudes? Do they differ from one another or is there one and the same rectitude for all?

S. I said earlier that, if there are as many rectitudes as there are things in which they are considered, it is necessary that they exist and vary as the things themselves do, but this has been shown not to be the case. So there are not many rectitudes just because rectitude is found in many things.

T. Do you have any argument other than the plurality of things why they seem to you to be many?

S. That having failed, I do not think any other argument could be found.

T. Therefore there is one and the same rectitude of all.

S. It seems to me we must say this.

T. Furthermore, if rectitude is not in the things that should have rectitude, except insofar as they are as they ought to be, and they are correct by this alone, clearly there is only one rectitude of them all.

S. That cannot be denied.

T. Therefore there is one truth in them all.

S. It is equally impossible to deny that. But show me why we say 'the truth of this or that thing', as if to distinguish differences of truth, if no diversity is derived from those things. For many would be reluctant to grant that there is no difference between the truth of will and that of action or of any of the others.

T. It is improperly said to be 'of this or that thing', since it does not have its existence in or from or through the things in which it is said to be. But when those things are said to be according to it—which always excels them—it is because they are as they ought to be, and then truth is said to be of this or that thing, e.g. the truth of will, the truth of action. So too we speak of the time of this or that thing although there is one and the same time of everything that is together at the same time. If this or that thing did not exist, there is still the same time. For we do not say the time of this or that thing because time is in those things but because they are in time. And just as time considered in itself is not the time of something, although

when we consider the things that are in it we speak of the time of
this thing or of that, so the highest truth subsists in itself and belongs
to no thing. But when something is in accord with it, we then speak
of its truth and rectitude.

ON FREE WILL

Chapters

1. *That the power of sinning does not pertain to free will*

Student. Since free will seems to be repugnant to grace, predestination and God's foreknowledge, I want to understand freedom of will and know whether we always have it. For if 'to be able to sin and not to sin' is due to free will, as some are accustomed to say, and we always have it, why do we sometimes need grace? But if we do not always have it, why is sin imputed to us when we sin without free will?

Teacher. I do not think free will is the power to sin or not to sin. Indeed if this were its definition, neither God nor the angels, who are unable to sin, would have free will, which it is impious to say.

S. But what if one were to say that the free will of God and the angels is different from ours?

T. Although the free will of men differs from the free will of God and the angels, the definition of freedom expressed by the word ought to be the same. For although one animal differs from another either substantially or accidentally, the definition attached to the word 'animal' is the same for all. That is why we must so define free will that the definition contains neither too little nor too much. Since the divine free will and that of the good angels cannot sin, to be able to sin does not belong in the definition of free will. Furthermore, the power to sin is neither liberty nor a part of liberty. Pay attention to what I am going to say and you will fully understand this.

S. That is why I am here.

T. Which free will seems more free to you, that which so wills that it cannot sin, such that it can in no way be deflected from the rectitude constituted by not sinning, or that which can in some way be deflected to sinning?

S. I do not see why that which is capable of both is not freer.

T. Do you not see that one who is as he ought to be, and as it is expedient for him to be, such that he is unable to lose this state, is freer than one who is such that he can lose it and be led into what is indecent and inexpedient for him?

S. I think there is no doubt that this is so.

T. And would you not say that it is no less doubtful that to sin is always indecent and harmful.

S. No one of healthy mind would think otherwise.

T. Therefore a will that cannot fall from rectitude into sin is more free than one that can desert it.

S. Nothing seems to me more reasonable to say.

T. Therefore, since the capacity to sin when added to will diminishes liberty, and its lack increases it, it is neither liberty nor a part of liberty.

S. Nothing is more obvious.

2. *Both the angel and man sinned by this capacity to sin and by
free will and, though they could have become slaves of sin,
sin did not have the power to dominate them*

T. What is extraneous to freedom does not pertain to free will.

S. I can contest none of your arguments, but I am not a little
swayed by the fact that in the beginning both the angelic nature and
ours had the capacity to sin, since without it, they would not have
sinned. Wherefore, if by this capacity, which is alien to free will, both
natures sinned, how can we say they sinned by free will? But if they
did not sin by free will, it seems they sinned necessarily. That is, they
sinned either willingly or necessarily. But if they sinned willingly,
how so if not by free will? And if not by free will, then indeed it
seems that they sinned necessarily.

And there is something else that strikes me in this ability to sin.
One who can sin, can be the slave of sin, since 'he who commits
sin, is the slave of sin' [John 8: 34]. But he who can be the slave of
sin, can be dominated by sin. How was that nature created free then,
and what kind of free will is it that can be dominated by sin?

T. It was through the capacity to sin willingly and freely and not
of necessity that ours and the angelic nature first sinned and were
able to serve sin, yet they cannot be dominated by sin in such a way
that they and their judgement can no longer be called free.

S. You must expand on what you said since it is opaque to me.

T. The apostate angel and the first man sinned through free will,
because they sinned through a judgement that is so free that it cannot
be coerced to sin by anything else. That is why they are justly rep-
rehended; when they had a free will that could not be coerced by
anything else, they willingly and without necessity sinned. They
sinned through their own free will, though not insofar as it was free,
that is, not through that thanks to which it was free and had the
power not to sin or to serve sin, but rather by the power it had of
sinning, unaided by its freedom not to sin or to be coerced into the
servitude of sin.

What seemed to you to follow does not, namely, that if will could
be a slave to sin it could be dominated by sin, and therefore neither
it nor its judgement are free. But this is not so. For what has it in its
power not to serve cannot be forced by another to serve, although it
can serve by its own power: for as long as the power uses that which

is for serving and not that which is for not serving, nothing can dominate it so that it should serve. For if the rich man is free to make a poor man his servant, as long as he does not do so, he does not lose the name of freedom nor is the poor man said to be able to be dominated or, if this is said, it is said improperly, for this is not in his power but in another's. Therefore nothing prevents either angel or man from being free prior to sin or from having had free will.

3. *How free will is had after they have made themselves slaves of sin and what free will is*

S. You have satisfied me that nothing certainly prevents this prior to sin, but how can they retain free will after they have made themselves slaves of sin?

T. Although they subjected themselves to sin, they were unable to lose natural free will. But now they cannot use that freedom without a grace other than that which they previously had.

S. I believe that, but I want to understand it.

T. Let us first consider the kind of free will they had before sin when they certainly had free will.

S. I am ready.

T. Why do you think they had free will: to attain what they want or to will what they ought and what is expedient for them to will?

S. The latter.

T. Therefore they had free will for the sake of rectitude of will. As long as they willed what they ought, they had rectitude of will.

S. That is so.

T. Still to say that they had free will for the sake of rectitude of will is open to doubt unless something is added. So I ask: How did they have free will for the sake of rectitude of will? To take it without any giver when they did not yet have it? To receive what they did not have when it was given to them? To abandon what they received and to get it back again after they had let it go? Or to receive it in order to keep it always?

S. I do not think they had the liberty for the sake of rectitude without a giver, since there is nothing they have that they have not received. We should not say that they had liberty to receive from a giver what they previously did not have, because we ought not to think that they were made without right will. Although it should not be denied that they had the freedom to receive this rectitude, if they abandon it it would be restored to them by the original giver. We often see men brought back from injustice to justice by heavenly grace.

T. It is true as you say that they can receive the lost rectitude if it is restored, but we are asking about the freedom they had before they sinned, since without any doubt they had free will then, and not about what no one would need if he had never abandoned the truth.

S. I will now respond to the other things you asked me. It is not true that they had liberty in order to abandon that rectitude, because to abandon the rectitude of the will is to sin, and we showed above that the power to sin is not liberty nor any part of it. They do not receive liberty in order to take on again a rectitude they had abandoned, since such rectitude is given in order that it might never be lost. The power of receiving again what is lost would bring about negligence in retaining what is had. It follows then that freedom of will was given to the rational nature in order that it might retain the rectitude of will it has received.

T. You have responded well to what was asked, but we must still consider for what purpose a rational nature ought to retain that rectitude, whether for the sake of the rectitude itself, or for the sake of something else.

S. If that liberty were not given to such a nature in order that it might preserve rectitude of will for the sake of rectitude, it would not avail for justice. Justice seems to be the retention of rectitude of will for its own sake. But we believe that free will is for the sake of justice. Therefore without a doubt we should assert that the rational nature receives liberty solely to preserve rectitude of will for its own sake.

T. Therefore, since all liberty is a capacity, the liberty of will is the capacity for preserving rectitude of the will for the sake of rectitude itself.

S. It cannot be otherwise.

T. So it is now clear that free judgement is nothing other than a judgement capable of preserving the rectitude of will for the sake of rectitude itself.

S. It is indeed clear. But as long as will has that rectitude it can preserve what it has. But how, after it has lost it, can it preserve what it does not have? In the absence of the rectitude that can be preserved, there is no free will capable of preserving it. For it does not avail for preserving what is not had.

T. But even if the rectitude of will is absent, the rational nature still has undiminished what is proper to it. I think we have no power sufficient unto itself for action, and yet when those things are lacking without which our powers can scarcely be led to act, we are no less said to have them insofar as they are in us. Just as no instrument suffices of itself to act, and yet when the conditions for using the instrument are wanting, it is not false to say that we have the instrument to do something. What you may observe in many things, I will show you in one. No one having sight is said to be incapable of seeing a mountain.

S. Indeed, one who cannot see a mountain, does not have sight.

T. He who has sight has the power and means of seeing a mountain. And yet if the mountain were absent and you said to him, 'Look at the mountain,' he would answer, 'I cannot, because it is not there. If it were there, I could see it.' Again, if the mountain were there and light absent, he would say that he could not see the mountain, meaning that without light he cannot, but he could if there were light. Again, if the mountain and light are present to one with sight but there is something blocking sight, as when one closes his eyes, he would say that he cannot see the mountain, although if nothing blocked sight, he could without any doubt see the mountain.

S. Everyone knows these things.

T. You see, then, that the power of seeing a body is (1) in the one seeing in one sense and (2) in another sense in the thing to be seen, and in yet another sense in the medium, which is neither the seeing nor the thing to be seen; and with respect to what is in the medium, there we must distinguish between (3) what helps and (4) what does not impede, that is, when nothing that can impede does impede.

S. I plainly see.

T. Therefore these powers are four, and if one of them is lacking the other three singly or together cannot bring it off; yet when the others are absent we do not deny either that he who has sight or the means or the power of seeing can see, or that the visible can be seen to be seen, or that light can aid sight.

4. *How those who do not have rectitude have the power to preserve it*

The fourth power is improperly so called. That which can impede sight, is said to give the power of seeing only because by being removed it does not impede. The power to see light [properly] consists in only three things because that which is seen and that which aids are the same. Is this not known to all?

S. Indeed it is unknown to none.

T. If then the visible thing is absent, or in the dark, or if those having sight have shut or covered their eyes, so far as we are concerned we have the power to see any visible thing. What then prevents us from having the power to preserve rectitude of will for its own sake, even if that rectitude is absent, so long as reason whereby we can know it and will whereby we can hold it are in us? It is in these—reason and will—that freedom of will consists.

S. You have put my mind at rest that this power of preserving rectitude of will is always in a rational nature, and that this is the power of free will in the first man and the angel, nor could rectitude of will be taken away from them unless they willed it.

5. *That no temptation forces one to sin unwillingly*

S. But how can the judgement of will be free because of this power, given the fact that often and without willing it a man who has right will is deprived of his own rectitude under the force of temptation?

T. No one is deprived of this rectitude except by his own will. One who acts unwillingly is said to act against what he wills; and no one is deprived of this rectitude against his will. But a man can be bound unwillingly, because he does not wish to be bound, and is tied up unwillingly; he can be killed unwillingly, because he can will not to be killed; but he cannot will unwillingly, because one cannot will to will against his will. Every willing person wills his own willing.

S. How can one be said to lie unwillingly when he lies to avoid being killed, something he only does willingly? For just as he unwillingly lies, so he unwillingly wills to lie. And he who wills unwillingly to lie, is not willing that he wills to lie.

T. Perhaps then he is said to lie unwillingly because he so wills the truth that he will only lie to save his life, and he wills the lie for the sake of life and not for the sake of the lie itself, since he wills the truth; and thus he lies both willingly and unwillingly. For to will something for its own sake, e.g. as we will health for its own sake, is different from willing something for the sake of something else, as when we will to drink absinthe for the sake of health. Perhaps with respect to these two kinds of willing one could be said to lie both willingly and unwillingly. He is said to lie unwillingly because he does not will it in the way he wills the truth, but that does not conflict with my view that no one unwillingly abandons rectitude of will. He wills to abandon it by lying for the sake of his life, according to which he does not unwillingly abandon it but wills to in the sense of will of which we now speak. That is, willing to lie for the sake of his life, not willing to lie for its own sake. Therefore either he certainly lies unwillingly, because he must either be killed or lie unwillingly, that is, he is not willingly in the anguish because either of these will necessarily come about. For although it is necessary that he be either killed or lie, yet it is not necessary that he be killed, because he can escape death if he lies, nor is it necessary for him to lie, because he could not lie and be killed. Neither of these is determinately necessary, because both are in his power. Therefore although he either lies or is killed unwillingly, it does not follow that he lies unwillingly or is killed unwillingly.

There is another argument frequently given to show why someone is said to do something unwillingly, against his grain and necessarily, yet does not want to. What we do not do because we can only do it with difficulty, we say we cannot do and necessarily turn away from. And what we can abandon only with difficulty we say we do unwillingly and necessarily. In this way, one who lies lest he be killed, is said to lie against his will, not willingly, and of necessity, given that he cannot avoid the falsehood without the penalty of death. He who lies in order to save his life is improperly said to lie against his will, because he willingly lies, and he is improperly said to will to lie against his will, because he wills it precisely by willing it. For just as when he lies he wills himself to lie, so when he wills to lie, he wills that willing.

S. I cannot deny what you say.

T. Why then not say that free will is that which another power cannot overcome without its assent?

S. Can we not for a similar reason say that the will of a horse is free because he only serves his appetite willingly?

T. It is not the same. For in the horse there is not the will to subject himself, but naturally, always and of necessity he is the slave of sense appetite, whereas in man, as long as his will is right, he does not serve nor is he subject to what he ought not to do, nor can he be diverted from that rectitude by any other force, unless he willingly consents to what he ought not to do, which consent does not come about naturally or of necessity as in the horse, but is clearly seen to be from itself.

S. You have taken care of my objection about the horse; let us go back to where we were.

T. Would you deny that every free being is such that it can only be moved or prevented willingly?

S. I do not see how I could.

T. Tell me how right will prevails and how it is conquered.

S. To will the preservation of rectitude for its own sake is for it to prevail, but to will what it ought not is for it to be conquered.

T. I think that temptation can only stop right will or force it to what it ought not to will willingly, such that it wills the one and not the other.

S. I do not see any way in which that could be false.

T. Who then can say that the will is not free to preserve rectitude, and free from temptation and sin, if no temptation can divert it save willingly from rectitude to sin, that is, to willing what it ought not? Therefore when it is conquered, it is not conquered by another power but by itself.

S. That demonstrates what has been said.

T. Do you see that from this it follows that no temptation can conquer right will? For if it could, it would have the power to conquer and would conquer by its own power. But this cannot be, since the will can only be conquered by itself. Wherefore temptation can in no way conquer right will, and it is only improperly said to conquer it. For it only means that the will can subject itself to temptation, just as conversely when the weak is said to be able to be conquered by the strong, he is said to be *able*, not by his own power but by another's, since it only means that the strong has the power to conquer the weak.

6. *How our will, although it seems powerless, is powerful against temptations*

S. Although you were to make subject to our will all the forces fighting against it and contend that no temptation can dominate it in such a way that I cannot counter your assertions, none the less I cannot agree that there is no impotence in the will, something nearly all experience when they are overcome by violent temptation. Therefore, unless you can reconcile the power that you prove and the impotence that we feel, my mind will not be at rest on this matter.

T. In what does the impotence of which you speak consist?

S. In the fact that I cannot adhere to rectitude with perseverance.

T. If you do not adhere because of impotence, you are turned away from rectitude by an alien force.

S. I admit it.

T. And what is this force?

S. The force of temptation.

T. This force does not turn the will from rectitude unless it wills what the temptation suggests.

S. That is so. But by its very force temptation prompts it to will what it suggests.

T. But how can it force willing? Because it can will only with great trouble or because it can in no way not will?

S. Although I have to admit that sometimes we are so oppressed by temptations that we cannot without difficulty manage not to will what they suggest, still I cannot say that they ever so oppress us that we can in no way not will what they inspire.

T. I do not see how that could be said. For if a man wills to lie in order that he not suffer death and live a little longer, who would say that to will not to lie is impossible for him in order that he might avoid eternal death and live eternally? So you should not doubt that the impotence in preserving rectitude, which you say is in our will when we consent to temptation, is a matter of difficulty rather than impossibility. We often say that we cannot do something, not because it is impossible for us, but because we can do it only with difficulty.

This difficulty does not destroy freedom of will. Temptation can fight against a will that does not give in but cannot conquer it against its will. In this way I think we can see how the power of the will as established by true arguments is compatible with the impotence our humanity experiences. For just as difficulty does not in any way destroy the freedom of will, so that impotence, which we assign to will because it can retain its rectitude only with difficulty, does not take away from the power to persevere in rectitude.

7. *How it is stronger than temptation even when it succumbs to it*

S. I am unable to deny what you prove but at the same time I cannot absolutely say that will is stronger than temptation when it is conquered by it. For if the will to preserve rectitude were stronger than the impetus of temptation, the will in willing what it keeps would be stronger as temptation is more insistent. For I do not otherwise know myself to have a more or less strong will except insofar as I more or less strongly will. Wherefore when I will less strongly than I ought because of the temptation to do what I ought not, I do not see how temptation is not stronger than my will.

T. I see that the equivocation of 'will' misleads you.

S. I would like to know this equivocation.

T. 'Will' is said equivocally much as 'sight' is. For we say that sight is an instrument of seeing, that is, a ray proceeding from the eyes whereby we sense light and the things that are in the light; and we also call sight the work of this instrument when we use it, that is, vision. In the same way the will means both the instrument of willing which is in the soul and our turning will to this or that as we turn sight to see different things. And this use of the will, which is the instrument of willing, is also called will, just as sight means both the use of sight and that which is the instrument of seeing. We have sight which is the instrument of seeing, even when we do not see, but the sight which is its work is only had when we see. So too will, namely the instrument of willing, is always in the soul even when it does not will something, as when it sleeps, but we only have the will that is the work of this instrument when we will something. Therefore what I call the instrument of willing is always one and the same whatever we will; but that which is its work is as many as the many things that we will. In this way sight is always the same whatever we see, or even in the dark or with closed eyes, but the sight which is its work and which is named vision is as numerous as are the things seen.

S. I see clearly and I love this distinction with respect to will, and I can see how I fell into error through deception. But do continue what you began.

T. Now that you see that there are two wills, namely the instrument of willing and its work, in which of the two do you find the strength of willing?

S. In that which is the instrument of willing.

T. If therefore you know a man to be strong, when he is holding a bull that was unable to escape and you saw the same man holding a ram who was able to free itself from his grasp, would you think him less strong in holding the ram than in holding the bull?

S. I would indeed judge him to be equally strong in both but that he did not use his strength equally in the two cases. For he acted more strongly with the bull than with the ram. But he is strong because he has strength and his act is called strong because it comes about strongly.

T. Understand that the will that I am calling the instrument of willing has an inalienable strength that cannot be overcome by any other force, but which it uses sometimes more and sometimes less when it wills. Hence it in no way abandons what it wills more strongly when what it wills less strongly is offered, and when what it wills with greater force offers itself it immediately drops what it does not will equally. And then the will, which we can call the action of this instrument, since it performs its act when it wills something, is said to be more or less strong in its action since it more or less strongly occurs.

S. I must admit that what you have explained is now clear to me.

T. Therefore you see that when a man, under the assault of temptation, abandons the rectitude of will that he has, he is not drawn away from it by any alien force, but he turns himself to that which he more strongly wills.

8. *That not even God can take away the rectitude of will*

S. Can even God take away rectitude from the will?

T. This cannot happen. God can reduce to nothing the whole substance that he made from nothing, but he cannot separate rectitude from a will that has it.

S. I am eager to have the reason for an assertion I have never before heard.

T. We are speaking of that rectitude of will thanks to which the will is called just, that is, which is preserved for its own sake. But no will is just unless it wills what God wants it to will.

S. One who does not will that is plainly unjust.

T. Therefore to preserve rectitude of will for its own sake is, for everyone who does so, to will what God wants him to will.

S. That must be said.

T. Should God remove this rectitude from anyone's will, he does this either willingly or unwillingly.

S. He could not do so unwillingly.

T. If then he removes this rectitude from someone's will he wills to do what he does.

S. Without any doubt.

T. But then he does not want the one from whom he removes this rectitude to preserve the rectitude of will for its own sake.

S. That follows.

T. But we already said that to preserve in this way the rectitude of will is for one to will what God wants him to will.

S. Even if we had not said it, it is so.

T. Hence if God were to take from something that rectitude of which we have so often spoken, he does not will one to will what he wants him to will.

S. An inevitable and impossible consequence.

T. Therefore nothing is more impossible than that God should take away the rectitude of will. Yet he is said to do this when he does not impede the abandonment of this rectitude. On the other hand, the devil and temptation are said to do this or to conquer the will and to remove from it the rectitude it has when they offer something or threaten to take away something that the will wants more than rectitude, but there is no way they can deprive it of that rectitude as long as the will wants it.

S. What you say is clear to me and I think nothing can be said against it.

9. *That nothing is more free than right will*

T. You can see that there is nothing freer than a right will since no alien power can take away its rectitude. To be sure, if we say that, when it wills to lie lest it lose life or safety, it is forced by the fear of death or torment to desert the truth, this is not true. It is not forced to will life rather than truth, but since an external force prevents it from preserving both at the same time, it chooses what it wants more—of itself that is and not unwillingly, although it would not of itself and willingly be placed in the necessity of abandoning both. It is not less able to will truth than safety, but it more strongly wills safety. For if it now should see the eternal glory which would immediately follow after preserving the truth, and the torments of hell to which it would be delivered over without delay after lying, without any doubt it would be seen to have a sufficiency for preserving the truth.

S. This is clear since it shows greater strength in willing eternal salvation for its own sake and truth for the sake of reward than for preserving temporal safety.

10. *How one who sins is a slave of sin, and that it is a greater miracle when God restores rectitude to one who has abandoned it than when he restores life to the dead*

T. The rational nature always has free will because it always has the power of preserving rectitude of will for the sake of rectitude itself, although sometimes with difficulty. But when free will abandons rectitude because of the difficulty of preserving it, it is afterward the slave of sin because of the impossibility of recovering it by itself. Thus it becomes 'a breath that goes forth and returns not' [Ps. 77: 39], since 'everyone who commits sin is a slave of sin' [John 8: 34]. Just as no will, before it has rectitude, can have it unless God gives it, so when it abandons what it has received, it cannot regain it unless God restores it. And I think it is a greater miracle when God restores rectitude to the will that has abandoned it than when he restores life to a dead man. For a body dying out of necessity does not sin such that it might never receive life, but the will which of itself abandons rectitude deserves that it should always lack it. And if one gave himself over to death voluntarily, he does not take from himself what he was destined never to lose, but he who abandons the rectitude of will casts aside what he has an obligation to preserve always.

S. I do indeed see what you mean by slavery, whereby he who commits sin becomes the slave of sin, and of the impossibility of recovering abandoned rectitude unless it be restored by him who first gave it, and I see that all those to whom it has been given ought to battle ceaselessly to preserve it always.

11. *That this slavery does not take away freedom of will*

S. But this opinion does much to depress me because I had thought myself to be a man sure to have free will always. So I ask that you explain to me how this slavery is compatible with what we said earlier. For it seems the opposite of liberty. For both freedom and slavery are in the will, thanks to which a man is called free or a slave. But if he is a slave, how can he be free, and if free, how can he be a slave?

T. If you think about it carefully you will see that when the will does not have the rectitude of which we speak, it is without contradiction both slave and free. For it is never within its power to acquire the rectitude it does not have, although it is always in its power to preserve what it once had. Because it cannot return from sin, it is a slave; because it cannot be robbed of rectitude, it is free. But from its sin and slavery it can return only by the help of another, although it can depart from rectitude only by itself. But neither by another or by itself can it be deprived of its freedom. For it is always naturally free to preserve rectitude if it has it, even when it does not have what it might preserve.

S. This suffices to show me that freedom and slavery can be in one and the same man without contradiction.

12. *Why a man who does not have rectitude is called free because if he had it no one could take it from him, and yet when he has rectitude he is not called a slave because if he loses it he cannot regain it by himself*

S. I very much want to know why one who has not rectitude is called free because when he has it no one can take it from him, and yet when he has rectitude he is not called a slave because he cannot regain it by himself if he lose it. In fact, because he cannot by himself come back from sin, he is a slave; because he cannot be robbed of rectitude he is called free, and just as no one can take it from him if he has it, so he can never himself regain it if he does not have it. Wherefore, just as he always has this freedom, it seems that he should always have this slavery.

T. This slavery is nothing other than the powerlessness not to sin. For whether we say this is powerlessness to return to rectitude or powerlessness of regaining or again having rectitude, man is not the slave of sin for any other reason than that, because he cannot return to rectitude or regain and have it, he cannot not sin. For when he has that same rectitude, he does not lack the power not to sin. Wherefore when he has that rectitude, he is not the slave of sin. He always has the power to preserve rectitude, both when he has rectitude and when he does not, and therefore he is always free.

As for your question why he is called free when he does not have rectitude, since it cannot be taken from him by another when he has it, and not called slave when he has rectitude because he cannot regain it by himself when he does not have it, this is as if you were to ask why a man when the sun is absent is said to have the power to see the sun because he can see it when it is present and when the sun is present is said to be powerless to see the sun because when it is absent he cannot make it present. For just as, even when the sun is absent, we have in us the sight whereby we see it when it is present, so too when the rectitude of will is lacking to us, we still have in us the aptitude to understand and will whereby we can preserve it for its own sake when we have it. And just as when nothing is lacking in us for seeing the sun except its presence, we only lack the power to make it present to us, so only when rectitude is lacking to us, do we have that powerlessness which its absence from us brings about.

S. If I ponder carefully what was said above when you distributed the power of seeing into four powers, I cannot doubt this now. So I confess the fault of doubting it.

T. I will pardon you now only if in what follows you have present to mind as needed what we have said before, so that there is no necessity for me to repeat it.

S. I am grateful for your indulgence, but you will not wonder that after having heard only once things of which I am not in the habit of thinking, they are not all always present in my heart to be inspected.

T. Tell me now if you have any doubt about the definition of free will we have given.

13. *That the power of preserving the rectitude of will for its own sake is a perfect definition of free will*

S. There is still something that troubles me. For we often have the power of preserving something which yet is not free because it can be impeded by another power. Therefore when you say that freedom of will is the power of preserving rectitude of will for the sake of rectitude itself, consider whether perhaps it should be added that this power is free in such a way that it can be overwhelmed by no other power.

T. If the power of preserving the rectitude of will for the sake of rectitude itself could sometimes be found without that liberty that we have succeeded in seeing clearly, your proposed addition would be fitting. But since the foregoing definition is perfected by genus and difference such that it can contain neither more nor less than what we call freedom, nothing should be added or subtracted from it. For 'power' is the genus of liberty. When 'of preserving' is added it separates it from every power which is not one of preserving, such as the power to laugh or walk. By adding 'rectitude' we separate it from the power of preserving gold and whatever else is not rectitude. By the addition of 'will' it is separated from the power of preserving the rectitude of other things, such as a stick or an opinion.

By saying that it is 'for the sake of rectitude itself' it is distinguished from the power of preserving rectitude for some other reason, for example for money, or just naturally. A dog preserves rectitude of will naturally when it loves its young or the master who cares for it. Therefore since there is nothing in this definition that is not necessary to embrace the free judgement of a rational creature and exclude the rest it sufficiently includes the one and excludes the other, nor is our definition too much or lacking anything. Does it not seem so to you?

S. It seems perfect to me.

T. Tell me then if you wish to know anything else of this freedom which is imputed to one having it whether he uses it well or badly. For our discourse is concerned only with that.

14. *The division of this freedom*

S. It now remains to divide this freedom. For although this definition is common to every rational nature, there is a good deal of difference between God and rational creatures and many differences among the latter.

T. There is a free will that is from itself, which is neither made nor received from another, which is of God alone; there is another made and received from God, which is found in angels and in men. That which is made or received is different in one having the rectitude which he preserves than in one lacking it. Those having it are on the one hand those who hold it separably and those who hold it inseparably. The former was the case with all the angels before the good were confirmed and the evil fell, and with all men prior to death who have this rectitude.

What is held inseparably is true of the chosen angels and men, but of angels after the ruin of the reprobate angels and of men after their death. Those who lack rectitude either lack it irrecoverably or recoverably. He who recoverably lacks it is one of the men in this life who lack it although many of them do not recover it.

Those who lack it irrecoverably are reprobate angels and men, angels after their ruin and men after this life.

S. You have satisfied me with God's help on the definition of liberty such that I can think of nothing to ask concerning such matters.

ON THE FALL OF THE DEVIL

Chapters

goods he received but abandoned, just as the good angel does who retained what he had received

19. That the will as such is good and that no thing is evil
20. How God is the cause of evil and willing and action, and how they are received from him
21. That the bad angel could not foresee that he would fall
22. That he knew that he ought not to will what he sinned by willing and that he ought to be punished if he were to sin
23. That he ought not to know that he would be punished if he sinned
24. That even the good angel ought not to know this
25. That the good angel by this fact alone that he now has knowledge of the fall of the devil is said no longer to be able to sin, though for him this works for glory
26. What horrifies us about the word 'evil' and the works that injustice is said to do if both are nothing
27. How evil came to an angel when he was good
28. That the power to will what is unfitting was always good, and willing itself is good insofar as it exists

1. *The verse 'What do you have that you have not received?' applies to angels too; from God come only good and being and every good is being and every being is good*

Student. Does the phrase from St Paul, 'What do you have that you have not received?' [1 Cor. 4: 7], apply only to men or to angels as well?

Teacher. No creature has anything of itself. How can something that does not have being of itself, have anything of itself? In short, if there is only one who creates and whatever is created is from that one, it is clear that he who creates and what he has created is all there is.

S. That is clear.

T. Also, the Creator himself and what has been created can only be from that same Creator.

S. That too is clear.

T. He alone has of himself all that he has, while other things have nothing of themselves. And other things, having nothing of themselves, have their only reality from him.

S. I do not quite see what you mean by 'other things have their only reality from him'. For who else brings it about that the many things we see pass from being to non-being are not what they were even if they do not pass wholly into nothingness? Or who else makes something not to be save the one who makes whatever is to be? Again, if something is only because God makes it, it is necessary that what is not is not because he does not make it. For just as the things which are from him have some being, so the things which are not or which pass from being to non-being have it from him that they are nothing.

T. It is not only the one who makes that which was not, to be, or that which is, not to be, who is said to make a thing to be or not to be. He who could bring it about that something is not, yet does not do so, is said to make it be, and he who could make something be, yet does not, is said to make it not be. Just as both he who strips someone and he who could prevent this but does not are said to cause someone to be nude or undressed. But the former is properly said to cause it and the latter improperly. When the latter is said to make another nude or unclothed, all that is meant is that when he could have he did not bring it about that the other was not stripped or remained dressed.

In this way God is said to do many things that he does not, as when he is said to lead us into temptation when he does not prevent temptation that he could, and to cause what is not since he could make it be and does not. But if you consider the things which pass into non-being, you will see that it is not God who causes them not to be. For not only is there no essence he does not make, but nothing he does make could last if he did not preserve it, for when he stops preserving what he made, it is not the case that he turns what was a being into non-being, as if he caused non-being, but only that he stops causing it to be. And even when in anger, as it were, he destroys something by taking away its existence, the non-being is not from him; rather when God's creative and preserving causality is removed, the thing reverts to the non-being it had of itself before it was created and does not have from God. If you were to ask someone for the cloak you had lent when he was naked, he does not receive his nakedness from you, but by the fact that you take back what is yours, he reverts to the condition that was his before you clothed him. Indeed, just as from the highest good only good comes, so from the highest being only being comes, and all being comes from the highest being.

Since the highest good is the highest being, it follows that every good is being and every being is good. Hence nothing and non-being do not come from God, from whom come only good and being.

S. I clearly see now that just as good and being are from God alone, so only good and being come from God.

T. Take care not to think, since we read in Sacred Scripture (or say in quoting it) that God causes evil or non-being, that I am criticizing or denying what is said there. But, in reading Scripture, we ought not to attend so much to the impropriety of the words that covers truth as pay attention to the propriety of the truth that is hidden under various kinds of verbal expression.

S. To do what you suggest would occur only to someone stupid or desirous of cavilling over Scripture.

T. Let us turn the discussion back to where it began and see if it can be maintained that only man, and not the angel, has all that he has from God.

S. It is obvious that the phrase applies to angels as well as men.

2. *Why it seems that the devil lacked perseverance because God did not give it to him*

S. It follows that the angel who perseveres in truth, does so because he has perseverance, and he has that because he received it, and he received it because God gave it to him. It also follows that he 'who does not persevere in the truth' [John 8: 44] does not persevere because he does not have perseverance, and he does not have it because he did not receive it, and he did not receive it because God did not give it to him. So tell me what his fault is, seeing that he did not persevere because he was not given perseverance, without which gift he could do nothing. I am in fact certain, unless I misunderstand, that the devil could only be justly damned by him who is supremely just and he could not be justly damned if the fault was not his.

T. Why do you conclude from the fact that the good angel receives perseverance because God gave it to him, that the bad angel does not receive it because God does not give it to him?

S. From this: if for the good angel the giving is the reason for its having received, the reason the bad angel lacks the gift will be that he has not received it; and given that the giving has not taken place, it follows necessarily that he has not received it. Indeed, we all know that when we do not receive what we want, its not being given is not a result of our not receiving it, but we do not receive it because it is not given. Those who raise this question do so, as far as I can see, because of this argument: If the good angel received perseverance because God gave it to him, then the bad angel did not receive it because God did not give it to him. I do not remember ever having heard a response to this.

3. *That God did not give it because he did not accept it*

T. But that does not follow. It can be the case that something's not being received is not explained by the fact that it was not given, even though the giving is always the cause of receiving.

S. Then, given the not-giving, it is not necessary that not-receiving follow, and then there could be a receiving even where there is no giving.

T. Not so.

S. Give me an example.

T. If I offer you something and you take it, my giving does not derive from your receiving, but you receive it because I offer it, and the giving is the cause of the receiving.

S. Right.

T. What if I offer the same thing to someone else and he does not take it? Is it because I do not give that he does not take?

S. It seems rather that you are said not to give it to him because he does not take it.

T. So here it is not non-giving that is the cause of the not-taking, whereas were I to imagine myself not to have given, that would indeed be the cause of your not receiving. It is one thing for something to be the cause of something else and another that, given the thing, something else does not follow. Burning is not the cause of the fire, but fire the cause of burning, but given burning, it is always the case that there is fire.

S. I will grant you that.

T. Do you see then that, if you have received because I have given, it does not follow that he who has not received has not received because I did not give to him, yet it follows logically that, if I had not given, he would not have received?

S. Happily I do see that.

T. Do you still doubt that just as an angel who perseveres does so because he accepts the perseverance that God gives him, so the angel who does not persevere is not given perseverance by God because he does not take it?

S. There is still something I do not understand. You have enabled me to see sufficiently only this, that, from the fact that the good angel receives because God gives, it does not follow that the bad angel did not receive because God did not offer it to him. If you indeed want to say that God did not give him the gift of perseverance because he did not receive it, I ask you why he does not take it. Either this is because he did not have the capacity or because he did not want to. If he did not have the capacity or the will to take it, God did not give it to him. And if God did give it to him, it is certain he would have had it. But if he cannot have the capacity or the will to accept perseverance save as a gift from God, in what did he sin by not taking that for which God did not give him either the capacity or the will to receive?

T. But God did give him the will and the capacity to receive perseverance.

S. Then he received what God gave him and he had what he received.

T. He received it and he had it.

S. Then he received and had perseverance.

T. He did not accept it and therefore did not have it.

S. But did you not say that God gave and that he received the will and capacity to accept perseverance?

T. Yes. But I did not say that God gave him the acceptance of perseverance, but only the will and the ability to accept it.

S. But if he willed to and could, he received perseverance.

T. The conclusion does not follow necessarily.

S. I do not see why if you will not show me.

T. Have you never undertaken something with the will and the capacity to carry it out and then not done so because you changed your mind before completing it?

S. Often.

T. Then you could have wanted to persevere in that in which effectively you did not persevere.

S. I willed but did not persevere in my desire and thus did not persevere in the activity.

T. Why did you not persevere in the desire?

S. Because I did not want to.

T. And yet as long as you did will to persevere in the activity, you willed to persevere in that will?

S. I cannot deny that.

T. Why then say that you did not will to persevere in that willing?

S. I would answer again that I wanted to persevere, but did not persevere in that willing, if I did not see the prospect of an infinite regress, with you forever asking me the same thing and I always answering the same.

T. Then you should not say, 'I did not will to persevere in willing because I did not will to persevere or to will my willing'. When you are asked why you did not persevere in the action that you had willed and could persevere in, answer, 'Because I did not persevere in willing it'. And if you are asked why you have not persevered in willing it, you should introduce another motive for the defect of that willing, and not the not persevering in the will to will. For your answer only repeats what was asked, that is, you did not persevere in the will to persevere in the activity.

S. I see that I did not understand what I was saying.

T. So tell me in a word what is persevering in the doing of something, as the argument requires.

S. I want to say, to bring it to term, to complete it.

T. Let us then say, in a similar fashion, that to persevere is to will it all the way.

S. All right.

T. When then you do not bring to term what you willed and could do, why did you not bring it to term?

S. Because I did not will it all the way.

T. Let us similarly say that the devil, who had the will and the capacity to receive perseverance and the will and the capacity to persevere, did not receive perseverance and did not persevere because he did not will it all the way.

S. But I will ask you again why he did not will it all the way. For when you say that he did not will all the way what he willed, that is like saying: what he willed before he did not will later. Why then is it the case that he no longer wills what he willed before, except that he does not have the will? I do not mean the will that he had before, when he willed, but the one he no longer has, when he does not will.

Why does he not have this will, save because he did not receive it? And why did he not receive it, except because God did not give it?

T. I say again: it is not the case that he does not have it because God did not give it, but God does not give it because he has not accepted it.

S. Show me that.

T. He freely abandons the will he had and, just as he accepted having it as long as he had it, so he was able to accept the hanging on to what he abandoned and because he abandoned it he does not accept it. Therefore his not accepting to hang on to what he abandoned is not because God did not give it, but God did not give it because he did not accept it.

S. But is it not clear that he does not will to keep it because he abandoned it, but he abandons it because he does not want to keep it? When something is had, not wanting to keep it precedes abandoning it, and one wills to let something go because he does not want to keep it.

T. The will to retain is not always prior to the will to abandon.

S. Show me when it is not.

T. When you do not want to retain something for its own sake but let it go, like a burning coal in the bare hand; then perhaps the not wishing to hang on to it is prior to the desire to abandon it, and thus you wish to abandon because you do not wish to retain. Before you have it, in fact, you do not want to hold it in your hand, and you could not let go of it before you had it. But when you hold something only for the sake of something else, you want to abandon it only for the sake of something else, and you want more the other thing that you cannot have unless you abandon what you have, then the will to abandon is prior to not wanting to retain. For when the miser wills to keep his money and prefers food which he can only have if he gives up some money, his will to give or abandon the money comes before his willing not to keep it. For he does not will to give because he does not will to keep it, but he wills not to keep it because he has to give it in order to get food. Prior to having money, he wants to have and keep it, and, when he has, it is not the case that he does not will to keep it when there is no need to let it go.

S. That is true.

T. So not wanting to keep does not always precede letting go, but sometimes wanting to let go comes first.

S. I cannot deny it.

T. So I say that the devil did not will what he should have willed when he should have willed it, not because he lacked the will (and lacked it because God did not give it to him), but because, willing what he ought not to have willed, he drove out the good will when the bad will supervened. Therefore God did not give him the good will to persevere, and he did not receive it, not because God did not give it, but on the contrary, God did not give it because he gave up willing what he should have willed, by abandoning and not retaining it.

S. I grasp what you say.

4. *How he sinned and wanted to be like God*

T. Do you still doubt that the devil did not will to keep what he had because he willed to abandon it and not vice versa, that is, that he willed to abandon what he had because he did not wish to keep it?

S. I do not doubt that it could be that way, but you have not yet made me certain that it was. First show what he wished to keep that he did not have, in order that he might will to abandon what he had, as you showed in the case of the miser. Then if nothing can be shown to contradict it, I will confess that I do not doubt.

T. You do not doubt that he sinned, because he could not be unjustly condemned by a just God, but you are asking how he sinned?

S. Yes.

T. If he had served justice with perseverance, he would neither sin nor be unhappy.

S. So we believe.

T. No one serves justice except by willing what he ought, nor abandons it save by willing what he ought not.

S. No one doubts that.

T. Therefore by willing something that at the time he ought not to will, he abandoned justice and thus sinned.

S. That follows, but I am asking what he willed.

T. Whatever he had, he should have willed.

S. Certainly he should have willed everything that he had received from God, nor could he have sinned by willing that.

T. Hence he willed something that he did not have and that he ought not to have willed then, as Eve willed to be like a god before God willed it.

S. I cannot deny that either.

T. But the only things he could will were justice, or what was useful to himself or the fitting.[1] And happiness, to which every creature aspires, is constituted by the fitting.

S. We can see this in ourselves, since we do in fact will only that which we see as just or pleasant.

T. The devil certainly could not have sinned by willing justice.

S. True.

T. So he sinned by willing something that pleased him and that he did not have and that he should not then have willed, but that could increase his happiness.

S. He could not sin in any other way.

T. And you recognize, I think, that, by inordinately willing more than he had received, his will exceeded the limits of justice.

S. I see clearly now that the devil sinned either by willing what he should not have or by willing what he should have. And it is evident enough that he willed more than what he should have, not because he did not will to maintain justice, but he did not maintain justice because he willed something else, something that required the abandonment of justice, as you have helped me see in the example of the miser apropos of money and food.

T. And when he willed what God did not want him to will, he inordinately willed to be like God.

S. But if God can only be thought of as unique, as that than which nothing greater can be thought, how could the devil will what he could not think? He was not so obtuse of mind that he failed to know that nothing other than God can be thought to be like him.

T. Even if he did not will to be wholly equal to God, but something less than God against the will of God, by that very fact he inordinately willed to be like God, because he willed something by his own will, as subject to no one. It is for God alone thus to will something by his own will such that he follows no higher will.

S. So it is.

T. Not only did he will to be equal to God in presuming to have

[1] The Latin is *commodum*. An Italian translator renders this as *piacere*. Sometimes 'pleasant' will be used when the context seems to support it.

his own will, but he even willed to be greater by willing what God did not want him to will, because he put his own will above God's.

S. I do not think anything could be clearer.

T. Therefore although the good angel accepted perseverance because God gave it, the bad angel did not receive it, not because God did not give it, but God did not give it because he did not receive it, and therefore he did not receive it because he did not will to.

S. You have responded so satisfactorily to what I asked that I cannot waver as to the truth of what you say or the rigour of your proof.

5. *That before the bad angels fell the good angels could sin*

T. Do you think that the good angels too could sin, before the bad angels fell?

S. I think so, but I would like an argument to that effect.

T. You know for certain that if they had not been able to sin, they would have served justice necessarily, not freely. But then they would not have merited from God the grace to be saved while the others fell, since they would have retained a rationality they could not have lost.

S. So reason shows.

T. Therefore [if that were the case], those who fell, if they had not sinned but could have, would have been so much greater than the others and more truly just and would have merited grace from God. From which it would follow that the elect among men would be better and higher than the good angels and would not substitute for the reprobate angels because men who take their place would not be as they should have been.

S. So those suppositions have to be rejected.

T. And the good angels could have sinned prior to the fall of the bad, in just the way that we have shown that the latter did in fact sin.

S. I do not see how it could be otherwise.

6. *How the good are confirmed in their condition and the evil in their fallen state*

T. Therefore, the angels that loved the justice that they had, rather than the more that they did not have, received as reward in justice that good their will renounced out of love of justice, and they remained in secure possession of what they had. And they were so elevated that they could have whatever they willed and not see what more they could have willed, and thus they cannot sin. But those who preferred to the stability of the justice in which they had been created what God did not yet will to give them according to his just decision, lost the good that they had and did not obtain that which induced them to depreciate justice. Thus the angels are divided into those who, adhering to justice, can enjoy all the goods they will, and those who, having abandoned justice, are deprived of whatever good they desire.

S. Nothing could be more just nor beautiful than this distinction. But if you can tell me, I would like to hear what the advantage was that the good angels justly renounced, thereby achieving perfection, and that the bad angels, by unjustly desiring, fell.

T. I do not know what it could have been, but whatever it was, it is sufficient to know that it was something that could have increased their greatness and which they had not received when they were created, in order that they might achieve it by merit.

S. Then we have looked into this matter sufficiently.

7. *The question whether the will and its turning toward what it should not is the very evil that makes them bad, and why it is that a rational creature cannot of himself turn from evil to good as he could from good to evil*

S. But I do not know how it is that, when I want to think we have exhausted the question, I then see other problems germinating, so to say, from the roots of the question resolved. Indeed, although I see clearly that the perverse angel could not have fallen into an immoderate demand of the good except through some immoderate desire, I am not a little worried as to whence comes this immoderate will. For if he was good, then he fell from so much good into so much evil on account of a good will. Again, if he was good, God gave it to him to be so, since he had nothing of himself. Therefore, if he willed what God gave him to will, how did he sin? Or if he had this will of himself, he had some good that he did not receive. But if it is evil, it is something, and so again it seems that it can only be from God, from whom is everything that is something. So too it can be asked how he sinned by having the will that God gave him, or how God could give him an evil will. Therefore if this evil will was from the devil himself, and is something, he has something of himself and not every essence is good, nor will evil be nothing, as we are wont to say, since a bad will is something. Or, if a bad will is nothing, he was gravely damned on account of nothing and for no reason. And what I say of will can be said of concupiscence or desire, since both concupiscence and desire are instances of willing, and just as there is a good and bad will, there is a good and bad concupiscence and a good and bad desire.

But if it is said that the will is a thing and is good when it turns to that which it ought to will, and is called an evil will when it turns to what it should not, it seems to me that what has been said of the will can be said of the turnings of the will. I am also puzzled when I consider this inclination to evil on the part of the will, because God makes such a nature, that he then raised to such a height, capable of turning from what it ought, yet incapable of returning to what it ought after having turned away, since it seems that such a creature ought to have from its Creator the power to do the good for which it was created rather than the evil it was created to avoid. This is something that can also be asked of our nature, since we believe that no man can have a single good will except as a gift from God, while he can always have a bad will if God should only permit it.

8. *That the will and its turning are not evil itself*

T. I do not think it can be denied that either the will or the turning of the will are real [things]. For although they are not substances, they cannot be shown not to be essences, since there are many essences besides what are properly called substances. Nor is a good will more real than a bad will, nor more good than the other is evil. For the will to give mercifully is not more real than the will to take violently, nor is the latter more evil than the former is good. If then an evil will is the same evil thanks to which one is called evil, the good will will be the same good whereby one is called good. But a bad will will be nothing if it is the very evil that we believe to be nothing. Therefore a good will will be nothing, since it is no more real than a bad will. And then we will not be able to deny that the good itself whereby the good are good is nothing, since it is a good will that will be nothing. But no one doubts that it is false that a good will or good itself is nothing. Therefore a bad will is not itself the evil which makes men evil, just as a good will is not itself the good which makes men good.

What I have said of will can also be said of the inclination of will. The conversion from theft to giving is no greater than that which converts the same will from generosity to avarice. And so too for the other things that I said of the will.

S. What you say is what I too think.

T. Therefore neither a bad will nor a depraved conversion of will is the very evil whereby an angel or man becomes evil, which we say to be nothing, nor a good will or a good conversion of will the good whereby they become good.

9. *That injustice is evil itself and is nothing*

S. So what is the evil that makes them bad and the good that makes them good?

T. We should hold that justice is the good whereby they are good or just, both angels and men, and that whereby the will itself is called good and just; and injustice is the evil that is only a privation of the good, and makes angels and men bad and makes their will bad. So we should say that injustice is nothing but the privation of justice. As long as the will originally given to a rational nature is simultaneously oriented to its rectitude by the same act with which God gives it, thus not only inclined to rectitude, but created right, that is, oriented to what it ought do, as long as, I say, the will remains in that rectitude that we call truth or justice, it was just. But when it distanced itself from what it ought and turned against it, it did not remain in the original rectitude in which it was created. And when it abandoned it, it lost something great, and acquired in exchange only the privation of justice we call injustice and that has no positive being.

10. *How evil seems to be something*

S. When you say that evil is the privation of the good, I agree, but none the less I see that good is a privation of evil. And just as I perceive in the privation of evil something else comes to be that we call good, so I note that in the privation of the good something comes to be that we call evil. Wherefore although evil can be shown by some arguments to be nothing, since evil is only vice or corruption, which are only in some essence,[2] and the more they are there, the more toward nothingness they turn it, and if the same essence came wholly to nothing, vice and corruption would be found to be nothing; although, I say, in these and other ways evil can be proved to be nothing, my mind cannot agree except on the basis of faith alone, unless we can eliminate the difficulties that prove to me on the contrary the reality of evil.

For when the word 'evil' is heard, our hearts irrationally tremble at what they understand in the meaning of this word, if it means only nothing. Again, if this word 'evil' is a noun, it is significant. But if it is significant, it signifies. But it can only signify something. How then can evil be nothing if its name signifies something? Finally since there seems to be such tranquillity and repose while justice remains, in many instances justice seems nothing more than the quieting of evil, as with charity and patience, whereas when justice goes, such diverse and onerous and multiple feelings occupy the mind which like a cruel master forces this poor homunculus to be concerned with so many laborious and base actions and to take on the grave burden of these actions: if it is thus, it will seem strange that nothing gives rise to all these.

11. *That evil and nothing cannot be shown from their names to be something but only a quasi-something*

T. I do not think it is absurd for you to say that nothing is something, since no one can deny that 'nothing' is a noun. If it cannot be shown that nothing is real just because there is the word 'nothing', how would one think to prove that evil is real just because there is the word 'evil'?

S. An example that solves a problem by raising another is worthless, but I do not know what this nothing itself would be. If you want to show me what I understand evil to be, show me first what I understand nothing to be, then you can deal with the other arguments rather than those having to do with the word 'evil' that lead me to think it is something.

---

[2] That is, inhere in something as its property or accident.

T. Since for nothing to be does not differ from something is not, how can we say what it is for something not to be?

S. If there is not anything signified by this word, it does not signify something. But if it does not signify something, it is not a noun. But it is a noun. Therefore, although no one says that nothing is something, but we are always driven to say that nothing is nothing, still no one can deny that the word 'nothing' is significant. But if this noun does not signify nothing but something, what it signifies seems to be something and not nothing. But if what it means is something and not nothing, how can it be signified by the word 'nothing'? Indeed, if 'nothing' is used correctly, nothing truly is, and therefore it is not something. Wherefore if what is signified by this word is something and not nothing, it follows that it is falsely and incongruously named by 'nothing'. But if, following common opinion, what is called 'nothing' is truly nothing and is not in fact real, the necessary consequence is that the word 'nothing' does not signify something and then it does not signify nothing. How is it then that the word 'nothing' is not devoid of meaning and signifies some thing, and does not signify some thing, that is, something real, but signifies nothing?

T. Perhaps there is no contradiction between signifying nothing and something.

S. But if there is no contradiction, either the word 'nothing' signifies nothing and something as taken differently, or we must find the reality that is something and nothing.

T. And if both conclusions can be affirmed, that is, if there are different ways of understanding the meaning of the word and that the same reality is both something and nothing?

S. Let us look at both.

T. It is clear that the word 'nothing' in no way differs in meaning from the expression 'not something'. Moreover it is evident that 'not something' indicates that every thing, whatever expresses any reality, should be excluded from the mind nor anything whatsoever of its meaning be retained. But since the negation of a thing must necessarily include in its meaning the thing negated—no one could understand what is meant by non-man unless he understands what man is—this term not-something, by negating what is, signifies something. Since then taking away everything that is something signifies nothing, it makes up the essence that must be retained in the mind of the listener: therefore 'not-something' signifies no thing or reality.

The expression 'non-being' then, according to these diverse considerations, in a way signifies reality and being and yet in no way signifies reality and being, for it signifies them by way of denial and not positively. Thus the word 'nothing' which does away with everything that is something and by so doing does not signify nothing but something, does not do so positively. So it is not necessary that nothing be something just because its name in a certain way signifies something; rather, it is necessary that nothing be nothing, because its name signifies something in this way. Similarly, there is nothing against the word 'evil' being meaningful if it thus signifies something by excluding it and positively signifies nothing.

S. I cannot deny that, following your argument, the word 'nothing' in some way signifies something, but it must be understood that the something which in this way is signified is not called 'nothing', nor when we hear the word do we take it for the reality that is signified in this way. So I ask why this name is spoken, and what do we understand when we hear it: what I want to ask is, what is it? This is what the word properly signifies and since a word is because it signifies it, not because in the way stated above it signifies by denying something. Indeed it is accounted a name of its signification, which is called 'nothing'. I ask how that can be something if it is properly called 'nothing', or how it is nothing if its name signifies something, or how something and nothing can be the same. That is what I am asking about 'evil' and of what it means and what 'evil' is the name of.

T. And you rightly pose this problem because although by the foregoing argument both 'nothing' and 'evil' signify something, evil and nothing are not what they signify. But there is another argument according to which they signify something and that something is signified, but not a true but a quasi-something.

There are many cases where the grammatical form does not correspond with the reality signified. For example, 'to fear' is an active verb, grammatically speaking, but in reality to fear is passive. So too 'blindness' grammatically indicates some thing, but in reality it is nothing positive. Just as we say that someone has sight and that sight is in him, so we say that he has blindness and that blindness is in him, although blindness is not something real but the lack of it, and to have blindness does not mean to say one has something but rather is deprived of it. In fact blindness is nothing other that non-sight or the absence of sight where it ought to be found. But non-sight or the absence of sight is certainly no more real where it ought to be found than where it ought not to be found. Many other things are expressed as reality from the point of view of the form of discourse, because we speak of them as if they existed, when no positive reality is involved.

It is in this way that 'evil' and 'nothing' signify things, that is, what is signified is not something in reality but only in grammatical form. 'Nothing' signifies simply non-being or the lack of all that is real. And evil is only non-good or the absence of good where good ought to be found. But that which is only an absence of reality is certainly not real. Hence evil in truth is nothing and nothing is not real, and yet in a way evil and nothing are something because we speak of them as if they were real, as when we say, 'He did nothing' and 'He did evil', that is, that what he did was nothing or evil—in the same way that we say 'I did something and I did a good thing'. So we deny that what someone says is in any way something: 'What you say is nothing.' For 'what' or 'this' which are properly said only of realities, here are not said of realities but of quasi-realities.

S. You have satisfied me with respect to 'evil' from whose meaning I sought to prove that it signifies something.

12. *That the angel cannot have its first act of willing from itself, and that many things can be said to be from an alien capacity but not from an alien incapacity*

S. But there remains for you to show me how I should respond to the other arguments that tend to persuade me that evil is a positive reality.

T. To get to the heart of the matter we must begin by backing up a bit. And you need to understand what I will say, not just in pieces, but remembering the whole as joined in a single intuition.

S. I will do all I can, but if at times I am slower than you might wish, do not fail to wait for me.

T. Let us then say that in this moment God creates an angel and wills to make him happy, not all at once, but in stages. So let us say that he has been created and is capable of volition but does not yet will anything determinate.

S. Stipulate what you like but keep my question in mind.

T. Do you think that the angel can of himself will anything?

S. I am not quite sure of what you mean by 'of himself'. Something that has nothing that it has not received, which we said above is true of every creature, cannot do anything 'of itself'.

T. By 'of himself' I mean with what he now has. For example, what has feet, and the other conditions for walking, can walk of itself. But what has feet, but unsound ones, cannot walk of itself. In this sense, then, I ask you if that angel, who is capable of willing, but does not yet will anything, can will something of himself.

S. I think he can, if he wills.

T. You are not answering my question.

S. Why?

T. I asked about one who does not yet will anything and about the capacity before it is used, and you answered with an example of one who wills and thus of an actuated capacity. Whatever is, by the very fact that it is, can be. But not everything that exists had the capacity to exist before it existed. So when I ask if he who does not will anything can will, I am asking you about the capacity that precedes willing, and what can move it to will. But you, when you answered that 'if he wills, he can', are speaking of the possibility which is actuated in the very act of willing. It is indeed necessary that he can will if he is willing.

S. I know that there are two kinds of power: one that is not yet actuated and one that is already actuated, but I also know that whatever can be, while it is, if at one time it was not, could be before it existed. If it had not the capacity to be, it would never have been. So I think I have answered well, since he who can will because he is willing, necessarily could have willed before he did so.

T. Do you not think that what is nothing has absolutely nothing and therefore has no capacity, and without a capacity it cannot in any way do anything?

S. I cannot deny that.

T. I think that before the world came to be it was nothing.

S. What you say is true.

T. Therefore it has no capacity of any sort before it is.

S. That follows.

T. So it did not have the capacity to be before it was.

S. But I say, if it was incapable of being, it was impossible for it to be at any time.

T. It was both possible and impossible before it was. That in which there was no capacity to exist before it was, was impossible; but for God, in whose capacity it was that it should come to be, it was possible. It is because God could make the world before it came to be that the world is, not because the world itself had the capacity before it was.

S. I am unable to counter your argument, but linguistic usage tells against it.

T. That is not surprising. Many things in common parlance are said improperly, but when we are trying to get to the bottom of the truth we must as far as possible and as the argument requires set aside the distracting improprieties. It is due to this impropriety of language that we often say, 'A thing can', not because it can, but because something else can. So too we say, 'A thing cannot', when in effect it is something else that cannot. If I should say, 'A book can be written by me', the book certainly can do nothing and it is I who can write the book. And when we say, 'That one cannot be conquered by the other', we intend to say that the latter cannot conquer the former.

This is the origin of our saying that God cannot do anything that is contradictory or perverse because God is so powerful in justice and beatitude, indeed, since beatitude and justice do not differ in him, but are one good, he is so omnipotent in simple goodness that no reality is capable of harming the highest good. That is why God cannot corrupt or lie. Very well, that which does not exist does not of itself have a capacity to exist, but if something else is capable of making it be, in that sense it can exist—by the capacity of the other.

Although capacity and incapacity can be of various kinds, for now it is sufficient to say that there are many things that *can*, not by their own power, but by that of another, and many things that *cannot*, not by their own incapacity but by that of another. Now, when I posed the problem about the hypothetical angel just created, and created capable of willing, but which does not yet will anything, and asked you if he can will anything of himself, I spoke of his own capacity, and it is with respect to it that I ask you to respond.

S. If he is capable of willing, if there is nothing lacking in him save actually willing, I do not see why he could not will of himself.

Anyone who is capable of seeing and is put in a bright place but with his eyes closed, sees nothing, but he can see of himself. Why then is one who does not will unable to will of himself in the way that one who does not see is able to see by himself?

T. Because one who does not see has sight and the will with which he can open his eyes, whereas we are speaking of one who has not yet any effective willing. Tell me then if a thing that moves itself from not willing to willing, wills of itself to move.

S. If I say that it moves without willing, it will follow that he moves because of another, not of himself, except perhaps in the manner of one who instantly closes his eyes to parry a blow or is forced to will what he did not before in order to avoid some harm. I do not know then if he first willed himself to move by this act of will.

T. No one is forced to will something out of fear or from the sense of some harm or the desire for some useful thing not had if he does not have a natural will to avoid that harm or pursue the useful things: that is what moves him to the further willing.

S. I cannot deny it.

T. Hence whatever is moved to will, first wills itself so to move.

S. It is so.

T. Therefore what wills nothing, can in no way move itself to will.

S. I cannot contradict that.

T. It follows that an angel already capable of willing, yet who wills nothing, cannot have its first willing from itself.

S. I must agree that a thing that wills nothing cannot of itself will anything.

T. But he cannot be happy if he does not will happiness. And I say happiness, not happiness with justice, but the happiness that all desire, even the bad. All in fact will to be well. Therefore prescinding from the fact that every nature is good [ontologically], two kinds of good and evil are usually distinguished: the moral good, which is called justice to which the evil that is injustice is opposed, and the good that it seems to me can be called the useful, to which the harmful is opposed. Not everyone wants justice nor do all flee injustice. On the other hand not only every rational nature, but every subject capable of sensation, tends to the useful and avoids the harmful. For no one wills but what he takes to be useful to him. In this sense all want things to be well with them and do not want things to go badly for them. It is of happiness in this sense that I now speak, because no one can be happy who does not will happiness. And no one can in fact be happy either by having what he does not want or by not having what he wants.

S. There is no denying that.

T. One who does not will justice ought not to be happy.

S. I will not deny that either.

13. *If it had only the will for happiness, it could neither will anything else nor not will it, and the will, whatever it willed, would be neither just nor unjust*

T. Let us say then that God gives him, as his first volition, only the will for happiness, and see whether because he has this volition, he is now capable of willing something other than what he has been given to will.

S. Go on. I am eager to hear.

T. It is obvious that he does not yet will anything other than happiness, because it has not been given to him to will anything else.

S. True.

T. So what I am asking is whether he is capable of moving himself to will something else.

S. I do not see how he can move himself to will something other than his happiness, since he does not will anything else. For if he wills to move himself to will something else, he already wants that something else.

T. Therefore just as when he has not received any volition he is not able of himself to will, so having received only the will for happiness, he is not able of himself to will anything else.

S. That is so.

T. And can he not determine himself to will that which he believes will lead to his happiness?

S. I do not know how to answer. If in fact he cannot, I do not see how one who cannot will what he believes leads to happiness can be said to will happiness. If he can, I do not see why he cannot will something else.

T. But what does he who seems to will something, not for its own sake, but for something else really will? That which he is said to will or that by means of which he wills it?

S. Certainly that which he wills by means of the other.

T. So one who wills something for the sake of his happiness, really wills nothing other than his happiness. Hence he can will that which leads to happiness while willing only his happiness.

S. That is clear enough.

T. Then I ask you if, having only the will for happiness, he is able not to will it.

S. He cannot simultaneously will and not will.

T. True, but that is not what I asked. I asked if he could abandon this will, to move himself to will not to will happiness.

S. If in fact he does this unwillingly, he does not do it. If willingly, he wills something other than happiness. But he does not. So it is clear, I think, that he can in no way of himself not will that which alone he is given to will.

T. You understand well, but tell me whether he who wills only happiness and cannot not will it, can will happiness more the more he understands it?

S. If he cannot will happiness more the more and better he understands it, either he does not will happiness at all or he wills something else for the sake of which he does not will the better. But we agreed that he loves happiness and nothing else.

T. Therefore he wills to be happy to the degree that he knows it.

S. Without a doubt.

T. Then he wills to be like God.

S. Nothing is clearer.

T. So what do you think, can the will to be like God be unjust?

S. I cannot call it just, because he would want what does not befit him, nor unjust, because he would will it necessarily.

T. But we said that one who wills only happiness, wills only the useful.

S. Yes.

T. If then he who wills only the useful cannot have something more and more truly useful, he would will a lesser advantage, but one accessible by him?

S. Indeed, he cannot not will the less, if the greater is impossible for him.

T. And would the will of one who wills the less useful and the unclean things in which irrational animals delight be unjust and blameworthy?

S. But how can his will be unjust and reprehensible if he wills that which he is not given the capacity not to will?

T. Yet it is obvious that the will itself that wills either the more or less useful is the work and gift of God, as are life and being endowed with senses, which do not involve morality and in which there is neither good nor evil.

S. There is no doubt there.

T. So to the degree that the will is a being, it is good, and so far as concerns morality it is neither good nor evil.

S. Nothing is clearer.

T. But the angel cannot be happy if he does not have a morally good will. If in fact he wills what he cannot and ought not to be, he cannot be perfectly and worthily happy.

S. That is obvious.

14. *And it would be the same if the angel were given only the will for rectitude; it is because it was given both that it can be just and happy*

T. Let us now consider the will for justice and see if the same angel to whom is given to will only what befits his nature, could will something else or could of himself not will what he has been given to will.

S. It must be exactly the same here as it was with the will for happiness.

T. Then this angel would have a will that is neither moral nor immoral. For just as above there could not be an unjust will if he willed something unfitting, since he could not not will it, so if he should will what is fitting, his will would not be just, since it was so given to him that he could not will otherwise.

S. That is so.

T. So neither by willing happiness alone nor by willing only that which befits its nature could that angel be called moral or immoral, because his will would be necessitated; on the other hand, if he neither can nor ought to be happy if he does not will and if his will is not morally good, God must harmonize the two wills in him such that he wills to be happy but wills it justly. Thus, when the moral good is present, his will to be happy is modified so as to eliminate going beyond, without destroying his capacity to go beyond. That is, although by willing to be happy he can surpass the measure, because his will is good he does not want to surpass it, and in this way, having a just will for happiness, he can be and ought to be happy. Such an angel, by not willing that which he ought not, although able to, would merit the capacity never to will that which he ought not and, always following justice, of never being deprived of any moderate desire; if he should abandon justice by an immoderate will, he would be deprived of all that he desires.

S. Nothing could be thought to be more fitting.

T. Remember that, when we first considered the will to be happy alone, without the limit we have added, that keeps it under the will of God, we said that there would be neither justice nor injustice in it, whatever it willed.

S. I remember.

15. *That justice is something real*

T. Do you think that that which when added to the will so moderates it that it can only will what it ought is something real?

S. No one who understands at all would think it nothing.

T. And I think that you have understood that this reality is nothing other than justice.

S. It could not be thought to be anything else.

T. So justice is certainly something.

S. And something very good.

16. *That injustice is only the absence of befitting justice*

T. Should that will will and not will according to justice before receiving justice?

S. There is no 'can' to entail the 'ought' because it has not received it.

T. But after it has, do you doubt that it should, at least when it is not subject to violence?

S. I think that will is always obligated, whether it retains what it accepted or willingly abandons it.

T. You judge rightly. But what would this will have if, without being forced either by need or violence, it should abandon the justice that has been attributed to it with such wisdom and with such usefulness for it? And abandon it by spontaneously using its power, or by willing more than it ought to? Would anything remain of this will beside what we first considered, before the addition of justice?

S. Since only justice was added, if justice is taken away, certainly nothing would remain but what was there before, but with this difference, that the justice received would make it indebted and the same justice abandoned would leave in it beautiful traces of itself. By the very fact that it remains indebted to justice it shows that it had been adorned by justice. It is only right that once it receives justice, it ought always to be just unless it lose it because of violence. A nature that received justice, if only at one time, is shown to be more noble and to bear the sign of always having a quasi absolute good than a nature that never had or ought to have had it.

T. You reason well. But add to this that the more a nature has this good, and ought to have it, it is praiseworthy, just as a person who ought to have it and does not is accounted more blameworthy.

S. I am in complete agreement.

T. Make clearer to me the good that reveals the nature praiseworthy and the person blameworthy.

S. To have and to ought to have justice shows the natural dignity of a nature, and not having it constitutes personal dishonour. For it was made worthy by him [God] who gave it but it does not have it because it abandons it. The obligation came from him who gave justice, the not-having it from him who abandoned it. He is obliged because he received it, he does not have it because he abandoned it.

T. Accordingly, what is blameworthy in that will is not that it did not remain in justice, but that it does not have justice.

S. The only thing I blame in it is the absence of justice, or not having justice. For as I already said, the worthiness adorns it, not having it demeans it, and the more the having adorns it the more not having demeans. Thus not having justice because of its own fault demeans the will only because being fit to have it, thanks to the goodness of the giver, constitutes its dignity.

T. So you do not think the will that lacks the justice it is not meant to have is unjust or that there is injustice in it?

S. Who would not agree?

T. If it should be unjust or if injustice be in it, I think you would have nothing to complain of it.

S. Nothing at all.

T. So the only thing you find reprehensible is its injustice and its being unjust.

S. There is nothing else with which I could find fault.

T. So if the only thing you find blameworthy is the absence of justice and its not having justice, as you said a short while ago, and again it is indeed the injustice in it and its being unjust that you find reprehensible, it is obvious that its injustice and being unjust are nothing other than the lack of justice and not having justice.

S. It could not be otherwise.

T. Therefore just as the absence of justice and not having justice have no essence, so injustice and being unjust have no being, and so are nothing rather than something.

S. No other conclusion is possible.

T. And you will also remember the conclusion to which we came that, once justice is lost, the justice received being abandoned, nothing remains but what was there prior to receiving justice.

S. That is what we concluded.

T. But the will is not unjust nor is there any injustice in it prior to receiving it.

S. No.

T. So, when it has lost justice, either there is no injustice in it and it is not unjust, or injustice and being unjust are nothing.

S. No conclusion seems more necessary.

T. But you conceded that this will has injustice in it and is unjust after it abandoned justice.

S. I must grant that.

T. So injustice and being unjust are nothing.

S. You make me think I understand what I thought I had not understood.

T. I think you have also grasped why the same absence of justice is not called injustice before justice has been given but only when justice has been abandoned, and not-having-justice is equivalent to being unjust, and both are blameworthy—although injustice is nothing other than the absence of justice and being unjust is nothing other than not having justice. The reason is that the absence of justice is not blamed where justice is not meant to be. Just as not having a beard is no disgrace in a man who does not yet have one, but when he should have one it is disgraceful that he does not; so not having justice does not deform a nature that ought not to have it, but debases one meant to have it. And just as having a beard denotes a virile nature, so not having one takes away from virile character.

S. I now see that injustice is only the absence of justice where justice ought to be.

17. *Why the angel that abandons it cannot regain justice*

T. When earlier we spoke of an angel that was given only the will for happiness, we saw that he would not be able to will anything else.

S. Yes.

T. Now, justice having been abandoned and only the prior will for happiness remaining, can the deserter go back to the will for justice by himself, something that was not given to him beforehand to do?

S. Much less. Before it was due to a condition of nature that he could not have it, but now it is by reason of his fault as well.

T. So there is no way in which he could acquire justice when he does not have it, either before receiving it or after having abandoned it.

S. He cannot have anything of himself.

18. *How the bad angel makes himself bad and the good angel makes himself good, and that the bad angel owes thanks to God for the goods he received but abandoned, just as the good angel does who retained what he had received*

T. But is there not some way, at least when he has it, that he can give himself justice?

S. How could he?

T. We use 'make' or 'do' in many ways. For we say that we make something when we make a thing to be and when we could make a thing not be and do not. In this second sense the angel could give himself justice, because he could take it away or not take it away. Similarly, one who remains in the truth in which he has been created and does not, as he could, cause himself not to have it, in a sense gives it to himself yet receives the whole from God. From him they receive both the having and the capacity to keep or abandon it. God gives the latter in order that they may give themselves justice in some sense. If they could in no way take justice away from themselves, there would be no sense in which they could give it. He who gives himself something in this sense, receives from God the capacity to do so.

S. I can see that by not taking it away they are able to give themselves justice, but they give it to themselves in one sense, and take it away in another.

T. Therefore you see that they should thank God for their goodness in either case, and the devil is not any less obligated to God for what is from God alone just because he threw away what God gave him and did not will to accept what God offered him.

S. I see.

T. Therefore the bad angel ought always to thank God for that happiness of which he is deprived just as the good angel for that which he gives himself.

S. Very true.

T. I think that you are aware that God can in no way make someone unjust save in the sense of not making him just when he could. Before receiving justice, in fact, no one is just or unjust and, after having received it, no one becomes unjust unless he willingly abandons justice. Thus just as the good angel is made just because he does not deprive himself of justice when he could, so God makes the bad angel unjust by not giving him justice when he could.

S. That is easily grasped.

19. *That the will as such is good and that no thing is evil*

T. Let us turn now to a consideration of the will and recall the conclusions to which we have come: namely, that the will for happiness, whatever it wills, is not an evil but a good before receiving justice. From which it follows that, when it abandons the justice received, if it is the same essence that it was before, it is something good insofar as it exists, but insofar as justice is not in the thing that it was in, it is called evil and unjust. For if to will to be like God were evil, the Son of God would not will to be like the Father. Or if to will lesser pleasures were evil, the will of brute animals would be called evil. But neither the will of the Son of God nor the will of the irrational animal is said to be evil because they are not unjust.

From this it follows that no will insofar as it exists is evil but is good because it is the work of God, nor is it evil except insofar as it is unjust. Therefore since only a bad will or what is due to a bad will is called evil, such as a bad man and a bad action, nothing is clearer than that no thing is evil nor that evil is anything but the absence in the will, or in something because of will, of that justice which has been abandoned.

20. *How God is the cause of evil and willing and action, and how they are received from him*

S. Your discourse is a concatenation of true, necessary and evident arguments, such that I can refute none of them, but I do see something following that I do not think I should allow and which does not seem avoidable if what you say is true. But if to want to be like God is not nothing nor is it evil but rather something good, this desire can only come from him from whom all that is comes. Therefore if the angel has nothing he has not received, what he has he received from the one who gave it. What could he receive from him that he did not give? So if he has a desire to be like God, he has it because God gave it.

T. But why wonder that, just as God is said to lead into temptation when he does not free from temptation, we admit that he gives a bad will by not impeding it when he could, since the capacity of willing anything depends on him alone?

S. So put, it does not seem impossible.

T. Therefore if there is no giving without a receiving, then just as we are accustomed to call giving both what is willingly conceded and what is permitted by not disapproving, so it is not incongruous that to receive should mean both one taking what is offered and presuming what is illicit.

S. What you say seems to me neither improper nor unusual.

T. So what do we say contrary to truth when we say that when the devil wills what he ought not, this is received by him because God permits it, and that he has not received it because God did not agree with it?

S. There seems nothing in conflict with the truth there.

T. So when the devil turned his will to what he should not, both his will and this turning were something real, and yet he could not have this reality except from God, since he could not will nor move his will if it had not been permitted by God, who causes all substantial and accidental natures to be, both universal and individual.

Insofar as the will and its movement or turning are real they are good and come from God. But insofar as they are deprived of some justice that they ought to have, they are not absolutely bad but bad in a sense, and what is bad in them does not come from the will of God or from God insofar as he moves the will. Evil is injustice, which is only evil and evil is nothing. But the nature in which injustice is found is something evil, because it is something real and differs from injustice which is evil and is nothing. Therefore, what is real is made by God and comes from him; what is nothing, that is evil, is caused by the guilty and comes from him.

S. It is certain that God creates the natures of all things, but who could admit that he causes the actions of a bad will or the depraved movement of the will by which the evil will moves itself?

T. What wonder if we say that God causes the singular actions that come from the bad will, when we allow that he makes the singular substances which come to be unjust by will and bad action.

S. I have nothing to say against it. I cannot in fact deny that every action is a reality nor that whatever is has its being from God. Your argument neither accuses God nor excuses the devil, but rather absolves God and accuses the devil.

21. *That the bad angel could not foresee that he would fall*

S. But I want to know whether the angel who abandoned justice foreknew this of himself.

T. When you ask if the angel who did not remain in the truth foresaw his fall, clarity must be had as to what prevision you mean. For if you mean a foreseeing that requires knowledge of an object founded in a certain concept, I reply that he cannot have known that which could equally well not have been. That which is capable of non-being cannot be foreseen with absolute certainty. Thus it is clear that he could not have foreseen with certainty his fall since it was not necessary. For let us suppose that in fact he did not fall, do you think he could have foreseen that which would not be?

S. It seems that that which in the future might not be cannot be foreseen, nor can that which is foreseen with certainty not be in the future. But now I recall that famous question concerning the divine foreknowledge and free will. For although it is asserted with such authority and is held with such profit that no human argument can put in doubt the compatibility of divine foreknowledge and free will, still, they do seem incompatible to reason when it thinks of them. That is why we find in this matter a tendency to affirm one of the two to the point of obscuring the other and thus run the risk of sinking in the sea of incredulity; others are in danger of falling while they fight against the adverse winds that buffet them. Thus although it is true that the divine foreknowledge embraces all the acts brought about by free will and that none of these acts is determined necessarily, none the less it seems that that which is foreseen by God might not come about.

T. I will answer briefly now: Divine foreknowledge is not properly called *fore*knowledge. He who has always present all things does not have foreknowledge of the future, but knowledge of the present. Therefore since foreknowledge of a future event is going to be considered differently than knowledge of a present thing, what is called divine foreknowledge and what is properly foreknowledge do not have the same consequences.

S. I agree.

T. So let us return to the question we have in hand.

S. What you say makes sense, but with the understanding that you do not refuse to tell me what God deigns to manifest to you when I ask you to respond to the problem that I have raised. Its solution is in fact most necessary, if anyone can find it or if it is possible to find it. Indeed I confess that, prescinding from the divine authority to which I defer without hesitation, I have not yet read a satisfying argument that enables me to grasp the solution.

T. When we get to it, if we do,[3] it will be as God gives; now however, by the argument given above it is clear that the apostate angel could not foresee his own ruin by that knowledge which makes what is known necessary. Hear another argument that excludes his foreseeing his own fall not only with secure foreknowledge but even with conjecture or presentiment.

S. I await that argument.

T. If, while still retaining a good will, he knew that he would fall, either he would have willed that it should come about or not.

S. One of the two must be true.

T. But if, along with foreknowledge, he also had the will to fall, he would already have fallen because of this bad will itself.

---

[3] See Anselm's *De Concordia.*

S. What you say is self-evident.

T. Therefore he did not know that he would be ruined before he fell, by willing his own ruin.

S. I have no objection to that conclusion.

T. But if he knew that he would fall and did not will it, he would be more miserable the more he willed to stand firm.

S. That cannot be denied.

T. And he would be more just the more he wished to stand firm and the more just he was the happier he deserved to be.

S. I cannot deny it.

T. So if he foresaw that he would fall while not willing to fall, he would be more unhappy because of that which should make him happier, which is absurd.

S. I cannot deny this consequence, but I see that it not only comes about without contradiction, but in a laudable way and by the disposition of divine grace. Often indeed—to cite only a couple of examples of the suffering of the just—the more one is virtuous, the more he is saddened, because of compassion, by the disgrace of another, and often he who has the greater constancy in virtue is persecuted with more insistence and cruelty by the unjust.

T. It is not the same with man and angel. Human nature, indeed, because of original sin has become subject to innumerable sufferings, and because of this capacity for suffering divine grace fashions our incorruptibility. But the angel, without any preceding sin, merited the suffering of some evil.

S. You have answered my difficulty. It is clear that this argument not only excludes that the bad angel foresaw with certainty his own fall, but also that he could foresee it with probability.

T. There is another argument that seems to me to demonstrate that he could not in any way foresee his own future prevarication. He would have had to foresee it either as forced or as spontaneous. But he had no reason to suspect that he could be forced and, as long as he willed to persevere in truth, he could not in any way think of abandoning it voluntarily. We already showed earlier in fact that so long as he had right will, he wanted to persevere in this will. And, willing to maintain with perseverance the rectitude he had, I do not see how he could have had even a remote suspicion that, without the intervention of any other cause, he would have abandoned it of his own will. I do not deny that he knew that he could change his will, but I say that he could not think of changing spontaneously, without some other motive, a will that he intended to maintain with perseverance.

S. He who listens carefully to what you say clearly sees that the bad angel could not in any way know with certainty or even only with probability that he would do the evil that he did.

22. *That he knew that he ought not to will what he sinned by willing and that he ought to be punished if he were to sin*

S. But I also want you to make me see if he knew that he ought not to will that which by prevaricating he willed.

T. There can be no doubt, if you recall what was said above. If he knew that he ought not to will what unjustly he willed, he would have been ignorant that he ought to retain the will that he abandoned. Wherefore he would neither be just in retaining it, nor unjust in abandoning a justice of which he was unaware. Nor could he not have willed more of that which he had if he had been unaware of having the obligation to be content with which he had received. Finally, since he was rational, and nothing prevented him from using reason, he could not be unaware what he should and what he should not will.

S. I do not see how your argument could be refuted, but it seems to me to give rise to a problem. If indeed he knew that he ought not to abandon what he had received, he knew that he would be punished if he abandoned it. So how could he spontaneously will that which would make him unhappy, he who had received as an inseparable inclination of his will to be happy?

23. *That he ought not to know that he would be punished if he sinned*

T. Just as it is certain that he could not be ignorant of the fact that he should be punished if he were to sin, so is it that he ought not to have known that having sinned he would be punished.

S. And how could he have ignored this, if he was so rational that his rationality could not be impeded from knowing the truth because it was weighed down as we are with a mortal body?

T. Because he was rational, he could understand that he would justly be punished if he sinned, but since God's judgements are a deep abyss and his ways inaccessible to us [Rom. 11: 33], he was unable to know whether God would do what he justly could do. But, even if one should say that he could not believe that God would have condemned the creature he had made with so much goodness because of his guilt, he would not in fact express something impossible, especially since no example of justice punishing injustice would have preceded, and the angel was certain that the number that were created to enjoy God had been established with so much wisdom as to have nothing superfluous and to be unable to be lessened without leaving something incomplete, and that God's wonderful work could not remain partially incomplete. On the other hand, he could in no way know, if man had already been created man, that God would put human nature in place of the angelic and the angelic in the place of the human should he fall. Rather he had to think God would reconstitute every nature in the way it had been made for itself and not for another; much less could he have thought, if man had not yet been created, that God would have created him to take the place of another nature. What is absurd about any of that?

S. That seems to me most probable.

T. Let us return then to what I said, that is, that the bad angel need not know that he would be damned. If indeed he had known it, he would have been unable to will spontaneously that which would render him unhappy while he had and willed felicity. And then he would not have been virtuous in not willing that which he ought not, because he could not do otherwise. And for the same reason consider if he should have known what you ask. For if he should know it, either he would have sinned or not.

S. One or the other.

T. If such punishment had been foreseen he would sin without need and without any contrary force and would be that much more deserving of punishment.

S. Yes.

T. So he could not have enjoyed such foreknowledge.

S. One who truly sinned ought not to have known the punishment.

T. And if he would not have sinned, he would have acted either because of a good will alone or out of fear of punishment.

S. No other hypothesis is admissible.

T. But that he had not avoided sin only out of love of justice, his very act demonstrates.

S. No doubt.

T. But if he avoided it out of fear, he would not have been just.

S. Thus it is clear that there is no way he could have known that an established penalty would have followed his sin.

24. *That even the good angel ought not to know this*

S. But since we think that the angel who remained in the truth and the one who did not were granted equal knowledge at the moment of their creation, I do not see why this knowledge must be denied to the one that had a good will so tenacious as to be sufficient to avoid sin.

T. Yet the good angel neither could have nor should have contemned the penalty he foresaw.

S. So it seems.

T. Therefore just as the love of justice alone, so the hatred of punishment alone, would have sufficed for not sinning.

S. Nothing is plainer.

T. He would therefore have had two reasons for not sinning, one honourable and useful, the other neither, that is, the love of justice and the hatred of punishment. For it is not honourable not to sin solely out of hatred of punishment, and such a hatred is useless to avoid sinning, where only the love of justice suffices.

S. There is nothing I can say against that.

T. What then? Is not his perseverance much more attractive with a single motive that is worthy and useful, because spontaneous, than if it is joined with another motive unworthy and useless?

S. What you say is so self-evident that, while earlier I wanted him to know, now I am content that he should have been unaware, except that now we cannot deny that he knew, because after the example of the fallen angel, he could not ignore it.

25. *That the good angel by this fact alone that he now has knowledge of the fall of the devil is said no longer to be able to sin, though for him this works for glory*

T. But if now both the one and the other, the good and bad angel, were certain that such a penalty would follow such a fault, just as the knowledge of one is different from that of the other, so the cause of their knowledge and its end differ. Indeed, what the one knows by his own experience, the other learns only from the example of the other. The first knows it because he did not persevere, the other in another way because he did persevere.

Wherefore just as the knowledge of the first redounds to his dishonour, because in a blameworthy way he did not persevere, so the knowledge of the other is to his glory, because he persevered in a manner worthy of praise. If then it is said that the second, by the sole fact that he has this knowledge, can then not sin, it is clear that, just as his knowledge acquired with a praiseworthy perseverance turns to his glory, so the impossibility of sinning due to this knowledge turns to his glory. Just as the bad angel is worthy of blame because he cannot return to justice, so the good angel is worthy of praise because he cannot depart from it. As the one cannot now return because he turned away from it solely because of a bad will, so the other can no longer depart from it because he is maintained in justice solely by a good will. Hence it is manifest that, just as the inability to recuperate what has been abandoned is due to the punishment for sin, so the reward of virtue in the other is that he cannot abandon what he has retained.

S. Your meditation on this knowledge and inability of the angel would be attractive if, as you say, this knowledge and this inability to sin were in the good angel as the proper result of his having persevered. But it does not now seem to me that he has acquired them because he has persevered, but because the other has not.

T. If it were as you say, the good angel would be able to rejoice in the fall of the apostate angel, because this fall enabled him to acquire the knowledge that now impedes him from sinning and from being unhappy, not because he merited it, but because the other did not. All of which is absurd.

S. It seems much more absurd that the virtuous angel rejoiced in the fall of the sinning angel, as you showed; so much more is it necessary that you make me see that the first did not acquire the knowledge of which we speak because of the sin of the other.

T. You need not say that the good angel came to this knowledge just because the bad angel sinned, but that the good angel came to it having seen the example of the one who fell because he sinned. If in fact neither had sinned, God would have given this knowledge to both of them, because of their perseverance, in another way, without the example of the fall. No one will say that God could not have given this knowledge to the angels in another way. When one sinned, God taught the other with the example of the first what he wanted to teach him, not by impotence, as if he could not teach him in another way, but through a greater power, that is by that which draws good even from evil, lest evil be deprived of meaning in the reign of omnipotent wisdom.

S. What you say pleases me very much.

T. It will please you too that the good angel cannot now sin for this reason alone: that he knows the sin of the bad angel to have been followed by punishment, which inability does not deprive him of praise, but is the reward for having served justice. But you know, because it was made clear above, that he cannot sin because, thanks to the merit of his perseverance, he has progressed to the point where he does not see what more he could desire.

S. I have forgotten nothing that you have achieved by your inquiring reason.

26. *What horrifies us about the word 'evil' and the works that injustice is said to do if both are nothing*

S. Although you have responded to all my questions, I still wait for you to explain what horrifies us when we hear the word 'evil' and what causes the actions of injustice such as in theft, and lust—if evil is nothing.

T. I will reply briefly. That evil which is vice is always nothing; the evil that is suffering is sometimes without doubt nothing, as with blindness, and sometimes real, like sadness and sorrow, and we always detest the suffering that is something real. When then we hear the word 'evil' we do not fear the evil that is nothing, but that which is something real and follows the lack of the good. Many sufferings follow on injustice and blindness and those in fact are nothing, but these sufferings are evil and are something real and it is these we fear when we hear the word 'evil'.

When we say that injustice causes theft or that blindness causes a man to fall in a ditch, we do not intend to say that injustice and blindness cause something real, but that if justice were in the will and sight in the eye, theft would not come about and one would not fall in the ditch. It is as when we say that the absence of the pilot causes the ship to go aground, or the absence of a bridle makes the horse run off, which are equivalent to: if the pilot and bridle had been present the wind would not have taken the ship nor the horse run off. For as the ship is governed by the pilot, so is the horse by the bridle; so too a man's will is governed by justice and his feet by sight.

S. You have satisfied me with respect to the evil that is injustice, such that all that this question raised in my mind has been clarified. The question concerning this evil seems to arise from the fact that, if it were some essence, it would be caused by God, from whom it is necessary that every thing that is comes, and from whom it is impossible that injustice and sin come. But the evil that in some way is something seems to cause difficulties for the true faith.

27. *How evil came to an angel when he was good*

S. So would you please reply briefly to my fatuous request, so that I can reply to one who asks me. It is not always easy to reply wisely to the questions of the unwise. So I ask you whence comes for the first time that evil which is called injustice or sin in the angel who was created just.

T. Tell me whence comes the non-being in something real.

S. That which is nothing neither comes nor goes.

T. Then why do you ask where the evil that is injustice comes from?

S. Because when justice departs from where it was, we say that injustice has come.

T. Speak more clearly and properly, and ask me about the departure of justice. A well-formed question is easier to answer, whereas the ill-formed one makes it more difficult.

S. Why does justice depart from the just angel?

T. Speaking properly, it does not depart from him, but he abandons it by willing what he ought not.

S. Why does he abandon it?

T. When I say that by willing what he ought not he abandons it, I show openly why and how he abandons it. He abandons it because he wills what he ought not to will, and in this way it is by willing what he ought not that he abandons it.

S. Why does he will what he ought not?

T. No cause precedes this will except that he can will.

S. And he wills because he can?

T. No. Because the good angel could will similarly yet does not. No one wills what he can will because he can, without some other cause, although if he is unable to will he never does.

S. Why then does he will?

T. Only because he wills. For this will has no other cause by which it is forced or attracted, but it was its own efficient cause, so to speak, as well as its own effect.

28. *That the power to will what is unfitting was always good, and willing itself is good insofar as it exists*

S. If the power to will and the willing itself are something real, they are good and come from God.

T. Both the one and the other are something real. And the power was only a good and spontaneous gift of God; the willing was good with respect to its being, but since it actuated unjustly it was an evil and in no way from God, from whom comes whatever is real. From God we have not only that which he gives us spontaneously but also that which we unjustly appropriate because God permits it. And insofar as God is said to do what he permits to come about, so he is said to give that which he permits to be stolen. Since therefore, God permitting, the bad angel abused the power God freely gave, he has from God the fact that he can use it, which is nothing other than his willing. For willing is nothing but using the power of willing, just as speaking is using the power of speech.

ON THE INCARNATION OF THE WORD

Brother Anselm, in way of life a sinner, by religious habit a monk, called by God (whether at his command or by his permission) to be bishop of the metropolitan see of Canterbury, with humble servitude and devout prayers duly submits himself to the lord and father of the universal Church pilgrimaging on earth, the Supreme Pontiff Urban.[1]

I

Since the providence of God has chosen your Holiness, to whom God entrusted the custody of the Christian faith and life, and the government of his Church, to no one else is it more properly referred, for his authority to correct, if anything contrary to faith arises in the Church. Nor is it more securely shown to anyone else, for his practical wisdom to consider, if there is anything answered against error. Therefore, as I cannot more worthily destine the present letter to any wisdom but yours, so I destine it to no wisdom more willingly, that your judgement may censure it if anything needs to be corrected, and that your authority may strengthen what adheres to the rule of truth.

While I was still abbot in the monastery of Bec,[2] a certain cleric in France[3] presumed to say this: 'If,' he said, 'the three persons are only one thing and not three things, each intrinsically separate, like three angels or three souls, such that they are none the less identical in will and power, then the Father and the Holy Spirit as well as the Son became flesh.' And when this was reported to me,[4] I began to compose a letter against this error, a letter that I held to be of little value after I composed part of it, believing there to be no need of it. I thought there to be no need of the letter both because the one against whom I was writing it had abjured his error in the council

---

[1] Urban II (Pope, AD 1088–99).
[2] Sometime before 5 March 1093, when Anselm became Archbishop of Canterbury.
[3] Roscelin of Compiègne.
[4] Letter of John to Anselm. *Florilegium patristicum*, fasc. 28, p. 37.

by the venerable Archbishop Rainald of Reims,[5] and ... there seemed to be no one who would not know that the indi- ... in question erred. But some brothers without my knowledge transcribed the part I had written and handed it over to others to read. And so I say this, that if that part should have come into the hands of anyone, although there is nothing false in it, it would none the less remain incomplete and unrefined, and what I began in that part would here need something more diligently begun and com- pleted. For after I was taken and bound to the episcopal office in England (by what disposition of God I do not know), I heard that the author of the aforementioned novelty, persevering in his opinion, claims that he had abjured what he said only because he feared that the populace would kill him. Therefore, for this reason, some broth- ers pressed me with their pleas to resolve the question with which he was so involved, so that he would acknowledge that he could not extricate himself except by entangling himself in the incarnation of God the Father and the Holy Spirit, or in a plurality of gods. And I ask this lest anyone think that I have been presumptuous, as if I should think that the strength of the Christian faith needs the help of my defence.

Indeed, if I, a despicable little man, were to attempt to write any- thing to so many holy and wise persons existing everywhere in order to strengthen the foundation of Christian faith, as if the faith should need my defence, I could of course be judged presumptuous and be perceived as someone to be laughed at. For if other human beings were to see me, bound by stakes and ropes and other things, with which tottering things are accustomed to be bound and stabilized, striving around Mount Olympus to strengthen it from tottering or being overturned by someone's force, it would be strange if they should restrain themselves from laughter and derision. How much more when the 'stone not hewn from a mountain by human hands struck and shattered the statue' that Nebuchadnezzar saw in a dream and, now 'become a great mountain, filled the whole earth' [Dan. 2: 34–5], can so many holy and wise persons, who rejoice in being estab- lished on the stone's eternal strength, be indignant with me and impute my efforts to boastful levity rather than earnest seriousness if I attempt to support the stone by my arguments and to stabilize it

---

[5] Council of Soissons (most probably AD 1092 or 1093).

as if it were tottering.)Therefore, if I have in this letter argued about the strength of our faith, it is not in order to confirm the faith but to satisfy the petitions of the brothers who begged me to write the letter.

But if he who proffered the aforementioned opinion, corrected by God, has returned to the truth, in no way should he think that I speak against him, since he is not what he was. For if he was 'once darkness and now is light in the Lord' [Eph. 5: 8], we should not accuse the darkness that does not now exist but approve the light that shines. None the less, whether or not he has up to now returned to the light, it does not seem to me superfluous to dissolve the repugnance of people troubled about this question, since I perceive that many are troubled about the matter, although their faith overcomes arguments that seem to them repugnant to faith.

And before I discuss the question, I shall make a prefatory comment. I do so to curb the presumption of those who, since they are unable to understand intellectually things the Christian faith professes, and with foolish pride think that there cannot in any way be things that they cannot understand, with unspeakable rashness dare to argue against such things rather than with humble wisdom admit their possibility. Indeed, no Christian ought to argue how things that the Catholic Church sincerely believes and verbally professes are not so, but by always adhering to the same faith without hesitation, by loving it, and by humbly living according to it, a Christian ought to argue how they are, inasmuch as one can look for reasons. If one can understand, one should thank God; if one cannot, one should bow one's head in veneration rather than sound off trumpets.

For a human wisdom trusting in itself can more swiftly pluck out its trumpets by pressing against them than it can roll such a stone by leaning on it. For some beginners, in presuming to rise to the loftiest questions about faith, typically produce trumpets, as it were, of knowledge trusting in itself. They do not know that if persons think they know something, they do not yet know, before they have spiritual wings through solidity of faith, how they should know it. And so it happens that when beginners foolishly try to ascend intellectually to those things that first need the ladder of faith (as Scripture says: 'Unless you have believed, you will not understand' [Isa. 7: 9][6]),

---

[6] Vulgate: 'Unless you have believed, you will not stand firm.'

they sink into many kinds of errors by reason of the deficiency of their intellect. For they evidently do not have the strength of faith who, since they cannot understand the things they believe, argue against the same faith's truth confirmed by the holy Fathers. This is as if bats and owls, who see the heavens only at night, should argue about the midday rays of the sun with eagles, who gaze on the very sun with undeflected vision.

Therefore, hearts need first to be cleansed by faith, as Scripture speaks of God 'cleansing their hearts by faith' [Acts 15: 9]. And eyes need first to be illumined by observance of the precepts of the Lord, since 'the precepts of the Lord are clear, illumining the eyes' [Ps. 19: 8]. And we ought to become little ones by humbly obeying the testimonies of God, so that we learn the wisdom that 'the trustworthy testimony of the Lord, manifesting wisdom to the little ones' [Ps. 19: 7], gives. And so the Lord says: 'I confess to you, Father, Lord of heaven and earth, that you have hidden these things from the wise and the clever, and you have revealed them to the little ones' [Matt. 11: 25]. We who govern the things of the flesh, I say, should live according to the spirit before we break down the deep things of faith by passing judgement. For those who live according to the flesh are carnal and animal. And Scripture says of them: 'Animal human beings do not perceive the things that belong to the spirit of God' [1 Cor. 2: 14], while those who 'by the spirit put to death deeds of the flesh' [Rom. 8: 13] are made spiritual. And we read of the latter that 'spiritual persons judge everything, and they are themselves judged by no one' [1 Cor. 2: 15]. For it is a fact that the more powerfully sacred Scripture nourishes us with things that feed us by obedience, the more acutely we are drawn to things that satisfy us intellectually. Indeed, one in vain attempts to say, 'I have understood more than my teachers' [Ps. 119: 99], who does not venture to add: 'because your testimonies are the object of my contemplation' [ibid.]. And one mendaciously proclaims, 'I have understood more than the elders' [Ps. 119: 100], who is not familiar with what follows: 'because I have sought your commandments' [ibid.]. This is surely the very thing that I am saying: those who have not believed will not understand. For those who have not believed will not find by experience, and those who have not found by experience will not know. For example, the more experience transcends hearing about things, the more the knowledge of those experiencing things surpasses the knowledge of those hearing about them.

And not only is the mind without faith and obedience to the commandments of God prevented from rising to understand higher things, but the mind's endowed understanding is also sometimes taken away, and faith itself subverted, when upright conscience is neglected. For example, the Apostle says of certain persons: 'Although they knew God, they did not honour him as God but vanished in their own thoughts, and their foolish hearts were darkened' [Rom. 1: 21]. And when he was instructing Timothy to serve as 'a good soldier' [1 Tim. 1: 18], he added: 'having faith and a good conscience. But some, rejecting these things, have made a shipwreck of their faith' [1 Tim. 1: 19]. Therefore, no one should rashly plunge into the complex things involved in questions about God unless the person first have a solid faith with the precious weight of character and wisdom, lest a persistent falsity ensnare the person who runs with careless levity through many little diverting sophisms.

And all should be warned to approach questions concerning the sacred text of Scripture carefully. Therefore, those contemporary logicians (rather, the heretical logicians) who consider universal essences to be merely vocal emanations, and who can understand colours only as material substances, and human wisdom only as the soul, should be altogether brushed aside from discussion of spiritual questions. Indeed, the power of reason in their souls, which ought to be the ruler and judge of everything in human beings, is so wrapped up in material fancies that they cannot extricate themselves from the fancies. Nor can they distinguish from the very fancies the things that, themselves alone and pure, they ought to contemplate. For in what way can those who do not yet understand how several specifically human beings are one human being understand in the most hidden and highest nature how several persons, each of whom is complete God, are one God? And in what way can those whose minds are darkened as to distinguishing their horse and its colour distinguish between one God and his several relations? Lastly, those who cannot understand anything to be a human being unless an individual will in no way understand a human being other than a human person. For every individual human being is a person. Therefore, how will they understand that the human being assumed by the Word is not a person, that is, that another nature, not another person, has been assumed?

I have said these things lest any presume to discuss the loftiest questions of faith before they are fit to do so. Or if they have presumed, lest any difficulty or incapacity of understanding avail to drive them away from the truth to which they adhere by faith. We now need to progress to the matter that prompted us to begin this letter.

2

As reported to me, the individual who people say asserts that the three persons are like three angels or three souls argues: 'Pagans defend their law; Jews defend theirs. Therefore, we Christians should also defend our faith.' Let us hear how these Christians should defend their faith. 'If,' he says, 'the three persons are only one thing, and there are not three things, each intrinsically distinct, like three angels or three souls, so that they are none the less completely one and the same in will and power, then the Father and the Holy Spirit became flesh with the Son.' See what these people say, how such Christians defend their faith! Surely either they intend to profess three gods, or they do not understand what they are saying. But if they profess three Gods, they are not Christians. And if they affirm what they do not understand, they should not believe it. The authority of Sacred Scripture is not a sufficient response to such persons, since they either do not believe in Scripture or interpret it in a perverse sense. For what does Sacred Scripture say more openly than that there is one and only one God? Therefore, their error is to be proved by the argument whereby they strive to defend themselves. And in order that I do this more easily and more briefly, I shall speak only of the Father and the Son, since these two persons by their own names are openly denoted as distinct from one another. (For the name 'Holy Spirit' is not foreign to the Father or the Son, since each of them is both spirit and holy.) And we shall undoubtedly know in the case of all three what we shall discover in the case of the Father and the Son regarding unity of substance and plurality of persons.

Therefore, he would say: 'If two persons, the Father and the Son, are not two things.' Let us first inquire what the expression 'two things' means here. For we believe that each of the two persons is what is common to both, and what is proper to each. For example, the Father's person is both God, which he shares with the Son, and Father, which is proper to him. Likewise, the Son's person is both God, which he shares with the Father, and Son, which we predicate only of this person. Therefore, these two persons have one thing in common (i.e. God), and two things as proper (i.e. Father and Son). For we understand everything common to them (e.g. almighty, eternal) only in regard to what is common. And we signify things proper to each (e.g. father or begetter to the Father, and word or begotten to the Son) by the two names, namely, Father and Son. Therefore, when he says that the two persons are two things, I ask what he claims the two things are, whether the two things there are what is common to the two persons, or the two things are individual things proper to the individual persons. And if he says that the two things are two proper things (i.e. Father and Son), so that what is common is not several things but one and only one thing, he says this superfluously. It is superfluous because no Christian professes that the Father and the Son as to their proper things are one thing; rather, Christians profess that the Father and the Son as to their proper things are two things. For we are accustomed to apply the term 'thing' to whatever we in any way assert to be something. And whoever predicates Father or Son of God says something about him. And everyone knows that, in the case of God, the Father is not the Son, and the Son is not the Father, although, in the case of human beings, if the same man is a father and a son, the father is a son, and the son a father. And this is so because we in the case of God predicate father and son in opposition to one another, while we in the case of human beings predicate father in relation to one man as son, and son in relation to another man as father, not father and son in relation to one another.

In this way, therefore, nothing prevents us saying that the two persons, the Father and the Son, are two things, provided that we none the less understand how they are things. For the Father and the Son are not two things in such a way that we in the case of these two things understand their substance, but that we understand their relations. But he clearly indicates by what he adds that he himself does not understand that the two persons are two things in the latter way. For when he says, 'If the three persons are only one thing and not three things,' he adds: 'intrinsically distinct'. Indeed, he seems to proclaim the kind of distinction that would prevent the same man being simultaneously a father and a son. For he thinks that he by this distinction alone frees the Father from sharing the incarnation with the Son. For if he believes that there is one and only one God who is Father and Son, he does not perceive that a father and a son can be distinct by reason of the distinction whereby it is one thing to be father, and another thing to be son. This is so because fatherhood and sonship differ from one another, without the same man being at the same time a father and a son. Therefore, he is talking about a different distinction of the persons of the Father and the Son than the one whereby the Father and the Son differ from one another by proper characteristics. He distinguishes in this way because he does not understand the incarnation to be unsuitable for the Father but rather thinks that, if the Father and the Son are not distinguished, the Father consequently shares the incarnation with the Son. Or else if he is talking about the distinction of the Father and the Son by proper characteristics, he toils needlessly, as I have just said, since the Christian faith thus understands that the Father and the Son are two things.

But when he says, 'as there are three angels or three souls', he clearly indicates that he is not speaking about the plurality or distinction that the persons have by proper characteristics. We surely do not predicate two angels or two souls of anything numerically one and the same, nor do we predicate anything numerically one of two angels or two souls, as we predicate Father and Son of numerically one God, and numerically one God of the Father and the Son. For we believe and affirm that God is Father, and that God is Son, and conversely, that the Father is God, and that the Son is God. And yet we neither believe nor affirm that there are several gods; rather, we believe and affirm that there is numerically one God as to substance, although the Father and the Son are two rather than one. For we speak of angels and animals as substances, not as relations. For although we understand the name 'angel' from the latter's office, since angel means messenger, none the less, as we understand souls as a species of substance, we also understand angels in the same way. And he himself indicates that he understands this when he in like manner says, 'as there are three angels or three souls'. And so he denotes the kind of plurality or distinction that several angels or souls have, that is, the kind that several substances have. And he seems even openly to show this when he adds 'so that they are none the less completely the same in will and power'. For he understands will and power in the plurality of the persons as in several angels or souls. And this is unintelligible if we consider the plurality of persons according to their proper characteristics, not according to what we predicate of them in common. For in no way does any willing or power belong to the Father and the Son by reason of their proper characteristics themselves, that is, fatherhood and sonship, but by reason of the substance of the divine nature, which is common to them. Therefore, if he says that the three persons are three things by reason of their proper characteristics themselves, it is clear how superfluously he would say this, how even inappropriately when he adds, 'as there are three angels or three souls'.

3

And if he says that the same persons are two things by reason of what is common to them, that is, as the one complete God is each individually and several together, I first ask whether he is a Christian. He will answer, as I estimate, that he is. Therefore, he believes that there is one God, and that God himself is three persons (i.e. Father and Son and Holy Spirit), and that only the person of the Son became flesh (although with the co-operation of the other two persons). And one who so believes affirms that those who deliberately assert anything contrary to these things are not Christians. Therefore, if he so believes, he denies that those who argue against these things are Christians. And let us see whether he is trying to subvert this faith. He says—to say about two persons what we may understand about all three, as I did at the start—'If two persons are one thing and not two, as there are two angels or two souls, the Father consequently also became flesh if the Son became flesh.' When he says this, I think that he reasons with himself as follows:

'If God is numerically one and the same thing, and if the very same thing is Father and is Son, how did the Father not also become flesh, since the Son did? Indeed, there is not at the same time a true affirmation of one and the same thing and a denial of it, but nothing prevents affirming something about one thing and denying the very same thing about another thing. For example, the same Peter is not (a) an apostle and (b) not an apostle. And if we both by one name affirm the very same person to be an apostle and by another name deny that the person is an apostle, as, for example, affirming that Peter is an apostle, and denying that Simon is, both are not true statements; rather, one of them is false. But it can be true that Peter is an apostle, and that Stephen is not, since Peter is one person, and Stephen another. Therefore, if the Father is numerically the same thing as, and not a distinct thing from, the Son, it is not true that something should be affirmed of the Son and denied of the Father, or affirmed of the Father and denied of the Son. Therefore, whatever the Father is, the Son is also, and what is affirmed of the Son should not be denied of the Father. But the Son became flesh. Therefore, the Father also became flesh.'

But such reasoning, if it is approved, is really the heresy of Sabellius. For if we also affirm of the other person everything we affirm of one person, since the two persons are one thing, then Son and Word and begotten should be affirmed of the Father in the same way that these things are affirmed of the Son. And both Father and begetter and unbegotten should be affirmed of the Son in the same way that the Father is such. But if this is so, the Father does not differ from the Son, nor the Son from the Father. Therefore, there is one person, not two. For although God will be Father and Son, we affirm two persons because we believe the Father and the Son to be distinct from one another. For a father is always the father of someone, and a son the son of someone, nor is a father ever the father of his very self, or a son the son of his very self; rather, a father is one person, and his son another person, and a son is likewise one person, and his father another person. Therefore, if the Father in God is not one person, and the one of whom he is the Father another person, and if the Son is not one person, and the one of whom he is the Son another person, we falsely call God a Father or a Son. For there can be no Father in God if the one of whom the Father is supposed to be the Father is not distinct from the Father. And likewise, there can be no Son in God if the one of whom the Son is supposed to be the Son is not distinct from the Son. Therefore, there will be no grounds for us to affirm that there are two persons in God, which we affirm because God is Father, and God is Son, and the Father is ever one person, and the Son another.

Therefore, do you perceive how our faith is destroyed by the opinion of the individual who thinks that, if the several persons in

God are one thing and not several, it logically follows that the Father became flesh along with the Son? For if this consequence of his is true, not only would what I have said about the Father and the Son follow, but so much confusion regarding all three persons that we would need to affirm as common to all of them everything we affirm as proper to each. Therefore, there will be no grounds for the Father and the Son and the Holy Spirit, who proceeds from both, to be distinct from one another, as I have demonstrated regarding the Father and the Son. Therefore, neither would there then be any relations, which are in God only by reason of that by which the persons are distinct from one another. Therefore, neither will there be several persons. For assuming that one thing is three persons, either what he says would not follow, or each and every one of the things I said would follow. For all those things have like consequential force. Therefore, why does he go no further than the incarnation, as if that alone poses the question, and not rather say: 'If the three persons are one thing, there are not three persons'? For he can pose this question no less before the incarnation than after it.

4

And if he means to assert this, namely, that the three persons as God severally are not one thing but three things, each of them intrinsically such, as there are three angels, he has most evidently set up three gods. But perhaps he himself does not say, 'as there are three angels', but only affirms that the three persons are three things without adding any comparison; rather, perhaps the one who relayed the latter's question to me posited this analogy on his own. Why then is the original proponent of the question misled, or does he mislead, by the word 'thing', since the word 'God' denotes the thing itself? Indeed, either he will deny that God is the thing in which the three persons exist (or rather the thing that we profess to be three persons), or if he does not deny this (since he asserts that the three persons are three things rather than one thing), so he should also affirm that the same persons are three gods rather than one God. And let Christians judge how impious these things are.

But he will say: 'By affirming "three things", I am not forced to admit three gods, since those three things together are one God.' And we answer: 'Then no single one of the three things, that is, no single

person, is God; rather, God is the product of the three things. Therefore, the Father is not God, the Son is not God, the Holy Spirit is
not God, since we should predicate God only of the three mentioned
together, and not of each of them or of pairs of them.' And this likewise is impious. For if it is thus, God is a substance composed
of parts and not a simple substance. But if my adversary has a pure
intellect and not one buried in a plethora of sense images, he understands that simple things as such surpass composite things as
such, since every composite thing of necessity can be actually or
conceptually divided into parts. And we cannot understand such
about simple things. For no intellect can dissolve into parts things
of which parts cannot be conceived. Therefore, if God is composed
of three things, either there is no simple substance, or there is
another substance that surpasses the substance of God in something.
And it is obvious how false both of these propositions are. And if he
is one of those modern logicians, who believe that only what they
can grasp in images exists, he does not think that anything without
parts exists. Or else he will admit that, were something that could
not be actually or conceptually divided to exist, it would be greater
than what can be, even conceptually. And so, if every composite thing
can be at least conceptually divided, he, when he says that God is
composite, says that he can understand something greater than God.
Therefore, his intellect penetrates beyond God, something no intellect can do.

5

And let us see what he adds as if to brush aside the impropriety that
seems to be generated if the three persons are three things. He says:
The three persons are three things 'in such a way that there is one
will and power of the three things'. We need to ask here whether the
three things belong to the divine substance because we conceive them
separately from one another; or because of their common will and
power; or neither only because of what they have separately, nor only
because of what is common to them, but because of both together.
Indeed, they will be three gods if they possess the divine nature by
reason of what they are separately, and we shall be able to understand the same ones apart from will and power. For proper things are
always understood as separate from common things, and common

things from separate things. But we can in no way understand the divine substance apart from will and power. And if both each person and pairs of persons and the three persons together are God by reason of will and power that are single and shared, what then do the three different things, which can harmonize into the unity of the divine nature only by something else, do, and avail neither to perfect nor to support God's existence? For if one will and power suffice to perfect God, what are these three things that God needs, or for what purpose does he need them? For we believe that God does not need anything. Therefore, there is no purpose in demanding that God have these three things. And if neither the three things alone nor will or power alone but all these things together bring about God, I again say that he is composite, and things not intrinsically God or gods produce God. Or if he says that the three things have the name 'God' by reason of their power and will, just as we call human beings kings by reason of their regal power, 'God' is not the name of a substance; rather, we by chance call these three (I know not what) things three gods, as we call three human beings possessing regal power three kings. For three human beings cannot be one king. And there is no need to say how impious this is.

I ought to fill a large volume if I wished to write down the absurdities and impieties that follow if it is true that when one divine person became flesh, the other two consequently did, since the three persons are one thing by reason of what we predicate of the three as common to them. Or the absurdities and impieties that follow if there are three separate things, as he against whom I have said these things thinks, since only the Son became flesh. Therefore, he evidently ought not to be ready to argue about profound things, especially things in which he does not stray without danger.

6

But perhaps he will say: 'As you think that the things you say necessarily follow if what I think follows, so the consequences I draw likewise seem necessary to me. Therefore, show that what I say does not follow, and I shall with you profess that nothing improper follows if only the Son became flesh, or if the three persons are one thing. And if you fail to demonstrate this, you do not resolve but rather tie up the question when you yourself are with me satisfied with the

source whence countless improprieties spring. And if these improprieties are to be denied, both of us ought likewise to conclude that
the three persons are not one thing if only the Son became flesh, or
that if they are one thing, all of them likewise became flesh.'

Therefore, we need to show in what he is mistaken, and how the
incarnation of the Son alone does not imply that the three persons
are three things, or that all three persons became flesh if the three
persons are one thing. And the irrefutable arguments of the holy
Fathers and especially blessed Augustine,[7] after the apostles and
evangelists, have argued that God is, of course, one and only one and
an individual and a simple substance, and three persons. And perhaps
some will deign to read two short works of mine, namely, the *Monologion* and the *Proslogion*. I composed these works especially to show
that compelling arguments apart from the authority of Scripture can
establish things that we by faith hold about the divine nature and the
divine persons besides the incarnation. If some wanted to read them,
I say, I think that they will discover in them regarding this matter
things that they will neither be able to disprove nor wish to make
little of. And to answer in defence of our faith against those who, not
wanting to believe what they do not understand, deride those who
do believe, or to aid the religious zeal of those who humbly seek to
understand what they most firmly believe, I may have posited in
these works things that I have not read, or do not remember having
read, elsewhere. (I have not written as if to teach what our teachers
did not know or to correct what they did not say well, but perhaps
to say things about which they were silent, things that agree rather
than disagree with their statements.) If I have said anything new, I
by no means think that I should be gainsaid for that reason. But lest
I impose the task of seeking other writings on readers of this letter,
that they may know both by faith and by clear argument that the
three persons are only one God, not three, and that when God
respecting one person became flesh, it was nevertheless not necessary that the same God respecting the other persons become flesh, I
shall add something here. This is as much as I believe sufficient for
our faith to refute the opinion of this 'defender of the faith', as he
considers himself.

He says openly that either the Father and the Holy Spirit became

[7] Especially in the work *On the Trinity* (*Patrologia Latina* 42: 819 ff.).

flesh with the Son, or those three persons are three separate things. And he indeed thinks this separateness to be such that neither the Father nor the Holy Spirit are in the Son. For if the other two persons are in the Son, and the Son in a human being, they too are in the human being. And so he thinks that, since the three persons together are in the same human being, it follows that the person of the Son in no way became flesh in the very human being apart from the other two persons. None the less, he does not deny that there are three persons, nor that the Son became flesh. I have demonstrated above [2–5] that if the three persons are three separate things, either it follows that there are three gods, or the other absurdities about which I have already spoken. Therefore, I, with the assistance of the one sole God, shall now briefly show: (1) that even if there be three gods, they will provide nothing for him to defend the Father and Holy Spirit from becoming flesh [7], and he thinks that this cannot be done without there being a plurality of gods; (2) that there is only one God, not several [8]. Then I shall make clear that although the one God is three persons, it is none the less not necessary that the other persons also become flesh if any one of them has; rather, to the contrary, I shall make clear that this is impossible [9].

7

It belongs to the divine substance, of course, that it always and everywhere exist, so that nothing ever or anywhere is apart from its presence. Otherwise, it is in no way everywhere and always powerful, and what is not everywhere and always powerful is in no way God. For if my adversary says that God's power and not his very substance is always and everywhere, he will still not deny that God's power is either accidental or substantial. God's power is indeed not accidental, since God can neither exist without power nor be conceived in such a way, although every subject can exist or be understood apart from accidents. And if God's power is substantial, it is either part of his essence or the very thing that is his whole essence. And it is not part of his essence, since, as I have said, what either actually or conceptually has parts can be divided into parts, and this is altogether foreign to God. Therefore, it is the same thing to belong to God and to belong to his power. And so, as God's power is always and everywhere, so whatever is God is everywhere and always. Therefore, when the aforementioned self-styled 'defender' of our faith says that there are three gods, he cannot show how they exist separately by the separation whereby he thinks that he delivers them from the incarnation. Therefore, a plurality of gods cannot help him to insulate the Father and the Holy Spirit from the incarnation, since there cannot be found in a plurality of gods the separation without which he thinks that that insulation can in no way be accomplished.

8

And that there is only one God and not several, we easily establish because either God is not the supreme good, or there are several supreme goods, or there is one sole God and not several. And no one denies that God is the supreme good, since anything less than something is in no way God, and anything not the supreme good is less than something, since it is less than the supreme good. The supreme good surely does not allow that there be duplication of itself, so that there be several supreme goods. For if there are several supreme goods, they are equal. But the supreme good is the good that surpasses other goods, so that it has neither an equal nor anything that surpasses it. Therefore, there is one and only one supreme good. Therefore, there is one and only one God and not several gods, just as there is one and only one supreme good, and as there is one and only one supreme substance or essence or nature (which the same argument as in the case of the supreme good proves cannot be in any way affirmed of several things).

9

And although this one sole God is three persons, namely, the Father and the Son and the Holy Spirit, it is none the less not necessary that when the Son became flesh, the other persons also do, as that disputant thinks; rather, it is impossible. For he does not deny that there are several persons, since they differ from one another. (For they would not be several unless they were to differ from one another.) But in order that I may explain more briefly and more easily what I mean, I shall only speak, as I did above [2–3], about the Father and the Son, since it will be clear through them what we need to understand regarding the Holy Spirit. Therefore, since the Father and the

Son are not two substances, they are not several and distinct from one another as to substance, nor the Father one substance, the Son another; rather, the Father and the Son are one and the same substance. And they are several and distinct from one another as to person, since the Father and the Son are two persons and distinct from one another, and not one and the same person. Therefore, my adversary says: 'If God the Son became flesh, and he is numerically one and the same thing as the Father, and not distinct from him, then the Father also necessarily became flesh. For it is impossible that a thing numerically one and the same both became flesh and did not become flesh in the same human being.' And I say: 'If the Son became flesh, and he is a different person than the Father is, and not numerically one and the same, then it is not necessary that the Father also became flesh. For it is possible that one person became flesh in a human being, and that another person did not become flesh in the same human being.' And he says: 'If God the Son became flesh, and the God who is Son is numerically one and the same God who is Father, and not distinct, it seems still more necessary because of the unity of the divine substance that, although the Father and the Son are different persons, the Father also became flesh with the Son, than it is possible because of the diversity of the persons that the Father did not become flesh together with the Son.'

See how he who says this limps on both feet in the matter of the incarnation of the Son of God. For one who correctly understands the Son's incarnation believes that the Son assumed a human being into the unity of his person and not into the unity of his substance. And my adversary foolishly thinks that the Son assumed a human being into the unity of his substance rather than into the unity of his person. For if he were not to think this, he would not say that it is more necessary that the Father became flesh with the Son, since the one God is Father and Son, than it is possible that the Father did not become flesh with the Son, since there are several persons. Therefore, whoever thinks that the Son of God became flesh by reason of a unity of substance, so that the Son could not become flesh apart from the Father becoming flesh, and does not understand that the Son became flesh by reason of a unity of person, so that the Father could not become flesh with the Son, limps on both feet, that is, in both parts, in the matter of the same incarnation of the Son, who is one substance with the Father and a different person than the

Father. Indeed, God did not assume a human being in such a way that the divine and human natures are one and the same, but in such a way that the divine and human person is one and the same. And this can only be in one divine person. For we cannot understand that different persons are one and the same person with one and the same human being. For if a human being is a person with several individual persons, the several persons that differ from one another are necessarily one and the same person, and this is impossible. Therefore, it is impossible that when God became flesh respecting any one person, God also becomes flesh respecting another person.

10

And although it is not our design to explain why God assumed a human being into the unity of the person of the Son rather than the unity of any one of the other persons, I none the less think that some reason should be given, since the mention of this matter presented itself. If the Holy Spirit became flesh, as the Son became flesh, surely the Holy Spirit would be the son of a human being. Therefore, there would be two sons in the divine Trinity, namely, the Son of God and the son of the human being. And so some mixture of doubt would be generated when we were speaking of God the 'son'. For both would be God and son, although one would be the Son of God, the other the son of a human being. There would also be a kind of inequality, as it were, of the different persons, who ought to be completely equal, by reason of the fact that they were sons, since one son would be greater by reason of the dignity of a superior parent, the other lesser by reason of an inferior parent. For as much as the nature of God is greater than the nature of a human being, so much is it more worthy to be the Son of God than to be the son of a human being. Therefore, if the Holy Spirit were to have been born of the Virgin, one person would be greater, and the other person lesser, by reason of the dignity of their origin, since the Son of God would have only the more excellent origin from God, and the Holy Spirit only the lesser origin from a human being. And this is inappropriate. And if the Father were to have assumed a human being into the unity of his person, the multiplication of sons would result in the same improprieties in God, and yet another. For if the Father were to be the son of the Virgin, two persons in the Trinity would take the name of grandson, since both the Father would be the grandson of the Virgin's parents, and the Father's Son would be the Virgin's grandson, although the Son himself would have no part of him from the Virgin.

Therefore, no divine person other than the Son ought to become flesh, since there cannot be any least inappropriate thing in God. For although we declare that the Son in his humanity is less than the Father and the Holy Spirit, yet the latter two persons do not on that account surpass the Son, since the Son also has the same majesty whereby they are greater than the Son's humanity, the same majesty whereby he himself with them is also superior to his humanity.

There is also another reason why the incarnation is more appropriate for the Son than another person. For the one who was to become flesh was to intercede for the human race, and the human mind more appropriately enough conceives a son pleading with his father than one individual pleading with another, although the human nature, not the divine nature, makes this supplication to the deity. And the Son of God achieves this because the human being is by reason of the unity of the person the Son of God.

Let me amplify. The one who was to assume a human being was to come to fight against the devil and, as I have said, to intercede for human beings. And both of these, namely, the devil and human beings, by exercising their wills as their own wished to make themselves like God by robbery. And because they wished to make themselves like God by robbery, they could do so only by falsehood, since they could do so only unjustly. For the will of an angel or a human being that is contrary to the will of God is its own. For those who will what God forbids them to will have only their very selves as the authors of their will, and so their will is their own. (For although human beings sometimes subject their will to the will of another human being, their will, if contrary to God, is none the less their own, since they subject their will to another only to attain what they will, and so have their very selves as the authors whereby they subject their will to another.) Therefore, a will subject to no one else's is one's own. But possessing a will as one's own (i.e. a will subject to no will) belongs to God alone. Therefore, all who exercise their will as their own strive to be like God by robbery and are guilty of depriving God of the dignity proper to him and of his unique excellence, insofar as it lies within their power to do so. For if there is any other will that be not subject to anyone, God's will will not be superior to all, nor will it be the only will with no other superior to it.

Therefore, none of the three divine persons more appropriately 'emptied his very self, taking the form of a slave' [Phil. 2: 7] in order to war against the devil and intercede for human beings, who had by robbery presumed falsely to be like God, than the Son. The Son, as the splendour of eternal light and the true image of the Father, 'did not think it plunder to be God's equal' [Phil. 2: 6] but by reason of true equality and likeness declared: 'I and the Father are one' [John 10: 30], and 'Those who see me see the Father also' [John 14: 9]. For no one more justly repels or punishes criminals, or more mercifully pardons or intercedes for them, than the one against whom injustice is more particularly demonstrated. Nor is anything more appropriately opposed to falsity in order to repel it, or more apposite for healing, than truth. For those presuming a false likeness to God seem to have sinned more particularly against him whom we profess to be the true likeness of the Father. And he assumed a human being into the unity of his person, so that the two natures, namely, the divine and the human, are one person, as I have said [1].

11

And yet it does not seem to me useless to say something about this unity of the person, which we most firmly profess not to be out of two persons in Christ, since we can articulate the reasons why Christ can seem to those reflecting less carefully to originate from and in two persons. For example, some say: 'How do we say that there are not two persons in Christ, as there are two natures in him? For God was a person even before he assumed a human being, nor did he cease to be a person after he assumed a human being, and the human being assumed is a person, since we know that every individual human being is a person. Therefore, there is one divine person that existed before the incarnation, another belonging to the assumed human being. Therefore, as Christ is God and a human being, so there seem to be two persons in him. And this argument seems to prove that there are two persons in Christ, since God is a person, and the assumed human being is a person.'

But such is not the case. For as there is one nature and several persons in God, and the several persons are one nature, so there is one person and several natures in Christ, and the several natures are one person. For as the Father is God, and the Son God, and the Holy Spirit God, and yet there is one God and not three gods, so, in Christ, God is person, and the human being is person, and yet there is one person and not two persons. For there is not in Christ one who is God, another one who is the human being, although there is one thing that is God, another thing that is the human being; rather, the very same one who is also the human being is God. For the 'Word made flesh' [John 1: 14] assumed another nature, not another person. For when we speak of 'human being', we signify only the nature that is common to all human beings. But when we speak of this or that human being particularly or Jesus by his proper name, we denote the person, which along with human nature has a combination of proper characteristics, and these characteristics individualize common human being and distinguish it from other individuals. For when we so designate Jesus, we understand the one whom the angel announced, the one who is God and the human being, the Son of God and the Son of the Virgin, and not any human being. And we truly predicate everything, whether regarding God or regarding the human being, of him. For we cannot designate or name the divine Son as person apart from the human son, nor the human son as person apart from the divine Son, since the very same one who is the human son is the divine Son, and the combination of proper characteristics of the Word and the assumed human being is the same. And different persons cannot have the same combination of individual characteristics, nor can we predicate different persons of one another. For example, Peter and Paul do not have the same combination of proper characteristics, and we do not call Peter Paul, or Paul Peter.

Therefore, when the 'Word became flesh' [John 1: 14], he assumed the nature that alone we signify by the term 'human being' and ever differs from the divine nature; he did not assume another person, since he has the same combination of proper characteristics with the assumed human being. For human being and the human being assumed by the Word (i.e. Jesus) are not the same, since, as I have said, we understand in the term 'human being' only a nature, while we understand in the assumed human being or the name 'Jesus' the combination of proper characteristics. And this combination is identical for the very human being assumed and the Word along with the nature (i.e. human being). Therefore, we do not say that the Word and human being in an absolute sense are the same person, lest we say that human being in an absolute sense rather than any one human being is the same person with the Word; rather, we say that the Word and the assumed human being (i.e. Jesus) are the same person. Just so, we do not profess that the very human being is the same person in an absolute sense with God; rather we profess that the very human being is the same person with the person that is Word and Son, lest we seem to profess that the very human being is the same person that is the Father or the Holy Spirit. But it is true to say that God and the human being are the same person, since both the Word is God, and the assumed human being is a human being. And we should implicitly understand the Word in the term 'God', and the son of the Virgin in the term 'human being'.

I have been unable to perceive anything concerning the writings of the one whom I answer in this letter besides what I have set down above [1]. And I think the things I have said make the truth of the matter so clear that it is evident to everyone with understanding that nothing expressed to the contrary has the force of truth.

12

But if my adversary, called back from the plurality of gods, denies the plurality of persons in God, he does so because he does not know whereof he speaks. For rather than thinking in terms of God and divine persons, he thinks in terms of things akin to several human persons. And because he perceives that one human being cannot be several persons, he denies the very same about God. For we affirm the three persons in God because they have some likeness to three separate persons, not because they are three separate things like three human beings. Let us consider this in the case of the Father and the Son, and let us understand the very same thing about the Holy Spirit.

Therefore, let us suppose a man who is only a father and not a son (i.e. Adam), and a son of his who is only a son and not a father (i.e. Abel). And so we predicate of Adam the father and Abel the son that the father is not a son, and that the son is not a father, since Adam and Abel are two human beings and separate persons. Nor is Adam the one to whom it should belong to be a son, or Abel the one to whom it should belong to be a father. And so we similarly in the case of God profess that although there are not two gods, the Father is not the Son, nor the Son the Father, since the Father does not have a father, nor the Son a son. Likewise, the Holy Spirit is not the Father or the Son, since the Holy Spirit is not one to whom it should belong to be a father or a son. Therefore, since the Father and the Son and the Holy Spirit are three and distinct from one another, and they cannot be predicated of one another, as we have shown about fathers and sons in the case of different human persons, we affirm that there are three persons in this way, not such that there be three separate things.

13

And perhaps my adversary, in order not to predicate three things of one another, denies that three things can be predicated of one thing, and one thing of three things, as we do in the case of the three persons and the one God, since he does not perceive such in the case of other things, and he cannot understand such in the case of God. If so, let him allow that there are things in God that his intellect could not understand, and let him not compare the nature that is superior to everything, the nature that is free from every law of time and space and composition of parts, to things that are. Rather, let him profess that there are in that nature what cannot be in the latter things, and let him accept Christian authority and not contest it.

None the less, let us see whether we can in some way find in created things, which are subject to the laws of space and time and composition of parts, what he denies in God. Let us suppose a source from which a river originates and flows, and let us suppose that the river later empties into a delta. And let the river's name be the Nile. And so we give the separate names 'source', 'river', 'delta' in such a way that we do not call the source the river or the delta, or the river either the source or the delta, or the delta the source or the river. But we call the source the Nile, and the river the Nile, and the delta the Nile, and both the source and the river together the Nile, both the source and the delta together the Nile, both the river and the delta together the Nile, and all three (the source and the river and the delta) together the Nile. We do so because there is still one and the same Nile, not one and another Nile, whether we call each one singly or pairs of them or all three the Nile. Therefore, the source, the river, the delta are three, and the Nile, the running water, the substance, the body of water one, and we cannot call anything three. For neither are there three Niles or three running waters or three bodies of water or three substances, nor are there three sources or three rivers or three deltas. Therefore, we here predicate one thing of three things, and three things of one thing, and yet not the three things of one another.

And if my adversary objects that any single one, whether the source or the river or the delta, or pairs of them, are part or parts of the Nile, not the complete Nile, let him reflect that the whole Nile, from its beginning to its end, consists of its entire span, as it were, since the Nile itself is not immediately entire, either spatially or temporally, but by reason of its parts, nor will it be complete until it ceases to be. (For the Nile is in this respect like speech, which is not complete as long as it flows out of a mouth as its source, as it were, and does not exist when it is complete.) For if one should so consider and carefully understand, such a one would know that the whole Nile is its source, the whole Nile its river, the whole Nile its delta, and that the source is not the river or the delta, nor the river the source or the delta, nor the delta the source or the river. For the source itself is not the same as the river or the delta, although the very same thing that is the source is the river and the delta, that is, the same Nile, the same running water, the same body of water, the same substance. Therefore, we predicate three things of one entire, complete thing, and one entire, complete thing of three things. And yet the three things themselves are not predicated of one another, although this exists in very different ways and more perfectly in the case of the simplest substance and the one freest from every spatial and temporal law. None the less, if this is in some way evident in something composed of parts, something spatial and temporal, it is credible that it exists perfectly in the substance that is supremely free from the laws of space and time.

We should also here consider that the source is not from the river or the delta, and the river is only from the source, not from the delta, and the delta is from the source and the river, and in such a way that the entire river is from the entire source, and the entire delta from the entire source and the entire river. Just so do we declare in the case of the Father and the Son and the Holy Spirit. And we should consider that the river is from the source in one way, and the delta from the source and the river in another way, so that we do not call the delta the river. Just so is the Word from the Father in one way, and the Holy Spirit from the Father and the Word in another way, so that the same Holy Spirit is not the Word or Son but proceeds from him.

14

I still want to say something that, despite its great dissimilitude, none the less is analogous to the incarnation of the Word. And some readers will perhaps look down on it. Nevertheless, I may say that I would not completely contemn it if another were to say it. For if the river should run through a pipe from the source down to the delta, is not the river alone, although no other Nile than the source and the delta, in the pipe, as I would so declare, just as the Son alone, although no other God than the Father and the Holy Spirit, became flesh?

15

But since these earthly things are so far removed from the highest nature, let us rise to that mind with its very assistance, and let us in some way and briefly consider what we are saying. God is nothing but pure eternity itself. And we cannot conceive of several eternities. For if there are several eternities, they are either without or within one another. But nothing is outside eternity. Therefore, neither is there an eternity outside eternity. Similarly, if eternities are outside one another, they are in different places or times, and this is unrelated to eternity. And so there are not several eternities outside one another. And if one asserts that there are several eternities within one another, such a one ought to know that there is only one and the same eternity, however many times eternity may be replicated upon itself. For a nature that, replicated upon itself, is always one with itself in complete unity is of higher rank than a nature that admits plurality of itself. For there is diversity where there is plurality. And where there is diversity, there is not complete agreement. For agreement is complete that agrees in one identity and the same unity. Therefore, if complete agreement is better than incomplete agreement—and there cannot be anything incomplete in the highest good (i.e. eternity itself)—the nature of eternity cannot admit plurality. Therefore, there is one and the same, and only one, eternity.

And we likewise say the same about many other things. For example, omnipotence upon omnipotence is only one omnipotence. And I shall propose as an example one of the things that do not have the divine nature, in which the case is similar: a point superimposed on a point is only one point. For points like the midpoint of the world and this moment of time (i.e., the present time) have some comparison to eternity, no small matter for the useful consideration of the same eternity. And so there is need to consider this more broadly in another place.[8] The consideration here suffices only to demonstrate that a simple point (i.e. one without parts), like eternity, is also indivisible, and so a point with a point superimposed without any interval is only one point, just as an eternity with an eternity superimposed is only one eternity.

Therefore, as God is eternity, there are not several gods, since there is no God outside of God, nor does God in God add plurality to God. Therefore, God is always one and the same, and only one. And so when God is generated from God, the offspring is in the parent, and the parent in the offspring (namely, one God the Father and the Son), since the generated is not outside the source of the generated. And when God proceeds from God the Father and the Son, he does not proceed outside God; God (i.e. the Holy Spirit) abides in God from whom he proceeds, and there is one God the Father and the Son and the Holy Spirit. And since this generation and procession are without beginning (otherwise, the eternity generated and the eternity proceeding have a beginning, and this is false), we neither ought nor can in any way conceive that God began to be the Father or the Son or the Holy Spirit.

16

And as the divine substance preserves an eternal and unique unity, so it has an inseparable plurality of these relations, namely, of Father and Son, of the one who proceeds and the one from whom the other's substance proceeds. For as God is necessarily always one and the same, and not one and another, so, by reason of these relations, the

---

[8] See *On the Procession of the Holy Spirit*, 9.

Father is never the same as his Son, nor the one who proceeds the same as the one from whom he proceeds. Rather, the Father is always one person, and the Son another, and the one who proceeds one person, and the one from whom he proceeds another, nor can they ever be predicated of one another. Therefore, since neither the divine substance can lose singularity, nor the divine relations plurality, when God is generated from God, or God proceeds from God, one thing in God is thus three, and three things are one, and yet the three things are not predicated of one another. Nor should it be incredible that there is in the substance that is superior to everything and dissimilar to everything else something whose imitation cannot be found perfectly in other things. And Latins call these three things persons, Greeks substances. For as we Latins call the one substance in God three persons, so the Greeks call the one person three substances, they meaning here by substance the very same thing that we mean by person, and not differing from us in faith in any way.

And the blessed Augustine carefully considered in his very work *On the Trinity*, 'as in a mirror and confusedly' [1 Cor. 13: 12], how the Son is generated from the Father, and how the Holy Spirit proceeds from the Father and Son and yet is not the Son, since we cannot in this life perceive God 'as he is' [1 John 3: 2]. And I in my *Monologion* [29 et seq.], which I recalled above [6], have so argued in proportion to my abilities. And if anyone wishes to know why we call the parent in God a father rather than a mother, or the offspring a son rather than a daughter (since there is no gender in the highest substance), or why the Father is the only unbegotten, the Son the only begotten, the Holy Spirit neither begotten nor unbegotten, such a one will find the answer explicitly in the same work [42].

WHY GOD BECAME MAN

[*Commendation of the work to Pope Urban II*]

Many of our holy Fathers and teachers, following the Apostles, speak frequently and on a grand scale about the logical principles[1] of our faith. Their aim in doing so is to confute unwisdom, to shatter the rigid resistance of unbelievers and to nourish those who, with cleansed hearts, already take delight in this same logic of the faith, for which, once we have reached certitude about it, we ought to hunger. Given the greatness and frequency of their utterances on this subject, neither in our times nor in times to come can we hope for anyone who will be their equal in the contemplation of the truth. All this I grant. Nevertheless, I do not think that anyone deserves to be rebuked, if, after becoming well-grounded in the faith, he has conceived a desire to exercise himself in the investigation of its logic.

For even the Fathers, because 'the days of men are short' [cf. Job 14: 1], were not able to say all that they could have said if they had lived longer; and the logic of the truth is so copious and profound that it cannot be exhausted by mortals. Moreover, the Lord, whose promise is to be with the Church 'until the end of the world' [Matt. 28: 20], does not cease to bestow his gifts within it. And where he says, 'Unless you have believed, you will not understand' [cf. Isa. 7: 9]—to make no mention of other places where the Sacred Page invites us to explore its rationale—he is plainly encouraging us to pay more attention to understanding, while teaching us the sort of method by which we must proceed towards it. Finally, I consider that the understanding which we gain in this life stands midway between faith and revelation. It follows, in my view, that, the nearer someone comes to attainment of this understanding, the nearer that person approaches to revelation, for which we all pant in anticipation.

I am comforted by this consideration, despite the fact that I am a man of inadequate knowledge. Hence I am attempting for a little

---

[1] Lat. *ratiopes*; 'logic' below is similarly a translation of *ratio*. In this translation of *Cur Deus Homo*, the term 'logic' and its cognates will be used interchangeably with 'reason', 'rational' and their cognates, to convey the meaning of Anselm's *ratio, rationalis*.

while, insofar as the heavenly grace deigns to allow me, to arise to contemplate the logic of our beliefs; and when I discover something which I used not previously to see, I am happy to disclose this to other people, my object being that I may learn through the judgement of others what I may confidently hold on to.

For this reason, my father and lord, Pope Urban, worthy as you are to be loved by all Christians with reverence and revered with love—you whom the providence of God has appointed as supreme pontiff in his Church—I present for the inspection of your Holiness, since there is no one to whom I can more rightly present it, the enclosed little work, with the aim that those items in it which are acceptable may receive approval on the authority of your Holiness, and those which are in need of correction may be put right.

Preface

Because of some people who, without my knowledge, began copying out the first parts of this work before it was finished and fully researched, I have been compelled to complete the work that follows, to the best of my ability, in greater haste than would have been opportune from my point of view. For, if I had been allowed to edit it in tranquillity and for the appropriate length of time, I would have included further additional material which I have left unmentioned. It has been amid great heartache—what the source of this has been, and the reason for it, God knows—that I began this work in England in response to a request, and have completed it, while on a journey, in the province of Capua. I have named it, in consideration of its subject-matter, *Why God Became Man*...,[2] and have divided it into two books. The first book contains the objections of unbelievers who reject the Christian faith because they think it militates against reason, and the answers given by the faithful. And eventually it proves, by unavoidable logical steps, that, supposing Christ were left out of the case, as if there had never existed anything to do with him, it is impossible that, without him, any member of the human race

---

[2] There is no verb 'became' in the Latin, but it is clear from *Cur Deus Homo* 1.1 (Schmitt 48.2 f.) and 2.18 (Schmitt 126.25 f.), where Anselm summarizes his subject-matter, that his title is an abbreviated version of the question, 'Why God became man in order that he might save mankind by his death, when it appears that he could have done this in another way'.

could be saved. In the second book, similarly, the supposition is made that nothing were known about Christ, and it is demonstrated with no less clear logic and truth: that human nature was instituted with the specific aim that at some stage the whole human being should enjoy blessed immortality, 'whole' meaning 'with both body and soul'; that it was inevitable that the outcome concerning mankind which was the reason behind man's creation should become a reality, but that this could only happen through the agency of a Man-God; and that it is from necessity that all the things which we believe about Christ have come to pass.

It is my earnest request that all who wish to copy this book should place before its opening this little preface, along with the chapter-headings of the whole work. My intention is that anyone into whose hands it comes may discern, as it were, from its facial appearance, whether there is anything, within the whole body of the work, which he may find worthy of respect.

Chapters of Book 1

1. The question on which the whole work hangs
2. How the things to be said are to be interpreted
3. Objections of unbelievers and answers of believers
4. That these replies seem to unbelievers to lack cogency and to resemble pictures
5. That the redemption of mankind could not have been brought about by any other than a divine person
6. How unbelievers find fault with our statement that God has ransomed us by his death, and that he has, in this way, showed his love towards us, and has come to drive out the devil on our behalf
7. That the devil had no jurisdiction over man. Why he might seem to have had it, causing God, as a result, to set us free in this way
8. How it is that, even granted that the lowly things of which we speak with reference to Christ do not pertain to his divinity, it may seem to unbelievers that it is inappropriate that they are said of him even with reference to his humanity. How it is, consequently, that it may seem to them that this same man did not die voluntarily
9. That he died voluntarily. Also the meaning of: 'He became obedient, even to death' [Phil. 2: 8] and 'Because of which God

has raised him up' [Phil. 2: 9], and 'I have not come to do my own will' [cf. John 6: 38], and 'He did not spare his own Son' [Rom. 8: 32] and 'Not according to my will, but yours' [Matt. 26: 39]

Chapters of Book 2

2. That he would not die if he had not sinned
3. That he rises with the body in which he lives in this life
4. That, with regard to the nature of mankind, God will bring to completion what he has begun
5. That, although it is a matter of necessity that this should happen, it will not be under compulsion of necessity that he will do this; that, moreover, there is a necessity which removes or diminishes graciousness and a necessity which increases it
6. That no one is capable of bringing about the recompense by which mankind may be saved except someone who is God and man
7. That it is necessary for one and the same person to be perfect God and perfect man
8. That it is right that God should assume human nature from the race of Adam and from a virgin woman
9. That it is necessary for the Word alone and man to combine in a single person
10. That this same man does not die obligatorily; and in what sense he is, or is not, capable of sinning, and why he, or an angel, should be praised for his righteousness, even though they are incapable of sinning
11. That it is of his own power that he dies, and that mortality is not a property of human nature which is pure
12. That, although he is a sharer in our discomforts, he is nevertheless not unhappy
13. That he does not have ignorance along with our other weaknesses
14. That his death outweighs the number and magnitude of all sins
15. That this same death destroys the sins even of those who put him to death
16. How God produced a man without sin out of sinful matter; also about the salvation of Adam and Eve
17. That in God no necessity or impossibility exists; and that there is a necessity which compels and a necessity which does not compel
18. How the life of Christ is recompense paid to God for the sins of mankind; and how Christ was obliged, and was not obliged, to suffer
19. With what very great logicality the salvation of mankind follows from his death

20. How great and just the mercy of God is
21. That it is impossible for the devil to receive reconciliation
22. That by the things which have been said, the truth of the Old Testament and the New has been proved

✳   BOOK 1

1. *The question on which the whole work hangs*

I have often been asked most earnestly, both by word of mouth and in writing, by many people, to set down a written record of the reasoned explanations with which I am in the habit of answering people who put enquiries to me about a certain question of Our Faith. For they say that these explanations please them, and they think them satisfactory. They make this request, not with a view to arriving at faith through reason, but in order that they may take delight in the understanding and contemplation of the things which they believe, and may be, as far as they are able, 'ready always to give satisfaction to all who ask the reason for the hope that is in us' [1 Pet. 3: 15]. The question is one which unbelievers, deriding Christian simplicity as foolish, are in the habit of raising as an objection against us, and many believers too are in the habit of pondering it in their hearts. The question is this. By what logic or necessity did God become man, and by his death, as we believe and profess, restore life to the world, when he could have done this through the agency of some other person, angelic or human, or simply by willing it? About this issue not only people who are literate, but many also who are unlettered, ask questions and long for a rational explanation. Many people, then, are asking for a treatment of this subject, and, although it is one which in the course of enquiry appears very difficult, in its solution it is intelligible to all, and appealing because of its utility and the beauty of its logic. With this in mind, I grant that what has been said about the matter by the holy Fathers ought to be sufficient, but I will nevertheless undertake to make plain to enquirers what God shall see fit to reveal to me about this subject. And since matters which are explored by means of question and answer are clearer to many people, particularly to slower intellects, and are correspondingly more pleasing, I will take, from among the people who importune me with this request, the one who is the most insistent of them all in goading me on to undertake this endeavour, and I shall have him dispute with me. And so, let *Boso* ask the questions, and let *Anselm* answer, as follows.

Boso. On the one hand, right order demands that we should believe the profundities of the Christian faith before we presume to discuss it logically, but, on the other, it seems to me negligence if, after we have been confirmed in the faith, we do not make an effort to understand what we believe. Thanks to the grace of God which goes before us, I think I adhere to faith in our redemption in such a way that, even though I cannot understand what I believe in any rational way, yet there is nothing which can tear me away from its steadfastness. I ask you, therefore, to reveal to me something which, as you know, many people besides me ask about, namely this: by what necessity or logic did God, almighty as he is, take upon himself the humble standing and weakness of human nature with a view to that nature's restoration?

Anselm. What you are asking of me is above me, and I am afraid of treating 'higher things' [Ecclus. 3: 22 Vulg.]. My fear is that someone thinking, or even seeing, that I am not giving him a satisfactory reply, may think that this is due to lack of truth where the actuality is concerned, rather than the insufficiency of my intellect to grasp it.

B. You ought not so much to be afraid of this as to remember also that it often comes about in discussions of some issue that God reveals what was previously hidden. And you ought to put your hope in the grace of God that, if you willingly share what you have freely received [cf. Matt. 10: 8], you will deserve to receive those 'higher things' to which you have so far not attained.

A. There is another factor, too, which I see making it scarcely, or not at all, possible for a joint treatment of this matter by us at this time to be exhaustive. For a complete treatment of it, it is essential to have an understanding of power and necessity and will and certain other things which are so constituted that no one of them can be fully considered without the others. And therefore the consideration of these matters demands a separate work, not an easy one, I think, and an extremely useful one too. For ignorance of these matters makes some things difficult which are made easy by a knowledge of them.

B. But you will be able to speak briefly about these matters in the places where they arise, in such a way that we may grasp what is sufficient for the present work and may defer until another time what more there remains to be said.

A. Something else which makes me hold back from complying with your request is that not only is the subject-matter precious, but, in conformity with the fact that it is about someone beautiful, 'with beauty excelling the sons of men' [Ps. 44: 3 Vulg.], it is itself correspondingly beautiful in its logic, beyond the reasoning of men. On this account, I am afraid that, just as I am invariably annoyed by bad painters when I see the Lord himself depicted as of ugly appearance, the same fault will be found with me, if I presume to plough through such beautiful subject-matter with an unpolished and contemptible style of writing.

B. This ought not to hold you back either. For you are leaving it open for anyone to speak who can do so better, and similarly you are not prohibiting anyone who does not like your style from writing more beautifully. But, so that I may put an end to all your excuses: you will be doing what I ask not for the learned, but for me, and for people who are making the selfsame request along with me.

2. *How the things to be said are to be interpreted*

A. In view of your importunate persistence and that of the people who, out of love and religious zeal, are making this request along with you, I shall attempt to grant what you are asking for to the best of my ability, with God's help, and with the support of your prayers which, at my request, you have often promised me with this specific undertaking in view. But my attempt will take the form not so much of a demonstration as of an enquiry undertaken jointly with you, and it will be made with the stipulation which I wish to be understood to apply to all that I say, namely, that if I say something which is not confirmed by a source of greater authority—even if I seem to be proving it by means of logic—it is to be accepted with only this degree of certainty: that it seems to be so provisionally, until God shall in some way reveal to me something better. If, moreover, it comes about that I seem to any extent to be replying satisfactorily to your question, it ought to be regarded as a certainty that someone wiser than I could do this more fully. Indeed, it is a matter of certain knowledge that, whatever a human being may say on this subject, there remain deeper reasons, as yet hidden from us, for a reality of such supreme importance.

3. *Objections of unbelievers and answers of believers*

B. Allow me, then, to use the words characteristic of unbelievers. For it is only fair, at a time when we are keen to explore the logic of our faith, to set out the objections of those who are totally unwilling to come to this faith without a logical reason for doing so. I grant that they are in search of logic because they do not believe, whereas we are seeking it because we do believe. Nevertheless, the object of our quest is one and the same. Again, if you give any reply which seems to be in contradiction to Sacred Authority, let me bring the authority to your notice, so that you may demonstrate how it is not contradictory.

A. Speak as you see fit.

B. Unbelievers, deriding us for our simplicity, object that we are inflicting injury and insult on God when we assert that he descended into a woman's womb; was born of a woman; grew up nurtured on milk and human food and—to say nothing of other things which do not seem suitable for God—was subject to weariness, hunger, thirst, scourging, crucifixion between thieves, and death.

A. We are not doing God any injury or insult, but are wholeheartedly giving him thanks and praise, and proclaiming the ineffable profundity of his mercy. For God has shown the magnitude of his love and devotion towards us by the magnitude of his act in most wonderfully and unexpectedly saving us from the evils, so great and so deserved, by which we used to be beset, and returning us to the enjoyment of the good things, so great and so undeserved, which we had lost. If then, they were to consider diligently how fitting it is that the restoration of mankind has been brought about in this way, they would not deride our simplicity, but would join us in praising God's wise benevolence. For it was appropriate that, just as death entered the human race through a man's disobedience, so life should be restored through a man's obedience; and that, just as the sin which was the cause of our damnation originated from a woman, similarly the originator of our justification and salvation should be born of a woman. Also that the devil, who defeated the man whom he beguiled through the taste of a tree, should himself similarly be defeated by a man through tree-induced suffering which he, the devil, inflicted. There are many other things, too, which, if carefully considered, display the indescribable beauty of the fact that our redemption was procured in this way.

4. *That these replies seem to unbelievers to lack cogency and to resemble pictures*

B. All these are beautiful notions, and are to be viewed like pictures. But if there is nothing solid underlying them, they do not seem to unbelievers to provide sufficient grounds why we should believe that God wished to suffer the things of which we are speaking. For someone who wishes to paint a picture chooses something solid on which to paint, so that his painting may have permanence. For nobody paints on water or on air, because on these no traces of painting last. Therefore, when we offer to unbelievers these notions which you say are 'appropriate', like pictorial representations of an actual past event, they think we are, as it were, painting on a cloud. This is the consequence of their view that what we believe is not an actual past event but a fiction. What has to be demonstrated, therefore, is the logical soundness of the truth, that is: a cogent reason which proves that God ought to have, or could have, humbled himself for the purposes which we proclaim. Then, in order that the physical reality[3] of the truth, so to speak, may shine forth all the more, these appropriatenesses may be set out as pictorial representations of this physical reality.

A. Surely there seems a sufficiently cogent reason why God had a need to do the things of which we are speaking: the human race, clearly his most precious piece of workmanship, had been completely ruined; it was not fitting that what God had planned for mankind should be utterly nullified, and the plan in question could not be brought into effect unless the human race were set free by its Creator in person.

---

[3] Lat. *corpus*: lit. 'body'.

5. *That the redemption of mankind could not have been brought about by any other than a divine person*

B. If it were said that this liberation had been brought about by a non-divine person—either by an angel or by a human being— the human mind would accept this far more readily. For God could have created some man without sin, not out of raw material that was sinful and not as the issue of another man, but in the same way in which he had created Adam. The work of liberation could, so it seems, have been accomplished through the agency of this man.

A. Do you not understand that, supposing any other person were to rescue man from eternal death, man would rightly be judged his bondslave?[4] If he were this, he would in no way have been restored to that dignity which he would have had in the future, if he had not sinned. For man, who had the prospect of being the bondsman of no one except God and the equal of the good angels in all respects, would be the bondslave of someone who was not God and to whom the angels were not in bondage.

6. *How unbelievers find fault with our statement that God has ransomed us by his death, and that he has, in this way, showed his love towards us, and has come to drive out the devil on our behalf*

B. Something which people are surprised at is that we call this liberation a 'ransoming'. They say to us, 'Now, in what captivity, or in what prison or in whose power were you held, from which God could not set you free without ransoming you by so many exertions and, in the end, by his own blood?' When we say to these people, 'It was from our sins and from his own anger and from hell and from the power of the devil that God ransomed us, and he came himself to drive out the devil on our behalf because we were ourselves incapable of this, and he bought back the kingdom of heaven for us, and, through the fact that he did all these things in this way, he showed us how much he loved us', they reply, 'If you say that God could not

---

[4] Lat. *servus*: 'slave', 'servant', 'serf', 'villein'.

have done all these things merely by commanding that they should be done—the same God whom you say created all things by issuing commands—you are contradicting yourselves, because you are making him out to be powerless. Alternatively, if you admit that he could have acted, but did not wish to act, other than in this way, how can you show him to be wise, while asserting that he wishes for no reason to suffer such indignities? For all the acts which you are postulating are matters of his will. Moreover, the anger of God is nothing other than a will to punish. Supposing, therefore, that God does not wish to punish the sins of mankind: man is free from sins, and from the anger of God and from hell and from the power of the devil, all of which things he suffers on account of his sins; and man gets back the things of which he is being deprived because of these same sins. For in whose power is hell or the devil, in whose power the kingdom of heaven, if not the power of him who created all things? Therefore, all the things you are afraid of, or long for, are subject to the will of him whom nothing can withstand. Consequently, if he was unwilling to save the human race in any way other than the one of which you speak, whereas he could have done so merely by willing it: to put the matter in the gentlest terms, see how you are impugning his wisdom! For, if a human being were, for no reason, to perform in a very laborious way an action which he could perform with ease, he would at all events not be judged by anyone to be wise. Certainly your statement that God, by so acting, showed how much he loved you, is not at all logically defensible, if it is not demonstrated that he could not have saved mankind in any other way. For, if he could not have done this by other means, then perhaps it would be necessary for him to display his love in this way. As it is, however, given that he was capable of saving mankind by other means: what reason is there why he should do, and suffer, the things of which you speak? For does he not show the good angels, for whom he endures no comparable sufferings, how much he loves them? As for your statement that he came for your sake to drive out the devil: what do you have in mind when daring to make this assertion? Does the omnipotence of God not rule everywhere? How was it, then, that God needed to come down from heaven in order to defeat the devil?' All these are objections which it seems unbelievers are able to put forward against us.

7. *That the devil had no jurisdiction over man. Why he might seem to have had it, causing God, as a result, to set us free in this way*

But, to proceed, take that other thing which we are in the habit of saying: that God, in order to set mankind free, was obliged to act against the devil by justice rather than mighty power.[5] We reason that thus the devil, having killed him in whom there was no guilt deserving death and who was God, would justly lose the power which he used to have over sinners. Otherwise, so we argue, God would have been doing unjust violence against the devil, since the latter was the lawful possessor of man; for the devil had not gained his hold over man with violence: rather it was man who had gone over to the devil of his own free will. I do not see what validity there is in that argument.

For, supposing that the devil, or man, were his own master, or belonged to someone other than God, or was permanently in the power of someone other than God, then perhaps one could justly speak in those terms. However, given that neither the devil nor man belongs to anyone but God, and that neither stands outside God's power: what action did God need to take with, concerning, or in the case of, someone who was his own, apart from punishing this bond-slave of his who had persuaded his fellow-bondslave to desert his master and come over to join him, and had treacherously taken in the fugitive and, a thief himself, had received a thief along with the stolen property of his master? For they were both thieves, since one was stealing his own person from his master at the instigation of the other. Supposing God were to act in this way, could any action be juster?

Alternatively, suppose that God, the judge of all, finding man thus in the devil's possession, were to seize him from the power of the one who was so unjustly possessing him, either with a view to punishing him by some means other than through the agency of the devil, or with a view to sparing him—what would be unjust about that? For although man was being justly tormented when he was tormented by the devil, the devil himself was not acting justly in tormenting him. For man had deserved to be punished, and there was no one by whom he could be more appropriately punished than by

---

[5] 'By... mighty power': Lat. *per fortitudinem*.

the one who had consented to his sin. But the devil had no merit whereby he deserved to inflict the punishment. Rather than being reluctantly drawn to act thus out of love of justice, he was impelled by the force of malice: there is a large difference, and the scale of his injustice was correspondingly large. For the devil was not acting in this way at the command of God, but with the permission of God's incomprehensible wisdom, by which he orders even bad things in a way that is good.

And I reckon that those people who are of the opinion that the devil has just cause for his possession of man are led to this conclusion by the fact that they see that man is justly subject to harassment by the devil and consequently reckon that the devil is acting justly in inflicting it. For it can happen that one and the same thing is, from different points of view, both just and unjust, and for this reason, is judged by people who are not considering the matter with care, to be entirely just or entirely unjust. For instance, someone unjustly strikes an innocent person, and hence justly deserves to be struck himself. If, however, the person who has been struck is under an obligation not to avenge himself, and strikes the person who strikes him, this action of his is unjust. The striking of the blow in this case is unjust where the person who strikes it is concerned, because he was under an obligation not to avenge himself: it is just where the person receiving the blow is concerned, because, through unjustly striking the blow, he has justly deserved to be struck. From different viewpoints, then, the same action is both just and unjust, and it is possible that it may be judged by one person just and by another, unjust. In this way, therefore, the devil is said to harass mankind justly, because God permits this justly, and man suffers it justly. But again, this so-called just suffering on the part of man: it is not in accordance with his own justice that he is said to suffer it, but because he is being punished according to the just judgement of God.

On the other hand, suppose one cites that 'bond of the decree'[6] which the Apostle says was against us and was annulled by the death of Christ, and suppose someone reckons that the meaning of this is that the devil, prior to the passion of Christ, used to demand sin from mankind justly, as if under the terms of a bond forming part of some agreement, as a sort of interest levied on the first sin which he

---

[6] Col. 2: 14, translating the variant on the Vulgate text read by Anselm: *chirographum decreti quod adversum nos* (instead of *chirographum decretis*).

persuaded man to commit, and that thus he appears to prove his jurisdiction over mankind: I do not believe this interpretation is at all correct. For this 'bond' is not a bond of the devil: it is a bond 'of the decree'. Now, that decree was not a decree of the devil but of God. For it was decreed by the just judgement of God and, as it were, confirmed by a bond, in order that man, having sinned of his own free will, would not be able, through his own efforts, to avoid either sin or the punishment for sin. For man is 'a breath that goes forth and does not return' [Ps. 77: 39 Vulg.] and 'he who commits a sin is a slave of sin' [John 8: 34], and a sinner is bound not to be set free without punishment, except in the event that mercy pardons the sinner and frees him and restores him. Consequently, we ought not to believe that any justification for the devil's harassment of mankind can be found to exist through this 'bond'. Finally, just as there is no injustice whatsoever in a good angel, similarly there is absolutely no justice in a bad one. There was nothing in the devil, therefore, which made God obliged not to use his mighty power against him for the purpose of liberating mankind.

8. *How it is that, even granted that the lowly things of which we speak with reference to Christ do not pertain to his divinity, it may seem to unbelievers that it is inappropriate that they are said of him even with reference to his humanity. How it is, consequently, that it may seem to them that this same man did not die voluntarily*

A. When God does something, 'the will of God' ought to be sufficient explanation for us, even if we do not see why it is his will; for the will of God is never irrational.

B. That is true, supposing it is agreed that God's will lay behind the action. The fact is that many people in no way accept that God wishes something, if reason seems to conflict with it.

A. What seems to you to be in conflict with reason, if we affirm that God willed the things which we believe about his incarnation?

B. In brief: that the Most High should stoop to such humble things; that the Almighty should do something with such great laboriousness.

A. People who say this do not understand what we believe. For we affirm that the divine nature is undoubtedly incapable of suffering, and cannot in any sense be brought low from its exalted standing, and cannot labour with difficulty over what it wishes to do. But we say that the Lord Jesus Christ is true God and true man, one person in two natures and two natures in one person. In view of this, when we say that God is suffering some humiliation or weakness, we do not understand this in terms of the exaltedness of his non-suffering nature, but in terms of the weakness of the human substance which he was taking upon himself. And thus it is seen that there is no rational objection to our faith. For we are not, in this way, implying lowliness on the part of the divine substance, but are making plain the existence of a single person comprising God and man. Therefore, in the incarnation of God it is understood that no humiliation of God came about: rather it is believed that human nature was exalted.

B. Very well. Let nothing which is said of Christ in terms of the weakness of mankind be reckoned to refer to his divine nature. But how will it possibly be proved a just and rational thing that God treated, and allowed to be treated, in this way, the man whom he, as Father, called his beloved Son in whom he was well pleased, and whose nature he, as Son, took upon himself? For what justice is it for the man who was of all the most just to be put to death for a sinner? What man would not be judged worthy of condemnation, if he were to condemn someone innocent and release the guilty party? For the argument seems to be moving towards the same unsatisfactory position which was referred to earlier. If God could not save sinners except by condemning a just man, where is his omnipotence? If, on the other hand, he was capable of doing so, but did not will it, how shall we defend his wisdom and justice?

A. God the Father did not treat that man as you apparently understand him to have done; nor did he hand over an innocent man to be killed in place of the guilty party. For the Father did not coerce Christ to face death against his will, or give permission for him to be killed, but Christ himself of his own volition underwent death in order to save mankind.   ✳

B. Even if it was not against the will of Christ, since he consented to the will of the Father, it nevertheless seems that the Father did coerce him, through the instructions he gave him. For it is said that Christ 'humbled himself, becoming obedient even to death, death, moreover, on the cross; because of which God has raised him

up on high' [Phil. 2: 8 f.], and that 'He learnt obedience from his sufferings' [Heb. 5: 8], and that the Father 'did not spare his only Son,
but handed him over on behalf of us all' [Rom. 8: 31]. And the Son
says the same: 'I have not come to do my own will, but the will of
him who sent me' [John 6: 38]. And, as he was about to go to his
passion, he said, 'I am acting in accordance with the command which
my Father gave me' [John 14: 31]. Likewise: 'The cup which my
Father gave me, shall I not drink it?' [John 18: 11] And in another
place: 'Father, if it is possible, let this cup pass from me; nevertheless, not in accordance with my will but yours' [Matt. 26: 39]. And:
'Father, if this cup cannot pass from me unless I drink it, let your
will be done' [Matt. 26: 42]. Everywhere here it is apparent that
Christ endured death under the compulsion of obedience, rather
than through the intention of his own free will.

9. *That he died voluntarily. Also the meaning of: 'He became*
   obedient, even to death' [Phil. 2: 8], and 'Because of which,
   God has raised him up' [Phil. 2: 9], and 'I have not come
   to do my own will' [cf. John 6: 38], and 'He did not spare
   his own Son' [Rom. 8: 32], and 'Not according to my will,
   but yours' [Matt. 26: 39]

A. You are not drawing a proper distinction, it seems to me,
between, on the one hand, what Christ did because of the demands
of his obedience, and, on the other, the suffering, inflicted upon him
because he maintained his obedience, which he underwent even
though his obedience did not demand it.

B. I need you to explain this more clearly.

A. Why did the Jews persecute Christ to the extent of killing him?

B. For no other reason than that he had maintained truth
and righteousness unflinchingly in his way of life and in what he
said.

A. This, I think, is what God demands from every rational creature, and every creature owes this to God as a matter of obedience.

B. That is what we ought to accept.

A. Therefore that particular man, Christ, owed this obedience to
God his Father, and his humanity owed it to his divinity, and the
Father was demanding this from him.

B. No one could doubt this.

A. See: here you have what Christ did because of the demands of his obedience.

B. That is true, and now I see what infliction it was that he underwent because he persevered in acting obediently. For it was death which was inflicted upon him owing to the fact that he remained steadfast in obedience, and it was this that he underwent. But I do not understand why his obedience does not demand this.

A. Supposing a man had never sinned: would he be under an obligation to suffer death? Would God be obliged to demand this from him?

B. In accordance with our beliefs, the man would not die, and neither would this be demanded from him. But I wish to hear a reasoned account of this matter from you.

A. You do not deny that rational creation was created righteous, and was so created for the purpose of being happy in the fact of God's delighted approval?

B. I do not deny this.

A. You will, moreover, not reckon it to be at all appropriate for God to force a creature—whom he has created righteous for the purpose of happiness—to be pitiably afflicted, in spite of an absence of guilt?

B. It is evident that, if the man had not sinned, God ought not to demand death from him.

A. God, therefore, did not force Christ to die, there being no sin in him. Rather, he underwent death of his own accord, not out of an obedience consisting in the abandonment of his life, but out of an obedience consisting in his upholding of righteousness so bravely and pertinaciously that as a result he incurred death.

It can also be said that the Father instructed him to die when he gave the instructions as a result of which he incurred death. In this way he acted 'in accordance with the command which his Father gave him' and he drank 'the cup which he gave' and he was 'made obedient' to the Father 'even to death' and he 'learnt obedience from his sufferings', that is, how obedience should be maintained. For the word 'learnt' which is used in this context can be understood in two ways. Either 'learnt' is said in place of 'he caused others to learn'[7] or it means: 'he learnt by experience something about which he used to

[7] *Discere* = 'to teach' is a recognized late-Latin usage.

have a theoretical awareness'. As for the assertion of the Apostle: after having said that Christ 'humbled himself, made obedient even to death, death, moreover, on the cross', he added, 'because of which God both raised him up and has given him a name which is above every name' [Phil. 2: 8 f.]—which is like the saying of David, 'He drank from the brook by the way, because of which he raised up his head' [Ps. 109 = 110: 7, with variants on the Vulgate text]. The wording used by the Apostle does not have the implication that Christ could in no way have arrived at the exalted position referred to except though this obedience involving death, and that this exalted position would not be granted to him except in return for this obedience. For before he had undergone his passion, Christ himself said that 'all things' had been 'handed over' to him 'by the Father' [Luke 10: 22] and that all things belonging to the Father were his [cf. John 16: 15]. Rather the Apostle's saying is so phrased in the light of the fact that Christ, along with the Father and the Holy Spirit, had determined that the way in which he would demonstrate the exaltedness of his omnipotence should be none other than through his death. For, seeing that it had been determined that this demonstration should come about by no other means than through his death, it is not inappropriate to say that it comes about 'because' of it.

As for what Christ himself says: 'I came not to do my will but the will of him who sent me' [John 6: 38], this is a saying of the same sort as 'My teaching is not my own' [John 7: 16]. For what a person possesses not from himself but from God, he ought to call not so much his own as God's. Indeed, no man possesses the truth that he teaches, or a just desire, from himself, but from God. Christ, therefore, did not come to do his will, but the will of his Father, because the just desire which he had came not from his humanity but from his divinity. Moreover, to say that God 'did not spare his Son but handed him over on our behalf', is the same as saying: he did not release him. For many sayings of this kind are found in Holy Scripture. And where he says, 'Father, if it is possible, let this cup pass from me: nevertheless, not according to my wish, but yours', and, 'If this cup cannot pass away unless I drink it, let your will be done', what he is meaning by his own will is the natural pursuit of safety whereby his human flesh was trying to escape the pain of death. And indeed he speaks of the will of his Father not because the Father willed his Son's death in preference to his life, but because the Father was unwilling for the restoration of the human race to be brought about by other means than that a man should perform an action of the magnitude of that death. Moreover, it is because reason did not absolutely require that another person could not perform the deed,[8] that the Son is saying that the Father wills his death, which he—the Son—himself prefers to suffer rather than allow the human race not to be saved. It is as if he were saying, 'Since you do not wish the reconciliation of the world to take place in any other way, I say that you are, in this way, willing my death. Let this will of yours come to pass, that is, let my death come to pass, so that the world may be reconciled to you.' For we often say that someone wishes something because there is something else that he does not wish for, the reasoning being that if he did wish for this second thing, his first alleged wish would not be fulfilled. For example we say, 'He wants the lamp to go out', when someone does not wish to close a window through which a draught is coming which is putting out the lamp. The Father, then, wished the death of the Son in the sense that it was not his will that the world should be saved by any means, as I have said, other than that a man should perform an action of this magnitude. Since no one else could perform the deed, this consideration was as weighty, from the point of view of the Son, in his desire for the salvation of mankind, as if the Father were instructing him to die. Hence he acted 'in accordance with the command that the Father gave' him, and 'he drank the cup which the Father gave' him, 'obedient even to death'.

10. *Once more on these same texts: other ways in which they can be correctly understood*

Another possible correct interpretation is this. It was through the channel of that dutiful willingness whereby the Son was willing to die for the salvation of the world that the Father 'gave' him a 'command'—not however coercing him—and the 'cup' of the passion, and 'did not spare' him 'but handed him over on our behalf', and also willed his Son's death. It was also through this willingness that the Son was 'obedient even to death' and 'learnt obedience from

---

[8] Lat. *quia non poscebat ratio quod alius facere non poterat*. But the first *non* is puzzling in view of the preceding argument and *quoniam alius hoc facere non valebat* below (Schmitt 64.9). Perhaps deletion of *non* should be considered.

the things which he suffered'. For, just as it was not in accordance
with human nature that he had the will to live righteously, correspondingly he could not have had that desire whereby he was willing
to die in order to bring about something so exceedingly good, from
any source other than from 'the Father of lights' by whom 'every
excellent gift and every perfect gift is given' [Jas. 1: 17]. And in the
same way that the Father is said to 'draw' a person by giving him a
desire, likewise it is not out of keeping for the assertion to be made
that he 'impels' him. For the Son says of the Father, 'No one comes
to me, unless the Father... has drawn him' [John 6: 44], and in just
the same way he could have said, 'unless he has impelled him'. Similarly, he could have asserted: 'No one incurs death for my name's
sake, unless the Father has impelled or drawn him.' For indeed, since
everyone is 'drawn' or 'impelled' to something which he steadfastly
desires, it is not inappropriate for it to be asserted of God that he
'draws' or 'impels' when he is the giver of such a desire. In this
'drawing' or 'impulsion' there is no inevitable element of violence
which is understood to be present: rather a spontaneous and heartfelt wish to hold on to the good desire which has been received. If,
then, it is an undeniable fact that the Father, by giving that desire,
had 'drawn' or 'impelled' his Son to his death, who will fail to see
that he gave him the 'command' to endure death willingly according
to the same logic whereby he gave him the 'cup' for him to drink not
unwillingly. And if it is correct to say that the Son did not spare
himself and handed himself over on our behalf, who will deny that
it is correct to say that 'the Father', from whom he had this kind of
desire, 'did not spare him, but handed him over on our behalf', and
willed his death? It was also in this way, by holding steadfastly and
of his own free will to a desire which he had received from the Father,
that the Son became 'obedient even to death' and 'learnt obedience
from the things which he suffered', that is to say, learnt the magnitude of the deed which had to be accomplished through obedience.
For absolute and true obedience is that which occurs when a rational
being, not under compulsion but voluntarily, keeps to a desire which
has been received from God.

    There are other ways, too, in which we can interpret the notion
that the Father willed the Son's death, although these ones may
suffice. For instance, when we see someone wishing to endure an
affliction bravely, in order that he may bring a good desire to

fulfilment, although we express a wish for him to endure that suffering, the object of our wish and our love is not his suffering, but his will-power. It is also our custom to say of someone who is capable of preventing something, but does not prevent it, that he 'wishes' for the thing which he does not prevent. In view of the fact, therefore, that the Son's will was pleasing to the Father, and the Father did not prevent him from willing or fulfilling what he desired, it is a correct assertion to say that he 'wished' his Son to endure death in this way, so dutifully and so beneficially—even though he did not like his punishment. It was not, however, because the Son could not avoid death if he wished to, that he said that his cup could not pass from him if he did not drink it, but rather on the reasoning that—as has been said—it was impossible otherwise for the world to be saved. Therefore, his purpose in speaking those words was to teach the human race that it could not have been saved by any means other than by his death. He was not meaning to express the notion that he was utterly incapable of avoiding death. For all the sayings about Christ which are phrased in ways similar to these are to be interpreted in the light of a belief that he died not under any compulsion but of his own free will. For he was omnipotent, and it is said of him that, 'he was sacrificed because he himself willed it' [Isa. 53: 7 Vulg.]. And he himself says, 'I lay down my life so that I may take it a second time. No one is taking it away from me, but I am laying it down of my own accord. I have the power to lay it down and I have the power to take it again' [John 10: 17]. It cannot, therefore, be correctly said of him that he is in any way compelled to this action which he performs by his own power and will.

B. There is just one thing that does not seem to be fitting for such a Father with regard to such a Son—the fact that God allows him to be treated in this way, even if it is with his consent.

A. On the contrary, it is most fitting that such a Father should agree with such a Son, if he has a desire which is praiseworthy in being conducive to the honour of God and useful in being aimed at the salvation of mankind, something which could not come about in any other way.

B. We are still involved in the question of how that death can be shown to be in accordance with reason, and necessary. For certainly, if it is not, it seems that the Son ought not to have wished it, nor the Father to have made it obligatory or permitted it. For the question is: why God could not save mankind in any other way. Now, it seems unfitting for God to have saved mankind in that way, and it is not self-evident how that death to which you refer is an effective means of saving mankind. For it is a surprising supposition that God takes delight in, or is in need of, the blood of an innocent man, so as to be unwilling or unable to spare the guilty except in the event that the innocent has been killed.

A. Since in this enquiry you are taking on the guise of the people who are unwilling to believe anything without a prior demonstration of its logicality, I wish to come to an agreement with you: that no inappropriateness where God is concerned—not even the smallest—shall be accepted by us, and that no logical consideration—not even the smallest—shall be rejected by us unless a more important logical consideration conflicts with it. For just as, in the case of God, what follows from any inappropriateness—however small—is impossibility, correspondingly what follows from a small logical consideration, if it is not defeated by a larger one, is inevitability.

B. Nothing could please me more in this undertaking than that this agreement should be adhered to by both of us.

A. Our enquiry is exclusively about the incarnation of God and the things which we believe about his having taken manhood upon himself?

B. Yes.

A. Let us posit, therefore, that the incarnation of God and the things which we say about him as man had never happened, and let it be agreed between us that man was created for a state of blessedness which cannot be had in this life, and that no one can arrive at that state if his sins have not been got rid of, and that no man can pass through this life without sin; let us also accept the other matters in which we need to have faith in order to attain eternal salvation.

B. Let this be done, because nothing in these stipulations seems impossible or inappropriate for God.

A. The remission of sins, therefore, is something absolutely necessary for man, so that he may arrive at blessed happiness.

B. This we all agree.

11. *What it is to sin and to give recompense for sin*

A. What we have to investigate, therefore, is the question: 'By what rationale does God forgive the sins of men?' And, so that we may do this more clearly, let us first see what it is to sin and what it is to give satisfaction for sin.

B. It is for you to demonstrate and for me to pay attention.

A. If an angel or a man were always to render to God what he owes, he would never sin.

B. I cannot contradict this.

A. Then, to sin is nothing other than not to give God what is owed to him.

B. What is the debt which we owe to God?

A. All the will of a rational creature ought to be subject to the will of God.

B. Perfectly true.

A. This is the debt which an angel, and likewise a man, owes to God. No one sins through paying it, and everyone who does not pay it, sins. This is righteousness or uprightness of the will. It makes individuals righteous or upright in their heart, that is, their will. This is the sole honour, the complete honour, which we owe to God and which God demands from us. For only such a will, when it can act, performs actions which are pleasing to God. Even when it cannot act, it is pleasing in itself, because no work without it is pleasing. Someone who does not render to God this honour due to him is taking away from God what is his, and dishonouring God, and this is what it is to sin. As long as he does not repay what he has taken away, he remains in a state of guilt. And it is not sufficient merely to repay what has been taken away: rather, he ought to pay back more than he took, in proportion to the insult which he has inflicted. For just as, in the case of someone who injures the health of another, it is not sufficient for him to restore that person's health, if he does not pay some compensation for the painful injury which has been inflicted, similarly it is not sufficient for someone who violates someone else's honour, to restore that person's honour, if he does not, in consequence of the harmful act of dishonour, give, as restitution to the person whom he has dishonoured, something pleasing to that person. One should also observe that when someone repays what he has unlawfully stolen, what he is under an obligation to give is not the same as what it would be possible to demand from him, were it not that he had seized the other person's property. Therefore, everyone who sins is under an obligation to repay to God the honour which he has violently taken from him, and this is the satisfaction which every sinner is obliged to give to God.

Summary

B. With regard to all these matters, seeing we have undertaken to adopt a logical approach, I have nothing to say in contradiction, though you frighten me a little.

12. *Whether it is fitting for God to forgive a sin out of mercy alone, without any restitution of what is owed to him*

A. Let us now return to the main argument and see whether it is fitting for God to forgive a sin out of mercy alone, without any restitution of the honour taken away from him.

B. I do not see why this should not be fitting.

A. To forgive a sin in this way is nothing other than to refrain from inflicting punishment. And if no satisfaction is given, the way to regulate sin correctly is none other than to punish it. If, therefore, it is not punished, it is forgiven without its having been regulated.

B. What you say is logical.

A. But it is not fitting for God to allow anything in his kingdom to slip by unregulated.

B. I am in fear of sinning, if I want to disagree.

A. Therefore, it is not fitting for God to forgive a sin without punishment.

B. That follows.

A. There is another thing which also follows, if a sin is forgiven without punishment: that the position of sinner and non-sinner before God will be similar—and this does not befit God.

B. I cannot deny it.

A. Consider this too. Everyone knows that the righteousness of mankind is subject to a law whereby it is rewarded by God with a recompense proportional to its magnitude.

B. This is our belief.

A. If, however, sin is neither paid for nor punished, it is subject to no law.

B. I cannot interpret the matter in any other way.

A. Therefore, sinfulness is in a position of greater freedom, if it is forgiven through mercy alone, than righteousness—and this seems extremely unfitting. And the incongruity extends even further: it makes sinfulness resemble God. For, just as God is subject to no law, the same is the case with sinfulness.

B. I cannot object to your reasoning. But, when God teaches us to forgive those who sin against us, he seems to be being contradictory—in teaching us to do something which it is not fitting for him to do himself.

A. There is no contradiction in this, because God is giving us this teaching in order that we should not presume to do something which belongs to God alone. For it belongs to no one to take vengeance, except to him who is Lord of all. I should explain that when earthly powers take action in this way in accordance with right, it is the Lord himself, by whom they have been appointed for the task, who is acting.

B. You have removed what I thought to be an inherent contradiction. But there is another matter about which I want your answer. For, since God is so free that he is subject to no law and no judgement, and is so benevolent that nothing can be conceived of more benevolent than he, and since there is nothing right or proper except what he wishes, it does seem surprising that we should be saying that he is in no way willing to forgive an injury to himself, or that it is not permissible for him to do so, whereas we are in the habit of seeking forgiveness from him even for things we do to other people.

A. What you say about God's freedom, his will and his benevolence is true, but we ought, in our reasoning, to understand these concepts in such a way as not to impugn his dignity. For the term 'freedom' relates only to the freedom to perform what is advantageous or fitting, and one should not give the name of 'benevolence' to something which brings about a result unfitting for God. A statement that, 'What God wills is just and what he does not will is unjust', is not to be understood as meaning that, 'If God wishes anything whatsoever that is unfitting, it is just, since it is he who wills it'. For the argument that, 'If it is God's will to tell a lie, it is just to tell a lie', is a *non sequitur*. Rather, the liar is not God. For a will cannot wish to tell a lie, if it is not one in which the truth has been corrupted, or, more accurately, one which has been corrupted by the fact of deserting the truth. When, therefore, one says, 'If it is God's will to tell a lie', this is no different from saying, 'If God is a being such as to wish to tell a lie'. It does not follow, then, that telling a lie is just. Unless, that is, we adopt an interpretation of the kind used when we say with reference to two impossibles, 'If this thing is so, then that thing is so', when neither 'this' nor 'that' is the case; for instance, if one were to say, 'If water is dry, then fire is wet', given that neither is true. It is therefore only true to make the statement, 'If it is God's will, then it is just', about things which it is not unfitting for God to wish. For if it is God's will that it should rain, then it is a just thing that it should rain; and if it is his will that some man should be killed, then it is just that he should be killed. In consequence of this reasoning, if it is not fitting for God to do anything in an unjust and unregulated manner, it does not belong to his freedom or benevolence or will to release unpunished a sinner who has not repaid to God what he has taken away from him.

B. You are removing all the objections which I thought could be raised against you.

A. Consider further why it is not fitting for God to act in this way.

B. I am happy to listen to whatever you say.

13. *That there is nothing in the universal order more intolerable than that a creature should take away from the Creator the honour due to him, and not repay what he takes away*

A. There is nothing more intolerable in the universal order than that a creature should take away honour from the creator and not repay what he takes away.

B. Nothing is more self-evident than this.

A. There is nothing, furthermore, which it is more unjust to tolerate than the most intolerable thing in the universal order.

B. That, too, is very clear.

A. I think, therefore, that you will not say that God ought to tolerate something which it is the greatest injustice in the universe to tolerate, namely: that a creature should not give back to God what he takes away.

B. No, on the contrary, I see that this needs to be utterly denied.

A. Likewise, if there is nothing greater and nothing better than God, then there is nothing, in the government of the universe, which the supreme justice, which is none other than God himself, preserves more justly than God's honour.

B. This too is perfectly plain.

A. There is nothing, therefore, which God preserves more justly than the honour of his dignity.

B. I must grant this to be so.

A. Does it seem to you that he is preserving his honour intact if he allows it to be taken from himself on such terms that, on the one hand, it is not repaid to him, and, on the other, he does not punish the person who takes it?

B. I dare not say so.

A. It is a necessary consequence, therefore, that either the honour which has been taken away should be repaid, or punishment should follow. Otherwise, either God will not be just to himself, or he will be without the power to enforce either of the two options; and it is an abominable sin even to consider this possibility.

14. *What sort of honouring of God the punishment of a sinner constitutes*

B. I realize that nothing more logical could be said. But I want to hear from you whether the punishment of a sinner redounds to God's honour, or what kind of honour it is. For, if the punishment of a sinner is not an honouring of God, since the sinner does not repay what he has taken from God, but instead is punished, God loses his honour without recovering it; and this seems contradictory to earlier assertions.

A. It is impossible for God to lose his honour. For either a sinner of his own accord repays what he owes or God takes it from him against his—the sinner's—will. This is because either a man of his own free will demonstrates the submission which he owes to God by not sinning, or alternatively by paying recompense for his sin, or else God brings him into submission to himself against his will, by subjecting him to torment, and in this way he shows that he is his Lord, something which the man himself refuses to admit voluntarily. In this connection, it needs to be borne in mind that, just as a man by sinning seizes what belongs to God, likewise God, by punishing him, takes away what belongs to man. For it is not just a person's present property which is said to belong to him, but what it is in his power to possess. Since, therefore, man was created in such a way as to be capable of possessing blessed happiness, if he were not to sin, when he is deprived of blessedness and of all that is good, on account of sin, he is paying back what he has violently seized from his own property, however much this is against his will. For, although God does not transfer what he seizes to a use which is to his own advantage, in the way that a man diverts to a use advantageous to himself money which he takes from another person, God nevertheless utilizes for his own honour what he takes away, through the fact of his taking it away. For by seizing the sinner and his belongings, he affirms that they are subject to himself.

15. *Whether God allows his honour to be violated even to a limited extent*

B. What you say pleases me. But there is another question to which I demand an answer. For, if it is right for God to preserve his honour in the way you affirm, why does he allow it to be violated even to a limited extent? For something which is allowed to be damaged in any way is not being guarded entirely or perfectly.

A. Nothing can be added to, or subtracted from, the honour of God, in so far as it relates to God himself. For this same honour is, in relation to him, inherently incorruptible and in no way capable of change. But when any creature whatever maintains, either by natural instinct or in response to reason, the station in life which belongs to it and has been, as it were, taught to it, this creature is said to be obeying God and honouring him. This is so most of all in the case of a rational being, to whom it has been given to understand what is right. When such a being desires what is right, he is honouring God, not because he is bestowing anything upon God, but because he is voluntarily subordinating himself to his will and governance, maintaining his own proper station in life within the natural universe, and, to the best of his ability, maintaining the beauty of the universe itself. But when a rational being does not wish for what is right, he dishonours God, with regard to himself, since he is not willingly subordinating himself to God's governance, and is disturbing, as far as he is able, the order and beauty of the universe. In spite of this, he does not harm or besmirch the honour of God to the slightest extent.

For, if those things which are contained within the ambit of heaven were to wish not to be under heaven, or to move away from heaven, it would in no way be possible for them to be anywhere other than under heaven, or to flee from heaven without approaching heaven. This is because, wherever they came from, and wherever they were going to, and by whatever route, they would be beneath heaven, and the further they would remove themselves from any part of heaven, the nearer they would approach to the part opposite. Thus, even should a human being or a bad angel not wish to be subject to the divine will or governance, he cannot flee from it, because, if he wishes to escape from a will that issues orders, he runs beneath a will that inflicts punishment; and if you ask by what route he passes from one to the other, it is nowhere other than beneath a will that gives permission; and the supreme Wisdom changes his wrong desire or action into the order and beauty of the universal scheme of things to which I have been referring. For—setting aside the fact that God does many good things, in all manner of ways, for the benefit of wrong-doers—the alternatives, voluntary recompense for wrongdoing, or the exaction of punishment from someone who does not give recompense, retain their own proper place in this same universal order and their own regulatory beauty. If the divine Wisdom did not impose these forms of recompense in cases where wrongdoing is endeavouring to upset the right order of things, there would be in the universe, which God ought to be regulating, a certain ugliness, resulting from the violation of the beauty of order, and God would appear to be failing in his governance. Since these two consequences are as impossible as they are unfitting, it is inevitable that recompense or punishment follows upon every sin.

B. You have given a satisfactory answer to my objection.

A. It is plain, therefore, that no one can honour or dishonour God, so far as God himself is concerned, but, in so far as the other party is concerned, a person appears to do this when he subjects himself to God's will, or does not subject himself.

B. I do not know what I can say to the contrary.

16. *The rationale whereby the number of angels who have fallen is to be made up for from mankind*

A. Let me add yet another point.

B. Keep talking until I am tired of listening.

A. It is agreed that it was God's plan to make up for the number of angels who had fallen, by drawing upon the human race, which he created sinless.

B. We believe this, but I would like some reasoned account of it.

A. You are cheating me! For we made it our plan to treat no subject other than the incarnation of God, and you are bringing in other questions for me.

B. Do not be angry. 'God loves a cheerful giver' [1 Cor. 9: 7]. Now, no one proves more emphatically that he is giving a promised gift cheerfully than someone who gives more than his promise entails. Please agree, then, to speak in answer to my question.

A. It should not be doubted that reasoning beings, who either are happy in the contemplation of God, or shall be happy, exist in a rationally calculated and perfect number known in advance by God, and that thus it would not be fitting for it to be greater or less. For either God does not know in what number it would be best[9] for reasoning beings to exist—a false supposition, or, if he does know, he will bring it about that they exist in the number which he will recognize to be most fitting for this purpose. Therefore, either the angels who have fallen were created so as to have their being within that number, or, alternatively, it was from necessity that they fell, because, being superfluous to that number, they could not keep their place— which is an absurd notion.

B. The truth of what you are saying is apparent.

A. Since, therefore, they must have been of that number, either their number has inevitably to be made up, or the number of rational beings will remain smaller than was foreseen previously in that perfect number—and that is impossible.

B. Beyond doubt, they have to be replaced.

A. It is necessary, therefore, that their number should be made up from the human race, because there is no other race from which it can be made complete.

17. *That other angels may not be put in their place*

B. Why cannot the fallen angels themselves be reinstated, or other angels reinstated in their place?

A. When you come to see the difficulty of our restoration, you

---

[9] Where 'best' and 'most fitting' are used it is assumed that the comparatives *melius* and *decentiorem* are used in a superlative sense.

will understand the impossibility of reconciliation with the fallen angels. And the reason why other angels cannot be reinstated in place of them—not to mention the consideration that this would seem to be contrary to the perfection of the original creation—is that it is not right that they should be put in their place if it is not possible for them to be such as those others would have been if they had not sinned. For supposing, in actuality, there exist two individuals, one who is unacquainted with the punishment of sin and another who looks all the time upon eternal punishment, both of whom remain steadfast, the two are not praiseworthy to an equal degree. Now, it is certainly not to be thought that the good angels were confirmed in their standing by the fall of the bad: rather it was by their own merit. For if the good had sinned along with the bad, they would have been condemned at the same time, and similarly the unrighteous, if they had kept their place along with the righteous, would have been confirmed in their standing. Indeed, if it were the case with any of them that the necessity for their being confirmed in standing depended solely on the fall of others, the consequence would be either that no one would ever receive this confirmation, or else that it would be necessary for one of them to fall in order that others should be confirmed. And both of these suppositions are absurd. Therefore, those who have retained their standing have been confirmed in the way in which all would have been confirmed if they had retained their standing. I have explained as far as I was able what this way would have been, in my treatment of the question why God did not give the devil perseverance.[10]

B. You have proved that bad angels ought to be replaced from the human race, and it is clear from the reasoning just presented that the human elect will not be fewer in number than the sinful angels. But are they to be more numerous? Clarify this, if you can.

18. *Whether there are to be more holy people than bad angels*

A. If the angels, before any of them fell, existed in that full number about which we have spoken, then human beings were created solely for the purpose of replacing the angels who had been brought to perdition, and it is plain that they will not be greater in

---

[10] i.e. in the treatise *On the Fall of the Devil*.

number than these. If, on the other hand, the number of all the angels in existence did not add up to that perfect number, what needs to be supplied is both the number of those who have been brought to perdition and the number which had previously been lacking. Moreover, there will be more elect people than sinful angels, and thus we shall say that human beings were not created solely for the restoration of a number which has been depleted, but also to make up a number which was not yet complete.

B. What position is one to prefer? Were the angels created previously in a number which was complete, or not?

A. I will say what seems right to me.

B. I cannot ask more from you.

A. If mankind was created after the fall of the bad angels, as some people take the text in Genesis to imply, I do not see that I can, on the strength of this, prove conclusively either of these alternatives. For it is a possibility, I think, that angels previously existed in their complete number, and that mankind was subsequently created in order to make up their depleted number; it is also a possibility that they did not exist in their full number, because God was delaying— just as he is still delaying—the completion of that number, intending to create the human race in his own good time, and it would follow that he would either only be making up a number not yet complete, or—an additional possibility—if the as yet incomplete number were depleted, restoring that number. However, suppose that the whole of creation happened at the same time, and those 'days' in which Moses appears to say this universe was created, not all of it simultaneously, are to be understood in a different way from the way in which we view the 'days' in which we live. In this case, I cannot see how angels were created in the complete number to which we have been referring. If this were so, it seems to me that either some angels or humans were of necessity going to fall in future, or they would be more numerous, in the renowned heavenly city, than was demanded by the inherent rightness of that perfect number. If, therefore, all things were created simultaneously, it appears that the angels and the first two human beings were comprised in a number which was incomplete to the extent that, if no angel were to fall, it would only be the deficiency inherent in the incomplete number that would be made up for from the human race, and, if any were to perish, the fact of his fall would also be made up for. Moreover, the fact that human nature is somewhat weak would, as it were, excuse God and confound the devil, supposing the devil were to attribute his fall to his own weakness, while human nature, though weaker, was standing firm. Furthermore, supposing it were human nature that fell, something which would all the more serve to vindicate God against the devil and against human nature itself, would be the consideration that, whereas humanity was itself very weak and mortal, the ascent which it would be making, in the case of the elect, would be from a position of such great weakness to a place which was higher than that from which the devil had fallen. For the elevation of the place which is humanity's due, on a level with the good angels, is higher than the devil's former place to the same degree that these good angels have earned higher standing as a result of their steadfastness after the ruin of the bad ones.

For these reasons, it seems to me that, in the case of the angels, the number whereby the city above is to be given its full complement was not complete. For, if mankind was not created at the same time as the angels, this is a possibility, and if both mankind and the angels were created simultaneously—a view which many people prefer, since one reads, 'He who lives for ever created all things at the same time' [Ecclus. 18: 1]—it appears to be an inevitability. But even if the 'completeness' of universal creation is not so much to be understood in terms of the number of individuals as in the number of races of creature in nature, it is inevitably the case either that the human race was created for the fulfilment of that 'completeness' of creation, or that it is superfluous to it—something which we dare not say of the existence in nature of the smallest worm. Consequently, the human race was created on that occasion for its own sake, and not just for the replacement of individuals of another race. Hence it is plain that, even if no angel had perished, human beings would none the less have had their place in the heavenly city. It follows, therefore, that, in the case of the angels, there was no full complement at the time before some of them fell. Otherwise, it would have been a matter of necessity that either some humans or some angels should fall, since no one could remain in their place in excess of the complete number.

B. You have been achieving some results.

A. There is another consideration, so it seems to me, which gives not a little support to the view which reckons that angels were not created in their full complement.

B. Tell me it.

A. If angels were created in their full complement, and human beings were created for no other reason than for the replacement of fallen angels, it is plain that, if the angels had not fallen from their former state of blessedness, humans would not be ascending to it.

B. That makes sense.

A. If someone were to say that elect human beings will be rejoicing as much on account of the perdition of the angels as about their own reception into heaven—since undoubtedly the one would not be happening if the other had not occurred—how will they be able to be kept from indulgence in this perverse joy? Again, how are we to say that the angels who have fallen have been replaced by human beings, given that, if they had not fallen, they would have been going to remain for ever without that sin, that is, the sin of rejoicing in the fall of others, whereas these humans cannot be without it? Indeed, how will it be these human beings' right to be happy? Furthermore, how dare we say that God is unwilling or unable to bring about the replacement of the angels without this wrong?

B. There is a comparable situation, is there not, in the case of the Gentiles who have been called to the faith because the Jews have rejected it?

A. No. For supposing all the Jews had believed, the Gentiles would nevertheless be called, because, 'In every race, he who fears God and does what is right is acceptable to him' [Acts 10: 35]. But it was because the Jews despised the apostles that the apostles had an opportunity at that time to turn to the Gentiles.

B. I cannot see at all what I can say in contradiction.

A. From what source does that rejoicing in the fall of another seem to you to originate?

B. From where else but from the fact that each individual will be certain that he would definitely not be in the place where he is, were it not that someone else had fallen from that place?

A. If, therefore, no one had this certainty, there would be no reason why anyone would rejoice in the ruination of someone else.

B. So it seems.

A. Do you think that any of them will have this certainty, if it comes about that they are much more numerous than those who have fallen?

B. I cannot at all imagine that any of them would have this certainty, or that it would be obligatory for him to have it. For how will anyone be able to know whether he has been created for the purpose of restoring a number previously depleted, or to make up an as yet incomplete part of the number required for the city's establishment? However, all of them will be certain that they have been made for the sake of bringing that city to completion.

A. Therefore, if it comes about that they are more numerous than the wicked angels, no one will be able to know, nor will anyone be obliged to know, that he has not been received into heaven for any other reason than because of someone else's fall.

B. That is true.

A. Consequently, there will be no reason for anyone to be obliged to rejoice in the ruination of someone else.

B. That follows.

A. We see, then, that, if there are to be more elect human beings than there are wicked angels, there does not arise as a consequence that incongruity which inevitably does result if they are not to be more numerous than the angels. Since, therefore, it is impossible that there is to be any incongruity in the city to which we have referred, it appears to be a necessary consequence that angels were not created in the aforesaid full complement, and that there are to be more humans in a state of blessedness than there are angels in a state of wretchedness.

B. I cannot see by what logic this can be denied.

A. I think one can state another line of reasoning in support of the same opinion.

B. You ought to present this line of reasoning too.

A. We believe that the present physical mass of the universe is to be changed anew into something better. We believe that this will not come to pass until the number of elect humans has reached its final total, and the blessed city to which we have referred has been brought to completion; also that, after the completion of the city, the renewal will follow without delay. Hence, it may be inferred that God from the beginning planned to bring both these things to fulfilment simultaneously. For lower nature—nature insensible to God—certainly ought not to be brought to perfection before higher[11] nature—nature with an obligation to rejoice in God. Moreover, lower nature, being

[11] To be more precise, Latin speaks of 'lesser' and 'greater' nature (*minor... maior*) rather than 'lower' and 'higher'.

itself changed at the bringing of higher nature to perfection, would, so to speak, rejoice in its own way. No, indeed: <u>every created thing would be happy, each in its own way joining in eternal rejoicing in its Creator and in itself and in their mutual relation to one another, upon this final fulfilment of itself, so glorious and so amazing</u>. This is because even an insensible creature would display naturally, through God's ordinance, what the will brings to pass in the case of a rational being. For it is our custom to rejoice in the exaltation of those greater than ourselves, for example when we take pleasure in festive exultation at the nativities of saints, rejoicing in their glory.[12]

A consideration which seems to support the opinion which we are discussing is that, <u>supposing Adam had not sinned, God would none the less be delaying the completion of the city referred to, until, on the completion from the human race of the number which he was waiting for, humans too would undergo change—to coin a phrase—into an undying bodily immortality</u>. For they used to have, in the Garden, a sort of immortality, that is, the power not to die; but this was not an undying power, because it could die—in the sense, I mean, that Adam and Eve could not not die. If it is the case that God planned from the outset to bring to completion simultaneously that blessed city characterized by rationality and this natural universe characterized by insensibility,[13] several possibilities seem to follow. Either that city was not complete in its number of angels before the fall of the bad ones, but God was waiting to fill up this number with humans at the time when he would be changing the physical nature of the universe into something better; or alternatively, supposing it was complete in its number of angels, it was not complete in the sense that its establishment had been confirmed, and the confirmation of its establishment,[14] even if no one within it had sinned, was to be delayed until the transformation of the universe which we are awaiting; otherwise, supposing this confirmation of its establishment could not be delayed any longer, that transformation of our universe would have to be hastened on, so that it would happen along with the confirming of the city's establishment. But it is a totally illogical supposition that God should have decided to renew immediately a newly created universe, and that he should at the very beginning have

---

[12] Here the paragraph division does not follow that of Schmitt.

[13] Lat. *rationalem illam et beatam civitatem et hanc mundanam insensibilemque naturam.*

[14] 'Confirmation of its establishment': Lat. simply *confirmatio.*

decided to destroy those things which will not exist after the renewal, before the reasons for their creation became apparent. It follows therefore that the angels did not exist in their full complement, the consequence of this state of affairs being that confirmation of their standing would not be long deferred. The reason why not is this: the renewal of the new universe would need to happen quickly—which is an incongruous notion. However, it seems unfitting that God should have wished to postpone that same confirmation until the future renewal of the universe, especially given that, in the case of some other creatures, he brought about this confirmation so swiftly that it is a reasonable notion that, where the first humans were concerned, it was at the time when they sinned that God would have brought about their confirmation, supposing they had not sinned— just as he did in the case of the angels who remained steadfast. For, even though they would not yet be promoted to that position of equality with the angels, to which human beings were to attain, since the full complement of the angels was to be made up from the human race, it appears that, by the terms of the justice under which they had their being, if they had been victorious in not sinning when tempted, they would be confirmed along with all their progeny, so as to be unable to sin any more. For, according to the same justice, because they were defeated and sinned, they went unconfirmed, as a consequence of which—insofar as it is a matter of their own power— they cannot be without sin. For who would dare to say that the power of unrighteousness to bind a person in servitude upon that person's consent to its first enticement, would be stronger than the power of righteousness to confirm a person in liberty as a result of his adherence to it when first tempted? Now, the whole nature of the human race was inherent in its first parents; human nature was as a result entirely defeated in them with the consequence that it became sinful—with the exception of that one man alone, whom God knew how to set apart from the sin of Adam, just as he knew how to create him of a virgin without the seed of a man. In just the same way, human nature would have been entirely victorious, if they had not sinned. It remains, therefore, for it to be stated that the heavenly city was not complete in that original number of angels, but had to have that number made up by humans. If this is established, there will be more elect human beings than wicked angels.

B. The things which you are saying seem very reasonable to me.

But what are we to say about the text where we read that God 'determined the limits of the peoples according to the number of the children of Israel' [Deut. 32: 8]. Some authorities, because the reading 'of the angels of God'[15] is found, explain this text as meaning that the number of elect humans to be received into heaven corresponds to the number of good angels.

A. This does not contradict the opinion previously stated, assuming it is not certain that the same number of angels remained steadfast as had fallen. For, if there are more elect angels than wicked ones, it is a necessity that elect humans should replace the wicked angels and it is a possibility that they will be equal to the number of the blessed ones; and thus there will be more righteous humans than unrighteous angels. But remember with what stipulation I have undertaken to reply to your questioning: namely that, if I say anything which is not confirmed by a greater authority—even if I may seem to be proving it logically—it is not to be accepted as having any validity beyond the fact that it seems to me for the moment to be so, until God reveals to me something in any way better. For I am sure that, if I say anything which is undoubtedly contradictory to Holy Scripture, it is wrong; and, if I become aware of such a contradiction, I do not wish to hold to that opinion. But there are matters about which different opinions can be held without danger, and one such is the issue which gave rise to our present enquiry. For, supposing we do not know whether or not there are to be more elect human beings than there are fallen angels, and supposing we rate one of these alternatives more highly than the other, I do not think this constitutes any danger to the soul. If, in the case of issues of this sort, we expound divine sayings in such a way that they seem to support differing opinions, and nowhere can any indication be found whereby they determine which opinion is uncontrovertibly to be held, I do not consider that adverse criticism is in order.

Take the text of which you spoke: 'He determined the limits of the peoples'—or Gentiles—'according to the number of the angels of God', or in the reading of another translation, 'according to the number of the children of Israel'. Since both translations either mean the same thing, or different, but not incompatible, things, it must be understood that the meaning of both 'the angels of God'

---

[15] The reading of the Septuagint.

and 'the children of Israel' is: good angels alone, or only elect human beings, or angels and elect human beings together, that is to say, the whole of the heavenly city; or else the meaning of 'the angels of God' is the holy angels alone, and 'the children of Israel' righteous people alone, or alternatively it is angels alone who are meant by 'the children of Israel' and righteous people by 'the angels of God'. If the meaning of both of the two expressions is good angels alone, the implication is the same as if only 'the angels of God' occurred; but if the meaning is the whole heavenly city, the sense is that 'peoples', that is, the multitudes of elect human beings, will be received into heaven, or alternatively, that there will be 'peoples' in this temporal world, for as long as it takes for the as yet incomplete, predestined number which is the full complement of that city, to be made up from the human race.

But, as things stand, I do not see how 'the children of Israel' can be understood to mean angels alone, or angels and holy people together. On the other hand, it is not inapposite for holy people to be called 'children of Israel', just as they are called 'children of Abraham'. Holy people can also be correctly called 'angels of God' because they imitate the angelic life, because comparability and equality with the angels is promised to them in heaven; also because all who live righteously are 'angels of God', and because of this are called 'confessors' or 'martyrs'. For someone who 'confesses' or 'bears witness' to the truth of God is his messenger, that is, his 'angel'. And if, in accordance with what the Lord says with reference to Judas [John 6: 70 f.], a wicked person is a devil, because of the comparability of his evil-doing, why shall a good person not be called an angel, because of his imitation of righteousness? For this reason, I think, we can say that God 'determined the limits of the peoples according to the number of' elect human beings, because there will be 'peoples', and there will be procreation of the human race in this world, for so long as it takes for the number of elect human beings to be brought to its final total; and, once this number is complete, the reproduction of mankind which takes place in this life will cease to occur.

But if we understand by 'the angels of God' the holy angels alone, and by 'the children of Israel', only righteous human beings, there are two possible interpretations of 'God determined the limits of the peoples according to the number of the angels of God'. One is that it will be a people of equivalent number who will be received into heaven, that is, as many humans as there are holy angels of God. The other interpretation is that the peoples will have their being until the full number of the angels of God is made up from out of the human race. And 'God determined the limits of the peoples according to the number of the children of Israel' can, as I see it, only be interpreted in one way, namely the one already stated, that there will be peoples in this temporal world until the full number of holy people has been received into heaven. It will, moreover, be inferred from both translations that as many human beings are to be taken into heaven as there are angels who have kept their place. It will not, however, follow from this, even though the lost angels are to be replaced by humans, that as many angels have fallen as have remained in their place. If, however, this view—that as many human beings are to be taken into heaven as there are angels who have kept their place[16]—is asserted, one will need to discover how it is that there is no confirmation here of the lines of reasoning set out earlier, which seem to show that, in the case of the angels, before they fell, there was not in existence that full complement of which I have spoken earlier; that, moreover, there are to be more elect humans than there are bad angels.

B. I am not sorry that I obliged you to discuss these issues about the angels. For it has not been a pointless undertaking. Now return to the point from which our digression began.

19. *That mankind cannot be saved without recompense for sin*

A. It is agreed that it was God's plan to replace the fallen angels from out of the human race.

B. That is a certainty.

A. The humans in that heavenly city—those who are to be taken up into that city in place of angels—ought to be of like character to those who were to be there, whose substitutes they are to be, that is, the same in character as the good angels now are. Otherwise, those who have fallen will not be 'replaced', and it will follow either that God will not be able to accomplish the good which he has begun, or he will come to regret that he had initiated such a good undertaking—both of which notions are absurd.

---

[16] The parenthesis here is the translator's expansion, aimed at clarity.

B. Certainly, the humans in question ought to be equals of the good angels.

A. Have the good angels ever sinned?

B. No.

A. Suppose there is a human being who has on any occasion sinned, and has on any occasion failed to give recompense to God for his sin, but is merely being let off unpunished: can you think that he is the equal of an angel who has never sinned?

B. I can 'think' the words you have uttered and say them, but I cannot 'think' their meaning, any more than I can understand falsehood to be true.

A. It is not fitting, then, for God to receive into heaven, for the replacement of the fallen angels, a human sinner who has not paid recompense. For truth does not allow him to be raised up to equality with the blessed ones.

B. Reason makes this clear.

A. Consider also—viewing man in isolation, without reference to the supposition that he ought to be made equal with the angels—whether it is right for God to promote him in such a way to any state of blessedness whatsoever, even to that which he enjoyed before he committed sin.

B. Put what you are thinking into words, and I will consider it to the best of my ability.

A. Let us imagine that some rich man is holding in his hand a precious pearl—one which no dirt has ever touched, and which no one else could remove from his hand without his permission—and he is planning to put it into his treasure-chest, which is where his dearest and most precious possessions are.

B. I am thinking of this, just as if it were happening before us.

A. What if he were to allow this same pearl to be knocked out of his hand into the mud by some malignant person, although it was in his power to prevent this, and afterwards, picking it up from the mud, dirty and unwashed, were to store it away in some clean and costly receptacle of his, intending to keep it there in that state. Will you think him wise?

B. How can I? For surely it would be an appreciably better course to keep and store his pearl clean, rather than dirtied, would it not?

A. Would God not be acting in a similar way? In the Garden, he used, as it were, to hold man in his hand, destined for fellowship with the angels. He allowed the devil, aflame with envy, to strike him down into the mud, admittedly with man's consent. For the devil would not have been able to tempt mankind if it had been God's will to prohibit him. Would God, I repeat, not be acting in a similar way if he were to bring man back to Paradise stained with the filth of sin without any washing, that is, in the absence of any recompense, at least supposing man were to remain in this state for ever?

B. I dare not say that there would not be a resemblance, supposing God were to do this, and consequently I do not accept that he is capable of so acting. For it would appear either that he had not been able to bring to completion something which he had undertaken to do, or that he had come to regret his good undertaking—and these are not things which can happen to God.

A. Consider it, then, an absolute certainty, that God cannot remit a sin unpunished, without recompense, that is, without the voluntary paying off of a debt, and that a sinner cannot, without this, attain to a state of blessedness, not even the state which was his before he sinned. For, in this case, the person would not be restored, even to being the kind of person he was before his sin.

B. I cannot in the least contradict your lines of reasoning.

But why is it that we say to God: 'Forgive us our debts' [Matt. 6: 12 Vulg.: *dimitte nobis debita nostra . . .*], and that every nation prays to the God in whom it believes, that he should forgive its sins? For if we are paying off a debt, why do we pray that he should remit it? Surely God is not unjust, so as to demand a second time recompense which has been paid? On the other hand, if we are not paying recompense, why are we praying, pointlessly, for him to do something which he is not able to do, owing to the fact that it is unfitting?

A. It is to no avail that someone who is not making payment says, 'Forgive', and the reason why someone who is making payment makes supplication is that this very fact of his supplication is a contingency of relevance to the repayment of the debt. For God owes nothing to anyone, but all creation is in debt to him, and therefore it is not expedient that a human being should deal with God as an equal deals with an equal. But there is no need for me to reply to you now about this issue. When you come to realize why it was that Christ died, perhaps you will see for yourself the answer to your question.

B. Very well: your present reply to my question is sufficient for me now. As for the fact that no man with sin can attain to blessedness, and that he cannot be absolved from sin unless he repays what he has violently taken away through his sin: you have given me such a clear demonstration of this that I could have no doubt about it, even supposing I wanted to.

20. *That the recompense should be proportional to the size of the sin, and that a human being cannot, of himself, make this recompense*

A. Another thing about which you will have no doubts, I imagine, is that recompense ought to be proportional to the magnitude of the sin.

B. If it were not so, the sin would remain to some extent unregulated, which cannot be the case if God leaves nothing unregulated in his kingdom. But it has previously been stipulated that no inappropriateness, however small, is possible where God is concerned.

A. Tell me, then: what payment will you give God in recompense for your sin?

B. Penitence, a contrite and humbled heart, fasting and many kinds of bodily labour, the showing of pity through giving and forgiveness, and obedience.

A. What is it that you are giving to God by all these means?

B. Am I not honouring God? For out of fear and love of him I am rejecting temporal happiness in heartfelt contrition; in fasting and labouring I am trampling underfoot the pleasures and ease of this life; in giving and forgiveness I am exercising generosity; and in obedience I am making myself subject to him.

A. When you are rendering to God something which you owe him, even if you have not sinned, you ought not to reckon this to be recompense for what you owe him for sin. For you owe to God all the things to which you refer. For, in this mortal life, your love and your yearning—here prayer is of relevance—to reach the state of being for which you were created; your grief because you are not yet there and your fear that you may not arrive at it: these feelings should be so strong that you ought not to feel any happiness except in things which assist you to reach your journey's end and give you hope of arriving there. For you do not deserve to have something which you do not love and yearn for in a way proportional to its importance,

and about which you are not grieved, because you do not yet have it
and are still in such jeopardy as to whether you will have it or not.
Moreover, to flee from ease and worldly pleasures which distract the
soul from what is true ease and pleasure—except to the extent which
you reckon suffices for your aim of reaching your goal—this also
contributes to your strivings towards an ultimate goal. However, you
ought to reckon that what you are giving is in payment of a debt.
You ought likewise to understand that the things you are giving are
not your property but the property of him whose bondslave you are,
and to whom you are making the gift. And nature teaches you to act
towards your fellow-bondslave, that is, as a human towards a fellow
human-being, as you wish to be treated by him, and that someone
who is unwilling to give what he possesses does not deserve to receive
what he does not have. Now, concerning forgiveness, what I say, in
brief, is that acts of vengeance are none of your business, since you
are not your own man, nor is a person who has done wrong owned
either by you or by himself. Rather, you are both the bondslaves of
one Lord, having been made by him out of nothing and, if you take
vengeance on your fellow-bondsman, you are arrogantly presuming
to exercise over him the justice which is the prerogative of the Lord
and Judge of all. And in obedience, when truth is told, what are you
giving God that you do not owe him, seeing that it is your obligation
to give him, at his command, all that you are and all that you have
and all that you are capable of?

B. I do not dare say that, in any of these actions, I am giving to
God what I do not owe him.

A. What payment, then, are you going to make to God in recompense for your sin?

B. If, in order that I may not sin, I owe to him my own being and
all that I am capable of, <u>even when I do not sin, I have nothing to
give him in recompense for sin.</u>

A. <u>What, then, will become of you? How will you be saved?</u>

B. If I take account of your lines of reasoning, I do not see how
I can be. But supposing I return to my faith: in the Christian faith,
'which operates through love' [Gal. 5: 6], it is my hope that I can be
saved, and, because we read, 'If the wicked man turns from his
wickedness and does what is right...' [Ezek. 18: 27], it is my hope
that all his wicked acts are consigned to oblivion.

A. This is not addressed to anyone apart from those who either looked forward in anticipation to Christ before his coming, or believe in him after his coming. We, however, have posited a hypothetical situation where Christ and the Christian faith had never existed, since we have made it our aim to discover by reason alone whether his coming was essential for the salvation of mankind.

B. So we have.

A. Let us proceed, then, by reason alone.

B. Never mind the fact that you are leading me into a tight corner: it is very much my desire that you should proceed just as you began.

21. *How heavy the weight of sin is*

A. Let us hypothesize that those things which you proposed you could offer in repayment for sin are not a debt which you owe, and let us see whether they can suffice as recompense for a single sin, even so small a sin as one glance contrary to the will of God.

B. Were it not that I hear you calling this matter into question, I would think that I cancel this sin by a single moment of repentance.

A. You have not yet considered how heavy the weight of sin is.

B. Explain this to me now.

A. If you were to see yourself in the sight of God, and someone were to say to you, 'Look over there', and God were to interject, 'It is totally against my will that you should look', consider for yourself in your own heart what contingency there is, in the totality of things which exist, on account of which you are obliged to take that look contrary to the will of God.

B. I can think of no contingency requiring me to do this, unless, maybe, I should be placed in an unavoidable situation where it would be absolutely necessary for me either to do this or commit a greater sin.

A. Set aside that case of absolute necessity, and consider, with exclusive reference to the particular sin in question, whether you can commit it in order to secure your own redemption.

B. I see clearly that I cannot.

A. To come to the point and not detain you further, what if it were necessary either for the whole universe and whatever is not God to perish and be brought to nothing, or for you to do this thing, such a little thing, against the will of God?

B. When I consider the action itself, I see that it is an extremely

lightweight matter—but if I consider that[17] it is contrary to the will
of God, I realize that it is something extremely grave, and incomparably greater than any loss. But we are in the habit of doing something occasionally against someone's will in a way which is not
reprehensible, with the aim that his interests may be protected; and
this deed afterwards pleases the person against whose will we are
acting.

A. This happens in the case of the person who sometimes does
not understand what is in his own interest, or is incapable of replacing what he loses. But God lacks for nothing and, if all things were
to perish, he would be capable of restoring them in the same way
that he created them.

B. I have no alternative but to admit that, for the sake even of preserving the whole of creation, there is nothing which I ought to do
contrary to the will of God.

A. What if there were several universes, full of created beings,
just like this one?

B. If there were an infinite multiplicity of universes, and they
were similarly laid out before me, this is the answer which I would
give.

A. You could not be more absolutely right. But consider, too, if it
came about that you took that glance contrary to the will of God:
what recompense could you make for this sin?

B. There is nothing I possess greater than what I have spoken of
earlier.

A. This is how seriously we sin, whenever we knowingly do anything, however small, contrary to the will of God. For we are always
in his sight, and it is always the teaching he gives us that we should
not sin.

B. To judge from what I am hearing, we live very dangerously.

A. It is obvious that God demands recompense in proportion to
the magnitude of the sin.

B. Undeniably.

A. You do not therefore give recompense if you do not give something greater than the entity on account of which you ought not to
have committed the sin.

---

[17] The translation here presupposes a conjectural reading, *quod sit contra voluntatem
dei* . . . in place of *quid sit contra voluntatem dei* (Schmitt, 89.5).

B. I see that logic demands this: I also see that it is utterly impossible.

A. And God cannot raise up to a state of blessedness anyone who is to any extent bound by indebtedness arising from sin.

B. This verdict is an extremely grave one.

22. *What an insult a human being inflicts on God when he allows himself to be conquered by the devil—one for which he is incapable of paying recompense*

A. Listen to another reason why it is equally difficult for a human being to be reconciled with God.

B. If it were not that faith were consoling me, just the one reason would force me to despair.

A. Listen, even so.

B. Speak.

A. In the Garden, man was created without sin, as if he were placed there as God's deputy, in a position between God and the devil, the intention being that he might overcome the devil by not consenting when the devil recommended sin by means of persuasion. In the event that man were not to sin despite the devil's persuasion, this would vindicate and honour God and confound the devil, who, despite his greater strength, committed sin in heaven as a consequence of no one's persuasion. And although man was easily capable of doing this, he allowed himself to be conquered by persuasion alone, not under forcible compulsion. He did this in accordance with the will of the devil and contrary to the will and honour of God.

B. Where do you intend this argument to lead?

A. Judge for yourself whether it is not contrary to the honour of God that man should be reconciled with him so long as he is subject to the charge[18] of having inflicted this insult upon God—unless he has previously honoured God by conquering the devil just as he has dishonoured him by having been conquered by the devil. Now, the character of this victory ought to be as follows. In the same way that man, when he was strong and potentially immortal, easily complied

---

[18] *Calumnia*: in classical Latin always a 'false charge'; in the Latin of Anselm's period it is sometimes used simply to mean any 'charge'.

with the devil's suggestion that he should commit a sin, and hence justly incurred the penalty of becoming mortal, correspondingly, now that he is weak and mortal, being himself responsible for having made himself like this, man needs to conquer the devil through the difficulty of death, and in so doing to sin in no way. He cannot do this, so long as he is conceived by the wound of primal sin, and so long as he is born in sin.

B. Once more I say that what you are saying is both logically proven and an impossibility.

23. *What it was that man stole from God when he sinned—* *something which he cannot give back*

A. Here is something else again—no less impossible—without which there is no way for mankind to be justly reconciled.

B. You have already put before us so many things which we are under an obligation to do, that nothing that you add could make me more terrified.

A. Listen, nevertheless.

B. I am listening.

A. What did man steal from God when he allowed himself to be conquered by the devil?

B. You do the talking, seeing that you have begun—for I do not know what he could have done additional to those evils which you have been disclosing.

A. Did he not steal from God whatever he planned to do with regard to the human species?[19]

B. This is undeniable.

A. Subject the matter to strict justice, and judge accordingly whether man may give recompense for his sin to a level commensurate with his sin, if he does not give back, by conquering the devil, what he has stolen from God by allowing himself to be conquered by the devil. Just as, through the fact of man's defeat, the devil took what belonged to God, and God lost it, so, correspondingly, in the event of man's victory, the devil would be the loser and God would regain what he had lost.

B. One can imagine nothing stricter or more just.

---

[19] 'With regard to the human species': Lat. *de humana natura*.

A. Do you think the supreme justice capable of violating this justice?

B. I dare not think so.

A. Man, therefore, neither ought nor can receive from God what God planned to give him, unless man returns to God all that he has taken away from him. In this way, just as God incurred loss through man, similarly, through man's agency, God would recover what he had lost. The only way in which this can be put into effect is as follows. Because of the man who was conquered, the whole of humanity[20] is rotten and, as it were, in a ferment with sin—and God raises up no one with sin to fill up the complement of the renowned heavenly city. Correspondingly, supposing a man were victorious, because of him as many humans would be brought out of sin into a state of righteousness[21] as would make up that full number to which I have referred, for the completion of which mankind was created. But a man who is a sinner is in no way capable of doing this, for one sinner cannot make another sinner righteous.

B. Nothing could be more just and, equally, nothing could be more impossible. Rather, what appears to be the case from all these considerations is that the mercy of God and the hope of man are dead, so far as the state of blessedness is concerned for which mankind was created.

24. *That, so long as a human being does not give back to God what he owes, he may not be blessedly happy, and his incapacity may not be excused*

A. Wait a little longer.

B. What further do you have in store?

A. If a man who returns what he owes to another man is said to be a wrongdoer, he is much more a wrongdoer if he does not return what he owes to God.

B. If he is capable of returning it and does not do so, he is certainly a wrongdoer. But if he does not have the capacity, in what sense is he a wrongdoer?

A. Perhaps, if the responsibility for his incapacity does not rest with him, he can be excused to some extent. But if there is blame

---

[20] 'Humanity', Lat. *humana natura*, so Migne edition.
[21] 'Brought . . . into a state of righteousness'; Lat. *iustificentur*.

inherent in the incapacity itself, the incapacity does not mitigate the sin itself, any more than it excuses the person who does not repay the debt. For suppose someone assigns his bondslave a task, and tells him not to leap into a pit from which he cannot by any means climb out, and that bondslave, despising the command and advice of his master, leaps into the pit which has been pointed out to him, so that he is completely unable to carry out the task assigned to him. Do you think that his incapacity serves in the slightest as a valid excuse for him not to perform the task assigned to him?

B. Not at all. It serves, rather, to increase his guilt, since he has brought the incapacity upon himself. For indeed he has sinned in two ways: in having not done what he was told to do, and in having done what he has been told not to do.

A. Thus, a person who has of his own accord bound himself by a debt which he cannot repay, has thrown himself into this state of incapacity by his guilt. As a result, he is unable to repay what he owed before his sin, that is, an obligation not to sin, and the fact that he is in debt as a consequence of his sin is inexcusable. For the very fact of his incapacity is blameworthy: because it is something he ought not to have, no indeed, he is under an obligation not to have it. Therefore, just as it is blameworthy for someone not to have that capacity which he received in order that he should be able to guard against sin, similarly it is blameworthy for him to have an incapacity as a result of which he cannot uphold righteousness and guard against sin and cannot, moreover, repay the debt which he owes on account of his sin. For he has acted of his own volition, and it is as a consequence that he has lost his former capability, and has arrived at his present state of incapacity. Now, it is the same thing for him not to have a capability which he ought to have, as it is for him to have an incapacity which he ought not to have. Consequently, a person's incapacity to repay to God what he owes—an incapacity which brings it about that he does not make repayment—does not excuse him, in the event that he does not make repayment. For the result[22] of a sin does not excuse a sin which it brings about.

B. This is an exceedingly grave consideration, and equally it is an unavoidable fact.

---

[22] Interpreting *effectum* as a neuter nominative.

A. A human being who does not give back to God what he owes is, therefore, a wrongdoer.

B. That is all too true. For he is a wrongdoer because he does not give it back, and he is a wrongdoer because he is unable to give it back.

A. No wrongdoer, moreover, will be admitted to a state of blessed happiness, since blessed happiness is sufficiency in which there is no want and, correspondingly, this state is appropriate for nobody except a person in whom there is such pure righteousness that there is no wrongdoing in him.

B. I do not have the audacity to believe otherwise.

A. A human being, therefore, who does not repay to God what he owes, will be incapable of being blessedly happy.

B. I am unable to deny that this too follows.

A. But if you want to say, 'A merciful God remits the debt of anyone who begs forgiveness on the ground that he is incapable of making repayment', God cannot be said to be remitting anything except either that which the person ought to repay and cannot, that is, recompense which he might hypothetically be able to give for his sin—sin which ought not to be committed even for the sake of preserving everything that exists which is not God—or alternatively: that which, by way of punishment, he was about to take away from a person against that person's will, that is, the state of blessed happiness. But if God remits what a person cannot give back of his own volition, for the reason that he is incapable of giving it back—how is this different from saying: 'God remits what he is not able to have'. But it is <u>mockery</u> for mercy of this kind to be attributed to God. If, however, God remits what he was about to take away from a person against his will, because of that person's incapacity to make payment—in that case he is making his punishment lax and making a person happy on account of his sin, in that the person has what he ought not to have. For his very incapacity is something he ought not to have, and therefore, so long as he has it without paying recompense, it is sin on his part. But mercy of this kind is absolutely contrary to God's justice, which does not allow anything to be given in repayment for sin except punishment. Hence, given that it is impossible for God to be self-contradictory, it is impossible for him to be merciful in this way.

B. I see that one has to look for some other 'mercy of God' than the 'mercy' to which you are referring.

A. Let it be true that God forgives a person who does not repay what he owes, for the reason that he is incapable of repaying.

B. I would wish this were the case.

A. So long, however, as he does not repay, he will either be wishing to repay, or not wishing to do so. But in the event that he has a desire to do what he is incapable of doing, he will be a person in want: in the event that he does not have this desire, he will be a wrongdoer.

B. Nothing could be clearer.

A. Now, whether he is in want or whether he is a wrongdoer—in neither case will he be blessedly happy.

B. If the God of justice acts according to logic, there is no route whereby wretched little man may escape, and it seems that the mercy of God is dead.

A. You asked for logic: here is logic. I do not deny that God is merciful, he who saves 'men and beasts in accordance with how' he has 'multiplied his mercy'.[23] Moreover, we are talking about that final mercy, whereby, after this life, he makes a human being blessedly happy. That this state of bliss ought not to be given to anyone whose sins have not been utterly forgiven, and that this forgiveness ought not to happen except on repayment of the debt which is owed because of his sin and which is proportional to the magnitude of his sin, I think I have demonstrated by the logical reasonings set out earlier. If it seems to you that any objection can be made to these logical reasonings, you ought to say so.

B. I see that I certainly cannot prove any of your logical reasonings in the slightest invalid.

A. Nor do I think them so, if they are properly considered. Nevertheless, if just one piece of reasoning, out of all those which I have set forth, has the corroboration of unassailable truth, that ought to suffice. For, whether the truth is unassailably demonstrated by one argument or by several, it is equally safeguarded from all doubt.

B. Self-evidently, this is the case.

---

[23] Cf. Vulgate, *Psalmi iuxta LXX*, 35 (=36), 7–8: *homines et iumenta salvabis, Domine, quemadmodum multiplicasti misericordiam tuam, Deus.*

25. *That it follows as a necessary consequence that mankind is saved by Christ*

B. How, then, will man be saved, if he does not himself pay what he owes, and is bound not to be saved if he does not pay? What effrontery it is on our part to assert that God, who is 'rich in mercy' [cf. Eph. 2: 4] beyond human understanding, cannot do this merciful thing!

A. You ought to demand an answer now from those people, on whose behalf you are speaking, who do not believe that Christ is necessary for the salvation of mankind. They should state by what kind of means mankind can be saved without Christ. If they are in no way able to do so, let them cease mocking us, and come and join those of us who have no doubt that mankind can be saved through Christ, or alternatively let them despair of the notion that salvation can ever happen by any means whatsoever. If they are horrified at the thought, let them believe, with us, in Christ, so that they be capable of being saved.

B. I shall make the same request as I did at the beginning: that you should explain for what reason it is that mankind is saved through Christ.

A. Surely it is sufficient proof that it is through Christ that mankind can be saved when even unbelievers affirm that there is some way in which man can become happy, and it has been adequately demonstrated that, if we posit the non-existence of Christ, the salvation of mankind cannot be effected by any means? For these are the alternatives: it will be possible for mankind to be saved through Christ, or by some other means, or by no means. Therefore, if it is untrue that this can happen by no means, or by some other means, it is necessary that it should come about through Christ.

B. Suppose someone were to see the validity of the reasoning that salvation cannot happen by any other means, while not understanding why it could happen through Christ. He would wish to assert that salvation could not happen through Christ or in any way at all. What shall we say in answer to him?

A. What answer is one to give to someone who, out of an inability to understand why it is, concludes that an inevitable fact is an impossibility?

B. The answer that he is a fool.

A. And so, what he says deserves contempt.

B. True. But one needs to make clear to him the reason why the thing that he reckons impossible is actually the case.

A. Do you not understand, on the basis of what we have already said, that it is a necessity that some human beings should attain to happiness? For let us assume that God created mankind without stain with this state of bliss in view and thus that it is unfitting for him to bring to this state a human being who is in any way stained— otherwise he might seem to be having regrets about his good undertaking and to be incapable of bringing his plan to fulfilment. If this is a correct assumption, the incongruity referred to makes it even more impossible that no human being can be brought forward to the state for which he was created. Consequently, one either has to look outside the Christian faith—and this is something for which no logic can offer demonstrative support— for the satisfaction for sin which, as we have demonstrated earlier, needs to come about, or, alternatively, one should have an undoubting belief in that faith. For something which is truthfully deduced to be the case by unavoidable logic ought not to be subjected to doubt, even if the reason why it should be the case is not perceived.

B. What you are saying is true.

A. So, what more are you asking for?

B. I have not come to this point with the aim that you should remove from me doubt about the faith, but so that you should reveal to me the logical basis for my certainty. You have brought me by logical reasoning to this point, so that I might see that man owes to God for his sin something which he is incapable of paying back, and cannot be saved unless he repays it. I wish you likewise to bring me to a position where I may understand that, in terms of logical necessity, all the things which the Catholic faith teaches us to believe have to be the case, if we wish to be saved; where I may understand, too, how it is that they are effective for the salvation of mankind, and how God in his mercy saves mankind, when he does not forgive a person for his sin, if the person in question does not give back what he owes on account of that sin. And, so that your arguments may be all the more certain, make your beginning a long way from your eventual point,[24] in such a way that you may build them on a firm foundation.

A. May God help me now, because, in setting me such a great task, you are not sparing me in the slightest and are not taking into account the weakness of my knowledge. Nevertheless, seeing that I have made a beginning, I shall make the attempt, not putting trust in myself but in God, and I shall do what I can with his help. But, to avoid causing the would-be reader tedium by too long a continuous argument, let us separate the things which remain to be said from those already said, by making another beginning.

BOOK 2

1. *That man was created righteous so that he might be blessedly happy*

A. It ought not to be doubted that the nature of rational beings[25] was created by God righteous[26] in order that, through rejoicing in him, it might be blessedly happy. For the reason why it is rational is in order that it may distinguish between right and wrong, and between the greater good and the lesser good. Otherwise it was created rational to no purpose. But God did not make it rational to no purpose. On the basis of similar logic there is proof that rational nature received the power of discrimination in order that it might hate and avoid what is bad, and love and choose the good, and, moreover, love and choose, for preference, the greater good. For otherwise it would have been to no purpose that God had given it that power of discrimination, if no love resulted from the discriminating, and no avoidance. But it is not fitting that God should have given such an important power to no purpose. It is a certainty, therefore, that rational nature was created to the end that it should love and choose, above all, the highest good, and that it should do this, not because of something else, but because of the highest good itself. For

---

[24] There is archaelogical evidence that it was common 12th-cent. bad building practice to erect buildings directly over the (rubbish-filled) quarry pits from which the stone for them had been excavated.

[25] Lat. *rationalem naturam*, lit. 'rational nature'.

[26] 'Righteous', Lat. *iustus, -a, -um*, also equivalent to 'just'.

if the loving were for the sake of something else, it would have as its object not the highest good itself but the other thing. But loving the highest good is something which rational nature cannot do unless it is righteous. In order, therefore, that its rationality should not be purposeless, it was simultaneously created rational and righteous. Now, it was created with these characteristics—if it was created for the purpose of choosing and loving the highest good—either so that it should attain to what it was loving and choosing, or, alternatively, so that it would not. But if it is not the case that rational nature has been created righteous in order that some day it may attain to what it loves and chooses, it has been created with this characteristic to no purpose, as a result loving and choosing the highest good without there being any reason why it will ever be its due to attain to it. For so long, then, as it performs righteous acts, loving and choosing the highest good—the purpose for which it was created—it will be miserable, because it will be in need against its will, not having what it yearns for. This is an extreme absurdity. Hence rational nature was created righteous to the end that it might be made happy by rejoicing in the highest good, that is, in God. Man, being rational by nature, was created righteous to the end that, through rejoicing in God, he might be blessedly happy.

2. *That he would not die if he had not sinned*

Furthermore, because man was created with this characteristic in order that he should not inevitably die, it is easily proved on this basis that, as we have already said, it is repugnant to the wisdom and justice of God that he should force him, if guiltless, to suffer death, having made him righteous for the purpose of eternal happiness. It follows, therefore, that if he had never sinned, he would never die.

3. *That he rises with the body in which he lives in this life*

Hence there is proof that there is to be at some time a resurrection of the dead. For if man is to be restored in perfection, he ought to be reconstituted as the sort of being he would have been if he had not sinned.

B. It cannot be otherwise.

A. In the same way, therefore, that if man had not sinned, he would have been bound to undergo change into incorruptibility, likewise it is right that, when in the future he is restored, he will be restored in the body in which he lives in this life.

B. What are we to answer, if someone should say that it is right that this should happen in the case of those in whom the human race is to be restored, but that it is not necessary where the wicked are concerned?

A. Nothing more just or appropriate can be conceived of than that, just as a human being, if he had persevered in righteousness, would have enjoyed eternal blessedness as an entirety, that is, with soul and body, similarly, if he perseveres in unrighteousness, he should, as an entirety, be eternally miserable.

B. You have not taken long to satisfy me about these matters.

4. *That, with regard to the nature of mankind, God will bring to completion what he has begun*

A. On the basis of these considerations it is easy to recognize, that with regard to the nature of mankind, there are two alternatives: either God will complete what he has begun, or it was to no avail that he created this life-form[27]—so sublime a life-form, and with such great good as its purpose. But, if it is recognized that God has made nothing more precious than rational nature, whose intended purpose is that it should rejoice in him, it is totally foreign to him to allow any rational type of creature to perish utterly.

B. A heart that is rational cannot think otherwise.

A. It is necessary, therefore, that, with regard to the nature of mankind, God should finish what he has begun. However, this cannot be done, as we have said, except through the paying of complete recompense for sin, something which no sinner can bring about.

B. I understand now that it is necessary that God should accomplish what he has begun, in order that he may not appear, unfittingly, to be failing in his undertaking.

---

[27] 'Life-form', Lat. *natura* again.

5. *That, although it is a matter of necessity that this should*
   happen, it will not be under compulsion of necessity that he
   will do this; that, moreover, there is a necessity which removes
   or diminishes graciousness and a necessity which increases it

But if this is so, God seems, as it were, to be forced to bring about
the salvation of mankind by the necessity for avoiding unfittingness.
How can it be denied, therefore, that he is taking this action for his
own sake rather than ours? Again, if this is the case, what gratitude[28]
do we owe him for this thing which he is doing for his own sake?
Furthermore, how is it that we are to attribute our salvation to his
grace, if it is of necessity that he saves us?

A. There is a necessity which removes graciousness from someone who is acting beneficently, or diminishes it, and there is a
necessity whereby the debt of gratitude owed for a benefaction is
increased. For when someone acts beneficently against his will due
to the unavoidable force of circumstances to which he is subject, he
is owed either no gratitude or less gratitude. When, on the other
hand, he subjects himself freely to a force which inevitably requires
him to do good, and is not reluctant to endure it, then he certainly
deserves greater gratitude for his good deed. Now, this action is not
to be called an act of necessity but an act of grace, because it is under
no one's compulsion that he undertakes it and carries it out, but
freely. For, suppose you promise today that you will give a present
tomorrow and tomorrow make the gift of your own free will: even
though it is a matter of necessity for you to keep your promise, if
you can—otherwise you will be a liar—the person to whom you are
making the gift is no less indebted to you than if you had not made
the promise, because you did not hesitate to make yourself his debtor
before presenting the gift. A comparable case is when someone of his
own free will makes a vow about holy living. It is true that he is of
necessity under an obligation to keep the vow after he has made it,
in order that he may not incur the condemnation due to an apostate;
it is true, also, that he can be forced to keep it, supposing he does not
wish to. But even so, if he keeps his vow willingly, he is not less, but
more, pleasing to God than if he had not made the vow, since what
he has renounced for the sake of God is not only life in ordinary

---

[28] Lat. *gratia* in this chapter is translated variously as 'gratitude', 'grace', 'graciousness' and 'an act of grace'.

society[29] but permission to participate in it. Moreover, it is not right to say of him that he is living a holy life as a matter of necessity, but in freedom, rather—the same freedom in which he made his vow.

Consequently, despite the fact that it is not fitting for God to fail to bring to completion a good beginning, we ought all the more to attribute it entirely to his grace if he completes the act of beneficence towards mankind which he has begun, seeing that he has begun it for our sake, not for his own, being himself in need of nothing. For it was no secret to God what man was going to do, when he created him, and yet, by his own goodness in creating him, he put himself under an obligation to bring his good beginning to fulfilment. Ultimately, God does nothing under compulsion of necessity—because he is in no way forced to do, or prohibited from doing, anything. And when we say that God is performing some action as if out of a necessary obligation to avoid what is dishonourable—something of which he certainly has no fear—what we should understand, rather, is that he is acting thus out of a necessary obligation to uphold what is honourable. The necessity to which I am referring is plainly nothing other than the unchangeability of God's honour, which he possesses of himself, and from no one apart from himself. For this reason, 'necessity' is a misnomer. Let us say, nevertheless, that it is a necessity that the goodness of God should bring to completion what it has begun with respect to mankind, because of his unchangeability, although the whole of what he does is grace.

B. You have my leave to say so.

6. *That no one is capable of bringing about the recompense by which mankind may be saved except someone who is God and man*

A. But this cannot come about unless there should be someone who would make a payment to God greater than everything that exists apart from God.

B. That is agreed.

A. It is also a necessity that someone who can give to God from his own property something which exceeds everything which is

---

[29] 'Life in ordinary society', Lat. *communem vitam*.

inferior to God, must himself be superior to everything that exists
apart from God.

B. I cannot deny it.

A. Now, there is nothing superior to all that exists which is not
God—except God.

B. That follows.

A. But the obligation rests with man, and no one else, to make the
payment referred to. Otherwise mankind is not making recompense.

B. This seems pre-eminently just.

A. If, therefore, as is agreed, it is necessary that the heavenly city
should have its full complement made up by members of the human
race, and this cannot be the case if the recompense of which we have
spoken is not paid, which no one can pay except God, and no one
ought to pay except man: it is necessary that a God-Man should pay
it.

B. Blessed be God! Now we have made a great discovery relating
to the object of our search. Continue, therefore, as you have begun.
For I have hope that God will help us.

7. *That it is necessary for one and the same person to be perfect*
   God and perfect man

A. What we now have to investigate is how it is possible for a God-
Man to exist. For it is not the case that divine nature and human
nature are mutually interchangeable so that divine nature may
become human or human, divine; nor can the two be mixed so that
some third nature might arise from them, a nature which would not
be divine—not at all—and not human either. To sum up, if it were
possible for one nature to be changed into another, the result would
be someone who would either be God and not man, or man and not
God. Alternatively, if they were mixed so that a third nature was
produced as the consequence of inter-contamination of the two
natures,[30] the result would be neither man nor God. We may compare
how the issue of two individual animals, male and female, of different species, is a third type of animal, which preserves neither the
nature of its father nor that of its mother in its entirety, but has a
third nature which is a mixture of both. The God-Man who is the

---

[30] 'Inter-contamination of the two natures', Lat. *ex duabus corruptis (sc. naturis)*.

object of our quest cannot, therefore, come into existence out of divine and human nature, or out of the changing of one into the other, or a contaminating mixture of the two resulting in a third nature. For these things cannot happen, or, supposing they were possibilities, they would not have the power to effect the outcome at which our enquiries are directed.

If, furthermore, these two natures, as wholes, are said to be somehow conjoined to a limited extent whereby man and God are distinct from one another and not one and the same, it is impossible that both should bring about what it is necessary should happen. For God will not do it because it will not be his obligation to do it, and a man will not do it because he will not be able to. In order, therefore, that a God-Man should bring about what is necessary, it is essential that the same one person who will make the recompense should be perfect God and perfect man. For he cannot do this if he is not true God, and he has no obligation to do so if he is not a true man. Given, therefore, that it is necessary for a God-Man to be found in whom the wholeness of both natures is kept intact, it is no less necessary for these two natures to combine, as wholes, in one person, in the same way as the body and the rational soul coalesce into one human being. For otherwise it cannot come about that one and the same person may be perfect God and perfect man.

B. I am happy with all that you are saying.

8. *That it is right that God should assume human nature from the race of Adam and from a virgin woman*

A. It remains now to investigate from what source, and how, God will take human nature upon himself. For either he will take on this nature from Adam, or he will create a new man, just as he created Adam from no other human being. But if he creates a new man who is not from the race of Adam, this new man will not belong to the human race which is descended from Adam. Consequently, he will not have an obligation to give recompense on behalf of this race, because he will not be from it. For, just as it is right that it should be a human being who should pay recompense for the guilt of humanity, it is likewise necessary that the person paying recompense should be identical with the sinner, or a member of the same race. Otherwise, it will be neither Adam nor his race who will be making recompense on Adam's behalf. Therefore, just as, starting from Adam and Eve, sin has been engendered in all human beings, similarly, no one except either these two themselves, or someone descended from them, has an obligation to pay recompense for the sin of mankind. As they themselves are not able to do so, it is necessary that the person who is to do this will be descended from them.

I will enlarge on this. If Adam had not sinned, he and all his race would have maintained their standing without the support of another creature: correspondingly, if this same race rises again after its fall, it is right that it should rise again, and be raised up again, through its own doing. For, whoever it is through whose agency man is restored to the standing which belongs to him, man will certainly owe his standing in future to this person through whose agency he recovers his standing. Moreover, it was in Adam alone that God originally created human nature, and it was God's will to create woman—in order that human beings of both sexes would be multiplied—from an origin which was none other than Adam. God therefore made it perfectly clear that it had not been his will that his future action regarding human nature would be without derivation from Adam. Consequently, supposing the race of Adam were to be raised up again by some man from a different race, it will not be restored to that dignity which it was to have had if Adam had not sinned. Hence it will not be completely restored; also God's plan will appear to be failing. Both of these consequences are unfitting. Therefore, it is necessary that the man through whom the race of Adam is to be restored should be taken from Adam's progeny.

B. If we maintain a logical approach, as we have proposed to do, this must inevitably be the case.

A. Let us now investigate the question of how God is to take human nature upon himself: whether from father and mother, as is the case with other human beings, or from a man without a woman, or from a woman without a man. For, in whichever of the ways it is to be, the human nature so assumed will derive from Adam and Eve, from whom every human being, of either sex, is descended. Moreover, it is not the case that one of these three ways of operating is easier for God than the others, so that it is in this way that human nature ought to be assumed by him in preference to the others.

B. The way in which you are proceeding is good.

A. But there is no need for great effort in order to demonstrate that the human being we have in mind will be more purely and honourably procreated from a man in isolation, or from a woman in isolation, than from an intermingling of the two like that whereby all other human children are procreated.

B. Enough said.

A. Therefore he must be taken either from a man in isolation or from a woman in isolation.

B. He can come from nowhere else.

A. God can create a human being by four methods. To be specific: he can do this either from a man and a woman together, as the usual practice demonstrates, or from neither a man nor a woman, as in the case of Adam's creation, or from a man without a woman, as in the creation of Eve, or from a woman without a man—which he has not yet done. In order, therefore, that he should prove that this method too is within his competence and that it has been kept in reserve for the very undertaking which we have in mind, it is pre-eminently fitting that he should take the man who is the object of our quest from a woman without a man.

B. You are speaking in accordance with my heart's desire.

A. Is what we have been saying something solid, or is it—as you have told me unbelievers allege in their criticisms of us—insubstantial like a cloud?

B. Nothing could be more solid.

A. Paint your picture, then, not upon an empty sham but upon solid truth, and say that it is extremely appropriate that, just as the sin of mankind and the cause of our damnation originated from a woman, correspondingly the medicine of sin and the cause of salvation should be born of a woman. Moreover, women might lose hope that they have a part in the destiny of the blessed ones, in view of the fact that such great evil proceeded from a woman: in order to prevent this, it is right that an equivalent great good should proceed from a woman, so as to rebuild their hope. Include this, too, in your picture: on the supposition that it was a virgin woman who has been the cause of all the evil besetting the human race, it is all the more appropriate that the woman who is to be the cause of all good should be a virgin. Another thing to include in your picture is this. One may presume that the woman whom God created from a man without a woman was created from someone who was a virgin: on this supposition, it is extremely fitting that the man who is to be created from a woman without a man, should be brought forth by a virgin. For the moment, however, let these considerations suffice with regard to the pictures which may be painted on the subject of how the God–Man ought to be born of a virgin woman.

B. These pictures of yours are extremely beautiful and in accordance with logic.

9. *That it is necessary for the Word alone and man to combine in a single person*

A. Something else which we must investigate now is this: in what person is God, who is three persons, to take manhood upon himself? For several persons cannot take upon themselves one and the same manhood with resultant unity of person. But I have said sufficient, I believe, for the purposes of our present enquiry, in the letter *On the Incarnation of the Word*, addressed to the lord Pope Urban, about this uniting of the person of God with man and the question in which person of God this ought best to come about.

B. Even so, do touch briefly, at this point, on the reasons why it is the person of the Son which ought to be made incarnate, rather than that of the Father or the Holy Spirit.

A. Supposing any other of the persons is to be made incarnate, there will be two sons in the Trinity, namely: the Son of God, who is Son even before the incarnation, and he who will be the Virgin's son through the incarnation. Moreover there will be, among persons who ought always to be equals, an inequality resulting from the distinction of their respective births. For the one who is born of God will have more distinguished birth than the one who is born of the Virgin. Also, if it is to be the Father who is made incarnate, there will be two grandsons in the Trinity, because, through his assumption of manhood, the Father will be the grandson of the parents of the Virgin, and the Word, despite having no trace of human nature in him, will none the less be the grandson of the Virgin, because he will be the son of her son. All these eventualities are incongruous, and do not come about if it is the Word who is made incarnate. And there is yet another reason why it is more appropriate for the Son to be made incarnate than the other persons: because it sounds more appropriate for the Son to make supplication to the Father than for any other of the persons to supplicate another. Also, both man, for whom the Son was to pray, and the devil, whom he was to defeat, had both wilfully taken upon themselves a false likeness of God. Hence they had sinned, as it were, most specifically against the person of the Son, who is believed to be the true likeness of the Father. The avenging or pardoning of a wrong, therefore, is most appropriately being assigned to the person on whom the injury is most specifically inflicted. Inescapable logic, then, has led us to the conclusion that it is necessary for divine and human nature to combine in one person, and that this cannot come about with respect to more than one person of God; moreover it is evident that it is more fitting for this to happen with respect to the person of the Word than to the other persons. It is, consequently, an inevitability that God the Word and a human being should combine in one person.

B. The road, fortified on both sides by logic, along which you are leading me is such that I see I cannot depart from it either to the right or to the left.

A. But it is not I who am leading you but the one about whom I am speaking, without whom we can do nothing, and who is our guide wherever we keep to the way of truth.

10. *That this same man does not die obligatorily; and in what sense he is, or is not, capable of sinning, and why he, or an angel, should be praised for his righteousness, even though they are incapable of sinning*

We must now investigate whether that man is obligatorily to die, just as all other men die obligatorily...[31] it is the case that Adam would not have been destined to die if he had not sinned, then this man, in whom it will be impossible for sin to exist because he is to be God, will have still less of an obligation to die.

B. I wish to detain you on this point for a little while. For whether it is said that he cannot sin, or that he can, in either case a question of considerable importance arises, as I see it. For if he is said to be incapable of sinning, it seems difficult to believe that he has this obligation. Let us speak, just for a moment, not as if with reference to a person who has never existed, which has been our procedure so far, but about the person whom we know, and whose deeds we are

---

[31] The thought-sequence here is elliptical, in a way uncharacteristic of Anselm, and it may be surmised that a sentence of his original may be missing.

acquainted with. Who will deny that he could have done many things which we call sins? For instance—not to mention other examples— how are we to say that he could not have lied, something which is always a sin. For, given that he says to the Jews, with reference to the Father, 'If I say that I do not know him, I shall be a liar, like you' [Joh. 8: 55], and he says in the course of this utterance, 'I do not know him'; who will be able to assert that he could not have uttered these five words[32] in isolation from the remainder of the utterance, so as to say, 'I do not know him'? If he were to do this, as he himself states, he would be a liar—and that is to be a sinner. Hence, since he could do this, he was capable of sin.

A. It was possible for him to say this and, at the same time, not to be capable of sin.

B. Demonstrate this.

A. All capability is consequent upon will. For when I say, 'I am capable of speaking' or 'walking', this contains an implicit subtext, 'If it is my will'. If will, then, is not implicit, what is being referred to is not capability but inevitability. For if I say, 'I am capable of being dragged away' or 'defeated', against my will, the reference is not to my capability, but to inevitability, and the capability of another individual. To be precise, to say, 'I am capable of being dragged away' or 'of being defeated' is no different from saying, 'Another person is capable of dragging me away' or 'defeating me'. We can therefore say of Christ that he could tell a lie, if this statement is recognized to contain the implication, 'If it were his will'. And since he could not lie unwillingly and it could not be his will to tell a lie, it can equally be stated that he was incapable of lying. It follows that thus he both could, and could not, tell a lie.

B. Let us now revert to making investigations about Christ in the manner we adopted at the outset: as if there were as yet no such person. What I say is this: if he is not going to be capable of sinning, because, as you say, he will not be capable of wishing to sin, he will be upholding righteousness as a matter of inevitable necessity. For this reason, he is not going to be righteous as a result of free will. What gratitude, then, will be due to him for his righteousness? For it is customary among us to say that God's purpose in making angels and human beings such as to be capable of sinning, was that, in the

---

[32] 'These five words': Lat. *tres . . . dictiones* with reference to the three words, *non scio eum*, translated as, 'I do not know him'.

event that they maintained righteousness while being capable of abandoning it, they should deserve gratitude and praise which they would not deserve if they were righteous as a matter of inevitability.

A. Are the angels, who are now incapable of sinning, not worthy of praise?

B. They certainly are, because the fact that they cannot now sin was their reward for not wishing to sin, when capable of doing so.

A. What about God, who cannot sin, and whose inability to sin has not been earned as a reward for not having sinned while being capable of sinning—what do you say about him? Is he not to be praised for his righteousness?

B. On this point my wish is that you should answer on my behalf. For if I say that he is not worthy of praise, I know that I am lying. But if I say that he is worthy of praise, I am afraid of invalidating the argument which I mentioned about the angels.

A. The reason why the angels are to be praised for their righteousness is not that they were in the past capable of sinning, but because in some way they possess—independently[33]—an inability to sin; in this respect they somewhat resemble God, who possesses whatever he possesses independently. Now, someone who does not take something away, when he is capable of doing so, is said to be 'making a gift of it', and a person who is capable of making something not be, but refrains from doing so, is said to be 'making do with it'. In this sense, then, it is correct to assert that an angel 'gave himself' righteousness and 'made himself' righteous, given that, while capable of depriving himself of righteousness, he did not do so and, while capable of making himself unrighteous, he did not make himself so. He therefore possesses righteousness 'independently' in this way, because it is impossible for a created being to possess anything 'independently' in any other way. As a consequence of this, he deserves to be praised for his righteousness. Furthermore he is not righteous as a matter of necessity but in freedom, because it is not correct to speak of necessity where there is neither any compulsion nor any prohibition.

It follows that, since God possesses to a perfect degree what he possesses independently, he most of all is worthy to be praised for the good things which he possesses and keeps in his possession, doing

---

[33] 'Independently' here and elsewhere in this passage: Lat. *a se*, lit. 'from themselves', 'from himself'.

this not out of any inevitable necessity, but as I have said earlier, out of an unchangeability which is his peculiar property and lasts for ever. Thus the man we have in mind, who is also to be God, will be righteous independently and therefore worthy of praise, since he will possess independently every good thing which he will possess, not out of necessity but in freedom. Even though his human nature will possess what he is to possess thanks to his divine nature, he will be possessing it 'independently', since his two natures will be one person.

B. You have satisfied me by means of this argument, and I see plainly both that it will not be possible for him to sin and that, even so, he will be worthy of praise for his righteousness.

But now I think the question has to be asked: given that God is capable of creating such a man, why did he not make the angels and the first two human beings such that they would likewise be both incapable of sinning and worthy of praise for their righteousness?

A. Do you understand what you are saying?

B. It seems to me that I understand it, and that is why I am asking why he did not make them like this.

A. This was because it was neither right nor possible for it to be brought about that any one of them should be identical with God, as is the case, so we are saying, with this man. And if you ask why he does not bring this about for as many such human beings as there are persons of God, or why he did not at least do it for one of them, I answer that reason did not at all demand that this should be done: rather, since God does nothing irrationally, it prohibited this.

B. I am ashamed at having asked this question.

A. Let us say, therefore, that the God-Man will be under no obligation to die, since he will not be a sinner.

B. I must admit this to be the case.

11. *That it is of his own power that he dies, and that mortality is not a property of human nature which is pure*

A. It now remains to investigate whether he is capable of dying as a consequence of his human nature; for, in consequence of his divine nature, he will always be incorruptible.

B. Why need we have doubt about this, seeing that he is to be a true man and all mankind is by nature mortal?

A. I do not think that mortality is a property of pure human nature, rather of human nature which is corrupt. Certainly, if man had never sinned and his immortality had been confirmed in such a way that it could not be changed, he would none the less have been truly human. Moreover, when mortals rise again into incorruptibility, they will be no less true human beings. Now, if mortality were a property essential for the genuineness of human nature, it would not be possible for someone immortal to be human. For corruptibility or incorruptibility is not a determinant of the genuineness of human nature, since neither makes or destroys a human being: rather, one has the power to cause him misery, the other happiness. But, on the reasoning that there is no human being who does not die, 'mortal' is specified in the definition of a man given by philosophers who did not believe that the whole man had ever been, or could be, immortal. Because of this, the fact that he is truly human is insufficient to prove that the man we have in mind need be mortal.

B. So, look for another line of reasoning. For I do not know of a way of proving that he is capable of dying, if you do not know one.

A. There is no doubt that he will be omnipotent, seeing that he is like God.

B. This is true.

A. If it is his will, then, he will be able to lay aside his soul and take it up again.

B. If he cannot do this, I do not see that he is omnipotent.

A. It will be in his power, therefore, never to die, if he wishes; it will also be in his power to die and rise again. Furthermore, it makes no difference, so far as his power is concerned, whether he lays his soul aside without involvement of any other person in the action, or whether it is another person who will bring it about that he lays it aside, having given his own consent.

B. This is undoubtedly the case.

A. If, therefore, it is his will to give his permission, it will be possible for him to be killed, and, if it is not, this will not be possible.

B. This is the conclusion to which logic unswervingly leads us.

A. Logic has also taught us that he ought to possess something greater than everything which is below God, which he may give to God voluntarily and not in repayment of a debt.

B. That is right.

A. But this cannot be found either below God or outside him.

B. True.

A. It is within the man himself, therefore, that it has to be found.

B. This follows.

A. What he will give, therefore, will either be himself or something from himself.

B. I cannot conceive it to be otherwise.

A. The question which now has to be asked is of what kind this giving ought to be. Now, he will not be able to give to God either himself or something from himself, as if he were making himself belong to one who does not own him—for every created being belongs to God.

B. This is so.

A. The way in which this giving has to be understood, therefore, is this: that in some way he will be laying aside himself, or something from himself, to the honour of God, since he will not be a debtor.

B. This follows from what has been said earlier.

A. If we say that he will make a present of himself as an act of obedience to God, in that he will be submitting himself to God's will by upholding righteousness with perseverance, this will not constitute giving something which God does not demand from him in repayment of a debt. For every rational creature owes this obedience to God.

B. It is impossible to deny this.

A. It ought to be in some other way, therefore, that he should give either himself or something from himself.

B. Reason impels us to this conclusion.

A. Let us see whether perhaps this may not be for him to give his life, or to lay aside his soul, or to hand himself over to death, for the honour of God. For this is not something which God will demand from him in repayment of a debt, given that, since there will be no sin in him, he will be under no obligation to die, as we have said.

B. I cannot interpret the matter differently.

A. Let us consider further whether it is logically appropriate for it to be so.

B. Speak, and I will be happy to listen.

A. If man sinned through pleasure, is it not fitting that he should give recompense through pain? And if it was in the easiest possible way that man was defeated by the devil, so as to dishonour God by his sinning, is it not justice that man, in giving recompense for sin, should, for the honour of God, defeat the devil with the greatest possible difficulty? Is it not fitting that man, who, by sinning, removed himself as far as he possibly could away from God, should, as recompense to God, make a gift of himself in an act of the greatest possible self-giving?

B. This is unsurpassable logic.

A. There can, moreover, be nothing that a man may suffer—voluntarily and without owing repayment of a debt—more painful or more difficult than death. And there is no act of self-giving whereby a man may give himself to God greater than when he hands himself over to death for God's glory.

B. All these things are true.

A. The one whose will it is to be to pay recompense for the sin of mankind ought therefore to have the characteristic of being able to die if he wishes.

B. I see clearly that the man whom we are seeking ought to have the following characteristics: it will not be as a matter of necessity that he will die, because he will be omnipotent; he will not be dying obligatorily, because he will never be a sinner, and it will be within his capacity to die of his own free will, because this will be necessary.

A. There are many other reasons too why it will be extremely appropriate for him to bear a resemblance to mankind and have the behaviour belonging to mankind—while being without sin. These reasons are more readily and clearly discernible in Christ's life and works than can be demonstrated by reason alone, hypothetically, as if before experience of the events. For who may explain how necessary and wise a thing it was for it to come about that he who was to redeem the human race and bring it back from the way of death and destruction to the way of life and eternal happiness, should live in the company of human beings and, while he was teaching them verbally how they ought to live, should, through his very behaviour, present himself as an example? Furthermore, how was he to present himself to weak and mortal humans as an example of the fact that they should not depart from righteousness on account of injustices, insults, pain or death, if they were not aware that he himself had experience of all these things?

12. *That, although he is a sharer in our discomforts, he is nevertheless not unhappy*

B. All these considerations make it patently obvious that it is right for him to be mortal and a sharer in our discomforts. But these are all circumstances which belong to our unhappiness. Will he not, therefore, be unhappy?

A. Not at all. For, just as a comfort which someone possesses against his will is not conducive to happiness, similarly it is not unhappiness to take upon oneself a discomfort willingly, out of wisdom, not out of any necessity.

B. This must be admitted.

13. *That he does not have ignorance along with our other weaknesses*

However, as regards the likeness which he needs to bear to members of the human race, say whether he is going to have ignorance in the same way as he is to have our other weaknesses.

A. Why do you have doubts with regard to God, as to whether he is omniscient?

B. Because, although he is to be immortal as a consequence of his divine nature, he will nevertheless be mortal as a consequence of his humanity. Why, in view of this, will it not be possible for the man we have in mind to be truly ignorant, just as he will be truly mortal?

A. The accepting of man into the unity of the person of God will not be brought about otherwise than wisely, by the highest wisdom, and therefore there will be no acceptance[34] of something which is in no way useful, but detrimental rather, for the work which the man is going to undertake. Now, there would be no purpose for which ignorance would be useful to him: rather it would be for many purposes detrimental. For how is he going to perform all the many great works which he is to perform, without immeasurable wisdom? Again, how are people going to believe in him, if they know he is ignorant? Moreover, supposing this is something they do not know: for what purpose will that ignorance be useful to him? And again, if it is the case that nothing is loved except that which is known: by the same

---

[34] For *non assumet* here (Schmitt, 112:23) perhaps we should read *non assumetur*.

token as it will be no good thing for him not to love, it will be no good thing for him to be ignorant. Furthermore, no one has a perfect knowledge of what is good who does not know how to distinguish it from what is bad. It is also the case that no one who is ignorant of the bad knows how to draw this distinction. The man we have in mind will therefore have all knowledge, even though he may not make this evident in public in his dealings with mankind.

B. What you are saying seems to hold good for his adulthood; but in his infancy it will not be the appropriate time for wisdom to appear in him, and similarly there will be no need, and consequently it will be incongruous, too, for him to have it.

A. Have I not said that the incarnation which we have in mind will be brought about in a way characterized by wisdom? Now, it will be in wisdom that God will take mortality upon himself, and it will be in wisdom that he will put it to use, because he will be using it to great advantage. But he will not be able to take ignorance upon himself in wisdom, because ignorance is never useful, always detrimental rather, except perhaps when an evil desire—something which will never be found in the God-Man—is prevented from being fulfilled. For even if sometimes ignorance is not detrimental in any other regard, it is nevertheless detrimental in the mere fact that it does away with the good which consists in knowledge. Moreover, to complete my brief reply to your enquiry: from the time when he becomes human, he will always be full of God, God's identity being his own. Hence he will never be without God's power and fortitude and wisdom.

B. I did not doubt that this was always the case with Christ but, even so, I none the less made this enquiry with the aim that I should hear a rational explanation for this fact also. For often we are certain that something is the case, but do not know how to prove it logically.

14. *That his death outweighs the number and magnitude of all sins*

Now my request is that you should teach me how it is that his death outweighs the number and magnitude of all sins, seeing that you make it clear that one sin which we consider the most lightweight is of such infinite magnitude that one ought not to take a glance contrary to the will of God, even supposing that an infinite number of universes, each full of creatures just as this one is, were to be laid out before one, and could not be kept from being reduced to nothing, except if someone were to take this glance.

A. If the man we have in mind were to be present, and you knew who he was, and someone were to say to you, 'If you do not kill this man, the whole of the universe will perish, and whatever is not God', would you do it in order to preserve the whole of the rest of creation?

B. I would not do it, even if an infinite number of universes were offered to me.

A. What if someone were to follow this up by saying, 'Either you will kill him or all the sins of the world will come upon you'?

B. I would answer that I would rather take upon myself all other sins, not just all the sins of this universe—both those committed in the past and those to be committed in the future—but whatever sins can be conceived of as existing in addition to these. And I think I ought to make this answer not only with regard to the act of killing him, but with respect to any small injury whatsoever which would harm him.

A. You are right in thinking so. But tell me why your heart makes such a judgement, being more horrified at one sin involving injury to this man than at all else that can be conceived of, given that all the sins ever committed are against him.

B. It is because a sin which is directed at this man's person is incomparably greater than all conceivable sins which are directed elsewhere than at his person.

A. What will you say to the objection that often someone willingly endures discomfiture to his own person so as not to endure greater discomfiture in his business dealings.

B. I will say that God has no need of this endurance, for all things are subject to his power, just as you said earlier in reply to some question of mine.

A. Your answer is a good one. We see, therefore, that no sins, no matter how immeasurably great or numerous, which are directed elsewhere than against the person of God, can be regarded as equal to the violation of the bodily life of the man whom we have in mind.

B. This is perfectly clear.

A. How great a good does he[35] seem to you to constitute, given that killing him is such a bad thing?

B. If every good is as good as its destruction is bad, he[36] is an incomparably greater good than the sins immeasurably outweighed by his killing are bad.

A. What you are saying is true. Consider also that sins are as hateful as they are bad and that the life which you have in mind is as loveable as it is good. Hence it follows that this life is more loveable than sins are hateful.

B. This is something which I cannot fail to appreciate.

A. Do you think that something which is so great a good and so loveable can suffice to pay the debt which is owed for the sins of the whole world?

B. Indeed, it is capable of paying infinitely more.

A. You see, therefore, how, if this life is given for all sins, it outweighs them all.

B. Plainly.

A. If, then, to accept death is to give one's life, just as his life outweighs all the sins of mankind, so does his acceptance of death.

B. It is established that this is the case with all sins which do not touch the person of God.

15. *That this same death destroys the sins even of those who put him to death*

But now I see that another question has to be asked. For if to kill him is as bad as his life is good, how can his death overcome and destroy the sins of those who killed him? Or, if it destroys the sin of any one of them, how can it destroy in addition any sin committed by other people? For we believe that many of the human race have been saved, and that countless others are being saved.

A. The Apostle who said, 'If they had known it, they would not have crucified the Lord of glory' [1 Cor. 2: 8], provided the answer to this question. For so great is the difference between a sin

[35] The text here raises suspicions: one would expect to read 'his life' rather than 'he', and it may be we should indeed read conjecturally: *Quantum bonum tibi videtur <huius vita> cuius interemptio tam mala est.*

[36] Or 'it', if we have read *<huius vita>*, 'his life'.

committed knowingly and one which is committed through ignorance, that an evil which, if it were recognized for what it was, they
would never be able to commit because of its enormity, is capable of
being pardoned because it was committed through ignorance. For no
member of the human race would ever wish to kill God, at least no
one would knowingly wish it, and therefore those who killed him
unknowingly did not fall headlong into that infinite sin with which
no other sins can be compared. Bear in mind that in order to see how
good his life was, we considered the magnitude of that sin not in relation to the fact that it was committed in ignorance, but as if it were
committed knowingly—something which no one has ever done or
would have been capable of doing.

B. You have demonstrated logically that it was possible for those
who killed Christ to attain to forgiveness of their sin.

A. What more are you asking now? Look! You recognize how
logical necessity makes it clear that the city above has to have its complement made up by members of the human race, and that this
cannot come about except through the remission of sins, which no
man can have except through a man who is identical with God and
who by his death reconciles sinners to God. We have clearly found
Christ, whom we acknowledge to be God and man and to have died
for our sakes. Be sure of this too, without any doubt: all that he says
is true, since God is incapable of lying, and the deeds he did were
done wisely, even though the reasoning behind them may not be
understood by us.

B. What you are saying is true, and I do not doubt that what he
said is true or that what he did was done in accordance with reason.
I nevertheless ask you to explain to me by what logic this truth, which
to those who do not believe in the Christian faith seems as if it were
not right and not possible, is in fact right and possible. I ask this not
in order that you should confirm me in the faith, rather so that you
should give one already confirmed in the faith the joy which comes
from an understanding of the absolute truth.

16. *How God produced a man without sin out of sinful matter;
    also about the salvation of Adam and Eve*

In view of this, it is my request that you should explain the reasoning behind the matters about which I have yet to ask you in the same

way as you have elucidated the reasoning behind the matters which we have spoken of up to now. My first question is: how did God produce a man without sin out of the human race, which is totally permeated with sin? This was like producing unleavened bread out of leavened dough. For, granted that the actual conception of this man was untainted and devoid of the sin of carnal pleasure, the Virgin from whom he was taken was conceived 'amid iniquities' and her mother 'conceived' her 'in sin' [cf. Ps. 50: 7 Vulg. = 51: 5], and she was born with original sin since she sinned in Adam, 'in whom all have sinned' [Rom. 15: 12].

A. Once it is agreed that the man whom we have in mind is God and the reconciler of sinners, there is no doubt that he is completely without sin. Moreover, this cannot be so if he has not been produced without sin out of sinful matter. Now, if we cannot understand the reasoning whereby the Wisdom of God did this, we ought not to express astonishment, but reverently bear with the fact that in the hidden recesses of so surpassingly great an actuality there is something which we do not know. Indeed, God's restoration of human nature was more miraculous than his creation of it. For the two acts—restoration and creation—are both equally easy for God. However, in the time before he was created, man did not sin, and hence there was no need for restoration to take place. But after he was created he sinned and, because of his sin, deserved to lose both the fact of being created and the destiny for which he was created. In fact, though, he did not entirely lose the fact of being created. This was so that he could be the object of God's punishment or of his mercy. For neither of these options could come about if he had been annihilated. It follows, then, that God's restoration of human nature was more miraculous than his action in bringing it into existence, to the extent that the restoration was concerned with man as sinner and was contrary to what he deserved, whereas the creation was concerned with man in a state of sinlessness, and was not contrary to what he deserved. What a great thing it is, too, for God and man to combine in One, in such a way that a man is identical with God, while the integrity of both natures is preserved! Who may presume even to think that a human intellect might be capable of fathoming how it is that such an act has been performed, so wisely and so wonderfully?

B. I agree that no human being can in this life disclose the

innermost depths of such a great mystery, and I am not asking you
to do what no human can do, only as much as you can do. For you
will be making a more persuasive case for there being deeper reasons
for this action if you show that you discern some reason for it, than
if, by saying nothing, you make it self-evident that you understand
no reason at all.

A. I see that I am unable to set myself free from your importun-
ity. But let us give thanks to God if I can to any extent make clear
the subject which you are demanding I should clarify. If, on the other
hand, I cannot, let the proofs arrived at earlier suffice. For if it is
established that God ought to become man, there is no doubt that he
does not lack the wisdom and the power whereby this may be effected
without sin.

B. I am happy to accept terms of this sort.

A. It was right, certainly, that the redemption which Christ
brought about should benefit not only the people in being at that
time, but others too.

Let us imagine that there is a king and that the entire populace of
one of his cities has sinned against him, with the exception of one
man, who is none the less of the same race. None of them, moreover, is capable of doing anything to escape from the death penalty.
Now, the man who is the only innocent party enjoys such favour with
the king that he has it in his power to bring about the reconciliation
of all those who believe in his advice, and he has such love towards
the guilty that he wishes to do this. This reconciliation will be
brought about by means of some service which will be very pleasing
to the king, and which he will perform on a stated day in accordance
with the king's desire. And, since not all who are in need of reconciliation are able to assemble on that day, the king makes the concession, in view of the magnitude of the service, that any people who
acknowledge before or after that day that they wish to receive pardon
through the act which is to be performed on that day, and that they
accede to the agreement concluded on that occasion, will be absolved
from all their past guilt. Furthermore, supposing it should come
about after this pardon that they should sin again, and provided that
they should then be willing to give satisfaction in a suitable way and
receive correction, they would receive pardon again through the
effective power of this same agreement. There would be this proviso:

that no one should enter his palace until the deed had been done whereby their wrongdoings were forgiven.

The thrust of this parable is that, when Christ brought about the redemption which we have in mind, not all those human beings who were to receive salvation were able to be present, and consequently there was such power in his death that its effect extends to those who were absent either geographically or temporally. ✓ That it would not be right for his death only to benefit those present is readily comprehensible from the fact that it was not possible for as many people to be present at his death as are needed for the building up of the heavenly city, even if all the people anywhere in existence at the time of his death were to be accepted for the redemption to which we have referred. For there are more evil angels than there would have been humans alive on that day, and it is from the human race that the full number of replacements for them has to be found.

Nor is it to be believed that, since mankind's first creation, there has been any time in which this world, filled as it is with creatures which were created for the use of mankind, has been so barren that there was no one in it from the human race bearing any relation to the purpose for which mankind was created. For it seems an incongruity that God should for one moment have permitted the human race, and all that he made for the use of the beings from whose ranks the heavenly city was to be completed, to exist, as it were, to no purpose. For they would seem to have their being in vain for as long as they did not seem to exist with a view to the purpose for which they were principally created.

B. You are demonstrating with consistent and apparently incontrovertible reasoning that, since mankind was first created, there has never been any time devoid of some person connected with that reconciliation without which all mankind was created in vain. And we can conclude that this is not only fitting, but a necessity. For, assume that this state of affairs is more fitting and logical than that there should have been at some time no one with regard to whom the intention of God in creating mankind was to be fulfilled; assume too that there is no obstacle to this logical state of affairs: in that case it is a necessary fact that there has always been someone connected with the reconciliation we have in mind. Hence it is not to be doubted that

Adam and Eve had a connection with that act of redemption, even though divine authority does not state this explicitly.

A. It also seems incredible that God excluded those two from his plan, in view of the fact that he created them and made it his plan, never deviating from it, to create from them all the human beings whom he was to take up into the heavenly city.

B. Indeed, what one ought to believe, rather, is that he created Adam and Eve particularly with the purpose in view that they should number among those for the sake of whom they were themselves created.

A. Your observation is a good one. But no soul could enter the heavenly Paradise before the death of Christ, in accordance with what I said earlier with reference to the 'king's palace'.

B. Such is the teaching which we hold to.

A. But that Virgin from whom the man about whom we are speaking was received was one of those who, before his birth, were cleansed of sins through him, and he was received from her in the state of cleanness which was hers.

B. What you are saying would please me greatly were it not for this: whereas he ought to have cleanness from sin in his own person and on his own account, he would appear to have it from his mother, and not to be clean on his own account, but through her.

A. It is not so. Rather, his mother's cleanness, whereby he is clean, would not have existed, if it had not come from him, and so he was clean on his own account and by his own agency.

B. Good—so far as that issue is concerned. But there seems to me another question to be asked. We have said earlier that he is not going to die as a matter of necessity, and now we see that his mother was clean because of his death which was to happen in the future. How, then, is it that this man, who could not have existed if it were not for the fact that he was going to die, did not die of necessity? For, if he had not been going to die, the Virgin from whom he was received would not have been clean, since this could in no way be so, except in the light of a belief in the reality of his death, and there was no other way in which he could have been received from her. Hence, if he did not die obligatorily, after he was received from the Virgin, the consequence is that he could not be received from the Virgin after he was, in fact, received—and this is an impossibility.

A. If you had considered well our previous discussions, you would have understood that in the course of them this question had been resolved.

B. I do not see how.

A. When we raised the question whether the God-Man could tell lies, did we not demonstrate that where telling lies was concerned there were two potentialities, one being a desire to tell lies, the other, actual lie-telling? Did we not also show that, while he had the capacity for telling lies, he had the characteristic inherent in himself of not being able to wish to lie, and that, for this reason, he was worthy of praise for the righteousness whereby he kept to the truth?

B. Yes.

A. Similarly, in the case of saving one's life, there is the capacity for wishing to save one's life and the capacity for saving it. When, therefore, the question is asked whether the same God-Man could have saved his life, so as never to die, it is not a matter for doubt that he always had the capacity for saving it, even though he was not capable of wishing to save it, so as never to die. And since this was something he had inherent in him—I mean, this inability to have this wish—he laid down his soul not obligatorily but by the free exercise of his power.

B. These potentialities in him to which you refer—that for telling lies and that for saving his life—were not in the least comparable. For in the one case, it is a logical consequence that he would be capable of telling a lie if he were to wish it, but in the other, it appears that, if he were to wish not to die, he would no more be capable of this than he could not be what he was. For the purpose of his being a man was this: for him to die; and it was because of the assuredness of his future death that it was possible for him to be received from a Virgin.

A. You think that he was incapable of not dying, or that it was a matter of necessity that he died, because he was incapable of not being what he was: you may just as well assert that he was incapable of wishing not to die or that he wished of necessity to die. For it was no more for the purpose that he should die that he was made a man than for the purpose that he should wish to die. Therefore, just as you ought not to say that he could not wish not to die, or that he wished to die obligatorily, similarly it ought not to be said that he could not not die, or that it was of necessity that he died.

B. No indeed. Since both these things—that is, dying and wishing to die—are subject to the same line of reasoning, and both of them seem to have been inherent in him of necessity.

A. Who was it who wished of his own volition to make himself a man, so that, by the same unchangeable will, he would die and the Virgin from whom he—that man—was to be received would be made clean through faith in the certitude in his death?

B. God, the Son of God.

A. Has it not been demonstrated earlier that when the will of God is said to do something of necessity, it is not actually coerced by necessity, but is maintaining itself by its own spontaneous unchangeability?

B. This has indeed been demonstrated. Rather we see, conversely, that something which is God's unchangeable will cannot not be and that it is necessary for it to be. Therefore, if it was God's will that the man we have in mind should die, he could not not die.

A. As an inference from the fact that the Son of God took manhood upon himself with the intention that he should die, you are asserting that the man in question could not not die?

B. That is how I understand the matter.

A. Has it not emerged likewise from our earlier discussions that the Son of God is one person with the manhood which he took upon himself, so that the Son of God and the son of the Virgin are identical?

B. Yes, it has.

A. The same man, therefore, of his own volition, could not not die and did, in fact, die.

B. I cannot deny it.

A. Since, therefore, it is not out of any necessity that the will of God performs any action, but on the strength of his own power, and since the will of that man was the will of God, it was not out of any necessity that he died but on the strength of his power alone.

B. I am incapable of rebutting your lines of argument. For I can in no way invalidate either the propositions which you are adducing as premises or the consequences which you are inferring. However, something which I have said keeps on coming back to me: that, if it were his will not to die, he would be no more capable of doing so than of not being what he was. For he was truly going to die since, if he had not been truly going to die, the faith in his future death would not be true, and it was through this faith that both the Virgin from whom he was born, and many others, have been cleansed from sin. Now, if it had not been true, it could not have been of any benefit. Consequently, if he was capable of not dying, he was capable of rendering untrue something which was the truth.

A. Why was it the truth, before he died, that he was going to die?

B. Because he wished for this spontaneously and with an unchangeable will.

A. If, therefore, as you say, he could not not die for the reason that he was truly going to die, and he was truly going to die owing to the fact that this was his spontaneous and unchangeable will, it follows that he could not not die for any other reason than because, by his unchangeable volition, it was his will to die.

B. That is right. But, whatever the reason may have been, it is nevertheless true that he could not not die and that it was necessary for him to die.

A. You are too persistent in grasping at nothingness and, as the saying goes, looking for a knot in a bulrush.

B. Have you forgotten what I said in the face of your excuses at the beginning of this disputation of ours, namely that it would not be for the learned that you would be doing what I asked, but for me and for those who were making the request along with me? Allow me therefore to ask questions corresponding to the slowness and dullness of our intelligence, so that in this way you may give me and those other people satisfaction even in the case of childish questioning, as you did at the outset.

17. *That in God no necessity or impossibility exists; and that there is a necessity which compels and a necessity which does not compel*

A. We have already said that it is incorrect to say of God that he 'cannot do something' or that he 'does it of necessity'. For all necessity, and all impossibility, is subject to his will. Moreover his will is not subject to any necessity or impossibility. For nothing is necessary or impossible for any reason other than that he himself so wills it. Indeed, for God himself to will something, or not will it, on account of necessity or impossibility, is a notion foreign to the truth. Hence, from the fact that he does all things which are his will and does nothing other than the things which are his will, two consequences follow: no necessity or impossibility precedes his volition or non-volition and, similarly, neither precedes his action or inaction, no matter how many things he may unchangeably wish or do. Moreover, when God does something, the deed cannot be undone after it has been done, but it is for ever the truth that it has been done; yet, despite this, it cannot be correctly stated that it is impossible for God to make a past event not a past event: neither the necessity for action or the impossibility of inaction is operative in this case, only the will of God who, being himself the Truth, always wishes the truth to be unchangeable, as he is. Correspondingly, in the event that God plans that he is unalterably going to do something, even though, in the time preceding his action, what he has in mind is not not going to happen, there is in him no necessity for action or impossibility of inaction, since in him it is the will alone which is operative. Now, on all occasions when it is stated that God is 'incapable' of something, this is not a negation of any capacity in him: rather, it is his insuperable power and might which is being signified. For the meaning is none other than that nothing can bring it about that he should do the thing which he is being said to be 'incapable' of doing. Now, much use is made of the type of expression whereby something is said to 'be possible', not because possibility is inherent in that thing, but because it is inherent in something else, and 'not to be possible', not because impossibility is inherent in that thing but because it is inherent in something else. For we say: 'This man is capable of being defeated', instead of 'Someone is capable of defeating him', and 'He cannot be defeated', instead of 'No one can defeat him'. For to be 'capable of being defeated' does not constitute a capability, but an incapability, and to be 'incapable of being defeated' does not constitute powerlessness, but power. Nor is it because there is any necessity inherent in him that we say that God does something 'of necessity', but rather because the necessity exists in something else; this is comparable to what I have said with reference to 'incapability' in statements to the effect that someone 'is incapable'. As for necessity, every case of it constitutes either compulsion or prohibition, and these two necessities are opposites, the converse of one another, as are 'necessity' and 'impossibility'. However, when we say with reference to God that something is, or is not, a necessity, the meaning is not that there exists in him either coercive or prohibitive necessity: the significance is that there is necessity inherent in all things other than himself which prevents him from acting—and compels him not to act—against what is predicated of God. For, when we say that it is a necessary fact that God always speaks the truth, and that it is a necessary fact that he never lies, all that is being said is that inherent in him there is such a high degree of constancy with regard to upholding the truth that nothing can make him not speak the truth, or tell lies.

Consequently, when with reference to the man we have in mind—who, in view of the unity of his person, as has been said earlier, is identical with the Son of God, God—we say that he could not not die, or could not wish not to die, after he was born of the Virgin, what is being signified is not any inability to preserve his own life, or to wish to preserve it, immortal. What is being signified, rather, is the unchangeability of his will, in response to which he had of his own volition made himself a man with the specific intent that he would die in the steadfast pursuance of that same will, and the fact that nothing could change that will. For it would be incapability more than capability, if he were to be capable of wishing to lie or to deceive or to change his will, having previously willed that it should be unalterable. Moreover, as I said earlier, when someone voluntarily plans to do some good thing, and afterwards, in accordance with the same will, completes what he planned, it is not right to say of him that he is doing what he is doing out of necessity, even though, supposing that he were unwilling to fulfil his promise, it would be possible for him to be compelled to do so. For one ought not to say that anything is being done, or not being done, out of necessity or incapability, when it is neither necessity nor incapability that is operative, but will. If, I say, this is so in the case of a human being, it is very much more the case that the terms 'necessity' and 'incapability' are not to be used at all with reference to God, who does nothing which is not his will, and whose will no force has the power to compel or prohibit. For, in the case of Christ, the difference between his natures and the unity of his person had the effect of making it possible for his divine nature to bring about what had to happen for the restoration of mankind, should his human nature not be capable of this, and for his human nature to show forth whatever was not at all appropriate for his divine nature. Moreover, it would not be a case of 'this man . . .' and 'the other . . .', but both would be himself, one and the same, and, being completely both human and divine, he would pay through his human nature the debt which human nature owed, and would be capable, through his divine nature, of what was expedient. Finally, the Virgin who was made clean through faith, so that he might be received from her, by no means believed that he was going to die for any reason other than that it was his will to do so, this being in accordance with the teaching of the prophet who said of him, 'He was made a sacrifice, because he willed it' [Isa. 53: 7 Vulg.]. Consequently, since her belief was true, it was a necessity that it would come about just as she believed. Now, if it troubles you once more that I am saying, 'It was a necessity', remember that the truth of the Virgin's belief was not the cause of his dying voluntarily: rather the belief was true because his dying voluntarily was in the future to be an actuality. Hence, supposing it is said, 'It was necessary that he should die only through his will, because prior belief or prophecy concerning it was true': this is no different from saying that it was necessary for it to come about thus in the future, since it was going to come about thus. Moreover, this sort of 'necessity' does not compel something to be: rather, the existence of an actuality makes it a necessary fact.

For there is a necessity which precedes, being the cause for an actuality's existence, and there is a necessity which is consequent, being caused by an actuality. It is a case of a necessity which precedes and effects when the statement is made that 'the sky revolves because it is a necessity that it should revolve'. It is a case of a necessity which is consequent and effects nothing but is itself caused when I say, 'You are, of necessity, speaking'. This is because when I say this, what I mean is that nothing can bring it about that, while you are speaking, you are not speaking; I do not mean that something is compelling you to speak. For the violence of a natural state of affairs compels the sky to revolve, but there is no necessity which is causing you to speak. Now, wherever there exists antecedent necessity, consequent necessity also exists. But it is not the case that where there is consequent necessity, there immediately exists antecedent necessity. For we can say, 'It is a necessity that the sky should turn, because it does turn', but it is not similarly true to say, 'You are speaking for the reason that it is a necessity for you to speak'. This consequent necessity occurs throughout the tenses, in this way. It is a necessity that whatever has been, has been. It is a necessity that whatever is, is. It is a necessity that whatever is, has been going to be. It is a necessity that everything that is going to be, is going to be. This is the necessity which, in Aristotle's treatment of singular and future propositions,[37] appears to deny the existence of alternatives and affirms that all things exist of necessity.

Since the conviction and the prophecy about Christ—that he was going to die voluntarily and not out of necessity—were true, it was on the strength of this consequent, non-effectual necessity that it was necessary that it should be so. This was the necessity whereby he was made man; whereby he did and had done to him[38] whatever he did and had done to him; whereby he willed whatever he willed. These things of necessity were, for the reason that they were going to be, and they were going to be because they were, and they were because they were. And if you want to know what the true necessity was behind all the things which he did and had done to him, know this: all these things of necessity were, because he himself so willed it. Indeed, no necessity is antecedent to his will. Hence, given that it was for no reason that these things were, other than that he willed it: if he had not so willed, they would not have been. In this way, therefore, no one took his life from him, but he himself laid it down and took it up again, because he had the 'power to lay down his life and take it up again', as he himself says [John 10: 18].

B. You have satisfied me that Christ cannot be proved to have undergone death out of any necessity, and I am not sorry that I was a nuisance to you, in order that you should do this.

A. We have made clear, I think, a definite logical explanation of how God raised up a man without sin out of sinful matter. I also think that one certainly must not deny there to be—apart from the consideration that God can do what human reasoning cannot comprehend—a logical explanation other than the one of which we have been speaking. But the explanation which I have given you seems sufficient to me, and also, if I were to wish to investigate another now, it would be necessary to look into what original sin is, and how it percolates through to the whole human race from our first ancestors, and it would be necessary to confront certain other questions which demand their own separate treatment. Let us be content, therefore, with the explanation of which we have been speaking, and

---

[37] Cf. Aristotle, *De Interpretatione*, cited by Boethius, *In De Interpretatione Aristotelis* Vol. 1: 9.31–10.1 Meiser, *PL* 64, 333, meaning, approximately, 'It is not the case, therefore, that anything exists or comes into being by chance, nor will it in future alternatively be or not be, but all things exist of necessity, and not as a matter of alternatives.'

[38] Lat. *passus est*; alternative translation, 'suffered'.

proceed to the remaining parts of the work which we have undertaken.

B. As you wish—but on condition that, with God's help, you will some time, as if in repayment of a debt, explore that other reason which you are avoiding looking into now.

A. I do not refuse your request, since I am aware that I have a desire to undertake this. But because I am uncertain about future events, I do not dare to make a promise, but place the matter at God's disposal.

18. *How the life of Christ is recompense paid to God for the sins*
    of mankind; and how Christ was obliged, and was not obliged,
    to suffer

In consequence of the question which you put forward at the beginning, many other questions have presented themselves. But say now what aspect of it seems to you in want of a complete solution.

B. The substance of the question was: why God became man, so that he might save mankind through his death, when it appears that he could have done this in another way. You have responded to this question with many cogent lines of reasoning, and have thereby shown that it was not right that the restoration of human nature should be left undone, and that it could not have been brought about unless man repaid what he owed to God. This debt was so large that, although no one but man owed it, only God was capable of repaying it, assuming that there should be a man identical with God. Hence it was a necessity that God should take man into the unity of his person, so that one who ought, by virtue of his nature, to make the repayment and was not capable of doing so, should be one who, by virtue of his person, was capable of it. Next, in view of the fact that the man who was God had to be taken from a Virgin and from the person of the Son of God, you have also shown how he could have been taken sinless from out of sinful matter. You have furthermore proved that the life of this man is so sublime and so precious that it can suffice to repay the debt owed for the sins of the whole world, and infinitely more besides. It now remains, therefore, to show how his life is recompense for the sins of mankind.

A. If he allowed himself to be killed on account of his righteousness, did he not give his life for God's honour?

B. If I can understand what I do not doubt, I will admit—although I do not see how he was acting rationally in doing this, seeing that he could have upheld righteousness unswervingly and could have preserved his life eternally—that he voluntarily gave to God, for his honour, some gift of the sort with which all that is not God cannot be compared, but which can be given as recompense for the debts of all mankind.

A. When Christ endured with kindly patience the sufferings—injuries and insults and death on the cross along with robbers—which were inflicted on him because of the righteousness which, as we have said earlier, he was obediently maintaining, he set an example to mankind, the purpose of which was that people should not turn aside, without the provocation of any perceptible discomforts, from the righteousness which they owe to God. He would certainly not have been setting this example if he had taken advantage of his power and turned aside from the death which, for such a reason, was being inflicted on him. Do you not understand this?

B. It does not seem that it was a matter of any necessity that he should personally have set this example, seeing that many people before his coming, and John the Baptist after his coming but before his death, are recognized to have done this adequately by enduring death bravely for the sake of the truth.

A. No member of the human race except Christ ever gave to God, by dying, anything which that person was not at some time going to lose as a matter of necessity. Nor did anyone ever pay a debt to God which he did not owe. But Christ of his own accord gave to his Father what he was never going to lose as a matter of necessity, and he paid, on behalf of sinners, a debt which he did not owe. In view of this, he was all the more setting an example, the purpose of this being that people would not, when there was a compelling reason, have doubts about giving to God something which each of them was some time before long to lose. He was in no way needy on his own account, or subject to compulsion from others, to whom he owed nothing, unless it was punishment that he owed them. Nevertheless, he gave his life, so precious; no, his very self; he gave his person—think of it—in all its greatness, in an act of his own, supremely great, volition.

B. You are approaching very close to my heart's desire. But be so patient as to allow me to ask a question which you may perhaps think me foolish to ask but to which it is not immediately obvious how I would reply, if I were to be asked it. You say that, when Christ died, he gave something which he did not owe. But no one will deny that, when he set this example in the way he did, he acted in a better way, and one more pleasing to God, than if he had not done this. And no one will say that he ought not to do something which he understood to be the better option and more pleasing to God. How, therefore, are we to assert that he did not owe to God what he did—namely, what he knew to be better and more pleasing to God—especially since a creature owes to God all that it is, and all that it knows and is capable of?

A. Although a creature possesses nothing of itself, none the less, when God gives it leave to do or not to do something with his permission, he is granting it the gift of having two options, under such terms that, although one option may be better, neither is definitely demanded. Instead, whether the creature does what is better, or the alternative, it is said that what it is doing is what it ought to do. Moreover, if it does what is better, it has a reward, because it is giving of its own accord what is its own. For instance, although virginity is better than marriage, neither is definitely demanded from a human being. Rather, it is said of a person who prefers to marry, and of one who prefers to preserve virginity, that this is what he ought to do. For no one says that a person ought not to choose virginity, or marriage. Rather, we say that what a person prefers, before choosing one of these options, he ought to do. And if he preserves his virginity, he looks forward to a reward for the voluntary gift which he is offering to God. When, therefore, you say that a creature owes to God what it knows is better and what it is capable of, this is not invariably true—not if you interpret the action as a matter of indebtedness, and do not read into your statement the unstated implication, 'If God commands it'. For indeed, as I have said, a person does not owe virginity as a debt. Rather, he ought to marry, if this is his preference.

But if the word 'ought' perturbs you and you cannot conceive of a meaning for it without any sense of 'owing', take note of the fact that, just as the words 'can' and 'cannot' and 'necessity' are sometimes uttered not because they apply to the subjects of the utterance in which they occur, but because they apply to something else, so it is with 'ought'. For instance, when we say that the poor 'ought' to receive alms from the rich, this is no different from saying that the rich 'ought' to give alms to the poor. For the debt owed here is not something to be exacted from a poor person, but from a rich one. It is said of God too that he 'ought' to be pre-eminent over all things, not because he is in this respect in any sense a debtor, but because all things 'ought' to be subordinate to him. It is said of him that he 'ought' to do what is his will, since that which is his will ought to be.

Thus, when some creature wishes to do something which it is its own prerogative to do or not to do, the reason why the expression 'ought to do' is used is that what it wishes ought to be. When, therefore, it was the will of the Lord Jesus, as we have said, to endure death, in view of the fact that it was his prerogative to suffer or not to suffer, the reason why he 'ought' then to do what he did was that what he wished ought to be. His action was not something that he owed, because it was not a matter of indebtedness. Indeed he is both God and man, so consequently, where his human nature was concerned, from the time when he became human, he received from his divine nature—which is different from human nature—the circumstance that whatever he had was his own. As a result, there was nothing which he 'ought' to give, except what he wished. But, where his person was concerned, he had what he had from himself, and thus was perfectly self-sufficient, and, as a result, neither owed recompense to anyone, nor needed to give recompense to himself.

B. I see plainly now that, contrary to what my reasoning seemed to indicate, there was no logical reason why it was as a result of an obligation owed that Christ gave himself up to death for the sake of God's honour—and that, nevertheless, what he did was something which he 'ought' to do.

A. That honour, to be sure, belongs to the whole of the Trinity. It follows that because Christ himself is God, the Son of God, the offering he made of himself was to his own honour as well as to the Father and the Holy Spirit; that is, he offered up his humanity to his divinity, the one selfsame divinity which belongs to the three persons. However, so that we may express our meaning more clearly, while remaining steadfast in the same truth, let us say, as customary usage has it, that the Son voluntarily offered himself to the Father. For it is most appropriate to speak in this way, because, in referring to the one person, one understands the whole God to whom Christ offered himself as a human being. Moreover, through the naming of Father and Son, a feeling of immense pious devotion is aroused in the hearts of listeners, since the Son is said in this way to be making supplication to the Father on our behalf.

B. I accept this most gladly.

19. *With what very great logicality the salvation of mankind follows from his death*

A. Let us contemplate now, as far as we are able, with what very great logicality human salvation follows from his death.

B. This is the direction towards which my heart inclines. For, although it seems to me that I understand this, I none the less want the structure of the logic to be worked out by you.

A. There is no need, however, to expound what a great gift it is that the Son voluntarily gave.

B. That is sufficiently clear.

A. Moreover, it will not be your judgement that someone who gives such a great gift to God ought to go without recompense.

B. No. I see that it is necessary that the Father should compensate the Son. Otherwise, he would seem unjust if he lacked the will, and powerless if he lacked the ability, to do so; both of which qualities are foreign to God.

A. Someone who gives recompense to another either gives what that person does not have or excuses what cannot be exacted from him. But before the Son performed his supremely great action, all things which belonged to the Father belonged to him, and he had no debt which he could be excused. What compensation is to be given, therefore, to someone who lacks nothing and to whom nothing can be given or excused?

B. On the one hand, I see the necessity for compensation and, on the other, its impossibility. For it is both necessary for God to give what he owes, and there is nothing for him to give as recompense.

A. If a reward, supremely great and supremely well-merited, is not given to him or to anyone else, the Son will seem to have done his supremely great act to no purpose.

B. It is an abomination to countenance this idea.

A. It is inevitable, therefore, that, because it cannot be given to him, it must be given to someone else.

B. This follows inevitably.

A. Supposing the Son wished that what was owed to him should be given to someone else, could the Father have justly prevented him, or denied the gift to the intended recipient?

B. No. I appreciate that it is both just and necessary that it should be handed over as recompense by the Father to the recipient to whom the Son wished to give it. This is for two reasons: it is permissible for the Son to give what is his own, and it is only to someone else that the Father can give what he owes.

A. On whom is it more appropriate for him to bestow the reward and recompense for his death than on those for whose salvation, as the logic of truth teaches us, he made himself a man, and for whom, as we have said, he set an example, by his death, of dying for the sake of righteousness? For they will be imitators of him in vain, if they are not to be sharers in his reward. Again, whom is he with greater justice to make heirs of the recompense due to him, and of the overflowing of his bounty, than those who are parents and brothers to him, whom he sees, bound by so many and such enormous debts, wasting away with deprivation in the depths of misery? The debt that they owe for their sins would, as a result, be excused and they would be given what, because of their sins, they are deprived of.

B. There can be nothing more logical, nothing sweeter, nothing more desirable that the world can hear. I indeed derive such confidence from this that I cannot now express in words with what joy my heart is rejoicing. For it seems to me that God rejects no member of the human race who approaches him on this authority.

A. So it is, if he makes the approach in the way that he should. Moreover, how one should approach the state of sharing in this grace, and how one should live once subject to that state, is something which Holy Scripture teaches, based as it is on the solid truth into which, with God's help, we have to some extent gained an insight, truth which is, as it were, a firm foundation.

B. Truly, whatever is built upon this foundation is founded on firm rock.

A. I think I have now gone some little way towards a satisfactory reply to your question, although someone better than I could do it more fully, and there are more, and greater, reasons for this thing than my intellect, or any mortal intellect, can comprehend. It is clear also that God in no way had a need which required him to perform the action of which we have been speaking: rather, it was

unchangeable truth that demanded that this be so. For, granted that
this was the action of the man of whom we have spoken and that it
may be said that God did it, in view of the unity of his person, it is
nevertheless not the case that God needed to come down from heaven
to conquer the devil, or to take action against him in order to set
mankind free. Rather, God demanded it of man that he should defeat
the devil and should pay recompense by means of righteousness,
having previously offended God through sin. Certainly God did not
owe the devil anything but punishment, nor did man owe him anything but retribution—to defeat in return him by whom he had been
defeated. But, whatever was demanded from man, his debt was to
God, not to the devil.

20. *How great and just the mercy of God is*

Now, the mercy of God which, when we were considering the justice
of God and the sin of mankind, seemed to you to be dead,[39] we have
found to be so great, and so consonant with justice, that a greater
and juster mercy cannot be imagined. What, indeed, can be conceived of more merciful than that God the Father should say to a
sinner condemned to eternal torments and lacking any means of
redeeming himself, 'Take my only-begotten Son and give him on
your behalf', and that the Son himself should say, 'Take me and
redeem yourself'. For it is something of this sort that they say when
they call us and draw us towards the Christian faith. What also could
be juster than that the one to whom is given a reward greater than
any debt should absolve all debt, if it is presented with the feeling
that is due?

21. *That it is impossible for the devil to receive reconciliation*

As for the reconciling of the devil about which you asked,[40] you will
understand this to be impossible if you carefully consider the reconciling of mankind. For just as man could not be reconciled except
by a man-God who was capable of dying, through whose righteousness what God lost through the sin of mankind might be restored,
likewise the condemned angels cannot be saved except by an angel-

[39] Cf. 1.25 above.
[40] Cf. 1.17.

God who would be capable of dying and who would restore by his righteousness what the sins of the others have stolen. Moreover, just as it was not right that man should be restored by another man who was not of the same race, even if he were of the same nature, similarly it is not right that an angel should be saved by another angel, even if he were of the same nature, since angels are not of one race as human beings are. For angels are not all descended from one angel in the same way that human beings are descended from one man. Another thing which rules out their restoration is that, just as they fell without having as the cause of their fall injury from anyone else, similarly they ought to rise once more without the assistance of anyone else—and this is impossible for them. For there is no other way in which they can be restored to the dignity which they were to have possessed, since, supposing they had not sinned, they would have been remaining steadfast in the truth without anyone else's assistance, through power which they had received as their own. Consequently, if anyone advances the opinion that our Saviour's redemption ought at some time to be extended to them, it is proved by logic that he is being deceived contrary to logic. I do not say this on the supposition that the value of the death of Christ does not outweigh in its magnitude all the sins of mankind and of the angels, but because unalterable logic opposes the granting of relief to the fallen angels.

22. *That by the things which have been said, the truth of the Old Testament and the New has been proved*

B. All the things which you say seem to me logical and incontrovertible. And my understanding is that, through the solution given to the single problem which we set ourselves, all that is contained in the New Testament and the Old has been proved. For you prove that it is a matter of necessity for God to become man, and you do so in such a way that, even if one were to remove the few things posited by you that come from books of ours, such as the material you have touched upon with regard to the three persons of God and with regard to Adam—you would be providing something which would satisfy not only Jews, but even pagans. The God-Man himself it is who establishes the New Testament and confirms the Old. Therefore, in the same way that it is a necessity to acknowledge that the

God–Man is truthful, likewise no one can fail to acknowledge that all that is contained in those Testaments is true.

A. If we have said anything that ought to be corrected, I do not refuse correction. But if it is corroborated by the Testimony of Truth, as we think we have by means of logic discovered, we ought to attribute this not to ourselves but to God, who is blessed throughout all ages. Amen.

ON THE VIRGIN CONCEPTION AND ORIGINAL SIN

As far as it is in my power to do so, I have always been anxious to comply with your thoroughly pious interests, my brother and dear son Boso, and since in this case it is I that have aroused your curiosity, I think that I owe you particular satisfaction. I have a strong impression that in my book *Why God Became Man*, which you more than any encouraged me to write, and which took the form of an imaginary dialogue between us, you have detected another argument besides the one I advanced, showing how God assumed sinless human nature from the sinful mass of humanity: and your lively intelligence has prompted you to try to find out what it is. Therefore, since I am afraid that I shall be doing you an injustice if I keep my thoughts on the subject to myself, I shall briefly summarize my thinking, in such a way that I shall not dismiss the faithful opinion of anyone, nor persist in defending my own view if it can reasonably be proved to be contrary to the truth. However, the reasoning which I set out in my work seems to me to be valid and sufficient if given careful thought. Nothing, after all, prevents the question from having several arguments running through it, each of which will·stand by itself.

Chapters

1. *A definition of original sin and personal justice and injustice*

So then, if we want to see how God assumed human nature without sin from the sinful mass of humanity, we shall first need to investigate original sin, because it is from this alone that our inquiry arises. If it can be seen how Christ could not be subject to it, it will be clear how his assumption or conception was entirely free from sin.

We can assume that the word 'original' comes from 'origin'. So, if original sin does not exist apart from human beings, it is likely to be called 'original' either after the origin of human nature, that is, original from its first beginning, in that it is contracted at the origin of human nature itself; or after each individual's origin or beginning, being contracted at that particular person's origin.

But since our first parents were created just and entirely sinless, the origin of human nature must have been just, and so I do not think that original sin descends to us from the origin of human nature. Therefore original sin would seem to take its name from the origin of each human person. However, I will not argue with anyone who says that sin is called original in that it descends to individuals from those from whom they have their original nature—as long as he concedes that each individual contracts original sin with his own origin. Let us consider that in each man there exist together both the nature which makes him a man like all other men, and the person which distinguishes him from others, so that he is called this or that man, or given a proper name, such as Adam or Abel; and also that each man's sin exists in his nature and his person—for the sin of Adam was both in the man, that is in his nature, and in the one who was called Adam, that is in the person. There is then a difference between the sin that each man contracts with his nature at his origin, and the sin that he does not contract with his own nature, but commits after he has become a person distinct from other persons. Indeed, the sin that is contracted at his origin is called 'original', which could also be expressed as 'natural' sin, not because it comes from the essence of nature, but because it is taken up with corrupted nature. But the sin that each man commits after he has become a person can be called 'personal' sin, because it comes about through a fault in the person. We can use the same terms to speak of 'original' and 'personal' justice: so Adam and Eve were 'originally' just, that is, they were just as soon as they began to exist as humans. But justice can be called personal, if an unjust man is given justice which he did not originally have.

2. *How human nature became corrupted*

Therefore, if Adam and Eve had retained their original justice, their descendants would, like them, have been originally just. But they committed personal sin, and so whereas originally they had the strength and integrity to remain just without trouble, their whole being was now weakened and corrupted. Their bodies after their sin became like those of brute beasts, subject to corruption and carnal appetites, and their souls, ruled by this bodily corruption and these appetites, and deprived of the gifts they had lost, were themselves infected with carnal appetites. And because the whole of human nature was contained in Adam and Eve, and nothing of it existed outside them, the whole of human nature was weakened and corrupted.

And so, along with the corruption which it incurred through sin, human nature was left with the obligation of possessing, whole and unadulterated, the justice which it had been given, and with the obligation to make satisfaction for having abandoned it. If human nature had not sinned, it would have been propagated as God had made it: thus after its sin it is propagated according to what it has made of itself by sinning. Human nature alone does not have the strength to make satisfaction for sin or to recover the justice it abandoned: 'the body which is corrupted burdens the soul', especially at times when it is particularly weak, for example in infancy and in its mother's womb, while the soul cannot even discern what is just. It would therefore seem inevitable that human nature should be born in infants with the obligation of making satisfaction for the first sin, which it has always had the potential to avoid, and with the obligation to possess original justice, which it has always had the power to keep.

Not even in the case of infants is human nature excused by weakness when it does not fulfil its debt, because it brought that weakness upon itself when it abandoned justice in our first parents in whom it entirely subsisted. The obligation persists for human nature to have the power it was given to be just. This is, I think, how infants come to have original sin.

Perhaps we might consider here the sins of our recent ancestors, which are 'reckoned unto the third and fourth generation'. It is arguable whether or not all these are to be included with original sin, but I do not wish to be seen to be trivializing the subject of my investigation, and so I shall say no more than that original sin is such that nothing can be shown to be graver.

3. *Sin exists only in the rational will*

If this has given a full account of original sin, or even if it has come short of one, I do not think that it is to any extent possible to assert that original sin exists in an infant before he has a rational soul, any more than there was justice in Adam before he became a rational man. For even if Adam and Eve had produced a child without their preceding sin, justice would not have been in their seed, nor could have been, before it was formed into a living man. Therefore, if a man's seed is not able to assume justice before it becomes a man, neither will it be able to assume original sin.

It must be agreed that original sin is injustice: if all sin is injustice, and original sin is sin, then it follows that original sin is also injustice. But anyone who states that not all sin is injustice is saying that in one person there can be sin and no injustice, which I find incredible.

It might be said that original sin is not sin absolutely speaking, but sin with the qualification 'original', in the way that a man in a painting is not really a man but a painted man; then surely it would follow that an infant that has no sin but original sin is free from sin; and that the Virgin's Son was not alone among men sinless in the womb and at his birth; and that a child that dies unbaptized and only having original sin either is not condemned or is condemned while sinless. But since we accept none of these, we can accept that all sin is injustice, and that original sin is absolutely sin. It follows then that original sin is also injustice.

Furthermore, if God does not condemn a man except because of injustice, but does condemn him because of original sin, original sin can only be injustice. If this is the case, and injustice is nothing but the absence of due justice—injustice being manifested only in a nature which lacks the justice it ought to have—then clearly original sin is included within the same definition of injustice.

But if justice is 'rectitude of the will preserved for its own sake', and that rectitude cannot exist except in rational nature, then it is only rational nature from which justice is due, since no nature is susceptible of justice except rational nature. Therefore, since injustice cannot exist except where justice ought to be, original sin, that is injustice, does not exist except in rational nature. But only God, angels and the soul of man, by which he is called a rational man, and without which he is not a man, are rational natures. Since neither God nor the angels have original sin, it cannot exist anywhere except in the rational nature of man.

We should also note that if justice is rectitude of the will preserved for its own sake, then justice can only exist in the will. If this is true, the same can be said of injustice, for the absence of justice is only called injustice when justice ought to be there.

So, apart from justice or injustice themselves, it is only the just or unjust will or its consequences that is called just or unjust. It is this that allows us to speak of a just or unjust man or angel, a just or unjust soul or action.

4. *That nothing is just or unjust by itself but justice and injustice themselves; and that nothing is punished but the will*

As I have said, nothing is considered just in itself but justice, and nothing is thought unjust or sinful but injustice: not substance nor action, nor even the will in which justice or injustice reside. For we should distinguish what we call the 'will': that power of the soul by which the soul wills anything, and which can be called the 'instrument' of willing, in the way that sight is the instrument of seeing, from justice, by whose presence the will is called 'just', and by whose absence it is called 'unjust'. The affections and uses of this instrument are also called 'wills', but this would take too long to explore here.

Nor do we consider just or unjust by themselves those appetites which the Apostle describes as 'the flesh which lusts against the spirit', and the 'law of sin which is in our members, fighting against the law of the mind' [Rom. 7: 23]. For a man is not made just or unjust simply by experiencing them: the unjust man is the one who consents to them willingly when he should not. For the same Apostle says, 'There is no condemnation for those who are in Christ Jesus, who do not walk according to the flesh' [Rom. 8: 1, 4], which is to say that they do not consent to the will of the flesh. For if such appetites were to make the man experiencing them unjust without his consent, they would bring condemnation.

So then, it is not in experiencing these appetites, but in consenting to them that the sin lies. For if the appetites were unjust in themselves, they would confer injustice whenever they were consented to. But when the beasts consent to them, they are not called unjust. Moreover, if they were sins, they would be removed at baptism, when all sin is wiped away, which is patently not the case.

From this we see that the injustice is not in the essence of these appetites, but in the uncontrolled rational will that follows them. For when the will resists them, 'delighting in the law of God according to the inner man', then the will is just. Indeed, the Apostle calls the justice commanded by the law both 'the law of God', because it comes from God, and 'the law of the mind', because it is understood by the mind; just as the old law is called 'the law of God', because it comes from God, and 'the law of Moses', because it was given through Moses.

My argument that an action is called unjust not in itself, but rather through an unjust will, is clearly demonstrated by those things that on occasion are done not entirely without justice, such as killing a man, as Phineas did; or sexual intercourse between married couples or between animals. However, it is less obvious in things which can never be done without injustice, such as perjury, and other actions which perhaps we will not name here.

We should consider, however, the kind of action by which something is done, and which exists only while that thing is being done, which thing once done the action passes away and no longer exists, along with the kind of work which is performed and remains—for example, when something is written which ought not to be written, the act of writing passes, while the characters written remain. If either of these were a sin, once the action had passed away and did not exist, the sin equally would no longer exist; or as long as what it had brought about remained, the sin would never be wiped out. But it often happens that sins are not removed when an action passes away, or that they are wiped out while a work remains. Therefore neither the action that passes nor the work that remains is ever itself a sin.

Finally, if the limbs and senses are accused of voluntary actions unjustly performed, they could answer: 'God subjected us and the power in us to the will, and when the will commands it is not possible for us not to move and do what it wishes. The will moves us as its instruments, and it does the works which we are seen to do. We cannot resist it by our own power, nor can the works which it does be prevented. God gave the will to us as our mistress, and we cannot and should not disobey it. When we obey it, we obey God who gave us this law.' So, then, how can the limbs sin, or the senses or the works, which God has thus subjected to the will, if they are carrying out what God has ordained for them? Whatever they do is entirely imputed to the will.

If this is the case, it might seem strange that it is the members and senses that are punished for the sins of the will. But this is really not the case. It is only the will that is punished. For a punishment is only effective because it is against the will, and only beings with a will feel punishment. The limbs and senses have no will of their own. So if the will is exercised in the members and senses, it will equally experience pleasure and pain in them. If anyone does not accept this, he should at least realize that the soul alone, in which the will resides, feels and works in the members and senses, and therefore feels pain or pleasure through them. Conventionally, however, we call sins those actions performed by an unjust will, because the sin is in the will by which they come about. We give names to some of these actions, such as fornication or lying, indicating that they are unjustly performed. But it is one thing to consider the action or utterance itself, and another to consider whether it is justly or unjustly done. In any case, since every being comes from God, from whom comes nothing unjust, no being is in itself unjust.

5. *That evil, that is sin or injustice, is nothing*

Injustice itself, however, does not exist, any more than blindness exists. For blindness is nothing but the absence of vision where vision should be. It is not something present in the eye where sight should be, any more than it would be present in a piece of wood where sight should not be. Injustice is not something which infects and corrupts the soul, as poison does the body, nor is it an agent, as we can see when a wicked man performs bad deeds. For when a beast breaks its chains and runs wild, or when a steersman has left the helm of his ship and abandoned it to the winds and currents to drift into all kinds of danger, we say that it is the absence of chains or a rudder that is the agent—not that this absence is something, or does something, but because if they had been there they would have prevented the beast from rampaging or the ship foundering. Thus when a wicked man rages and is driven into the various dangers posed by his evil deeds, we protest that injustice does these deeds; not that injustice is something in itself or does anything, but because the will to which all voluntary movements of every man is subject, without justice, inconstant, unrestrained and ungoverned, throws itself and every-thing subject to it into all kinds of evil, all of which justice, had it been present, would have prevented from happening.

From all of this it can easily be seen that injustice has no being, although we are accustomed to give this name to the effects and acts of the unjust will, which considered by themselves are something. By the same argument, we understand that evil is nothing. For as injustice is nothing but the absence of the justice that ought to be there, evil is nothing but the absence of the good that ought to be there. But no being, however evil it may be said to be, is nothing, nor is it being evil that makes it something. For it is nothing for any being to be evil, other than to lack that good which it ought to have. The absence of the good that ought to be there is not what makes some-thing exist. So being evil does not mean being something.

I have sketched out here a few ideas on evil, or rather injustice, which is indubitably nothing. For incommodity is an evil, from which incommodities are called evils; sometimes, as in the case of blindness or deafness, these are nothing, while sometimes they seem to have some substance, as with pain and grief. But my treatise *On the Fall of the Devil* has, I think, adequately shown that justice is uprightness of will kept for its own sake, and that injustice is nothing but the absence of justice that should be there, and has no being: that every being comes from God, and that nothing that is not good comes from God. Justice is dealt with in greater depth in my work *On Truth*.

6. *When God punishes sin, he does not punish for nothing at all*

There are some who, when they are told that sin is nothing, reply 'If sin is nothing, why does God punish man for sin, when nobody ought to be punished for nothing?' This is a minor point, but since these people do not understand what they are asking, some brief answer should be made here.

We will assume that the absence of justice is nothing, both where justice ought to be and where it ought not to be. But God rightly punishes sinners, not for nothing but for something: for, as I have said in my book mentioned above, he demands the honour due to him from unwilling sinners which they did not wish to render freely, and he places them apart from the just in due order so that nothing should be out of place in his kingdom. But he does not punish those creatures in which there is no obligation for justice, for the absence of justice is nothing, because there is nothing that he requires from them, nor does the order of the universe require it. Therefore, although the absence of due justice is itself nothing, God cannot be said to punish for nothing when he punishes for sin, and it is true to say that unless there is something which deserves punishment, he will never punish for nothing.

7. *How human nature can be called unclean and conceived in sin*

I think that it is now clear from what has been said that sin and injustice are nothing, and only exist as attributes of the rational will, and that no being but the will is properly called unjust. From this it would seem to follow either that from its very conception a foetus has a rational soul, without which it cannot have a rational will, or that there is no original sin at the moment of its conception. But no reasonable man accepts that a foetus has a rational soul at the moment of its conception. It would therefore follow that if at any time from the moment it was taken up, the foetus were to die before it achieved human shape, the human soul in it would be damned, because it was not reconciled through Christ. As this is clearly absurd, we should perhaps leave aside this part of the argument.

But if a foetus does not have sin at the moment of its conception, what does Job mean when he says to God: 'who but you who alone are can make clean one conceived from unclean seed' [Job 14: 4]? And how can David say: 'I was conceived in iniquity and my mother conceived me in sin' [Ps. 51: 5]? I will investigate, therefore, how, if sin is not in infants immediately at conception, they can be said to be conceived of impure seed in iniquity and sin.

Often divine Scripture asserts something that is not actually so, meaning that it is certain that it will be so. Thus God spoke to Adam of the forbidden tree: on the day that you eat of it you will die the death—not that he would die on that day, but that on that day he incurred the necessity that one day he would die. Paul, likewise, says of the inevitability of dying one day: if Christ is in you, your body is indeed dead unto sin, but your spirit is alive through justification. For those he addressed were not in fact dead, but they were destined to die through sin, because 'sin entered this world through one man, and through sin, death'. Thus when Adam sinned we all sinned in him, not because we ourselves, who did not yet exist, sinned, but because we were to be born from him: it was then that the necessity was created that when we came to be we should sin, because 'through the sin of one disobedient man many were made sinners'.

Similarly, man can be said to be conceived of impure seed in iniquity and sin, not because his seed contains the uncleanness of sin or iniquity, but because from that seed and that conception from which he began to be a man he took on the necessity that when he gained a rational soul he would gain with it the uncleanness of sin, which is nothing other than sin and iniquity. For if an infant is generated even in wicked concupiscence, the sin is no more in the seed than it would be in the spittle or blood, if someone in ill-will were to spit or bleed. For the blame attaches not to the blood or spittle but to the ill-will. I have thus made it clear how there is no sin in infants at the very moment of conception, and demonstrated the truth of the texts that I have quoted from Scripture. Indeed there is no sin in these infants, because they do not have that will, without which they can have no sin; however, sin is said to be in them, because with the seed they assume the necessity that when they become human beings they will sin.

8. *That in the seed taken up from the virgin there is neither sin nor the necessity for future sin*

Therefore if all this is true—and I believe it is—if what is taken up from the parent to the offspring has no will, it has no sin. It is then clear that whatever the Son of God took to his person from the Virgin could contain no stain of sin. But I have said that seed is taken from the parents along with the necessity of future sin when it becomes animated by a rational soul. This is simply because, as I have said, human nature is born in infants with the obligation to make satisfaction for the sin of Adam, and, according to what I have argued, of recent ancestors. This is impossible for human nature to achieve, and as long as it does not achieve it it sins: alone it does not have the strength to have the justice which it has abandoned, and the soul, burdened by the corruptible body, cannot even comprehend justice, which if not comprehended cannot be kept nor possessed. Because of this, if we can show that the seed taken from the Virgin was free from these obligations, it will be clear that Our Lord derived no necessity of sin from it.

If we accept that the assumed and assuming nature are a personal unity, and then exclude that necessity by which human nature appears to be bound to make satisfaction for the sins of its first and more recent ancestors, it will be easily shown that the seed taken from the Virgin has no relation either to that necessity by which human nature alone is unable to recover justice, or to that necessity by which the corruptible body so burdens the soul that even if justice were granted to human nature in the fullness of age we could not keep it without the help of grace, while in infancy we could not even comprehend it. But as for any debt incurred by any more recent ancestors, there will be no doubt that the seed is not bound by any such obligation, if it can be seen to be free from the obligation of our first parents. With God's help, therefore, I shall try first to find out how it can be established firmly enough to make any further elaboration unnecessary.

9. *Why the sin by which the human race is condemned is imputed more to Adam than to Eve, when he sinned after and because of her*

To this end it seems to me that the first question to ask is why the sin by which the human race was condemned is more frequently and more particularly imputed to Adam than to Eve, when Eve sinned first and Adam after and through her. For the Apostle says: 'But Death reigned from Adam to Moses, even in those who did not sin according to the likeness of Adam's transgression' [Rom. 5: 14]. We can find many other texts which seem to condemn Adam rather than Eve.

I think this comes about because the couple is thought of under the name of the principal party, in the same way that we often use a part to signify the whole; or in that Adam along with his rib, even though a woman was created from it, can be called 'Adam', as we read that God 'male and female he created them and blessed them and called them Adam on the day they were created' [cf. Gen. 1: 27, 28]; or because, if Eve alone and not Adam had sinned, it would not have been the fate of the whole human race to die, but Eve's alone. For God could then have fulfilled his purpose by making another woman from Adam, in whom he had created the seed of every human being. By the same reasoning I shall indicate both under the name of Adam, unless I need to distinguish between them.

10. *How men who were not accessories to it are burdened with the sin of Adam*

Indeed each son of Adam is a man by his creation in Adam through propagation and a person through the individuation by which he is distinguished from others. He has been given his being as a man not by Adam, but through Adam. For as Adam did not make himself a man, likewise he did not create in himself the property of generation, but God who made him a man created this nature in him so that men might be generated from him. There can however be no doubt about the origin of the obligation in question that binds each human being. It does not arise because he is a man, nor because he is a person. For if each individual is guilty of this debt because he is a man or a person it was necessary for Adam, before he sinned, to be bound by this debt because he was a man and a person; which is quite absurd. It remains therefore that he is a debtor simply because he is Adam, and not only because he is Adam, but because he is Adam the sinner. It would otherwise follow that if Adam had never sinned, those who were to be propagated from him would still be born with this debt, and this would be an impious belief.

It would not be out of place here to repeat what I have said above, on why each man is burdened with the sin or debt of Adam, each being propagated from Adam, although he is not implicated in the sin itself. When God made Adam, he created in him the property of generation which he placed under Adam's power so that he should use it according to his own will for as long as he wished to be subject to God. He was not to use it in bestial and unreasoning pleasure but according to a humane and rational will. For as it is characteristic of beasts to want nothing reasonably, it is characteristic of humans to want nothing without reason: this has always been their duty, because they accepted this power from Adam, and Adam could always have kept it. God also gave Adam this grace, that when he created him without the operation of the property of generation or the will of a creature, at the same time he made him rational and just. Thus those whom he begot by operation of nature and the will would have been just from the moment that they had a rational soul—if only he had not sinned.

By the same argument by which rational nature is proved to have been created just—as I have shown in my previous book—it is also proved that anyone propagated from human nature without forego-ing sin would necessarily be endowed with justice, and indeed God who created the first man without the generation of parents, also created those who are made through the property of generation that he created. Therefore, if sin had not come first, every man would have been, like Adam, just and reasonable. But Adam declined to be subject to the will of God, so that the property of generation, although it remained, was not subjected to his will, as it would have been had he not sinned. He lost the grace which he was in a position to keep for those begotten from him, so that everyone generated through the nature given to him are born bound by his debt. Through this needless sin, from which it could not redeem itself, human nature, which was entire in Adam so that nothing of it existed beyond him, dishonoured God. It lost the grace given to it which it was always able to keep for those to be propagated from it, and it brings on the sin with the accompanying penalty for sin whenever it is propagated by the property of generation given to it.

11. *Why the sin by which the human race was condemned is imputed to Adam rather than to Eve, when he sinned after her and because of her*

Our next task is to consider carefully whether this inheritance of sin and the punishment for sin should duly cross to the man propagated from Adam through the Virgin. We can assume that the nature of propagation given to Adam operated only through the union of a man and a woman. Indeed it is not in the power of human nature for a man alone or a woman alone to beget a human being merely by the operation of nature and his own will, and it is generally understood to be quite impossible. For the clay of the earth was not given a nature or a will, by whose operation the first man might be made from it, although it was the material from which God could make him; nor was the first woman made from the man's rib or a man from a woman alone by the operation of nature or the will of man, but God by his own power and will made one man from clay, and another man from a woman alone and a woman from a man alone. Allowing that nothing is done entirely without the action or permission of the will of God, some things his power and will alone perform, some things created nature, and some things the will of a creature.

But since created nature can do nothing alone, except for what has been granted it by the will of God, then the will of the creature cannot perform anything by itself except with the permission and aid of nature. God's will alone made the nature of things in the beginning, allotting wills appropriate to each creature, so that these natures and wills would perform their tasks in due course according to the ordinance given to them; and still it often happens that the will of God is effective where the natures and wills achieve things that they would never have done following their own uses and purposes.

It has been the work of God's will alone that the sea opened up a dry way for his people, that the dead rise, that water was turned suddenly into wine, that by the Holy Spirit the hearts of men are taught things which they knew neither from themselves nor from any other creature, that vicious wills guided by grace alone are turned to profitable actions, that many other things come about, which are worked neither through a creature nor its will. Nature draws light things upwards, heavy things downwards; makes the earth produce plants and innumerable trees and makes them fruitful, sometimes when a will has tilled and sown it, and sometimes with no operation of the will: and there are many other examples which are better observed than known by learning; the kind of things imputed to the will, including travelling, building, writing, speaking, and similar actions which are only done through the will.

Everything that takes place, if carefully considered, comes about by the will of God alone, by nature according to the power accorded it by God, or by the will of a creature; and those things which neither created nature nor the will of a creature but only God does are always miraculous. It is therefore apparent that there are three ranks of events: the miraculous, the natural and the voluntary. And the miraculous is not at all governed by the others or their laws, but freely governs; nor does it harm them, when it seems to come up against them, because they have nothing but what they have received from it, nor has it given to them anything except what is under it. Thus if the propagation of a man from a virgin is not voluntary or natural but miraculous, like that which brought forth a woman from a man alone, and like the creation of man from clay, it is clear that it cannot submit to the laws and merits of that propagation which nature and the will—although separately—work. For here the will does one thing and nature another. But equally Adam is a man taken from a non-human, and Jesus from a woman alone and Eve from a man alone, as much as any man or woman from a man and a woman. But every man is either Adam or born of Adam; but Eve is from Adam alone, and all others from Adam and Eve. Mary, from whom alone Jesus comes, is of Adam and Eve; therefore he cannot but be born of them. Thus it was expedient that he who was to redeem the human race should have his being and birth from the father and mother of us all.

12. *That it would be wrong for the ills of Adam to transfer to that man*

It will also be clear from this that the Son of the Virgin is not subject to the sin or debt of Adam. For Adam was made just and free from sin and the debt to which I have frequently referred and from the penalty of sin: he was happy and had the power to retain for ever the justice he was given, and through that justice liberty and happiness. Still, although he had the ability to keep these blessings without trouble he did not keep them for himself: he robbed himself of them and subjected himself to their opposites. Thus he became enslaved to sin—or injustice—and to debts which he could not repay, and the misery of being unable to recover the blessings he had lost.

Therefore, as it was not for him to deprive himself of the blessings that he had, or bring upon himself the evils he did not yet have, unless he let go of those gifts by his own choice, he could not remove those same gifts from another person and bring evils on him, except by not keeping those gifts for him for whom he could keep them. But he was in a position only to keep these gifts for those for whose generation he accepted the power subjected to his will. Therefore he could not transfer these evils I have spoken of to any person, although propagated from him, in whose generation neither the propagating nature given to him nor his will worked anything or had the power to work anything. Thus it is neither reasonable nor right that these evils of Adam should descend to the man born of the Virgin.

13. *Even if Christ were not God but a mere man, it would still have been necessary for him to be created in the same state as the first man*

To make another point: if with the pure insight of reason we consider the providence of God, it will be seen as absurd that, even if Christ were not assumed into the person of God, but had been made a mere man, any binding debt or punishment for sin should pass to him. It was not created nature, nor the will of a creature, nor a power given to any being that bore or sowed that seed; the will of God alone used a new power to set it aside from the Virgin for the procreation of a man free from sin. For by the same argument according to which God needed to make Adam entirely just and unhindered by any failing or debt, it will be plain to the rational mind that he could not make a man, created likewise through his own will and power, subject to any evil: it would be grossly unfitting to the omnipotent and wise providence of God to make such a rational nature by his own will alone from material in which there is no sin. Anyone who does not perceive this has no conception of what is unfitting to God. Therefore even if God had made a mere man in the way that I have suggested, it would be necessary for him to be endowed with no less justice and happiness than Adam had when he was first created.

14. *Texts in Scripture stating that man is conceived of unclean seed and in iniquity do not affect our argument, even though there are cases where these are appropriate*

There may still be somebody who does not grasp what I have said about human seed, that there is no sin in it before there is a rational soul, but that it is called impure in sin and iniquity because of its future impurity when it becomes a man: he thinks that it is impure at the moment of conception because he has read: 'who can make something clean conceived of unclean seed?' and: 'I was conceived in iniquity and in sin hath my mother conceived me'—texts that I have brought in to test my own argument. I do not need to spend much labour here to make him understand something he is not capable of understanding, and I will not try: but I will ask him to consider this brief explanation.

The writers of these texts wanted them either to be understood of every man's seed, or only of that seed which is sown with the sense of pleasure which would only have belonged to brute beasts, if man had not sinned. But if they meant this of every seed, then the seed taken from the Virgin alone was unclean, and this belief would be blasphemous. Therefore they did not write of this, but if they spoke of the seed of a man according to the second sense, they meant it to be understood that it was conceived in the pleasure I was speaking of. This in no way contradicts our argument that the seed taken from the Virgin is clean, although it is taken from the mass of sin.

15. *How the sinful mass is not entirely sinful*

For when we call a man blind, we do not locate his blindness in a part of his body such as his hand or his foot but in the eyes where sight ought to be—likewise the deafness of a deaf man resides only in his ears: thus although the mass of the human race is called sinful, it is only, as I have said, in the will that sin is to be found: and the embryo is understood not to have a will at conception. Therefore if we consider what has been said hitherto, we can conclude without contradiction of any true or apparently true argument that no reason, no truth, no thought can allow the man conceived by the Virgin alone to be tainted by the sin of the sinful mass, although it is assumed from it, and that this would be the case even if he were not God.

16. *Why John the Baptist and others who were similarly miraculously conceived, are not themselves free from sin*

What then if someone brings up the example of some, such as John the Baptist, who were propagated from women who were barren and whose nature of generation had passed away in their old age: if these were conceived miraculously, it is suggested, perhaps by a similar argument they should be considered to have been born without sin and the punishment for sin. In fact, the argument which shows that the virginal conception was free from all necessity of sin is to be understood quite differently for these cases. It is one thing to perform something unheard of, unexpected and unknown to nature, but something different to recover nature weakened by age or some other defect and recall it to its task. For if Adam had not sinned, just as he would have been weakened by no old age or any cause, the property of generation created in him and, as we have said, subjected to his power for his own use would not have been deflected from its course by his fall. For these people, therefore, no new element has been added to Adam's nature, as was given to the Virgin's son, but what in their case was weak is known to have been repaired. Therefore, because they were generated through the nature of propagation given to Adam, the fact that their conceptions were miraculous does not and should not in any way free them from original sin.

17. *Why God should become incarnate, when from Adam he could make enough sinless men who were not also God*

Perhaps someone will ask: You have said that a mere man who was not God could be made from Adam untouched by sin. Why then was it necessary for God to become incarnate? God could redeem sinners through one such who was without sin, or perform a similar miracle and make as many men as were necessary to complete the heavenly city. I shall reply briefly. As I have shown in my widely-known little work, *Why God Became Man*, it was because a man who was not God was not sufficient to redeem other men. He did not make as many such men as were necessary lest, if no one propagated naturally from Adam were saved he would have created that nature in vain and would seem to be correcting something he had made badly—something that would not be fitting for the highest wisdom to do for any nature.

Not far back I proposed to investigate how the seed taken from the Virgin, seed in which it was shown that there was no sin, could be understood to be free from the aforementioned necessity in which I proposed that all other men were conceived. I was confident, if by argument I could remove the sin and debt of Adam and our near ancestors, that the seed could be freed from that necessity by which human nature cannot recover the justice which it abandoned, and from that necessity by which the corruptible body burdens the soul, especially in infants, because that man was God. Therefore I began to inquire how it could be established that this seed was free from the necessity of the sin and the debt of Adam, so that I could more easily pursue my enquiry with respect to the others. At this, by the abundant grace of him the purity of whose conception we are proving, it was granted not only that he should be seen to be free from all the sin and debt that I have already mentioned, but further that it should be rationally proved that a man thus conceived ought to be endowed with no less justice or happiness than was Adam's lot when he was created, whether he was God or a mere man. Indeed, it was clearly irrational in either case that on the one hand sin or the penalty for sin should descend to him from any of his ancestors through such a propagation, or on the other that God should deliberately make a rational nature that was unjust, or unhappy where there was no injustice to merit its unhappiness.

18. *God was not conceived from a just Virgin out of necessity, as if it were impossible from a sinful woman, but rather because this was fitting*

Therefore although it is true that the Son of God was born of a spotless Virgin, this was not out of necessity, as if a just offspring could not be generated by this method of propagation from a sinful parent, but because it was fitting that the conception of this man should be of a pure mother. Indeed it was fitting that that Virgin should shine with a purity which was only exceeded by God's own, because it was to her that God the Father disposed to give his only Son, whom he loved in his heart as equal to himself, begotten equal to himself, so that in nature he should be at the same time the Son of God and of the Virgin; the Son himself substantially chose her for himself to be his mother, and from her the Holy Spirit willed and was to effect the conception and birth of the Son from whom the Spirit should proceed. Of how the Virgin was cleansed by faith before this conception I have spoken in the course of another treatise on this subject.

19. *How the present argument is consistent with the other and where they differ*

Either of these two arguments to my mind seem to suffice alone for this enquiry, but both together should amply satisfy the mind of anyone searching for a forceful argument and proper dignity in the agents. And although they move to the same end, they do differ in this: the one which I have put forward here shows beyond any contradiction that God ought to produce a just offspring, and none other than a just offspring, by such a propagation—for nowhere in human nature is there any sin except in the will—but the other proves that, even if sin pervaded the entire being of the Virgin, she could still be made clean by faith to purify her for this mode of conception. And in this argument all necessity of death and sin and any form of corruption or hardship are clearly excluded; in the second a question arises about this which, however, will be cleared up by adequate reasoning if examined carefully. Therefore it is clear from both that in all that he suffered, Our Lord endured nothing but in his obedient will.

20. *The Virgin's son had original justice instead of original sin*

As it seems to me, on the question of original sin it has been sufficiently demonstrated—as I proposed—how no reasoning could show that it descended from his parents to the man conceived of the Virgin, but rather that reason demands that he should have been made just and happy. Therefore because according to his divine nature he was born of a just father, and a just mother according to his human nature, he was born just from his very origin, as we might say: it would not be out of place to say that he had original justice instead of the original sin which all Adam's sons have from their origin.

21. *He could not have had personal injustice*

But it would be unnecessary to dispute over a personal injustice which does not touch on Christ, because the human nature was never in him without the divine, nor was his soul weighed down against his will or in any way hindered by a corruptible body. Since that soul existed as one person, while he was fully man and fully Word of God, he was never without perfect justice and wisdom and power, which he always had from himself according to his person as God, although between his natures whatever he had of the human he accepted from the divine.

I do not deny that there may be a deeper reasoning to show how God assumed sinless humanity from the sinful mass, as if something unleavened were taken from leaven, beyond that which I have presented here as well as the one I gave elsewhere. If someone can show me such an argument, I will accept it freely and I will not cling to my own reasonings if they can be shown to be contrary to the truth—although I doubt that they can.

22. *The magnitude of original sin*

Furthermore, original sin cannot be greater in magnitude than I have said, nor any less: because as soon as an infant is rational, human nature in it does not have the justice it accepted in Adam and which it ought always to have: nor, as I have stated above, does weakness excuse this lack of justice. However I do not think original sin is entirely as grave as I have represented it above. For, wanting to show that it did not pertain to the man begotten of the Virgin, I presented it in a way that allowed nothing more to be added to it lest, as I said, I should be seen to be trivializing it for the sake of my enquiry. I shall briefly explain what I now think.

I do not think that the sin of Adam descends to infants so that they ought to be punished for it, as if they had each personally acted as Adam did, although because of his sin it came about that none of them is born without sin, or the condemnation following it. For when the Apostle says that 'death reigned from Adam to Moses, even in those who have not sinned like Adam' [Rom. 5: 14], he clearly signifies that nothing as great as the actual sin of Adam is imputed to them personally, although all Adam's sons—except the Virgin's son—are denoted 'sinners' and 'sons of wrath' in his writings. For when he says 'even in those who have not sinned according to the transgression of Adam', he can be understood to be saying: even in those who have not sinned as much as Adam sinned in transgressing. And when he says: 'but the law entered in so that the offence might abound' [Rom. 5: 20], we should either understand that the sin before the law in those 'who had not sinned according to the transgression of Adam' was less than the sin of Adam; or if it was not less, sin abounded in them after the law beyond the sin of Adam; which when I give it any thought I cannot bring myself to believe. In *Why God Became Man* I set out my ideas on this weight of sin and its satisfaction, as you have already read. But it is true that nobody is restored to that state for which man was made and the power of propagation given to him; nor is human nature rescued from the evils into which it has fallen except through satisfaction for that sin by which it has thrown itself into those evils.

Somebody might say: if individuals are not guilty of the sin of Adam, how can you assert that nobody is saved without satisfaction for the sin of Adam? For how does a just God demand from them satisfaction for a sin of which they are not guilty? I would say that God does not demand more from a sinner than he owes, but since no one can repay as much as he owes, only Christ renders on behalf of all who are saved more than they owe, as I have explained in my well-quoted little work.

Furthermore we should look at another argument by which sin is less in children than it is in Adam, although it descends to them from him. For, 'through one man'—that is, through Adam—'sin came into the world, and by sin death' [Rom. 5: 12].

23. *Why and how it comes down to infants*

Still, we will not know why sin is less in infants if we do not understand why and how it is present in them. It will not be superfluous to repeat here what I said earlier, where I said as much as I felt was necessary for the present investigation. Indeed it cannot be denied that infants were in Adam when he sinned. But they existed causally or materially in him, as they would in the seed, though in themselves they exist personally: for in him they existed as seed but in themselves they exist as individual diverse persons. In him they were not other than him, in themselves they are other than him. In him they were he, in themselves they are they. More simply, they were in him, but they did not exist as themselves, because they were not yet themselves.

Perhaps someone will say that the being according to which other men are said to have been in Adam is really 'nothing', an 'empty' proposition, and should not be called 'being'. Let him then call 'nothing' or 'empty' or 'false' the being by which Christ existed as seed in Abraham, in David and in his other forefathers, and by which everything that comes from a seed exists in seeds. Let him say that God did 'nothing' when he made first in the seed everything that is procreated from seed, and let him call 'nothing' or 'vain' a state if which were not the case, the things which we see to be would not be. For if it is not true that everything that nature procreates from seeds has had some kind of existence in those seeds, they could not have been said to have come from those seeds. If, however, this objection is an absurdity, then it was not a false or vain being but a true and substantial being, by which all other men were in Adam; nor did God do something empty when he caused them to be in him. But, as I have said, in him they were not other than him, and therefore their existence was quite different from their being in themselves.

Although it can be agreed that all men existed in Adam, the son of the Virgin alone, however, existed in him in quite a different mode. All other men existed in Adam in such a way that they came to be from him through the property of generation which was subdued to his will and power; Christ alone did not exist in Adam in that he would be born through Adam's nature and will. For it had been given to Adam at the time of his sin that he would be the one from whom they would come to be born, and that he would be the cause of their existence; but as for Christ, while Adam was the one from whom he would come to be born, he was not able to cause him to come into being, because it was not in his power that he should be begotten from him. But it was no more in Adam's power that Christ should be made from some other being or from nothing at all: indeed it was not in Adam's power that he, Christ, should exist in any mode at all, for it was possible neither through any natural power nor through the power of the will that Christ could come to exist. What Adam did have was the nature by which Christ was to be propagated, though not through his own power, but through God's.

Down the line of our ancestors, as far as the Virgin his Mother, the will sowed the seed and nature brought it to life, so that the Virgin herself, partly in the natural course and partly in the course of the will, took her being from Adam, like all the others: but in her neither the will of a creature sowed her offspring, nor did nature nurture it, but the Holy Spirit and the Power of the Highest effected the miraculous propagation of a man from a virgin woman. Therefore in the case of the rest of humanity, it was in Adam, that is in Adam's power, that they should come from him; but in Christ's case it was not in Adam's power that he should come to be in any way, as it was not in the power of the clay from which the first man was made to bring about that miraculous creation, nor was it in the first man that Eve should come from him—however she was made. Neither was it any more in the power of any of those in whom he existed from Adam to Mary, that he should exist. He was however in them, because there was in them that from which he was to be assumed in the way that there was that in the clay from which the first man was made, and in him, that from which Eve was made, not by the will or power of a creature but by divine power alone; but this God-Man was made far more miraculously and with greater grace than those mere men. It is clear, then, that he was in Adam when Adam sinned in a different mode from those who are procreated voluntarily in the course of nature. Therefore in a sense Adam made those whom the human will through the power it has accepted and human nature through germination have procreated; but only God made the Son of the Virgin, in a sense from Adam, although not through Adam but through his own power, as it were from himself.

Therefore what is more fitting for showing the great goodness of God and the abundance of the grace that he gave to Adam, than that those whose being was so in his power that through him they would be what by nature he was, would also likewise have their being governed by his free will so that what he was by nature they through him could be, and so that whatever he was in justice and happiness, thus he would reproduce them? This therefore was the gift given to him. Then while he was placed on such a pinnacle of grace, he wilfully abandoned the gifts which he had been given to keep for himself and his offspring: thus his children lost what their father, when he was able to give it to them by keeping it, took away by not keeping it. This is, I think, sufficient reason why the sin and evils of Adam descend to children if we resolutely distance our own inclinations, which often and significantly hinder the mind from perceiving what is right, and consider all this as a matter of pure justice. But I will say a few words on how that same sin descends to them.

As I have said, there is the sin committed by the nature, and there is sin committed by the person. Therefore what is committed by the person can be called 'personal', while what comes from nature is called 'natural' sin; which is called original sin. And as the personal sin crosses to nature, so natural sin crosses to the person, thus: it was Adam's nature that demanded that he eat; it was created so that it had that need. However, when he ate from the forbidden tree, this was not natural will but personal—his own will. But what the person did was not done without the nature. For he was a person, with the name Adam; a nature because he was a man. Therefore his person made the nature sinful, because when Adam sinned, the man sinned. Indeed it was not because he was a man that he was impelled to eat the forbidden fruit, but he was drawn to it by his own will, which nature did not require but which the person committed.

It is similar, while converse, in infants. Indeed the fact that the justice that they ought to have is not in them is not due to personal will, as in Adam, but a lacking in nature, which their nature took on from Adam. For in Adam, outside whom there was nothing of human nature, human nature was stripped of the justice that it had, and continues to lack it unless it is aided. By this argument since nature subsists in persons, and there are no persons without nature, nature makes the persons of infants sinful. Thus the sin of Adam is transmitted personally in all those who are by nature propagated from him, and is in them original, or natural.

Clearly, a wide distance appears between the sin of Adam and the sin of these infants; because he sinned through his own will, while they sin through the natural necessity which is the outcome of his own personal will. But while no one can doubt that equal punishment does not follow unequal sins, still in this respect the condemnation is the same for personal and original sin, that no one is admitted to the kingdom of God, for which man was made, except by the death of Christ, without which there can be no rendering of what is owed through the sin of Adam, although not all deserve the same punishment in hell. For after the day of judgement there will be no creature, angel or man, except either in the kingdom of God or in hell. Therefore it is true to say both that the sin of infants is less than the sin of Adam, and that none is saved without that universal satisfaction, by which great and small sin is remitted. However, the question of why this could not come about without that death, and how man is saved through it, has been researched and set out in my aforementioned book, as far as God has given me the power.

24. *The sins of ancestors after Adam are not counted with the original sin of their descendants*

I do not think that the sins of our near ancestors have any bearing on original sin. If Adam was unable to pass on his own justice to those whom he was to generate, he could not possibly pass on his injustice. Therefore since no one after Adam was able to keep his justice for his children, I see no reason why the sins of our near ancestors should be imputed to the souls of their descendants. Finally, there is no doubt that no infant keeps rectitude of will for the sake of rectitude itself. Therefore all infants are equally unjust, because they have none of the justice which it is each man's duty to have. This destitution of justice has descended to all infants from Adam, in whom human nature had robbed itself of that justice. For in Adam a certain measure of justice remained to human nature so that he kept a right will in some things, but it was so bereft of that grace by which Adam could himself retain justice for his descendants that in none of them can it reproduce itself with any justice. Indeed, in infants it could not remove from itself more than all the justice and beatitude which is given to no one who lacks any of the justice required.

I do not see that it is possible for the injustice of its near ancestors to increase this bereftness of justice when no greater indigence can descend to an infant than that brought by the sin of Adam. For if there is no justice, no justice can be taken away. But where justice cannot be removed, no injustice can be added. Therefore unjust parents cannot add any injustice to their children beyond the destitution of justice we have mentioned. But where there is no justice nothing prevents the deposit of some justice. Therefore it is more likely and more probable—if unjust parents are said to add some injustice to their children—that just ones can give their infants some measure of justice. If this is the case, the children of just parents have some justice. And if this is true, they are less heavily judged than the children of unjust parents if they die unbaptized; or if they are saved they would be elected with some pre-existing merit of their own. This is denied by the Apostle Paul, where he uses the example of Jacob and Esau to prove that no man is saved except by grace preceding each man's merits. Since therefore just parents do not give any justice to their children before baptism, surely unjust parents add no injustice to theirs.

What then if someone says: even if unjust parents do not add any injustice to their children, from whom they cannot remove any injustice, still they aggravate the original sin which they have from Adam. Therefore, just parents relieve it in their children, and so if the children of just parents are less unjust than those of unjust parents, they should be less culpable than the latter. If anyone has the courage to say this and prove it let him do so: he is braver than I am, because I see the children of just and unjust parents equally elected to the grace of baptism and rejected from it. But even if anyone asserts this, it cannot be proved. Indeed just as the only man who is more just than another just man is one who by his will either praises more or avoids more all those things that he should, the only man more unjust than the unjust man is the one who loves more and condemns more the things he should not. Therefore if it cannot be shown that infants as soon as they have a soul want more or less one than another what they should or should not, no one can prove that among infants one is born more or less just than another. Equally, therefore, it seems neither that the just by their justice lighten the burden of original sin on their children nor that unjust parents make it heavier by their injustice. Therefore if unjust parents cannot by number or magnitude increase the original sin in their children by their sin, I do not see that the sin of parents after Adam is counted with the original sin of infants.

I will not deny that many and great benefits to the body and soul come from the merits of ancestors, and that because of sins of ancestors sons and grandsons are afflicted 'unto the third and fourth generation', and perhaps further. More, I do not deny that, by diverse tribulation in this life, they lose those gifts—spiritual gifts no less—which might have come to them if they had been just—there is no space here to give examples—but I do assert that original sin is exactly the same in all infants conceived in nature, as much as the sin of Adam, which is the cause of their birth in sin, pertains equally to all.

25. *How their sins harm the souls of their descendants*

However, if the sins of parents do sometimes harm the souls of their children, I think it rather comes about in this way: not because God imputes the sins to them, or because he leads them into any transgression because of their parents, but because, as he often rescues the sons of the just because of the merits of their parents, so he sometimes leaves the children of the unjust in their sins because of their parents' deserts. For since no one is free from sin unless God frees him, when he does not free him he is said to be leading him into it, and when he does not soften, he is said to harden. For it seems more reasonable that God should leave in its sin a sinful soul on account of its parent's sin—after all he owes it nothing but punishment—so that it is punished for its sins, than that he should burden it with others, so that it should suffer for those. Thus, therefore, it can be said without contradiction that original sin is the same in everyone, and that 'the son will not bear the iniquity of the father', and 'each will bear his own burden', and will receive 'according to his deeds' in his body 'whether good or evil', *and* that God visits the sins of parents on their children 'unto the third and fourth generation', even if only in their souls, and anything we read which seems to indicate that the sins of ancestors harm the souls of their descendants. Indeed, the soul of a descendant dies not because of his father's sin but because of his own, nor does anyone bear 'the iniquity of the father', when he is left in iniquity, but his own, nor does he receive according to what his father has done in the body, but according to what he has done; but because on account of the sins of his ancestors he is not free from his evils, the evils he bears are imputed to the sins of his ancestors.

26. *Still, everyone bears their own sins rather than those of their ancestors*

But if it is contended that all who are not saved by faith in Christ bear the iniquity and the burden of Adam, with the intention of proving thereby that infants ought either to bear the iniquities of their other ancestors similarly, or not to bear those of Adam: let him then consider that infants do not bear Adam's sin but their own. For, as we have said, there is a difference between the sin of Adam on the one hand, and the sins of children on the other: one is the cause and one is the effect. Adam lacked the justice that he owed, because he and no other had abandoned it: infants lack it because another and not they abandoned it. For the sin of Adam is not identical with the sin of infants. And when the Apostle says, as I have said above, that death reigned from Adam to Moses, also in those who have not sinned in the likeness of the sin of Adam, he thus clearly shows it to be something different.

Therefore, when an infant is condemned for original sin, he is not condemned for the sin of Adam but for his own. For if he did not have his own sin, he would not be condemned. In this way, then, he bears his own sin, not Adam's, although it is he that is said to bear it, because his first parent's sin was the cause of his sin. But this cause of infants being born in sin was in Adam, but not in their other ancestors, because human nature in them does not have the potential, as I have said, to procreate just children. Thus it does not follow that sin is in infants because of their sin as it does for the sin of Adam.

27. *What original sin is; that it is equal in all human beings*

Therefore I understand original sin to be simply the sin which is in an infant as soon as he has a rational soul, whatever may have taken place in his body before he had that soul—some corruption of the members, for example—and whatever may become of his body or soul. Because of the reasons I have given I think that the original sin is equal in all infants naturally propagated, and that all those who die in original sin alone are equally condemned. Whatever sin is added to this in a man is personal sin: and since according to its nature a person is born sinful, the nature is thus rendered the more sinful by the person, because when the person sins, the whole man sins.

The only way that I can understand this sin, which I call original sin, in the case of these infants, is as that destitution of due virtue created by the disobedience of Adam, through which all have become the sons of wrath; for the wilful desertion of justice which his nature caused in Adam accuses it, and, as I have said, the inability to recover justice does not excuse persons. This inability is accompanied by destitution of blessings, so that they are as bereft of happiness as of justice. Because of these two destitutions they are in exile in this life, and unless they have the protection of divine providence, they are open to sin and misery incessantly and everywhere meeting and attacking them from all sides.

28. *An answer to those who think that infants ought not to be condemned*

There are those who cannot bring themselves to accept that children who die unbaptized are condemned on account of that injustice alone which I described, because no man judges them to be culpable of the sin of another person, and because at such an age children are not just and have no discernment, and furthermore they do not think that God should judge innocent children more strictly than men judge them. In answer to these, it needs to be explained that God ought to act towards children in one way, and man another. For man should not demand from a nature what he has not given and is not due to him, nor is it any more just for a man to accuse a man of being born with a fault which he was not born without and from which he cannot be healed without the help of another. Rightly, God demands from a nature what he has given, and what is justly owed to him.

But this judgement by which infants are condemned, if given some thought, is not very far removed from the judgement of man. Suppose that a man and his wife, promoted to some great dignity and possession not on their own merit but through grace and favour alone, then commit a grave crime for which they cannot be excused, and for it are duly deposed and cast into servitude. Who will say that the children that they generate after their condemnation should not suffer the same servitude, but rather by grace be restored to those possessions which their parents rightly lost? It is no different for our first parents and the children whom they generated in exile, when they had been rightly sent from blessedness to misery for their fault. Therefore the judgement ought to be similar for similar cases, but for them it should be as severe as their misdeed can be proved indefensible.

In the end every man is either saved or damned. But every man who is saved is admitted to the kingdom of heaven, and every man who is damned is shut out from it. Whoever is admitted is brought to the likeness of the angels, in whom there was never nor shall be any sin; this cannot happen while there is any stain of sin in him.

Since, therefore, it is impossible for any man to be saved with any sin, however small, if what I have called original sin is any sin at all, it is necessary for every man born into it to be condemned unless he is forgiven.

29. *How the inability to have justice excuses infants after baptism*

I said that the lack of power to retain justice did not excuse injustice in infants. Somebody might ask, therefore: You have said that sin, that is injustice, exists in an infant before its baptism, and that the lack of power to have justice is not excused, and that furthermore in baptism sin is not remitted except for the sin that existed before: if after baptism he is without justice for as long as he is an infant, and cannot understand the justice which he should keep—if indeed justice is uprightness of will kept for its own sake—how can he fail to be unjust even after he is baptized? If then a baptized infant dies in infancy a little after his baptism, when he does not yet know how to repent since he does not have the justice he ought to have, and since weakness is not an excuse, he leaves this life unjust, as he would have done had he died before baptism, and is not admitted to the kingdom of God, into which no unjust man is received—and this is not a tenet of the Catholic Church. So if a sin to be committed in infancy is remitted for infants in baptism, why not those too which are committed at a later age?

To this I would reply that in baptism the sins as far as those that existed before baptism are wiped out, and so the original inability to have justice is not imputed a sin in those already baptized as it was before. Therefore, as before the inability did not stand as an excuse for the absence of justice, because it was itself at fault, thus after baptism it dispenses it absolutely because the inability remains, but with no accompanying fault. Hence it happens that justice, which before baptism was required from infants without any dispensation, is not required of them after baptism as an obligation. Therefore as long as they have no justice through original impotence alone they are not unjust, because there is no absence in them of justice which should be present. For no one requires what is impossible and free from blame. Therefore if they die in this state they are not unjust and therefore are not condemned: but they are saved through the justice of Christ who gave himself for them, and the justice of the faith of their mother the Church which keeps the faith for them as if they were just.

I have given you this summary of what I have to say on original sin as far as my understanding will allow, more as conjecture than assertion; God may one day reveal it to me more fully in some way. If any person has another view and can demonstrate its truth, I will not reject his opinion.

ON THE PROCESSION OF THE
HOLY SPIRIT

I

The Greeks deny that the Holy Spirit proceeds from the Son, a procession that we Latins profess. Nor do they accept the Latin teachers that we follow in this matter. And they with us honour the Gospels, and they believe in other things concerning the one and triune God the very same in everything that we do, we who are certain about the same things. Therefore, I with the help of the same Holy Spirit hope that they, if they prefer acknowledgement of solid truth to contention for empty victory, can be led by reason from what they unambiguously profess, to what they do not accept. Therefore, although there are many who may be better able to do this, I none the less invoke the same Holy Spirit to deign to direct me to this end, since many enjoin me to undertake it, and I, both out of love for them and a pious desire, do not dare to resist their request. And so I, with such hope in proportion to the lowliness of my knowledge, leaving loftier things to those more knowledgeable, should get to work on what they ask. And I should make use of the faith of the Greeks and the things that they undoubtedly believe and profess, as the surest arguments to prove what they do not profess.

They indeed profess that there is one and only one God, and that he is perfect, and that he has no parts, and that the whole of him is whatever he is. They also profess that God is Father and Son and Holy Spirit, so that if we should call him Father or Son or Holy Spirit alone, or if we should call him two of these simultaneously (Father and Son, or Father and Holy Spirit, or Son and Holy Spirit), or if we should call him all three simultaneously (Father and Son and Holy Spirit), we would designate the same God integrally and perfectly. This is true although the term 'Father' or the term 'Son' would not signify the same thing as the term 'God'. For it is not the same thing to be God as it is to be Father or Son. And we posit the title 'Holy Spirit' as a relational term, so that we understand the Holy Spirit as the spirit of someone. For although the Father is spirit and holy, and the Son is spirit and holy, the Father is not the spirit of anyone, nor is the Son the spirit of anyone, in the way in which the Holy Spirit is the spirit of someone, since the Holy Spirit is the Spirit of God and the Spirit of the Father and the Son. For the Greeks, although they deny that the Holy Spirit proceeds from the Son, none the less do not deny that the Holy Spirit is the Spirit of the Son.

The Greeks also believe and profess that there is God from God by generation, and that there is God from God by procession, since the Son is God from God the Father by generation, and the Holy Spirit is God from God by procession. Nor do the Greeks think that God who is generated is other than God from whom he is generated, or other than God who proceeds. This is true although God admits plurality insofar as the Father and the Son and the Holy Spirit are several and distinct from one another by reason of the significance of their names, since there is one from whom someone is generated, and one who is generated from someone, and one who proceeds from someone. For when we call God the Father, we mean that there is one from whom someone is generated. And when we call God the Son, we understand that there is one who is generated from someone. And when we call God the Holy Spirit, we indicate that there is one who proceeds from someone, since we understand the Holy Spirit as the Spirit of God and not as spirit in an absolute sense. And when we say that the Son is from the Father, and that the Holy Spirit is from the Father, we understand that the Son and the Holy Spirit have from the Father what constitutes the Son or the Holy Spirit. But we understand that the Son is from the Father in one way, and that the Holy Spirit is from the Father in another way. For the Son is from his Father, that is, from God who is his Father, while the Holy Spirit is not from God as his Father but only from God who is Father. Therefore, we call the Son, as he is from God, God's Son, and we call the one from whom the Son is, the Son's Father. And the Holy Spirit, as he is from God, is not God's Son, nor is the one from whom the Holy Spirit is, the Spirit's Father.

It is also certain that God is not the Father or the Son or the Spirit of anyone but God, and that nothing is God but the same Father and Son and Holy Spirit. And as there is one God, so there is only one Father, one Son, and one Holy Spirit. And so it happens that there is in the Trinity no Father except the Father of the same Son, and no Son except the Son of the same Father, nor the Holy Spirit of anyone except the same Father and Son. Therefore, the only cause of plurality in God is such that we cannot predicate Father and Son and Holy Spirit of one another, and that the Son and Holy Spirit are distinct from one another, since there is God from God in the two aforementioned ways.

And we can call the whole of this a set of relations. For as the Son originates from God by generation, and the Holy Spirit from God by procession, the very difference between generation and procession are related to one another, so that the Son and the Holy Spirit are different and distinct from one another. And when a substance has existence from a substance, there are then two dissociable relations if their names should posit substances. For when a man is from another by generation, we call the man from whom the other is, the father, and we call the man who is from the other, the son. Therefore, a father cannot be the son of the man of whom he is the father, and a son cannot be the father of the man of whom he is the son, although nothing prevents a father being a son or a son being a father when one and the same man is a father and a son, since the man is a father in relation to one man, and a son in relation to another. For example, since Isaac is the father of Jacob and the son of Abraham, a father is a son, and a son is a father, without contradiction, since we call Isaac a father in relation to a man who is not his father, and we call Isaac a son in relation to a man who is not his son. And it is impossible that, in the case of the same Isaac, the father be the son of the man of whom Isaac is the father, or that the son be the father of whom Isaac is the son.

Therefore, so in the case of God, although he is Father and Son and Holy Spirit, there is the Father of only the same Son and the Son of only the same Father and the Holy Spirit of only the same Father and Son. The Father is not the Son or the Holy Spirit, the Son is not the Father, and the Holy Spirit is not the Father. Indeed, since the Son is from the Father, and the Holy Spirit is from the Father, the one from whom someone is cannot be the one who is from him, nor can the one who is from someone be the one from whom he is, as I have already said. Therefore, the Father is not the Son or the Holy Spirit, nor are the Son and the Holy Spirit the Father. And so (to mention a different reason provisorily, since we have not yet shown that the Holy Spirit exists and proceeds from the Son) the Son is not the Holy Spirit, nor is the Holy Spirit the Son, since the

Son has existence from the Father by generation, and the Holy Spirit has existence from the Father by procession and not by generation. Nor can the Son be his own Spirit, nor can the Holy Spirit be the one of whom he is the Spirit.

With these things established, let us inquire how the indivisible unity and the dissociable plurality in God are interrelated. And since both we, who affirm that the Holy Spirit proceeds from the Son, and the Greeks, who disagree with us in this matter, alike undoubtedly believe and profess the things that I have said, we should with one mind unambiguously accept the necessary consequences of those things. For it follows logically from the characteristic of God's unity, which has no parts, that whatever we say about the one God, who in his entirety is whatever he is, we say about the entire God, the Father and the Son and the Holy Spirit, since each is the sole and whole and complete God. And the aforementioned relational opposition, which results from the fact that God is from God in the two afore-mentioned ways, prevents us from predicating Father and Son and Holy Spirit of one another, and from attributing the properties of each to the others. Therefore, the consequences of this unity and this set of relations are so harmoniously mixed that neither the plurality resulting from the relations is transferable to the things in which the simplicity of the aforementioned unity resounds, nor does the unity suppress the plurality whereby we signify the same relations. The unity should never lose its consequences except when a rela-tional opposition stands in the way, nor should the relations lose what belongs to them except when the indivisible unity stands in the way.

And if we should consider this by examples, it will be more clearly evident. Indeed, as the simplicity of the unity excludes from itself the plurality contained in the meaning of the relational terms, it is easy to know. For we profess that the Father is not the Son or the Holy Spirit, and that the Son is not the Father or the Holy Spirit, and that the Holy Spirit is not the Father or the Son. Therefore, the Father and the Son and the Holy Spirit are distinct from one another and are several. But the Father is God, and the Son is God, and the Holy Spirit is God. And so, if the aforementioned plurality preserves its characteristic, what is more a consequence than that the Father and the Son and the Holy Spirit be several Gods and Gods distinct from one another? But the inviolable simplicity of the divine nature, which we profess to be only one God, in no way permits this. Thus the unity of God's substance rejects a consequence of the relational terms.

Let us also consider how the plurality in the relations opposes consequences of the unity after we have established some things in which no opposition stands in the way. We say that the one God is the Father and the Son and the Holy Spirit, and we may say that they, whether singly or in pairs or all three, are one and the same God. Therefore, if God is eternal, it necessarily follows from the unity of the divine nature that the Father is eternal, that the Son is eternal, that the Holy Spirit is eternal. And since they, whether singly or several together, are one God, there is only one eternal God. The consequences are the same if we call God creator or just or any of the other things in which we understand none of the aforementioned relations.

We may now perceive how the relations restrict consequences of God's unity. For example, we say that God is the Father. Therefore, since there is one God the Father and the Son and the Holy Spirit, God's unity requires that the Son be the Father, and that the Holy Spirit be the Father. But the relations that prevent the Son or the Holy Spirit being the Father stand in the way. Indeed, nature does not permit, nor does the intellect comprehend, that the person originating from another is the one from whom the person originates, or that the one from whom the person originates is the person originating from that one. And so neither the Son nor the Holy Spirit can be the Father, although God is the Father, and one and the same God is the Father and the Son and the Holy Spirit. We know the very same thing when we say that God is the Son. For a consequence of God's unity implies that both the Father and the Holy Spirit are the Son. But the Father, from whom the Son is, cannot be the one who is from the Father himself. And the Holy Spirit, who originates from the Father by procession, is not the one who is from the Father by generation. Likewise, when we say that God is the Holy Spirit, the aforementioned unity requires that the Father and the Son also be the Holy Spirit. But neither can the Father, from whom the Holy Spirit is, be the one who is from the Father himself, nor is the Son, who originates from the Father by generation, the one who is from the Father by procession, that is, the Holy Spirit. And when we shall make evident that the Holy Spirit is from the Son, then it will also be clear that the Son for that reason cannot be the Holy Spirit, nor the Holy Spirit the Son.

Let us further consider how the aforementioned oppositions stand in the way of the consequences of the aforementioned unity. God is from God. Therefore, once we accept this, since the same God is Father and Son and Holy Spirit, it follows from this identity that God the Father is God from God, and God from whom God is, and likewise that the Son is God from God, and God from whom God is, and that the Holy Spirit is God in the same way. And to ask whether each is God from whom God is, is simply to consider whether each one singly is God from God. For there can be no God from God except the Father or the Son or the Holy Spirit, and except from the Father or the Son or the Holy Spirit. Therefore, we should inquire whether every single one is God from whom God is.

But the Father cannot be from God because of the aforementioned opposition. For God the Father can be from God only either from the Father (i.e. his very self) or from the Son or from the Holy Spirit, or from two of them, or from all three, since God is only either the Father or the Son or the Holy Spirit or two of them or all three. The Father cannot be from his very self, since one originating from another, and the other from whom the first originates cannot be the same. The Father is not from the Son, since the Son is from the Father himself, and so the Father cannot be from the Son. The Father is not from the Holy Spirit, since the Holy Spirit is from him, and he cannot be the one who is from himself. The Father cannot be from two or all three of the Trinity because of the same aspect of opposition. And God the Son is necessarily from God the Father, since the Father is not from the Son. And the Son cannot be from the Son (i.e. from his very self), since one originating from another, and the other from whom the first originates, are not the same. And we shall later show whether the Son is from the Holy Spirit, or the Holy Spirit from the Son. But we shall first speak about the Holy Spirit, inquiring whether he, by reason of the aforementioned consequence, is from the Father or from his very self. The Holy Spirit is indeed necessarily from the Father, since no opposition stands in the way. For the Holy Spirit is not the Father of the Father. And the Holy Spirit cannot be from his very self, since one who originates from another, and the other from whom the first originates, cannot be the same.

In all these things, nothing except an opposition regarding the aforementioned stands in the way of the consequences of the one identity. And there necessarily results in everything immutably predicated about God what we know in their regard.

We need now to inquire by the aforementioned irrefutable arguments whether the Son is from the Holy Spirit, or the Holy Spirit from the Son. I say that, just as, by the aforementioned argument, either the Father is from the Son or the Son from the Father, and likewise either the Father is from the Holy Spirit or the Holy Spirit from the Father, so either the Son is from the Holy Spirit or the Holy Spirit from the Son. And anyone who denies this, should also deny the necessity that there be only one God, or that the Son be God, or that the Holy Spirit be God, or that there be God from God, since what I say results from these things. Let me amplify. The Son or the Holy Spirit is from the Father only from the Father's substance, which is one substance that belongs to the Father and the Son and the Holy Spirit. Therefore, when we say that the Son is from God the Father, it follows from the unity of the divine nature, if the same God is Father and Holy Spirit, that the Son is also from the Holy Spirit. In the same way, when we profess that the Holy Spirit is from God the Father, it follows from the same unity of the divine nature, if the same God is Father and Son, that the Holy Spirit is from the Son. Therefore, we know from these things that either the Son is from the Holy Spirit, or the Holy Spirit is from the Son, since both propositions cannot be true, or both false.

Therefore, the Holy Spirit is necessarily from the Son if we can demonstrate that the Son is not from the Holy Spirit. Someone may say that it does not follow that the Son is from the Father and the Holy Spirit because the Father and the Holy Spirit are one God, although nothing else is opposed, or that it does follow that the Holy Spirit is from the Father and the Son because the Father and the Son are one God, although the Son is not from the Holy Spirit. If someone so says, the person should consider that, if there is God from God, either the whole God is from the whole God, or part of God is from part of God, or the whole God is from part of God, or part of God is from the whole God. But God has no parts. Therefore, there cannot be God from God as whole from part, or as part from whole, or as part from part. Therefore, if there is God from God, the whole God is from the whole God. Therefore, when we say that the Son is from God, who is Father and Holy Spirit, either one whole God will be the Father, the other whole God the Holy Spirit, so that the Son will be from the whole Father and not from the whole Holy Spirit; or if the same whole God is Father and Holy Spirit, the Son, if he is from the whole God, and the one whole God is the Father and the Holy Spirit, is likewise necessarily from the Father and the Holy Spirit, provided that nothing else is incompatible. Similarly, if we say that the Holy Spirit is from the whole God who is Father and Son, either one whole God will be the Father, the other whole God the Son, so that the Holy Spirit is from the whole Father and not from the whole Son, or if the Holy Spirit is from the Father, the Holy Spirit cannot not be from the Son if the Son is not from the Holy Spirit. For we can by no other argument deny that the Holy Spirit is from the Son.

Someone will say: 'Perhaps, since the one God is Father and Holy Spirit, it follows that the Son is from the Holy Spirit if the Son is from the Father, or the Holy Spirit is also from the Son if the Holy Spirit is from the Father, since the same God is Father and Son. If so, the Father necessarily also generates the Holy Spirit if he generates the Son, since one and the same God is Son and Holy Spirit. And the Son as well as the Holy Spirit proceed from the Father if the Holy Spirit proceeds from the Father, because of the same unity of the divine nature of the Son and the Holy Spirit. And if God's unity in the Son and the Holy Spirit does not have the power to entail the consequence that both are generated and proceed in like manner, it does not seem to follow from the fact that the Father and the Holy Spirit are one God that the Son is from the Holy Spirit, or that the Holy Spirit is from the Son because the same God is Father and Son, as you say.'

And I answer to this objection: The Son and the Holy Spirit, of course, have existence from the Father but in different ways, since one is from the Father by generation, the other from the Father by procession, so that the Son and the Holy Spirit are on that account distinct from one another, as I have said. And so, if one is generated, there cannot be generated with him the one who is distinct from him by reason of the fact that the second proceeds and is not generated like the first. And if one proceeds, the one who is distinct from him by reason of the fact that the second is generated and does not proceed cannot proceed with the first. And so the unity does not here have the power to entail the indicated consequence, since the plurality resulting from the generation and the procession stands in the way. For even if the Son and the Holy Spirit were not several by reason of something else, they would be distinct by reason of this fact alone. And when I say that it follows from the fact that the Father is one God with the Son and the Holy Spirit that the Son is from the Holy Spirit, or that the Holy Spirit is from the Son, there results no plurality that obstructs a consequence of God's unity, since I do not say that both propositions are true, but only that one of them is.

Therefore, we conclude by universal and irrefutable logic that, if those things are true that I previously said that we as well as the Greeks believe, either the Son is from the Holy Spirit, or the Holy Spirit is from the Son. And it is clearly part of the universal faith that the Son is not from the Holy Spirit. For there is God from God only either by generation, as the Son is generated, or by procession, as the Holy Spirit proceeds. For if the Son is generated from the Holy Spirit, the Son is the Son of the Holy Spirit, and the Holy Spirit is the Son's Father. But neither one is the Father or the Son of the other. Therefore, the Son is not generated from the Holy Spirit. Nor is it less clear that the Son does not proceed from the Holy Spirit. For the Son would be the Spirit of the same Holy Spirit. And we clearly deny this when we say and profess that the Holy Spirit is the Spirit of the Son. For the Holy Spirit cannot be the Spirit of his own Spirit. And so the Son does not proceed from the Holy Spirit. Therefore, the Son is in no way from the Holy Spirit. And so it follows by irrefutable logic that the Holy Spirit is from the Son as well as from the Father.

2

Perhaps the Greeks will say that the Holy Spirit, unlike the Son, is not God from God, since we prove from this that the Holy Spirit exists and proceeds from the Son. Nor does the creed[1] posit this, and they in such regard reproach us for having added the procession of the Holy Spirit from the Son. But anyone who thinks this, either denies that the Father is God from whom the Holy Spirit is, or denies

---

[1] The creed cited in this work is the Nicene-Constantinopolitan.

that the very substance of the Holy Spirit is from the Father. And no Christian denies that the Father or the Holy Spirit is God.

Therefore, let us see whether the very substance of the Holy Spirit is from the Father, regarding which I have noticed that a bishop in the town of Bari,[2] one perhaps supporting the Greeks, refused to agree. For if the very substance of the Holy Spirit is not from the Father, we cannot discover the reason why the Holy Spirit is distinct from the Father, since there is one and the same God who is Father. For the Holy Spirit is not distinct from the Father because the Father begets the Son, and the Holy Spirit does not. For we can by the begetting and non-begetting of the Son prove that the Father and the Holy Spirit are distinct from one another, but this does not cause them to be distinct persons. Indeed, if there should be two human beings, one of whom should beget a son, and the other of whom should not, although the begetting and non-begetting of a son can show them to be distinct, yet it is not for that reason that they are distinct from one another, since they do not lose their distinctness no matter how they are disposed with respect to begetting or not begetting a son. So in the case of the Father and the Holy Spirit, they are not distinct because one begets the Son and the other does not; rather, it is because they are distinct that nothing prevents them being dissimilar in begetting and not begetting the Son.

We can answer similarly if one calls the Son distinct from the Holy Spirit because the Spirit does not proceed from the Son as the Spirit himself does from the Father. Indeed (to speak as do those who deny that the Holy Spirit proceeds from the Son), the Son's distinctness from the Father is not the reason why the Son does not have the Holy Spirit proceeding from himself as the Father does (for it would follow from such reasoning that there would be no Son distinct from the Father if the Holy Spirit were to proceed from the Son). Just so, the Holy Spirit is not distinct from the Father by reason of the fact that the Holy Spirit does not have the Son or the Spirit proceeding from himself as the Father does. And the Son is not distinct from the Father by reason of the fact that the Son has a father while the Father does not (for the Father would still be distinct from the Son if the Father were to have a father). Just so, the Holy Spirit is not distinct from the Father by reason of the fact that the Holy Spirit

---

[2] The reference is to the regional Council of Bari (AD 1098). The name of the bishop is not known.

proceeds from someone while the Father proceeds from no one, since, were the Father to proceed from someone, the Holy Spirit would still be no less distinct from the Father from whom he proceeds. Therefore, it is clear that the Holy Spirit is not distinct from the Father by reason of the fact that the Holy Spirit does not have the Son or the Spirit proceeding from himself as the Father does, nor by reason of the fact that he proceeds from someone while the Father proceeds from no one.

But neither can we understand that the Holy Spirit is distinct from the Father by reason of the fact that the Holy Spirit is the Father's Spirit unless the Holy Spirit has existence from the Father. For we can understand someone as distinct from another before we understand such a one as belonging to the other, although one cannot belong to another unless the one be distinct from the other. For example, if we say that a human being is the master or slave of another, we understand the slave to be distinct from the one called master before we understand the one to be the slave's master, or the other to be the master's slave. Therefore, nothing prevents us from understanding the Holy Spirit as distinct from the Father before we understand the Holy Spirit as belonging to the Father. And so the fact that the Holy Spirit belongs to the Father does not cause the Holy Spirit to be distinct from the Father unless the Holy Spirit has being distinct from the Father by reason of that by which the Holy Spirit is the Father's Spirit. Just so, the Son is distinct from the Father by reason of that by which the Son is the Father's Son, which is simply the fact that the Son originates from the very Father by generation.

And so we perceive that the Holy Spirit is distinct from the Father only by reason of the fact that the Holy Spirit has his substance from the Father, although in his own way, a way different from the Son's way. None the less, let us look into this matter more carefully. To be sure, the Holy Spirit may be distinct from the Father after having been constituted what he is, or the Holy Spirit has in his origins the reason why he is distinct from the Father. For a person may be what the person is before being distinct from another, and a person may in the course of originating be constituted distinct from another, but no person can be distinct from another before being what the person is. For example, the first human being was that very human being and no other before there was any second human being from the first.

And when someone first originated from the first human being, both the first from whom the second originated, after the second existed, became distinct from the second, and the second who originated from the first had at the same time both existence and being distinct from the first. Therefore, as I have said, either the Holy Spirit, after he existed, became distinct from the Father, or the Holy Spirit has in his origins the reason why we say that he is distinct from the Father. But if the Holy Spirit comes to be distinct from the Father after the Holy Spirit existed, there were not always three persons (there being other persons only because the others are from the Father), since the Holy Spirit did not always exist, as he was not always distinct from the Father. And so, since these things are false, the Holy Spirit evidently has in his origins the reason why he is distinct from the Father.

And the Holy Spirit can only be, like the Son, from someone, or, like the Father, from no one. And if the Holy Spirit is from no one, as the Father originates, each originates intrinsically so that neither has anything from the other, and there are two Gods, the Father and the Holy Spirit. Or else, they being one God, we can find absolutely nothing in the Christian faith whereby they are distinct from one another if each is from no one, and the Father and the Holy Spirit are one and the same, and one person. And the true faith abhors such things. Therefore, it is false that the Holy Spirit is from no one. And if he is from someone, he is only from God, who is the Father and the Son and the Holy Spirit. But the Holy Spirit cannot be from his very self, since no person can originate from the person's very self. And so no one who denies that the Holy Spirit is from the Son can deny that the Holy Spirit is from the Father.

And if anyone says that we can understand the Holy Spirit as distinct from the Father by reason of the Spirit's procession even though the Holy Spirit does not have existence from the Father, I think that I also need to answer this objection, lest there may be in this matter any objection to our position that our response would not obviate. Nor should anyone wonder that I dwell so much on this point, since there was among the Greeks one of great authority whom I perceived not to agree that the Holy Spirit has his substance from the Father,[3] and I did not then have the opportunity to reply.

---

[3] The reference is to the unnamed bishop at the Council of Bari mentioned earlier.

Therefore, one who wishes to say that the Holy Spirit is distinct from the Father only by reason of the Spirit's procession, granted that the Father is not from the Holy Spirit, either understands that the Spirit's procession consists only of his being sent or given by the Father, so that the Holy Spirit only proceeds from the Father when the Father sends or gives him; or else such a person understands that the Spirit's procession consists of his being from the Father. But if the Spirit's procession is identified with his being given or sent, the Holy Spirit proceeds from the Son as well as from the Father, since the Son as well sends and gives the Holy Spirit. Likewise, if the Holy Spirit's procession is only his being sent or given, he is distinct from the Father and proceeds from the Father only when he is given or sent, something that no one to my knowledge understands. For the Holy Spirit is always distinct from the Father, even before creatures, and the Holy Spirit is given or sent only to creatures. Nor should we even say that being given or sent happens to him. For nothing previously non-existent regarding the Holy Spirit comes to be, since he himself is everywhere and unchangeable; something indeed happens to those who receive the Holy Spirit, since there is something regarding them that previously was not and can be missing. For example, when a blind man in the presence of light does not perceive the light, the light does not have more or less of anything. But if the man, with his blindness removed, perceives the light, there is change regarding him, not regarding the light. And so the Holy Spirit is evidently not distinct from the Father by reason of the Spirit's procession understood in such a way that his procession consists only of his being given or sent. Therefore, the Spirit by procession evidently has existence from the Father and is thereby distinct from the Father, just as the Son is distinct from the Father only by reason of the fact that the Son originates from the Father. Therefore, the Holy Spirit is God from God and proceeds from God, since both he himself is God, and the Father from whom he exists and proceeds is God.

And if we say that we can refer to two processions of the Holy Spirit, one when he originates from the Father, the other when he is given or sent, I do not think that we can deny this if we understand each procession in its own signification. Indeed, of the procession whereby the Holy Spirit is given or sent, we understand that the Lord has appropriately spoken thus: 'The Spirit breathes where he wills, and you hear his voice, and you do not know whence he comes, or whither he goes' [John 3: 8]. For the Lord thus seems effectively to say this: 'You do not know whence the Holy Spirit comes, or whither he withdraws. For when he is given, he comes and goes as if from a secret place, and when he is taken away, he goes away and withdraws as if to a secret place.' We can say of this procession that his proceeding is the same as his being sent.

Therefore, whether he should proceed only by originating from the Father, or only when he is given or sent and proceeds to sanctify creatures, or in both ways, it follows that he proceeds from the Son. For if the Holy Spirit is from the Father, the Holy Spirit is God from God, whereby, as I have said, he is proved also to exist and proceed from the Son. For the Holy Spirit proceeds from the one from whom he exists, and he originates from the one from whom he proceeds. And if he proceeds only when he is sent or given, he proceeds from the Son, who gives and sends him. And if the Holy Spirit proceeds in both ways, we know that he also proceeds in both ways from the Son. Note that we perceive that the Holy Spirit is God from God and proceeds from God, and the aforementioned creed does not posit such. Therefore, if the Greeks deny that the Holy Spirit exists and proceeds from the Son because the creed is silent about the matter, they should likewise deny that the Holy Spirit exists and proceeds from God because the same creed is silent about the matter. Or if they cannot disavow the latter, they should not be afraid to profess with us that the Holy Spirit exists and proceeds from the Son, since they do not find this statement in the same creed.

But the Greeks will say: 'The creed sufficiently indicates that the Holy Spirit exists and proceeds from God when it states that the Holy Spirit proceeds from the Father, since the Father is God.' And we likewise say that the procession of the Holy Spirit from the Son is clearly demonstrated when the creed states that the Holy Spirit proceeds from God, since the Son is God. For I ask whether we should understand that the Holy Spirit is from the Father because he is from God, or that the Holy Spirit is from God because he is from the Father. For, although one proposition in turn proves the other (since the Holy Spirit is from God if he is from the Father, and he is from the Father if he is from God, as no aforementioned relation stands opposed), the one proposition is none the less not reciprocally the reason for the other in the same way. For if the Holy

Spirit's being from the Father is the reason why he is from God, we should, when we say he is from the Father, understand that this is so by reason of the fact that God is Father (i.e. by reason of the Father's relation to the Son), not by reason of the fact that the Father is God (i.e. by reason of the divine substance). Therefore, the Holy Spirit will not have the divine substance from the Father's divine nature but from the Father's relation to the Son. And to say this is very foolish.

And as you please, if one should be willing to accept this, it follows no less that the Holy Spirit proceeds from the Son than that he proceeds from the Father. There is surely no relation of father apart from the relation of son, just as there is no relation of son apart from the relation of father. Therefore, if one relation is nothing apart from the other relation, there can be nothing from the relation of Father apart from the relation of Son. And so it will follow that the Holy Spirit is from both relations if he is from one of them. And so, if he is from the Father by the Father's relation to the Son, he will likewise be from the Son by the same signification. And since no one is so stupid as to think this, we should believe and profess that the Holy Spirit is from the Father because he is from God. And the Father is God no more than the Son is, and there is only one true God the Father and the Son. Therefore, if the Holy Spirit is from the Father, since he is from God who is the Father, we cannot deny that the Holy Spirit is also from the Son, since he is from God who is the Son.

3

Let us also consider what the Lord says in the Gospel. For example, he says: 'And this is eternal life, that they may know you, the only true God, and the one you have sent, Jesus Christ' [John 17: 3]. Therefore, we should understand the expression 'the only true God' in such a way that we do not signify the only true God when we refer to the Father alone, nor when we refer to the Son alone, but we understand the only true God only when we are talking about the Father and the Son. Or else we understand the only true God when we refer to the Father alone or the Son alone. And if, when we refer to the Father alone or the Son alone, we do not understand the only true God unless we add the name of the other, the Father is not complete God, nor is the Son complete God; rather, God is composed of Father and Son. But we believe that the Father is the complete and only true God, and that the Son is likewise the complete and only true God. Therefore, when we refer to the Father alone or the Son alone, we understand nothing (except the relation whereby they are related to one another) other than the same and only true God that we know when we mention each one.

And so, when the Lord said, 'And this is eternal life, that they may know you, the only true God, and the one you have sent, Jesus Christ' [John 17: 3], if he were to have added the words 'and the Holy Spirit proceeds from the only true God', who would dare to exclude the Son from that procession, since the Father is not the only true God more or less than the Son is? And so, if we understand the same only true God when we are talking about the Father alone or the Son alone, and when we are referring to both together, what is more evident than that the Holy Spirit, when we say that he proceeds from the Father, proceeds from the only true God, who is the Father and the Son? And so we would understand that the Holy Spirit proceeds from the Son if the same Son, when he said that he and the Father are the only true God, were to have said that the Spirit proceeds from the only true God. Just so, the Son, when he says that the Holy Spirit proceeds from the Father, undoubtedly signifies that the Holy Spirit proceeds from himself.

4

The Lord also says: 'And the Paraclete, the Holy Spirit, whom the Father will send in my name' [John 14: 26], and: 'When the Paraclete, whom I shall send to you from the Father, has come' [John 15: 26]. Therefore, what should we understand when he speaks of the Paraclete 'whom the Father will send in my name'? Is the fact that the Holy Spirit will have the Son's name, as when the Father will send the Holy Spirit, the same as to send the Son? But what he says, the Paraclete 'whom I shall send to you from the Father', does not allow this sense, since the Son also sends the very same Spirit that the Father sends, nor does the Son send the Son. Lastly, we never read, and we altogether deny, that the Holy Spirit is the Son. And so what do the words 'whom the Father will send in my name' mean except that the Son will also send the one whom the Father will send, as, when the Lord says, 'Whom I shall send from the Father', the words mean the same as 'I and the Father shall send'? For the Son is the name of him who said: 'The Father will send in my name.' Therefore, the words 'The Father will send in my name' are the same as to say that the Father will send in the name of the Son. Therefore, what is the statement 'The Father will send in the name of the Son' except that the Father will send as if the Son should send, so that we understand sending by the Son in the sending by the Father? And how should we understand what the Lord says, the Paraclete 'whom I shall send from the Father'? The Spirit is of course sent from the one from whom the Son sends him. And the Son sends the Spirit from the Father. Therefore, the Spirit is sent from the Father. But the one from whom the Spirit is sent sends. And so, when the Son says, 'I shall send from the Father', we understand that the Father sends. Therefore, what do the words 'I shall send from the Father' mean except 'I shall send as if the Father should send, so that my sending of the Spirit and the Father's sending of the Spirit are one and the same'?

And so the Son shows with so much care that there is one sending by the Father and himself, so that both the Father sends only when the Son sends, and the Son sends only when the Father sends. Therefore, what does the Son mean to signify or for us to understand except that the Holy Spirit is not related in one way to the Father and in another way to the Son, and that the Holy Spirit does not belong more to the one than to the other? And so it is too difficult, even impossible, to show how the Holy Spirit does not proceed from both. For why does the Son along with the Father give and send the Holy Spirit, and why does the Holy Spirit belong to both, if the Holy Spirit is not from both together? For why does the Son give the Holy Spirit rather than the Holy Spirit give the Son, or why does the Holy Spirit belong to the Son rather than the Son to the Holy Spirit, except because the Son is not from the Father and the Holy Spirit together as the Holy Spirit is from the Father and the Son together? Therefore, the Holy Spirit, if he is not from the Son, would not be given by the Son, nor would we say that the Holy Spirit belongs to the Son, since the Holy Spirit does not give the Son, nor do we say that the Son belongs to the Holy Spirit, since the Son is not from the Holy Spirit. And the Greeks may say that the Holy Spirit also sends the Son, as the same Son says through the mouth of the prophet: 'And now the Lord God sent me, and his Spirit sent me' [Isa. 48: 16]. But we should understand this according to the human being that the Son assumed, the human being who, destined to redeem the world by the one will and disposition of the Father and the Holy Spirit, was manifest in the world.

None the less, I ask of those who deny that the Holy Spirit exists and proceeds from the Son how they understand that the Spirit is the Spirit of the Son, so that the Son sends the Spirit as his Spirit. Do they think that the Father gave his Spirit to the Son as one who does not have the Spirit from himself? For the Son has the Spirit either from himself or from another. But the Son can have the Spirit from another only from the Father. Therefore, the Son received the Holy Spirit from the Father, from whom he has the Spirit, and the Father gave the Spirit to him as one who does not have the Spirit from himself. Since the Father and the Son and the Holy Spirit are equal, and each is self-sufficient, let them show here what reason or what need of the Son there was that the Father gave his Spirit to the Son rather than his Son to the Holy Spirit.

We do not deny that the Son has the Holy Spirit from the Father in such a way that the Son has from the Father from whom he has existence that he, like the Father, has the Spirit originating from himself, since the same existence belongs to the Father and the Son. For receiving from the Father the substance from which the Holy Spirit proceeds is not the same as receiving the Holy Spirit from the Father. For if we say that the Son has from the Father the substance from which the Holy Spirit proceeds, we do not indicate anything lacking in the Son. But if we say that the Son receives from the Father the Holy Spirit, whom the Son does not have from himself as the Father does, we seem to signify the Son as having something less than the Father does, and as being given the Holy Spirit to supply that lack.

But it is not clear why the Son needs the Holy Spirit rather than the Holy Spirit needs the Son. For if one replies to this objection that the Holy Spirit has been given to the Son so that, since the Son himself along with the Father gives the same Holy Spirit, the favour is imputed equally to the Father and the Son, such an opinion is crude and far removed from understanding the divine nature. And the consequence would be that God comes to the aid of God as if of one in need, as human beings come to the aid of human beings. For if the Father gives the Holy Spirit to the Son, God gives God to God. For the Father is God, and the Son is God, and the Holy Spirit is God, and they are one and the same God. And we do not understand that God receives God from God except we should say this when, in the case of the Son and the Holy Spirit, there is God from God. Therefore, we say that the Holy Spirit is the Spirit of the Son only because the Holy Spirit is from the Son himself.

5

We read that the Lord after the resurrection 'breathed' on his disciples and said to them: 'Receive the Holy Spirit' [John 20: 22]. What does this breathing mean? For we know that the breath that came out of his mouth on that occasion was not the Holy Spirit. Therefore, we do not believe that that breathing transpired without a secret meaning. Therefore, what can we understand here more correctly or more appropriately than that the Lord did this so that we understand that the Holy Spirit proceeds from him? This is as if he were to say: 'As you perceive this breath, whereby I indicate to you that, since perceptible things can signify imperceptible things, the Holy Spirit comes out of the depths of my body and from my person, in like manner know that the Holy Spirit, whom I indicate to you by this breath, comes out of the recesses of my divinity and from my person.' For we believe and profess that there is one person of the Word and the human being, and in that person two natures, namely, the divine and the human.

But the Greeks will perhaps say: 'That breath, of course, was not part of his human substance, and yet he emitted the breath as his. And so such giving of the Holy Spirit teaches us that the Son, when he gives the Holy Spirit, gives and sends his Spirit but not from the substance of his divine nature.' Therefore, if any are of this opinion, they may say that, as the breath emitted by human beings is not their human substance, so the Holy Spirit, when given or sent by God the Son, is not the divine substance. But no Christian professes this. They may also, when we hear, 'the word of the Lord established the heavens, and the breath of his mouth all of their powers' [Ps. 33: 6], if they do not deny in that text that we should understand the breath of the Lord's mouth as the Holy Spirit, say that the Holy Spirit is not from the substance of the Lord, of whom the Spirit is called the breath. They may say this because the breath that is accustomed to come out of the mouths of human beings is not from the substance of those from whom the breath comes out.

But they should not dare to say that the Spirit, namely, the Spirit of God, is not from the substance of God, and they should understand by the words about perceptible things, that is, by the mouth's breath, that the Holy Spirit proceeds from the recesses of the substance of the one of whose mouth the Spirit is called the breath. If so, they should also admit that the Holy Spirit proceeds from the substance of the one of whose lips the Spirit is called the breath. For we read in the prophet about Christ that 'he shall slay the impious with the breath of his lips' [Isa. 11: 4]. Therefore, either they should show the difference between the breath of his mouth and the breath of his lips, something that cannot be done, or they should likewise admit that the Holy Spirit proceeds from the one of whose mouth, and of whose lips, the Spirit is designated. And they may say that we should in no way understand the words 'the breath of his lips' in the text as the Holy Spirit but as the words of his statement, which he fashioned out of that heavenly breath in a human way, since he slays the impious by his words when he by his teaching removes impiety from human beings. But the perceptible words and the perceptible breath, of course, do not accomplish this. Rather, this is accomplished by the Holy Spirit, about whom God says through the prophet: 'I shall remove the heart of stone from your flesh, and I shall give you a heart of flesh, and I shall implant my Spirit within you' [Ezek. 36: 26–7]. Therefore, the Holy Spirit slays the impious when he converts the heart of the impious from impiety to piety. And if we understand in the impious one the Antichrist, 'whom the Lord Jesus will slay with the breath of his mouth' [2 Thess. 2: 8], I do not think that anyone would attribute that power as much to the breath of the human voice as to the Spirit of God.

Therefore, if we understand the Holy Spirit in these statements, since he is in like manner called the breath of the mouth of the Lord (i.e. the Father), whose word 'established the heavens', and the breath of the mouth and lips of the Lord Jesus, there is no apparent reason why we should understand that the Holy Spirit proceeds from the mouth of the Father more than from the mouth of the Son. And let us understand the mouth of the Father as the substance of the Father, since his mouth is simply his substance, so that, as the word of the Lord is from his substance, so the breath of his mouth is simply from his substance. What is then more evident than, as the breath of the Father's mouth exists and proceeds from the Father's substance, so the breath of the Son's mouth and lips exists and proceeds from the Son's substance? For I think that when the text says, 'The word of the Lord established the heavens, and the breath of his mouth all of their powers' [Ps. 33: 6], no one understands the words as simply transitory, or the breath as a breath taken from the atmosphere that is emitted through the speaker's mouth.

But howsoever one attempts to explain these things, it suffices to say that that breathing of the Lord on the disciples, which I have mentioned, transpired to signify that the breath that he gave came out of the recesses of the same person, from the recesses of whom proceeded the breath that he breathed. Lastly, when divine Scripture signifies things hidden in perceptible things, the things cannot be like in everything that they signify, and that are signified. For such would be sameness, not likeness, unless one perchance wished to say that the breathing, by the wisdom of God, transpired so artlessly as to be without any spiritual significance. But I do not think that anyone is so foolish as to think that.

6

The Son likewise says of the Holy Spirit: 'For he will not speak from his very self, but he will speak whatever he hears' [John 16: 13]. What is 'He will not speak from his very self' except that he will have from another what he will speak? And what is 'He will have from another what he will speak' except that he will from another have knowledge of the things about which he will speak? And so, after the Son says, 'He will not speak from his very self', he adds, 'but he will speak whatever he hears'. What is it for the Holy Spirit to hear except to learn, as it were, and what is it to learn except to receive knowledge? Therefore, if his knowledge is simply his substance, he has his substance from the one from whom he hears what he speaks and teaches, since it is the same thing for him to speak and to teach. And he hears and has his substance from another only either from the Father or from the Son. And if the Spirit has existence from the Father, he by the previously mentioned argument [2] also has existence from the Son as well. And so the Son also says the same thing: 'The Spirit will glorify me, since he will receive from what belongs to me and declare it to you' [John 16: 14]. Indeed, what else is this except to say: 'He will hear from me' (i.e. he will know from me) what he declares to you? When the Son said, 'He will speak whatever he hears', the Son did not specify from whom the Spirit will hear. But when the Son says, 'He will receive from me', the Son shows openly that the Son is the one from whom, as from the Father, the Spirit receives his knowledge or substance, lest anyone attribute to the Father alone what the Spirit hears from another. For when the Son says, 'He will not speak from his very self, but he will speak whatever he hears', and 'he will declare it to you', the Son signifies that the Spirit exists and proceeds from the one from whom the Spirit hears. Just so, when the Son says, 'He will receive from what belongs to me, and he will declare it to you', the Son shows openly that the Spirit has his substance and proceeds from what belongs to the Son, that is, from the Son's substance. For things not the divine substance are subject to the Holy Spirit, and he himself does not receive anything from things subject to himself. And so, when the Son says, 'He will receive from what belongs to me', the Son does not on that occasion signify anything of his other than his substance.

7

Perhaps the Greeks will attempt to understand what the Son says, 'He will receive from what belongs to me, and he will declare it to you', in ways other than I have explained. But what will they say about the text where the Son says, 'No one knows the Son except the Father, and no one knows the Father except the Son and those to whom the Son wished to reveal them' [Matt. 11: 27]? We hear that no one knows the Father or the Son except the Father or the Son, and those to whom the Son reveals them. And the Son does not say 'no one' as if to say 'no human being', but as if to say 'no one at all'. Indeed, if the Son were to understand 'no one' to mean 'no human being', he would not add 'except the Father', since the Father is not a human being. And when the Son says, 'And no one knows the Father', we do not understand in the subject of the sentence, namely, 'no one', a reference to human persons but a reference to any person. Therefore, no one has such knowledge except the Father and the Son and those to whom the Son reveals the same. And so either the Holy

Spirit does not know the Father and the Son, which it is impious to think, or the Son reveals to the Holy Spirit knowledge of the Son and the Father, and the Holy Spirit's knowledge of the Son and the Father is nothing other than the substance of the same Holy Spirit.

But perhaps they say that, although the Son, as regards this declaration, admits to such knowledge no one except himself and the Father and those to whom he himself reveals it, we should none the less not allow either that the Holy Spirit is distinct from that knowledge, or that the Holy Spirit receives the knowledge from the Son. They may say this because the Father and the Son know themselves only because they are one with the Holy Spirit. And so, when the Son says that the Father and the Son know one another, we should understand the Holy Spirit at the same time, and the Son, when he reveals, reveals to creatures and not to the Holy Spirit. If they say this, I say, we evidently draw an immediate inference as follows. Truth, as the words of the Son's mouth declare, affirms that the Holy Spirit knows the Father and the Son only with the Son revealing them. Therefore, if the Greeks say that we ought not to pay as much attention to the words as to the unity of the Trinity's substance, which is one and indivisible for all three persons, we ought much more to pay heed to this unity's consequences, about which I have spoken before [1]. And no authority either in word or meaning denies them, nor advances anything contrary to them or in any way inconsistent with them.

And so the Greeks, if they wish openly to resist the truth, may choose one of two things, namely, either that the Holy Spirit knows the Father and the Son only with the Son revealing them, or that, when the very Father and Son are said to know themselves, it necessarily follows that we understand the Holy Spirit in the same knowing, since they are one with the Holy Spirit in that by which they know themselves. There is, of course, no middle way if they are unwilling completely to disavow such knowledge by the Holy Spirit or truth from the words of Truth. And the true profession of faith anathematizes both of the alternatives. For Truth speaks thus: 'No one knows the Son except the Father, and no one knows the Father except the Son and those to whom the Son wished to reveal them' [Matt. 11: 27]. If they indeed choose to say that the Holy Spirit knows the Father and the Son by the revelation of the Son, the Holy Spirit has knowledge from the Son, which is simply for the Holy

Spirit to have existing from the Son. Therefore, the Holy Spirit exists and proceeds from the Son, since the Spirit proceeds from the one from whom he exists. And let us suppose they say that, when the Father and Son are said to know themselves, it follows that the Holy Spirit has an equal share in the knowledge, since the substance by which the Father and the Son know themselves is the same as the Holy Spirit's substance. Then they, when they read that the Holy Spirit proceeds from the Father, of whom the Son says, 'I and the Father are one' [John 10: 30], should profess with us that the Holy Spirit undoubtedly also proceeds from the Son, since the Father and the Son have the same substance.

8

And someone may object that, when we say that the Father generates the Son, and that the Holy Spirit proceeds from the Father and the Son, we constitute certain grades and intervals, as if the Holy Spirit could not exist unless the Father first generates the Son. And the consequence would be that the Holy Spirit is subsequent to the Son, and we should accordingly say more correctly that both the Son and the Holy Spirit are from the Father, the Son by generation and the Holy Spirit by procession, so that neither is the Son from the Holy Spirit, nor the Holy Spirit from the Son. Just so, both brightness and heat are from one and the same sun, and the brightness is not from the heat, nor the heat from the brightness.

If anyone poses such an objection to our position, I say, we answer: We neither posit grades of dignity in God (who is one) nor constitute intervals in eternity (which is outside every point of time) in originating the Son from the Father, or the Holy Spirit from the Father and the Son. For all of us holding the Christian faith alike profess that the Son is neither less than nor subsequent to the Father, although the Son exists only from the Father. So also we who say that the Holy Spirit exists or proceeds from the Son profess that the Holy Spirit is neither less than nor subsequent to the Son. Although brightness and heat, of course, come from the sun and cannot exist unless there exist the thing from which they exist, we none the less do not understand before and after in the three, namely, the sun and the brightness and the heat. And so, since these things are so in temporal things, much less can we understand the aforementioned three persons in their originating to be susceptible of intervals in the course of eternity, which time does not encompass.

And to say that the Son and the Holy Spirit can be from the Father alone, so that neither the Son is from the Holy Spirit, nor the Holy Spirit from the Son, as brightness and heat come from the sun alone in such a way that the one is not from the other, is not properly alleged as an objection to our position. For when we say that the Son and the Holy Spirit are from the Father, we profess that God the Son and God the Holy Spirit are from God the Father, and that these three persons are only one God, and that the very thing is from the very same thing. And in the case of the sun, we do not say that the sun is from the sun when brightness or heat is from the sun, nor that the very thing is the sun and what comes from the sun, nor that the three things are one and the same sun. For suppose that the sun and the brightness were to be one and the same sun, or that the sun and the heat were to be one and the same sun. It would then be necessary either that the brightness be from the heat, since the brightness would be from the whole sun that would be the very heat, or that the heat would be from the brightness, since the heat would have existence from the sun, which would not differ substantially from the brightness.

Let us none the less suppose that both the Son and the Holy Spirit are from the Father alone just as heat and brightness are from one and the same sun. And if this is so, why do those who hold this hold that they profess that the Holy Spirit belongs to the Son, and deny that the Son belongs to the Holy Spirit? For as no reasoning allows that heat belongs to brightness, or brightness to heat, so honesty does not allow them to say that the Holy Spirit belongs to the Son rather than that the Son belongs to the Holy Spirit. And so, if they do not dare to deny that the Holy Spirit belongs to the Son, they should deny that the Son and the Holy Spirit are both from the Father alone in the same way that brightness and heat are from the one sun. And so, if they pose as an objection to our position what I have said about the brightness and heat of the sun, the objection is neither consistent with their position nor contrary to ours.

9

The Greeks, as they tell us, in order not to exclude the Son entirely from communion with the Father in the procession of the Holy

Spirit, assert that the Holy Spirit proceeds from the Father through the Son. But it is not clear how we can understand this, especially since they never recite from what source they can openly demonstrate this. For they may think favourable to their position what we read about God, that 'all things are from himself and through himself and in himself' [Rom. 11: 36], so that the Father is from whom all things exist, and the Son is through whom all things exist, and the Holy Spirit is in whom all things exist, and we understand the Holy Spirit to be among the 'all things' that exist through the Son. If they so think, we accept without any qualm the fact that all things are from the Father and through the Son and in the Holy Spirit, but it is too exacting to say that the Holy Spirit is among all the things about which St Paul so speaks. For we cannot include any one of the three persons among those things and exclude the other two. But if the Father and the Son and the Holy Spirit are among all the things that are from the Father and through the Son and in the Holy Spirit, the rational mind should perceive how great would be the confusion that would result. Therefore, when the Apostle says, 'All things are from himself and through himself and in himself', we should undoubtedly understand all the things created by God, which are thus 'from himself and through himself and in himself', as things from something else and through something else and in something else. For things produced are not identical with God but distinct from him. And the Holy Spirit is not distinct but the very same thing that is the Father and the Son.

Of course, we can understand nothing else by which they can show that the Holy Spirit proceeds from the Father through the Son, as they express it. For the Father and the Son do not differ in the one divine nature, and the Holy Spirit proceeds from the Father only from the divine nature. Therefore, we cannot understand how, if the same divine nature belongs to the Son, the Holy Spirit proceeds from the divine nature of the Father through the divine nature of the Son and not from the divine nature of the Son, unless someone perchance should say that the Holy Spirit does not proceed from the divine nature of the Father but from his paternity, nor through the divine nature of the Son but through his filiation. And the latter opinion suffocates itself with its obvious foolishness.

But someone may say that when I say that the Holy Spirit proceeds from the divine nature of the Father and the Son, I cannot exclude the divine nature of the Holy Spirit from the divine nature of the Father and the Son, since one and the same divine nature belongs to the three. And such a person may conclude that if the Holy Spirit proceeds from the divine nature of the Father and the Son, he also proceeds from his own divine substance and thereby from his very self [1]. If anyone so says, I recall that I have already sufficiently replied to such an objection that no person can be from that person's very self. For the Son, while he is from the substance of the Father, although the substance of the Son is not distinct but the same as the substance that belongs to the Father, is none the less not from his very self but from the Father alone. Just so, the Holy Spirit, while he is from the substance of the Father and the Son and has the same substance, is none the less not from his very self but only from the Father and the Son.

The Greeks will say: 'Why can we not say that the Holy Spirit proceeds from the Father through the Son just as we say that all things have been made by the Father through the Word that is the Son? For when the Father produces through his Word, he produces only through what he himself is, that is, through the substantial power that is the same substantial power of the Word, and yet is said to produce through the Word. Why do we not similarly say that the Holy Spirit proceeds from the Father through the Word, since the Holy Spirit proceeds from the Father only from and through what is the same for the Father as well as the Son, although not as creatures do but as the very same thing from the very same thing?'

Let us see what follows if we say this, and let there be peace among us. The things done by the Father through the Word, of course, are done by the very Word. For the Word himself says: 'For all the things he [the Father] has done, the Son likewise does' [John 5: 19]. Therefore, we should say that the Holy Spirit, when he proceeds from the Father through the Son, also proceeds from the Son in the same way as things done by the Father through the Word are done by the very Word.

Unless perchance the Greeks understand that the Holy Spirit proceeds from the Father through the Son just as, when a spring flows into a stream, and a stream collects in a lake, we say that the lake is from the spring through the stream. But the stream in that case is outside the spring and not in the spring, whereas the Son is in the Father and not outside the Father. And so the Holy Spirit is not from the Father through the Son exactly as the lake is from the spring through the stream. None the less, if this is so, we cannot deny that the Holy Spirit is from the Son, although he is from the Father through the Son, as we need to admit that the lake is from the stream, although the lake is from the spring through the stream. For those who deny that the lake is from the stream, since the stream is from the spring, should say that they are not from their fathers but from Adam, since they are from Adam through their fathers. They should also say that the Virgin's son is not from Mary, nor from David or Abraham, since these were from Adam. And they should call false what is said of Abraham, 'All nations will be blessed in your seed' [Gen. 22: 18], and to David, 'I shall place on your throne one from the fruit of your loins' [Ps. 132: 11], and to Mary, 'Blessed is the fruit of your womb' [Luke 1: 42]. And they should say that Christ is not the seed or fruit of Abraham or David or Mary but of Adam, since Abraham and David and Mary descend from Adam. But the Virgin's son is not from Adam in this sense; rather, the Virgin's son is from the slime of the earth from which Adam was made.

But they will argue: 'We rightly say that the Holy Spirit proceeds not from the Son but from the Father through the Son, although the Holy Spirit is from the Father and the Son, as you say that the lake is from a spring and a stream. For we disagree about the word "procession", which you affirm, and we deny, to be from the Son. For note that you perceive that a stream comes from a spring as its initial source. And the lake does not come from the stream but is collected from it, although the lake has its existing from the stream. Therefore, even if the Holy Spirit should have existence from the Son, we still do not, strictly speaking, say that the Holy Spirit proceeds from the Son; rather, we say that the Holy Spirit proceeds from the Father as his source.'

They would perhaps correctly say this if the Son generated from the Father were to proceed outside the Father, and, with some space intervening, we were to understand that the Holy Spirit is from the Father before he is from the Son. Just so, a stream flowing from a spring proceeds outside the spring and is collected after an interval into a lake, and the lake is from the spring before it is from the stream, and so the lake is from the spring through the stream, not from the stream through the spring. But since the Son generated from the Father does not go outside the Father and, remaining in him, is neither spatially nor temporally nor substantially distinct from the

Father, and since that from which the Holy Spirit proceeds is one and the same thing for the Father and the Son, we neither can understand nor ought to say that the Holy Spirit proceeds from the Father and not from the Son. Therefore, there seems to be no reason why we should say that the Holy Spirit does not proceed from the Son, but that he proceeds from the Father through the Son, since the Holy Spirit cannot not be from the Son, even if he be through the Son.

Perhaps someone none the less wishes to say that the Son proceeds from the Father in a stricter sense than the Holy Spirit proceeds from the Son, although the Spirit is from the Son, as the stream seems to that person to come from the spring more than the lake comes from the stream. The person may wish to say this in order not to admit that the Holy Spirit proceeds from the Son from whom he has existing, as the lake comes from the stream. We do not deny that the Son generated proceeds in one way from the Father generating. And we affirm that the Holy Spirit truly proceeds in his own way from one source, not as if from two sources, and in such a way that neither the procession of the Son loses, nor the procession of the Holy Spirit receives, the name 'generation'. Therefore, there is no reason why we ought more to say that the Son proceeds from the Father than we ought to say that the Holy Spirit proceeds from the Son.

Let us consider more carefully how the lake is both from the spring and from the stream, so that we may thereby know that the Holy Spirit is from the Father and the Son, inasmuch as we can understand what is eternal by what is temporal and spatial. For, as I wrote to Pope Urban of venerable memory in my letter *On the Incarnation of the Word*,[4] we discover many things in considering temporal and spatial things that are analogously fit for the one God and the three persons. One and the same water is evidently what we call the spring and the stream and the lake, not three waters, although the spring and the stream and the lake are three. And so we should distinguish between the spring and the stream and the lake, and we should perceive that we should understand these individual things, although they be three, to be in the one water.

Indeed, water rising from the depths bubbles up in the spring, descending from the spring flows in the stream, is collected and stays in the lake. Therefore, we understand by the spring the water bub-

---

[4] *On the Incarnation of the Word*, 13.

bling up from the depths, by the stream that the water flows from the spring, by the lake that the water then coalesces together. And we perceive that the stream is not such from the condition by reason of which we call water a spring, but from what the stream is, that is, water, nor is the lake such from the condition by reason of which we call water a spring or a stream, but from the very water, which is one and the same in the spring and the stream. Therefore, the lake does not originate from the condition by reason of which the spring and the stream differ, but from the condition in which the spring and the stream are the same. Therefore, if the spring is no more than the stream the reason why the lake exists, we cannot understand the lake to be more from the spring than from the stream. And so, when we call God the Father or the Son or the Holy Spirit, we understand in the three persons one substance and one God (which title signifies the very substance). But we understand in the Father the one who begets, and in the Son the one who is begotten, and in the Holy Spirit the one who proceeds in a singular and ineffable way. Therefore, as the lake is not such from the condition by reason of which the spring and the stream differ from one another, but from the water in which they are the same, so the Holy Spirit is not such from the condition by reason of which the Father and the Son differ from one another, but from the divine substance in which the Father and the Son are the same. Therefore, if the Father is not more than the Son that by reason of which the Holy Spirit exists, we cannot understand why the Holy Spirit is more from the Father than from the Son.

10

But if the Greeks say that the Holy Spirit cannot be from two causes or two sources, we answer that, as we do not believe that the Holy Spirit is such from the condition by reason of which the Father and the Son are two, but from that in which they are one, so we do not say that there are two sources of the Spirit, but that there is one source. Indeed, when we call God the source of creatures, we understand the Father and the Son and the Holy Spirit to be one source, not three, as one Creator, not three. This is true although the Father and the Son and the Holy Spirit are three, since the Father or the Son or the Holy Spirit is the source or Creator by reason of that in which they are one and not by reason of that whereby they are three.

Therefore, the Father and the Son and the Holy Spirit, although each is the source of creatures, are none the less not three sources but one. Just so, the Holy Spirit, when we say that he is from the Father and the Son, is not from two sources but one, which is the Father and the Son, as the Spirit is from God, who is Father and Son—if it is notwithstanding proper for us to say that God has a source or cause.

For we perceive sources only of things that begin to exist, and causes only of effects, and the Holy Spirit never began to exist, nor is he the effect of anything. For things that begin to exist go from non-existing to existing, and the word 'effect' in the strict sense seems to be applicable to things that come into existence. None the less, since it is true that the Son is from the Father, and the Holy Spirit is from the Father and the Son, we can, if we understand each procession in its own ineffable way (since it could not otherwise be revealed), appropriately say that the Father is in one way the source of the Son, and that the Father and the Son are in another way the source of the Holy Spirit. And yet we do not profess two sources, one the Father for the Son, the other the Father and the Son for the Holy Spirit. Just so, we do not believe that there is one God the Father from whom the Son is, and another God the Father and the Son from whom the Holy Spirit is, although each is from the same God or source in his own way, namely, one by generation and the other by procession, provided that we understand that procession in a unique and ineffable way. For we speak of procession in many ways, of which we understand the one of the Spirit to be unique, just as we know the generation of the Son to be unique. We understand the very same thing if we say that the Father causes the Son, and that the Father and the Son cause the Holy Spirit. For we cannot speak of two causes, namely, one of the Son and the other of the Holy Spirit, but of one cause, just as there are not two Gods but one God, from whom the Son and the Holy Spirit are.

11

And when the Lord said, 'When the Paraclete, the Spirit of Truth, who proceeds from the Father has come' [John 15: 26], one may ask why he did not add, 'and from the Son', or 'from me'. I answer that it is not unusual in his statements that, when he attributes something to the Father as if only to the Father, or to himself, or to the Holy

Spirit, he wishes what he says in the case of one to be understood in the case of the others. For example, when he says, 'Blessed are you, Simon Bar-Jonah, because flesh and blood have not revealed this to you, but my Father who is in heaven' [Matt. 16: 17], should we not understand that the Son and the Holy Spirit along with the Father have revealed it? For, since the Father does not reveal things by reason of the fact that he is the Father, but by reason of the fact that he is God, and since the same God is the Son and the Holy Spirit, it follows that the Son and the Holy Spirit reveal what the Father reveals.

Likewise, the Lord says, 'No one knows the Son except the Father, nor does anyone know the Father except the Son and those to whom the Son wished to reveal them' [Matt. 11: 27], as if the Son alone should know and reveal the Father and himself, and that the Father alone should know the Son. But we should understand in the passage that the revealing and knowing is common to the three persons, since they do not know and reveal things by reason of the fact that they differ from one another, but by reason of the fact that the Father and the Son and the Holy Spirit are one. Also, when the Lord says that the Father knows the Son, and that the Son knows and reveals himself and the Father, he evidently wishes us to understand that the Father knows the Holy Spirit, and that the Son knows and reveals the Holy Spirit, since the very substance that constitutes the Father constitutes the Holy Spirit.

Likewise, when the Lord says, 'Who sees me sees the Father also' [John 14: 9], we should not exclude the Holy Spirit, since those who see that in which the Father and the Son and the Holy Spirit are one cannot see one of the three apart from the other two.

The Lord also says of the Holy Spirit to the apostles, 'And when the Spirit of Truth has come, he will teach you all truth' [John 16: 13], as if the Holy Spirit should be the one who teaches all truth, although he teaches all truth neither apart from the Father nor apart from the Son. For he does not teach all truth by reason of the fact that he is the Spirit of someone, namely, the Spirit of the Father and the Son, but by reason of the fact that the Holy Spirit is one with the Father and the Son, that is, by reason of the fact that he is God.

Therefore, do you perceive how, in the things I have presented, things attributed to one person as if only to the one person cannot be excluded from the other two persons? We read many such things in Sacred Scripture, so that we understand about the three persons without distinction what we say uniquely about one person. For everything we say about the one person we ought likewise to understand of the other persons, except when we know that, as I have said [1], whereby the three persons differ from one another. And so, when we profess that the Holy Spirit proceeds from the Father, since the Holy Spirit is God from God, that is, when we understand that the substance of the Holy Spirit is from the substance of the Father, which substance is common to the three persons, we need to profess that the Holy Spirit is likewise from the Son if the Son is not from the Holy Spirit. For the Holy Spirit is from the substance of the Son and the substance of the Father.

But someone will say: 'We understand that the Son and the Holy Spirit reveal what the Father alone is said to reveal, and that the Father and the Holy Spirit reveal and know what the Son alone is said to reveal and know, and that the Father and the Son teach what instruction the Holy Spirit is sent to cause, because other citations clearly signify what we read in a particular citation. And while the Lord says that the Holy Spirit proceeds from the Father, we do not read elsewhere that the Holy Spirit proceeds from the Son, whereby we are put on notice never to assert the Lord's statement in our sense.'

And we reply to this objection that things so expressed, to the contrary, teach us to understand in like fashion things unexpressed in like expressed things, especially when we have clearly perceived that the unexpressed things follow with logical necessity, with no argument to the contrary, from the expressed things. For example, when the Lord says to the Father, 'And this is eternal life, that they know you, the only true God, and the one whom you have sent, Jesus Christ' [John 17: 3], ought we to exclude the Holy Spirit from this wholesome and vital knowledge because we never read, 'And this is eternal life, that they know the only true God the Father and the Holy Spirit,' or, 'This is eternal life, that they know the only true God the Son and the Holy Spirit'? Or when we read, 'As the Father has life in his very self, so he also gave the Son to have life in his very self' [John 5: 26], shall we say that the Holy Spirit does not have from the Father, from whom he is, that he have life in his very self, as the Father and Son do, since the Son never says this about the Holy Spirit, as the Son does about his very self? Likewise, when the

Lord says, 'The Father is in me, and I am in the Father' [John 14: 10], and, 'Those who see me see the Father also' [John 14: 9], shall we deny that the Holy Spirit is in the Father and the Son, and that the Father and the Son are in the Holy Spirit, or that those who see the Son see the Holy Spirit, as they see the Father, unless we read such things in the same statement that mentions them regarding the Father and the Son?

But since one and the same God is the Father and the Son and the Holy Spirit, when the cited text says that to know the 'one true God', the Father and the Son, is life eternal, we should inclusively understand the Holy Spirit in such knowledge. And when we read, 'As the Father has life in his very self, so he gave the Son to have life in his very self', we ought not to judge the same life to be foreign to the Holy Spirit, or that the Holy Spirit does not have that life in his very self. And when we hear, 'The Father is in me, and I am in the Father', and, 'Those who see me see the Father also', we should know by the things so expressed that the Holy Spirit is not outside the Father and the Son, or the Father and the Son outside the Holy Spirit, and that those who see the Son see the Holy Spirit as well as the Father. For as the Father is not one God, the Son another God, the Holy Spirit another God, so God has nothing in his very self other than God, nor is there God outside of God, nor is there God unlike God.

Lastly, where do we in so many words read in the prophets or the evangelists or the apostle that the one God is three persons, or that the one God is the Trinity, or that there is God from God? And neither do we find the name 'person' or 'Trinity' in the creed, in which the procession of the Holy Spirit is not mentioned. None the less, since these things follow from the things that we read, we firmly both from the heart believe and in words profess such things. And so we ought to accept as certain not only the things that we read in Holy Scripture but also the things that follow from them with logical necessity, with no other argument to the contrary.

12

Although the things that I have already said may be sufficient, I none the less shall still add something else whereby we know that the Holy Spirit is from the Son. We and the Greeks profess that the Holy Spirit is the Spirit of God and the Spirit of the Father and the Spirit of the Son. And so I ask if they understand in the same way or a different way that the Holy Spirit is the Spirit of God and the Spirit of the Father and the Spirit of the Son. And it is certain that we do not call the Holy Spirit the Spirit of God to indicate that the Spirit is a possession of God, as when we call a horse or house the horse or house of someone. For possessors are greater than the things they possess. And God is not greater than the Holy Spirit, since the Holy Spirit is God, and God is not greater than God. Nor do we call the Holy Spirit the Spirit of God to indicate that the Spirit is a part of God like the hand or foot of a human being. For God has no members or parts. Therefore, how should we understand that the Holy Spirit is the Spirit of God other than that the substance of the Holy Spirit is from God? And the name 'Father' signifies only God who is the Father, or his relation to the Son, from which relation he acquires the name 'Father'. We should speak in like manner about the Son. For what do we understand in the name 'Son' other than God who is the Son, or the relation whereby the Son is related to the Father, the relation whereby we call the Son the Son? But no meaning of the Holy Spirit understands that he is the Spirit of the Father or the Son as the one is Father, the other the Son, but as both are one and the same God. And so we have understood the same thing when we call the Holy Spirit the Spirit of God and the Spirit of the Father and the Spirit of the Son.

But we call the Holy Spirit the Spirit of God and the Spirit of the Father because the Holy Spirit exists and proceeds from God and the Father. And so the Holy Spirit exists and proceeds from the Son, since we in the same sense call the Holy Spirit the Spirit of the Son. For when we call the Holy Spirit the Spirit of God and the Spirit of the Lord, if we do not there understand the Spirit of the Son in the same sense as the Spirit of the Father, either we shall exclude the Son from the title of God or Lord, or we shall understand the Spirit of God or the Spirit of the Lord in two senses. But from what do those titles have this sense, or where do we read in Sacred Scripture that, when we read Spirit of God or Spirit of the Lord, we do not understand the titles to regard the Father and the Son? Or what do we find from which such follows? For the Greeks may say: 'When we call the Holy Spirit the Spirit of the Father, we understand this in two ways, that the Holy Spirit is from the Father, and that he is given by the Father, while the Holy Spirit is the Spirit of the Son only because the Holy Spirit is given by the Son.' If they so say, I ask from what source they know this. And if they say that no authentic page of Scripture says this, nor does it follow from what is written there, why do they, because they do not read the words in Scripture, censure us when we say that the Holy Spirit proceeds from the Son, since we understand that such procession necessarily follows from the things that they read and profess?

Therefore, let the Greeks themselves judge what they should rather accept: either what we say, that the Holy Spirit proceeds from the Son, which we have demonstrated to follow from things that we truly believe, or what they themselves say, that the Holy Spirit is in one way the Spirit of the Father and in another way the Spirit of the Son, which they can demonstrate neither by authority nor by argument nor by things that are certain. To be sure, they ought to abandon this opinion of theirs, if, as I hear, they say that the Holy Spirit is the Spirit of the Son in a different way than he is the Spirit of the Father, since they never read it in Scripture or show from what source they derive it. Or else they at least ought not to censure us for saying that the Holy Spirit proceeds from the Son in spite of the fact that we do not read such in the words of Scripture, since we demonstrate that such follows from things that we, like them, believe. And if they abandon this assertion of theirs, they should likewise with us profess that the Holy Spirit is in like manner the Spirit of the Father and the Son, and understand that the Holy Spirit proceeds from the Son as well as the Father. And if they cease to censure us, they should profess with us the source from which they know that we ought not to be censured.

13

As to their censure of us for having added the profession of the Holy Spirit in the creed, which we and they accept and hold, and their inquiry why we have done this, and why we have not first informed their church of this, so that what was added would be jointly considered and added by common consent, to this, I say, we have a sufficient answer.

For if one inquires why we did this, we say that it was necessary because of certain less understanding persons, who were not attentive in things that the universal Church believes to be firmly established (and from which the procession of the Holy Spirit from the Son follows), lest they perchance hesitate to believe that the Holy Spirit so proceeds. And we know how necessary this was by reason of those who deny that the Holy Spirit proceeds from the Son because the creed has not posited such procession. Therefore, since both necessity compelled this, and no argument prevented it, and the true faith admitted it, the Latin church faithfully asserted that it knew that we should believe and profess it. For we know that the creed has not expressed everything that we ought to believe and profess, nor did those who prescribed the creed wish that the Christian faith be content to believe and profess the things that the creed posited. For example, not to mention other things, the creed does not say that the Lord descended into hell, something that both we and the Greeks alike believe. And if they say that a creed weighted with so much authority ought in no way to have been corrupted, we do not judge that there is corruption when we add nothing contrary to the things said in the creed. And although we can defend the position that this addition is not a corruption, if anyone still wished contentiously to assert the contrary, we answer that we have not corrupted the creed but presented something else new. For we with the Greeks preserve and reverence the whole creed as conveyed by the character of Greek speech, and we have set it forth, transcribed in the Latin idiom with the aforementioned addition, as we more frequently use it in ordinary speech.

And because they ask why we have not done this with the consent of the Greek church, we answer that it was both too difficult for the Latins to assemble the Greek bishops to deliberate on this matter and not necessary to debate the matter when the Latins had no doubt. For what church, especially one that is spread throughout the breadth of one kingdom, is there to which it is not permitted to establish things regarding the orthodox faith that assemblies of the people should profitably read and sing? Therefore, how much more was it permitted to the Latins to make clearly known that on which all the peoples and all the kingdoms using the Latin language alike agree?

14

Let us briefly summarize what the several arguments advanced above have produced. Irrefutable logic makes it evident that the Holy Spirit is from the Son, just as he is from the Father, and yet he is not from them as if from two different sources but as from one. For the Holy Spirit is from the Father and the Son being the same, that is, from the Father and the Son being God, not from that whereby the Father and the Son differ from one another. But since God (from whom the Holy Spirit is) is Father and Son, we on that account truly say that the Holy Spirit is from the Father and the Son (who are two). And since the Father is not antecedent or subsequent to, or greater or lesser than, the Son, nor is one more or less God than the other, the Holy Spirit is not from the Father before he is from the Son. Nor is he from the Son before he is from the Father. Nor is his originating from the Father greater or lesser than his originating from the Son. Nor is he more or less from one than from the other. For if he were to be before or after, or greater or lesser, or more or less from one than from the other, it would necessarily follow that the Holy Spirit would not be from that in which the Father and the Son are one. Or else it would follow that their very unity would not be complete and absolute, and there would then be some diversity, regarding which there would be the difference I mentioned, the difference in originating the Holy Spirit from the same unity. But we cannot say that the Holy Spirit is not from that in which the Father and Son are one (otherwise, the Holy Spirit would not be from God), nor ought we to believe that there is in the very unity any difference. And so the Holy Spirit is not from the Father before or after, or greater or lesser, or more or less than he is from the Son, or vice versa. For the one and same Holy Spirit, the whole of whom is once for all from the whole God, cannot be more or less from the one and supremely simple God.

And if one says that the Holy Spirit is chiefly from the Father, as if he is more from the Father than from the Son, we should not say this so as to understand that any of the aforementioned differences are present. But since the Son has his substance from the Father, one on that account appropriately affirms that the Holy Spirit has the very fact that he is from the Son from the Father, from whom the Son has existence. And the Son has existence from the Father such that that very existence is completely what the Father and the one and same God have, as the unique and simple God cannot be greater or lesser than his very self, nor before or after his very self, or have any different part in himself. Therefore, the Son is neither antecedent or subsequent to, nor greater or lesser than, the Father, nor does the Son have any part in himself different from the Father. Rather, as the Son has existence completely from the Father, so the Son has from the same Father equality with him in everything and indeed the very like existence.

Therefore, as the Father is not more God than the Son is, although the Son has existence from the Father, so the Holy Spirit is not more from the Father than from the Son, although the Son has from the Father that the Holy Spirit is from the Son. For in that in which the Son is one and the same with the Father, that is, in what is God, the Son is not one God, and the Father another God. Nor do they have anything in unlike ways, since there is not one God the Father and another God the Son. Nor are they in unlike ways what they are, but the Father is distinctive in being the Father, and the Son is distinctive in being the Son. And as the Son is not a different God than the Father, so, insofar as the Son is God, he has nothing from anyone other than his very self. For when we call him God from God, Son from the Father, we do not understand one God from another God but the very same God from the very same God, although we say that one is from the other, namely, the Son from the Father. For, as I have said before [1], as God receives differences by names that do not signify any unity, so God necessarily admits plurality by names that signify that God is from God.

Therefore, if we say that the Holy Spirit is chiefly from the Father, we signify only that the Son himself from whom the Holy Spirit is has from the Father the very fact that the Holy Spirit is from the Son, since the Son has his substance from the Father. This is not the way in which we mean to signify in the case of created things, when we say that something is chiefly such, that what we say is chiefly such is more than that to which the chief thing is related. For example, when the steward of a master provides food for the family of a household at the master's bidding, we correctly say that the master chiefly and more than the steward provides food for the household. For not everything that belongs to a master belongs equally to his steward, while things belonging to the Father also belong equally to the Son.

Perhaps someone will ask and express bewilderment: 'How can we understand that something has existence from something, and that the latter is not in some way more the chief thing and more worthy, and that the former is in some way less and, as it were, secondary? One may especially ask this because what originates from something seems necessarily to belong to the source, and the source in no way needs the thing that originates from the source.' And we should reply to this objection that, as God's substance is very different and other than created substances, so, when we say that God originates from God by generation or procession, we should understand the generation or procession far differently than when we in the case of other things say that things are generated or proceed. For in the case of generation or procession from God, nothing either by nature or by time or by any compulsion is before or after, more or less, or for any reason needs anything. Rather, there is a whole that is not so uniform, or even like itself, and coeternal as to be the same as its very self, and that is altogether intrinsically sufficient for its very self, nor is there generated or does there proceed in the case of generation and procession from God anything as if going from non-existing to existing. Therefore, as our intellect cannot go beyond eternity so as to judge about the beginning of eternity, as it were, so our intellect cannot about the generation or procession from God, nor should our intellect think or judge by analogy to creatures. But both what is generated and what proceeds is only that from which there is the generating or proceeding, that is, the one and only God, as the same God is not greater or lesser than his very self. Just so, in the three persons, that is, the Father and the Son and the Holy Spirit, nothing is greater or lesser, nor is one anything that is more or less than the other, although it is true that there is God from God by generation and procession.

Note that we perceive with how much truth and necessity it follows that the Holy Spirit proceeds from the Son. But if this conclusion is not true, either one of the things from which we have said the conclusion follows is false, and this is contrary to the Christian faith that we with the Greeks hold, or we have improperly drawn a conclusion that we cannot demonstrate. Therefore, if the conclusion is not true, the Christian faith is destroyed. It is also clear to those who understand, that, if we hold the conclusion to be false, no truth is thereby generated. Let us also consider what happens if we assert the conclusion to be true. If it is true that the Holy Spirit proceeds from the Son as he does from the Father, it of course follows that the Spirit is the Spirit of the Son as well as of the Father, and that the Spirit is given and sent by the Son as well as by the Father, which things divine authority teaches, and absolutely no falsity results. And denial of the procession of the Holy Spirit from the Son entails such falsity that the denial, contrary to Christian faith, destroys the things from which we have demonstrated that the procession from the Son results, and generates no truth. And affirmation of the procession from the Son proves so much truth, as we have demonstrated, and in no way entails any falsity with it. Therefore, the reasonable mind should consider on what ground it excludes from the Christian faith the procession from the Son. Lastly, if it is error to believe this procession of the Holy Spirit from the Son, divine authority itself leads us into error when divine authority teaches us both the things from which such procession results and the things that result from such procession. Nor does divine authority anywhere either deny such procession or say anything in any way contrary to it. Therefore, if one argues that we should not affirm the procession of the Holy Spirit from the Son, since divine authority never mentions it, one may likewise say that that procession should not be denied, since divine authority never denies it or says anything contrary. We also say that divine authority affirms that procession sufficiently when it affirms the sources whence it is proved, and in no way signifies anything whereby it may be denied.

15

Therefore, it is evident, as I assured you before [1], that the Son and the Holy Spirit, besides the fact that the former originates by generation and the latter by procession, also cannot be said to be from one another for this reason, namely, that the Holy Spirit is from the Son, and the Son cannot be from the Holy Spirit for this reason alone. For if the Holy Spirit were not from the Son, it would follow that the Son is from the Holy Spirit, since either the Son is from the Holy Spirit, or the Holy Spirit is from the Son, as I have said [1]. And so it is evident by the aforementioned arguments that the Father is God from whom God is, and is not God from God, and that the Son is God from God, and is God from whom God is, and that the Holy Spirit is God from God, and is not God from whom God is. And although two persons, that is, the Son and the Holy Spirit, are from the Father, there are none the less not two Gods from the Father but one God, who is the Son and the Holy Spirit. And although the one from whom the Son is, and the one who is from the Son, that is, the Father and the Holy Spirit, are two, they are none the less not two Gods but one God, who is the Father and the Holy Spirit. And although the Holy Spirit is from two persons, that is, the Father and the Son, the Holy Spirit is none the less not from two Gods but one God, who is the Father and the Son.

And if we should consider the Father and the Son and the Holy Spirit in pairs, it is clear from what I have said that it is necessary either that one of the pair is from the other, since the other is not from that one, or that that one is not from the other, since the other is from that one. For example, if we should pair the Father and the Son, we perceive that the Son is from the Father, since the Father is not from him, and that the Father is not from the Son, since the Son is from the Father. And similarly, if we should consider the Father and the Holy Spirit, we find that the Holy Spirit is from the Father, since the Father is not from him, and that the Father is not from the Holy Spirit, since the Holy Spirit is from him. So also, if we should explore how the Son and the Holy Spirit are related to one another, we shall understand that the Holy Spirit is from the Son, since the Son is not from him, and that the Son is not from the Holy Spirit, since the Holy Spirit is from the Son. Therefore, what I said before [1] is evident, that the aforementioned relations, although they are in one thing, cannot let their plurality be absorbed in the unity, nor can the unity let its uniqueness be absorbed in the relations.

16

Moreover, there are six differences between the Father and the Son and the Holy Spirit that arise from these names, namely: to have the Father as Father, and not to have the Father as Father; to have the Son as Son, and not to have the Son as Son; to have the Spirit proceeding from oneself, and not to have the Spirit proceeding from oneself. Each person has one of these differences as a proper characteristic by which each one differs from the other two, has two of the differences as common and proper characteristics such that the characteristic imparted to one person differs from another person. For example, the Father alone has the Son, and the Father thereby differs from the other two persons. The Father has the Holy Spirit proceeding from himself, and he shares this with the Son, and he thereby differs from the Holy Spirit. And the Father, like the Holy

Spirit, does not have a father. The Son alone has the Father as Father, and he thereby differs from the Father and the Holy Spirit. The Son shares with the Father that the Holy Spirit proceeds from himself, as I have said, and the Son thereby differs from the same Holy Spirit. And the Holy Spirit as Holy Spirit lacks the Son as Son, and the Holy Spirit thereby differs from the Father. The Holy Spirit alone is one from whom no other proceeds. He shares with the Father that he does not have the Father as Father, as I have said, and he differs from the Son in this. The Holy Spirit also shares with the Son that the Holy Spirit does not have a son, as I have already demonstrated [15], and the Holy Spirit thereby differs from the Father. And so the Father alone is one who is from no one, and from whom the other two are; conversely, the Holy Spirit alone is one who is from two, and from whom no one is. The Son alone is one who is from one, and from whom one is. And it is common to the three to have relations to the two other persons. For the Father is related to the Son and the Holy Spirit, as those who are from himself. The Son is related to the Father and the Holy Spirit, since the Son is from the Father, and the Holy Spirit is from the Son. The Holy Spirit is related to the Father and the Son, since the Holy Spirit is from both.

Therefore, each person possesses his own characteristics, the conjuncture of which differs in the others, by analogy to different human persons. For human persons differ from one another by reason of the fact that the conjuncture of characteristics of each is different in others. Nevertheless, there is a difference between human persons and the divine persons. For in the case of human persons, there is one human being if there is one person, and there is one person if there is one human being. Likewise, there are also several human beings if there are several persons, and persons also do not escape plurality if there are several human beings. But in the case of God, although there are three persons, there is none the less one God, and although there is one God, the persons none the less never lose their plurality. And so God, like several human beings, admits diversity of persons in what we call God in relation to God, and God by analogy to one human being preserves indivisible uniqueness in what he is as such, that is, in being God. For there is plurality of human persons only in several human beings, nor does one human being take on plurality of persons, while one God is three persons, and the three persons one God. And so God preserves the characteristics of the different persons in this way neither simply of one God nor simply of different persons.

And although I have said a little about why this is so in the aforementioned letter *On the Incarnation of the Word*,[5] I shall none the less briefly repeat it here. It often happens that several things become one thing under the same name and with the same quantity that each had before the several things became one. Indeed, if we add one point to another without an interval, or if we lay an equal line on an equal line, or if we lay an equal surface on an equal surface, there is constituted only one point, one line, one surface. Anyone, if such a one wished to inquire, will find the like in many things. And so, although there are not several eternities, if we none the less speak of eternity upon eternity, there is in the aforementioned way only one eternity. And if we speak of light upon light, there is only one light. In the same way, everything we say about God's substance, if in itself duplicated, neither increases the quantity nor admits plurality. And since God is eternity, as there is altogether nothing of eternity outside of eternity, so there is absolutely nothing of God outside of God, and as eternity upon eternity is only one eternity, so God in God is only one God.

And we have from the true faith that God is from God by generation, and that God is from God by procession. But since there is nothing of God outside of God, when God is generated from God, or when God proceeds from God, the generation and procession do not go outside of God but remain in him. Therefore, since God in God is only one God, when God is generated from God, there is only one God who generates and is generated. And when God proceeds from God, there is only one God who proceeds and from whom he proceeds. And so it inevitably follows that, since God has no parts, and the whole of him is whatever he is, the whole God, one and the same and not one and another, is the Father, is the Son, is the Holy Spirit. And so, by analogy to one human being, the Father and the Son and the Holy Spirit preserve the uniqueness in the divine nature by reason of the fact that there is only one God if God from God is God in God. And like different human persons, the Father and the Son and the Holy Spirit have plurality of persons by reason of names

---

[5] *On the Incarnation of the Word*, 15.

signifying the relations of generation and procession, since one who is from another, and one from whom another is cannot be one and the same if there is God from God, whether by generation or procession.

Nevertheless, we should note that neither is there God without the persons, nor the persons without God, and that we sometimes attribute to individual persons the characteristics proper to the persons, sometimes characteristics common to the others as if proper to one. For example, when we say that, of the three persons, only the Father is one who is from no one, only the Son is one who is from one, and from whom one is, only the Holy Spirit is one from whom no one is, we attribute to individual persons proper characteristics denominating the individual persons. And when we read, 'No one knows the Son except the Father, and no one knows the Father except the Son' [Matt. 11: 27], and, 'No one except the Spirit of God knows the things belonging to God' [1 Cor. 2: 11], although Scripture seems to deny about the other persons what it says about one person, the characteristics attributed to individual persons as if proper to them are none the less common to all the persons. For example, the Father and the Son know their very selves, and the Holy Spirit knows the Father and the Son. And I have previously said enough about why and when we understand about the other persons [1; 11] what Scripture says about one person as if only about that person.

I, trusting in the Holy Spirit rather than myself, have presumed to write these things about the procession of the same Holy Spirit, with other compelling things, in favour of the Latins against the Greeks, and on this occasion to add a few things about the unity of the divine nature and the Trinity of the persons, although there are countless individuals skilled in the Latin language who could do this better than I. Therefore, let every statement of mine that should be maintained be attributed to the Spirit of Truth rather than to myself. And if I have expressed anything that needs in some measure to be corrected, let it be imputed to me, not to the way the Latin Church thinks.

DE CONCORDIA

THE COMPATIBILITY OF GOD'S FOREKNOWLEDGE, PREDESTINATION, AND GRACE WITH HUMAN FREEDOM

With God's help I shall try to put in writing what he shall be pleased to show me concerning those three areas in which his foreknowledge, predestination, and grace seem to conflict with human free choice.

1. *God's Foreknowledge and Human Freedom*

I

It certainly seems as though divine foreknowledge is incompatible with there being human free choice. For what God foreknows shall necessarily come to be in the future, while the things brought about by free choice do not issue from any necessity. And, if divine foreknowledge and human free choice cannot both exist, it is impossible for God's foreknowledge, which foresees all things, to coexist with something happening through free choice. Yet if it can be shown that the 'impossibility' here is apparent rather than real, the seeming opposition between God's knowledge and human freedom would be shown to be unreal.

So let us affirm the coexistence both of divine foreknowledge (which seems to require the necessary existence of future things) and of free choice (by which many things are believed to occur apart from any necessity), and let us see whether it is impossible for these to be coexistent. If they cannot, there arises as a consequence a second 'impossibility'. For that which entails an impossibility is itself impossible. But if something is going to occur freely, God, who foreknows all that shall be, foreknows this very fact. And whatever God foreknows shall necessarily happen in the way in which it is foreknown. So it is necessary that it shall happen freely, and there is therefore no conflict whatsoever between a foreknowledge which entails a

necessary occurrence and a free exercise of an uncoerced will. For it
is both necessary that God foreknows what shall come to be and that
God foreknows that something shall freely come to be.

You may say to me: 'You are still not removing from me the necessity of sinning or not sinning since God foreknows that I am going
to sin or not sin, and it is therefore necessary that I sin, if I sin, or
that I not sin if I do not sin.' But then I, in turn, respond: 'You should
not say: "God only foreknows that I am going to sin or not." You
should say: "God foreknows that I am going freely to sin or not."
From this it follows that I am free to sin or not to sin because God
knows that what shall come to pass shall be free. Do you see, then,
that it is not impossible for God's foreknowledge (through which he
foreknows the future events which are said to happen necessarily) to
coexist with freedom of choice (by which much is done freely)? For
if this is impossible, the consequence is something impossible.'

You might reply by saying: 'You do not yet remove from my will
the weight of necessity when you say that it is necessary that I shall
sin or not sin freely because God foreknows this. For necessity seems
to imply coercion or prevention. So if it is necessary that I sin voluntarily, I conclude that I am compelled by some hidden power to
will the sin; and if I do not sin, that I am prevented from willing to
sin. Therefore it seems to me that it is by necessity that I sin, if I
sin, or do not sin, if I do not.'

2

Yet I reply: Note that we often say that something is necessary which
is not compelled by any force, and that something is not necessary
which is not impeded by any obstacle. We say, for instance, that God
is necessarily immortal and is necessarily not unjust, not because
some force compels him to be immortal or blocks him from being
unjust, but because nothing can cause him not to be immortal or to
be unjust. So if I say 'It is necessary that you shall sin or not by free
choice alone, just as God foreknows', my statement should not be
thought to mean that something is preventing a choice which is not
to be, or compelling the one which shall be. For God, who foresees
that some act shall occur only by free choice, surely foreknows that
the choice is not compelled or prevented by something or other. So
what is done by the will is freely done.

Once these points are carefully pondered, I think that no incongruity rules out the coexistence of God's foreknowledge and freedom of the will. Finally, if one rightly grasps the meaning of the word *foreknown*, by the very fact that something is said to be foreknown, its future existence is declared. For it is not foreknown unless it shall actually be, since the object of knowledge is what is actually the case.

So 'If God foreknows something, then it happens necessarily' is equivalent to 'If it shall be, it shall be of necessity'. Yet this sort of necessity neither compels nor prevents the future existence or non-existence of anything. For it is precisely because the existence of a thing is asserted as a fact that its existence is said to be necessary, or because its non-existence is so asserted that its non-existence is affirmed to be necessary—and not because necessity compels or prevents its existence or non-existence.

When I say 'If a thing shall be, it shall be of necessity', the necessity does not precede but follows upon the assertion of the thing as a fact. The same holds if I say 'That which shall be, shall necessarily be'. For this sort of necessity means nothing else than that what shall be shall not be able at the same time not to be. And it is equally true to say both that something has been, is, and shall be necessarily, and also that everything that has been has been necessarily, that what is necessarily is, and that what shall be necessarily shall be. For it is, of course, not the same for a thing to be past as for a past thing to be past, or for a thing to be present as for a present thing to be present, or for a thing to be future as for a future thing to be future.

To take a parallel example: it is not the same to say that a thing is white and that a white thing is white. A piece of wood is not always necessarily white, since before it was whitened it was possible for it not to be made white, and after it was white, it is possible for it to be made non-white. But a white piece of wood is always necessarily white since, both before and after it is white, it is impossible that it be white and non-white at the same time. Similarly, a thing is not necessarily present, since before it was present it could have been that it would not be present; and after it is present, it can be no longer present. However, it is always necessary that a present thing be present because, both before and after it is present, it could not be both present and non-present at the same time.

In the same way, something, such as a certain action, shall not necessarily happen in the future, because it is possible that it shall not come to be before it is. But it is necessary that a future action be future, because it cannot both be future and non-future at the same time. This is similarly true with respect to the past. A certain thing is not necessarily past, because before it was past, it was possible that it would not be past. And a past thing is always necessarily past, because it cannot simultaneously be non-past and present. But in the case of the past thing there is a distinguishing feature not found in a present or future thing. For it is never possible for a past thing to become not-past in the way in which something which is present can become non-present, or something which is not necessarily future may not be future. So when a future thing is termed to be future, it is necessary that it be what it is termed to be, because the future is never a not-future—just as is the case as often as we identify a subject simply by repeating an identical term. For when we say 'Every human being is a human being', or, 'If X is a human being, then X is a human being', or, 'Every white object is white', or, 'If X is white, then X is white', what we affirm is necessarily true since it is impossible for something to be and not be at the same time. Clearly, if it is not necessary that everything which is going to occur is going to occur, then something which is going to occur is not going to occur, which is impossible. Therefore it is necessary that everything which is going to occur is going to occur, and if it is going to occur, it is going to occur, since 'going to occur' is attributed to something which is 'going to occur'—but with subsequent or after-the-fact necessity, which does not compel anything to be.

3

Moreover, to say that a thing is going to happen does not always imply that it is going to happen by necessity, even if it is actually going to happen. For if I say 'A rebellion shall take place tomorrow', it does not follow that the rebellion shall happen of necessity. For before it happens it is possible that it shall not happen even if it is actually going to happen. Yet sometimes what I say is going to happen does come to pass by necessity—e.g. when I say that tomorrow the sun shall rise. Talk of a future rebellion as being necessary is talk about a necessity which is future (i.e. 'If it shall happen, it shall happen'—as in 'If it has happened, it has happened'). By contrast, however, talk of tomorrow's sun rising is a way of reporting what happens by necessity in the natural order (in terms of physical laws). The rebellion which shall not happen as a result of any natural necessity is claimed to be going to happen by a merely consequent necessity, in that we simply speak of a future thing as something which is to be. Obviously, if the rebellion is in fact to happen tomorrow, then some necessity is present since it shall be. But a future sunrise is something understood to be necessary in view of two necessities—with a preceding one which causes something to be (it shall happen because it is causally necessary that it happen), and with an after-the-fact necessity, which does not compel anything to happen, because the sunrise is also going to happen necessarily since it is going to happen.

Therefore, when we say that what God foreknows is going to happen is necessarily going to happen, we are not asserting always that it is going to happen by necessity but simply that it is necessary that what is going to happen is going to happen. For it is impossible that what is going to happen is simultaneously not going to happen. The meaning is the same of the wording 'if God foreknows something' even if we do not add the word 'future', because 'future' is already connoted in the verb 'foreknow'. For to 'foreknow' is to know something as 'future', and therefore if God foreknows something, it is necessary that it is going to happen. Therefore it does not always follow from God's foreknowledge that something is going to happen by necessity. For although God foreknows all that will happen, he does not foreknow that absolutely all will happen by necessity, but that some things will happen by the free choice of his rational creatures.

We should, of course, note that just as it is not necessary that God wills as he does, it is not necessary that you or I will as we do. And just as whatever God wills necessarily happens, what we will necessarily happens in those cases when, for example, God brings what we will about in accordance with our willing or not willing. For since what God wills cannot not happen, when he wills that our will shall not be compelled or prevented by any necessity either to will or not will, and when he wills that an effect should follow from a human choice, it is necessary that the human chioce will be free, and it is necessary that what it wills should actually happen.

From all of this it would seem to follow that people who sin do what they do necessarily even though they act freely. And if, regarding the sin of the will considered as sinning willingly, it is asked whether it happens by necessity, the proper reply is that just as the will does not sin by necessity, so too the will's sin does not happen by necessity. And this same kind of volition operates by necessity, for if it did not operate freely, it would not be operating at all—even if what it wills must necessarily occur, as I said previously. For in this case since to commit sin is the same as to will what one ought not, then just as the act of will is not necessary, so too the will's sin is not necessary. And yet, however, it is true that if human beings will to sin they are necessarily sinning, with that kind of necessity which, as I have said above, does not in any way compel or prevent the sin. So free choice is able to will what it does will and unable not to will what it wills, and it is necessary that it wills this. It has the power not to will of course before it does will, because it is free, and when it is now willing it cannot be not willing, but it is necessary that it be willing, for it is impossible for it to be willing and not willing the very same thing at the same time. Indeed the activity of the will, enjoying the gift that what it wills happens and what it does not will does not happen, is voluntary and free because it is done by a free choice. But this activity is also necessary in two respects: both inasmuch as it is compelled by the will to be done, and inasmuch as what is done cannot at the same time not be done. It is, however, free choice which causes these very necessities, and it is able to avoid them before they happen. God, who knows all truth and nothing but the truth, sees the will's activities in the ways they are free or necessary. And as he sees them, so they are. By such careful consideration, therefore, it is plain that without any incompatibility God both foreknows all things, and that many things are the result of free choice. With respect to the latter we have to say that before they happen it is possible for them never to happen and that, in a certain respect, they happen necessarily, which, as I have said, is a consequence of freedom of the will.

4

That not everything which God foreknows happens by necessity, but that certain things happen as a result of free will, may also be seen from the following. When God wills or causes something, he cannot be denied to know what he wills and causes or to foreknow what he is going to will and create. This is true whether we speak according to the unchangeable present of eternity (in which nothing is past or future but all things exist simultaneously without any change—as when we say of God, not that he *has* willed or caused or *is going to* will or cause, but only that he wills or causes something), or whether we speak according to the realm of time—when we state, for example, that God is going to will or cause that which we know has not yet happened. Now if God's knowledge and foreknowledge of itself enforces necessity upon all things that he knows or foreknows, then he himself neither wills nor causes anything freely but necessarily, whether from the aspect of eternity or any conceivable time. If this conclusion is absurd even to suppose, we ought not to think that everything which God knows or foreknows to happen or not to happen thereby happens or does not happen by necessity. Therefore nothing precludes God's knowing or foreknowing that something is caused in our wills or actions or is about to happen through our free will. Even though it is necessary that what God knows or foreknows shall happen, many things happen not by any necessity but by free will, as I have shown above.

It is not surprising if in this way something happens both freely and necessarily, for many things allow of opposite attributions in different respects. For instance what are more opposed than going toward and going away from? Nevertheless we see that when someone crosses from one place to another, the same action is both an approaching and a departing, for the person is departing from one place and approaching another. Similarly, if we observe the sun in some quarter of the sky when it is hastening toward the same quarter while always lighting up the sky, we see that the area from which it is receding is the same one as the one for which it is heading, and it is continually and simultaneously approaching the area from which it is departing. It is evident to those who know the sun's course that if we are observing the sky, it is always crossing from the western sector to the eastern; if, however, we focus upon the earth, it is always crossing only from east to west. In this way the sun always proceeds both contrary to the firmament and—although more slowly—along with the firmament, the very phenomenon which is perceived in the case of the planets.[1] So then no incompatibility arises if, in accordance with the explanations just noted, we assert that one and the same thing is going to happen necessarily just because it is going to happen, and also that it is not compelled to be going to happen by any necessity—except by the kind of necessity which I have described above as being caused by free will.

5

Referring to human beings, Job says to God: 'You have determined the bounds of their lives, which they shall not be able to pass beyond' [Job 14: 5]. Suppose that someone wishes to show by quoting this text that no one has been able either to hasten or postpone the day of his or her death—even though people sometimes seem freely to bring about the cause of their death. This citation does not counter what I have said above. For since God is not deceived and sees only what is really so in fact, whether it issues from free will or by necessity, he is said to have situated immutably with regard to himself that which is mutable with regard to the human being before it is done. St Paul speaks in the same vein about those who, according to God's purpose, are called to be holy: 'Those whom he foreknew, he also foreordained to become conformed to the likeness of his Son, so that his Son would be the firstborn among many brethren. Moreover, those whom he foreordained, these he also called. And those whom he called, these he also justified. Moreover, those whom he justified, he also glorified' [Rom. 1: 7; 8: 28–9]. Indeed within eternity, in which there is no past or future but only a present, this purpose in accordance to which they are called to be holy, is immutable; but within human beings it is sometimes mutable because of free will. For in eternity a thing has no past or future but only an (eternal) present, though in the realm of time things move from past to future without any contradiction arising. Similarly, that which cannot be changed in eternity sometimes, before it occurs, proves to be, without involving any incongruity, changeable because of free will. Moreover, although in eternity there is only a present, nevertheless it is not a temporal present as ours is, only an eternal one in which all periods

---

[1] Anselm seems to mean that as the sun moves across the sky, so the earth, moving beneath it, appears to travel in the opposite direction against the sun.

of time are contained. Indeed, just as our present time envelops every place and whatever is in every place, so in the eternal present all time is encompassed along with whatever exists at any time. Therefore when St Paul says that God foreknew, predestined, called, justified, and glorified his saints, none of these actions happen before or after on God's part. They must all be understood as existing simultaneously in an eternal present. For eternity has its own unique simultaneity which contains both all things that happen at the same time and place and that happen at different times and places.

However, in order to show that he was not using those verbs in their temporal signification, St Paul described future happenings in the past tense. For, temporally speaking, God had not already called, justified and glorified those whom he foreknew were yet to be born. We can therefore understand that it was for want of a verb signifying the eternal present that St Paul used verbs of the past tense. The reason is that things which are past in time are wholly immutable— like those in the present of eternity. Indeed, in this respect things which are past in time more resemble the eternal present than do things which are present in time; for all that is present in eternity can never be anything but present, just as in time the past can never be anything but past, whereas all transitory things in time become non-present.

In this way therefore whenever Sacred Scripture speaks of things which occur by free will as though they were necessary, it is speaking according to the eternity in which all truth, and nothing but the truth, is present immutably. It is not speaking of the temporal world in which the acts of our will and behaviour are not everlasting; and just as, while they do not exist, there is no necessity for them to do so, so too it is often not necessary that they occur at some time. For instance, I am not always writing or willing to write. In the same way, while I am not writing or willing to write, there is no necessity that I write or will to write. Similarly, it is not at all necessary that at some time I write or will to write.

Moreover, since we know that a thing exists so differently in time than in eternity that sometimes it is true that there does not exist in time something which exists in eternity (and true too that in time something is not present which is present in eternity, or not past in time which is past in eternity, or future in time which is not future in eternity), it seems that it cannot be denied on any grounds that something is mutable in time which is immutable in eternity. Surely mutability in time and immutability in eternity are no more contra-dictory than are non-existence at some point in time and everlasting existence in eternity, or than past and future existence in time and the absence of both in eternity.

I am not saying that something never exists in time that exists forever in eternity. My point is just that it does not exist at some point in time. I am not saying that my action of tomorrow is not existing at any time. I am merely saying that it does not exist today even though it exists always in eternity. And when we say that some-thing which has past and future existence in time does not have a past or future existence in eternity, we are not asserting that what has a past or future does not exist in any fashion in eternity but simply that it does not exist there in a past or future fashion since it exists there unceasingly in its eternal-present fashion. But we see noth-ing to gainsay these statements. Thus, surely, no contradiction is involved in saying that something is mutable in time before it happens, something which is immutably in eternity. In eternity there is no time before or after. Something in eternity exists unceasingly now, since in eternity there is no temporary existence. What truly exists there eternally is this and nothing more: that in time some-thing both exists and, before it exists, it is possible that it fail to exist, as I have already said. From what I have said I think it is clear that God's foreknowledge and human free choice involve no contradic-tion at all in their relation to one another. This is due to the nature of eternity which embraces all time and all that occurs at any point in time.

6

Since, however, we do not employ free choice on all occasions, we must examine the sphere and nature of the freedom of will which we believe people always possess. And we must ask what sort of faculty it is. For the will and the freedom by which it is free are not simply identical. In many cases we speak of freedom and choice in one way—for instance, when we say that people enjoy freedom to speak or remain silent, and that what they decide lies within their free choice. Similarly we also speak of freedom and free choice in very many other cases when they are not always present or not necessary to us for the soul's salvation. However, our present exploration is being aired only in regard to that choice and freedom without which people cannot attain salvation once they have the power to use them. For many people are distressed because they hold the belief that free choice plays no role in our salvation or damnation and that necessity alone rules since God foreknows both. For this reason, since people are not saved, after reaching the age of reason, unless they are personally just, both the source and the foundation of this freedom and choice of justice should be examined at this point. And so the nature of justice must be clarified first, and then the nature of that freedom and that choice.

Any justice—in large or small measure—consists of that moral uprightness of will that is maintained for its intrinsic worth. Moreover, the freedom also under discussion is the power to preserve uprightness of will for the sake of that very same uprightness. I think I have explained these definitions with clear accounts, the former, in fact, in the treatise I wrote *On Truth*, the latter in the one I published *On Free Will* in this specific regard. The latter also showed the manner in which this kind of freedom exists naturally in and inseparably from human beings even though they do not always exercise it. I showed as well that this specific freedom is so enduring that nothing has the power to take away from people the aforesaid uprightness, that is, their just state, for as long as they shall have willed to exercise this kind of freedom. Indeed, the state of justice is not present by nature, but has proved to be separable from the beginning both in the case of the angels in heaven and of human beings in Paradise. This is still the case in this life not by necessity; it belongs to those who possess it by their own free will. Now it is apparent that the state of justice which constitutes the just person is precisely that uprightness of will I have described—an uprightness which is present in people only when they, for their part, will what God wants them to will. Consequently it is obvious that God cannot remove this uprightness from people against their will for the reason that God is unable to will anything like this. Neither can God will that someone possessing their uprightness should lose it against the person's will but owing to any kind of necessity. For then God would be willing that the person not will what God wants the person to will—which is impossible. Therefore it follows in this way that God wills that an upright will be free indeed for willing rightly and for maintaining this uprightness, with the kind of freedom which, since it does have the power to will what it wills, freely does what it does. Consequently it is eminently clear to the mind that both a will and its action are free, and that consistently with God's foreknowledge, as I have shown above.

Let us now cite a particular example in which there appears an upright (i.e. a just) will, freedom of choice, and an actual choice. And let us consider both the way in which the upright will is assaulted and the fashion in which it maintains its uprightness by its free decision. Suppose someone yearns to adhere to truth while realizing that it is right to love truth. This person surely has an upright will as well as uprightness of will. Yet the will in question is one thing, the uprightness by which it is upright another. Another person approaches and threatens the first person with death unless that person tells a lie. We see that the latter is free now to decide whether to value life before uprightness of will or uprightness before life. This decision, which also might be called a verdict, is free, because the reason by which the value of uprightness is grasped, teaches that this uprightness ought always to be preserved out of love for that very uprightness—teaches too that whatever is spread before one as a pretext for abandoning it ought to be spurned, and that it is the duty of the will also promptly to reject or choose the one to which rational grasp points the way. It is to this end above all that will and mind have been given to a rational creature. Therefore an equivalent decision of the will to abandon this same uprightness is also free and not forced by any necessity, even though it is assailed by the harsh alternative of death.

For although it is necessary to abandon either life or uprightness, nevertheless no necessity determines which of the two is maintained or abandoned. Without doubt the will alone determines which one is to be preserved in this situation and the power of necessity effects nothing when the will's choice alone is operative. But people are under no necessity to abandon the uprightness of will which they possess; they do not lack the power or freedom to maintain it. For such a power is always free. For this is the nature of the freedom I have described as the power to maintain the uprightness of will purely for the sake of its uprightness. It is in this sense of the freedom characteristic of the rational creature that both its decision and its will is called free.

7

Since God is believed to foreknow or know all things, we have still to consider whether his knowledge results from things or whether the existence of things results from his knowledge. For if God owes his knowledge to things, it follows that they exist prior to his knowledge of them and that their existence is not owed to God. For they cannot owe their existence to God if he does not know them. But if everything that exists derives its existence from God's knowledge, then God is the Creator and author also of evil works and, by inference, unjustly punishes the wicked—a conclusion that is unacceptable.

However, this problem is easily solved if it is first recognized that the goodness which consists of uprightness is really something that exists, whereas the evil which is called unrighteousness lacks existence entirely. This I made very plain in the treatise *On the Fall of the Devil* and the essay which I entitled *On the Virgin Conception and Original Sin*. For unrighteousness is not a quality nor an action nor a being but merely the absence of something which ought to be present and occurs only in the will where righteousness ought to exist. It is owing to that righteous or unrighteous will that every rational creature and each and every one of its deeds is called righteous or unrighteous. Of course every quality, every action, everything that has existence owes its being at all to God, who is the source of all uprightness but not of unrighteousness. Therefore, although God is a factor in all that is done by a righteous or unrighteous will in its good and evil acts, nevertheless, in the case of its good acts he effects both their existence and their goodness, whereas in the case of its evil acts he causes them to be, but not to be evil. Indeed for every real thing its being righteous or good requires its being something, but for no thing does its being something require that it be unrighteous or evil. Moreover, to be good or upright requires the possession of uprightness which is a particular thing. To be evil or unjust, however, is to lack righteousness which ought to be present. Righteousness truly is a kind of thing, whereas unrighteousness is not a thing at all, as I have said.

But there is another kind of good which is called a 'benefit', whose contrary is bad, which is called 'affliction'. Sometimes this 'affliction' is the absence of something, as with blindness; sometimes it is a real thing, as with pain. We do not deny that God causes this kind of evil when it exists because we read in Scripture [Isa. 45: 7] that he himself 'brings peace and causes woes'. Assuredly, he causes the afflictions by which he tries and purifies the just and punishes the wicked. And so only in the kind of evil that is unrighteousness by which a person is termed unrighteous is it never the fact that it is an actual thing; and for something to be unrighteous it is not necessary for unrighteousness to be an actual thing. And just as God does not cause unrighteousness, so too he does not cause something to be unrighteous. On the other hand he does cause all actions and movements since he causes the things by which, from which, through which, and in which they are done. Nothing has any power at all to will or act unless God bestows it. The very act of willing, which is sometimes righteous, sometimes unrighteous, and is nothing other than the employment of the will and power given by God, insofar as it exists, is something good and proceeds from God. And in this case when its existence is upright, it is both good and upright; but when its existence is unrighteous, it is evil and unrighteous solely because of its unrighteousness. However, existing rightly is something and is owed to God, but not existing rightly is not something and is not due to God. When, for instance, someone uses sword, tongue, or oratorical power, the sword or the tongue or the oratorical ability as such is the same thing when used rightly or wrongly. In the same way the will we use for willing (like the faculty of reason we use for reasoning) is the same thing as such whether we use it rightly or wrongly. But the will because of which a person or an action is termed righteous or unrighteous is neither more nor less precisely what it is existentially, when it is righteous or unrighteous. So in this fashion God causes in all volitions and good actions both that they actually exist and that they are good, while in evil actions he is not the cause of their evil but only that they exist. Just as the existence of things is owed only to God, so too their righteous existence is impossible without him.

The absence of this uprightness, this lack of justice, is found only in the will of the rational creature which ought always to preserve justice. But why does a rational creature lack what it ought to have? And how is it that the goodness of our actions is the result of God's goodness and their evil the result of our own fault alone or the devil's? And in what way do human beings do good deeds by their free choice under the direction of divine grace and evil deeds owing only to the exercise of their own characteristically free will? And why is God's contribution to our evil deeds blameless and our part in our own good deeds praiseworthy so that, as a consequence, their goodness is clearly seen to be imputable to God and their evil to us? Answers to all these queries shall, I think, appear even more clearly with the help of God, when we treat of grace and freedom of will. At this point, however, I am content to remark only that an evil angel is lacking in justice precisely because that angel abandoned it and did not receive it back afterward, whereas human beings lack it because they threw it away in the person of their first parents and afterwards either did not recover it or threw it away after receiving it.

I think I have demonstrated with the help of God's grace that no impossibility is involved in the coexistence of God's foreknowledge and our free choice and that no unsolvable objection can be raised if someone carefully weighs my words.

2. *Predestination and Free Choice*

I

So with hope in him who has guided us up to now, let us at this point tackle the challenge to resolve the conflict which apparently exists between predestination and free choice. We have advanced no little distance toward this goal by our previous discourse, as shall be apparent in what follows.

Predestination is the equivalent of pre-ordination or pre-establishment; and therefore to say that God predestines means that he pre-ordains, that is, to bring it about that something happen in the future. But it seems that whatever God decrees to happen in the future shall necessarily happen. Therefore, whatever God predestines shall happen of necessity. If then he predestines the good and evil acts that we do, no room is left for the action of a free choice but all occur of necessity. Now if God predestines only good deeds, then only the latter occur of necessity and there is freedom of choice only in the case of evil ones—which is incredibly absurd. Therefore God does not predestine only in the case of good actions. Moreover, if a free choice performs certain good actions by which people become just apart from God's pre-ordaining, then God does not predestine all the good deeds which justify people, nor does he justify those just people who are so through their free choice. So then God did not foreknow them, since, according to Scripture, it was actually those 'whom he predestined that he foreknew' [Rom. 8: 29]. But it is false to say that God does not foreknow some good actions or some just people. Therefore it is not true that there are some good deeds which are the work of free choice acting all alone that justify us; rather is it true to say that only those good works justify us that God predestines. Therefore if God predestines all things, and if what is predestined shall happen of necessity, and since no act of free choice is done by necessity, it seems to follow that in the presence of predestination no freedom of will is possible. Even if we maintain that free choice still operates in some cases, we must hold that in those cases any predestination is cancelled out.

2

To begin with, before a resolution of the point at issue, it should be recognized that God's predestination attaches not only to our good actions but, it is possible to say, to our evil ones in the sense that it is by permitting the latter that God is said to be the cause of evils which he does not actually cause. In fact he is said to harden people when he does not soften them and to lead them into temptation when he does not release them from it. Therefore there is no problem in saying that in this sense God predestines evil people and their evil acts when he does not straighten them out along with their evil acts. He is, however, more precisely said to foreknow and predestine their good works because in their case he causes both that they exist and that they are good, whereas in the case of the evil ones he is only the cause that they simply exist and not that they are evil, as said above. It should also be understood that the word '*fore*knowledge', as also the word '*pre*destine' are not used of God literally, for in him there is no before or after, but all things are present to him at once.

3

Let us now consider whether some things that shall happen by free choice can be predestined. It is, of course, beyond question that God's foreknowledge and predestination do not conflict; rather, even as God foreknows, so he predestines. In regard to the dispute over his foreknowledge, we clearly ascertained that some things that shall happen as a result of free choice are in fact foreknown by him without entailing any contradiction at all. Therefore, the plain truth and reason also teach that certain results of free choice are predestined by him without entailing any inconsistency. For God neither foreknows nor predestines that anyone shall be just out of any necessity. For those who do not preserve their uprightness by their own free choice lose it. Therefore, although things foreknown and predestined are bound to happen, still it is equally true that some things foreknown and predestined do not happen by the type of necessity which precedes and causes something. They happen, as we have said above, by the kind that follows upon something. Even though God predestines actions of that nature, he causes them not by compelling or constraining the will but by leaving it to its own devices. And even though the will employs its own power, it still causes nothing which God does not also cause by his grace in the case of good deeds. In the case of evil ones, however, the evil is not due to any fault of God, but to the same free choice. This shall appear more clearly when, as we have promised, we shall be speaking of God's grace. And just as his foreknowledge, which is not deceived, foreknows the true nature of an event, whether necessary or free, so too his predestination, which is immutable, preordains something exactly as he foreknows it. And although that which he foreknows in his eternity is immutable, in time it is mutable at some point before it happens. This is true of all cases where he predestines.

It is clear, then, from what has been said, if thoroughly considered, that predestination does not exclude free choice and that free choice is not opposed to predestination. Indeed all those means by which we have shown that free choice is not inimical to foreknowledge equally show that the former is compatible with predetermination. So whenever something happens by the exercise of free choice, for example, when A harms B and B kills A in retaliation, it is unreasonable for some to say loudly: 'This was foreknown and predestined by God and therefore it happened by necessity and could not have happened otherwise.' Indeed, neither A nor B acted by necessity but with free will alone, for if they had not acted voluntarily they would not have done what they did.

3. *Grace and Free Choice*

I

With the help of divine grace, we must now consider the question of the relation of that same grace to free choice. The question arises from the fact that the Bible speaks at times as if that grace alone seems to avail for salvation and free choice not at all, but at other times as though our salvation entirely depends on free choice. Indeed the Lord says concerning grace: 'Without me you can do nothing' [John 15: 5]. Also: 'No one comes to me unless my father draws him' [John 6: 44]. And the Apostle Paul says: 'What do you have that you have not received?' [1 Cor. 4: 7]. And also with regard to God: 'he takes pity on whom he pleases and hardens whom he pleases' [Rom. 9: 18]. Also: 'So it is not of the one who wills, nor of the one who runs, but of God, who shows mercy' [Rom. 9: 16 in the Vulgate text]. We also read many other verses which seem to attribute our good works and salvation to grace alone without free choice. Many people even claim to demonstrate from experience that no human being is fortified at all by freedom of choice. They are of the opinion that an unlimited number of persons strive with an extraordinary effort of body and mind but overwhelmed by some intractable or even impossible situation they either make no progress at all or after a substantial advance suddenly fail beyond recall.

However, the same Scripture demonstrates that we do possess freedom of choice by what follows. Thus God speaks through Isaiah: 'If you are willing and listen to me, you shall dine on the good things of the land' [Isa. 1: 19]. And David says: 'Who is it who chooses life, who loves to see good days? Keep your tongue from evil and let not your lips speak guile. Turn away from evil and do good' [Ps. 34: 12–14]. And the Lord says in the Gospel: 'Come to me all you who toil and are oppressed and I shall refresh you. Take my yoke upon you and learn from me, that I am gentle and lowly of heart, and you shall find rest for your souls' [Matt. 11: 28, 29]. There are very many other passages which are seen to arouse free choice to do good and to reproach it for ignoring right advice. And God would in no wise give warrant to such passages if there were no freedom of choice in human beings. And there would be no reason at all why a just God would reward the good or punish the evil according to individuals' merits if no one did good or evil by freedom of choice.

Therefore since we come upon some passages in Sacred Scripture which seem to recommend grace alone and some which are considered to uphold free choice without grace, there have been certain proud individuals who have decided that the entire efficacy of our virtues rests upon our free choice alone and in our own day there are many who retain no hope whatsoever of the very existence of free choice. Therefore in this investigation of ours, our aim shall be the following: to show that free choice in many instances coexists with grace and co-operates with it, just as we have discovered it to be compatible with foreknowledge and predetermination.

2

It should be understood that just as this investigation, as I said above, is only concerned with the freedom without which no one, having arrived at the age of reason, merits salvation, so too is it concerned with no other grace than that without which nobody is saved. For every creature owes its existence to divine grace, since every creature was created by grace; and God bestows many good things in this life by his grace without which a human being can be saved. In fact in the case of infants who die after baptism before they are able to employ freedom of choice, the compatibility we are examining does not arise, because in such cases grace alone effects salvation for them in the absence of their free choice. To be sure, a further grace is given to others, namely, to will to substitute for them by their own faith. Therefore our investigation must be directed to those who have reached the age of reason, because the problem we are addressing has to do with them alone.

Moreover, there is no question but that all of the latter, who are saved, are saved by their being in a state of justice. It is to the just, in fact, to whom eternal life is promised, since 'the just shall live forever and their reward is in the house of the Lord' [Wisd. 5: 15]. Sacred authority often instructs us that justice consists in uprightness of will. In this regard it suffices to cite a single example. After David had asserted: 'The Lord shall not desert his people nor abandon his inheritance until their justice is transformed into judgement' [Ps. 94: 14–15], in order to teach us what justice is, he continues with the question: 'And who are in accord with justice?' To which he responds in answer to himself: 'All the upright of heart', that is, upright of will. For even though we believe and understand with our heart, nevertheless the Holy Spirit does not judge someone to be upright of heart who only believes rightly and understands rightly. Right will is necessary as well. Without this, one is not using the rightness of belief and mind for rightly willing, which is why right belief and understanding are granted to the rational creature. Someone ought not to be said to have right understanding unless that person rightly wills as a result of it. People have nothing but a dead faith unless they rightly will in accordance with that faith to bring about that for which faith was given them. Therefore we correctly understand David to have meant by the 'upright in heart' the upright in will. Furthermore, lest anyone imagine that divine authority implies that someone is just or upright who maintains it for some other end, we say that justice is that rightness of will which is kept for its own sake. For people who preserve it only for some other end do not love it; rather, they love that for the sake of which they preserve it. Such people are not to be called just and their uprightness is not to be termed justice.

When we were dealing with foreknowledge and free choice we showed by an example that uprightness of will, which I call justice, can coexist with freedom of will. That example made it plain to see that the same is true in many other cases. Therefore if we now can show that no creature can attain to uprightness of will except by grace, then the concordance we look for between grace and free choice for the sake of our salvation will become clear.

3

It is certainly beyond doubt that the will does not will rightly unless it is itself upright. For just as our vision is not sharp because it sees sharply, but sees sharply because it is sharp, so the will is not upright because it wills rightly but wills rightly because it is upright. Moreover, when it wills uprightness of will, then it is surely willing rightly. Therefore it wills uprightness only because it is upright. For the will to be upright, however, is the same as for it to possess uprightness. Obviously, then, it does will uprightness only because it has uprightness. I admit that an upright will wills an uprightness that it does not yet have when it is willing a greater uprightness than it has, but I am merely saying that it cannot will any uprightness at all unless it possesses the uprightness in order to will it.

Now let us consider whether people who do not have this uprightness of will can acquire it in some fashion by themselves. Surely they can acquire it by themselves only by willing or not willing it. But no one who does not possess uprightness of will is equipped to acquire it alone with an act of the will. And it is absurd to think that people who lack uprightness of will should be able to attain it by themselves by not willing it. So there is no way by which creatures can have it on their own. Yet neither can a creature have it from another creature. Just as creatures cannot save other creatures, they cannot give them the means necessary for salvation. So it follows that a creature possesses the uprightness which I have called uprightness of the will only by the grace of God. Now we have shown that this kind of uprightness can be preserved by free choice, as I said above. Therefore we have found, with God's gracious help, that his grace harmonizes with free choice to achieve salvation for people. To resume, then, grace alone can save someone when free choice can do nothing, as happens in the case of infants, whereas in the case of those who have the use of reason, grace always aids one's innate free choice by giving it the uprightness which it may preserve by free choice, because without grace it achieves nothing toward salvation.

And even if God does not give grace to everyone, for 'He shows compassion to whom he wills and hardens those he wills to harden' [Rom. 9: 18], still he does not give to anyone in return for some antecedent merit, for 'who has first given to God and he shall be rewarded?' [Rom. 11: 35]. But if by its free choice the will maintains what it has received and so merits either an increase of the justice received or power by way of a good will or some kind of reward, all these are the fruits of the first grace and are 'grace upon grace' [John 1: 16]. It must all be attributed to grace, too, because 'it is not of the one who wills, nor of the one who runs, but of God, who shows mercy' [Rom. 9: 16]. For to all, except God alone, it is said: 'What do you have that you have not received? And if you have received it all, why do you boast as though you had not received it?' [1 Cor. 4: 7].

4

I believe that I have shown in the treatise *On Free Will* how in fact freedom of the will that maintains its received uprightness is not destroyed by any necessity to abandon it but is instead daunted when the choice is difficult and may yield to this difficulty, not involuntarily but voluntarily. But there are ways in which grace helps free choice to preserve the uprightness once it has received it. This it does in a host of ways; though I cannot list them all, nevertheless it will be useful to say something in regard to that.

Assuredly, no one preserves this received uprightness without willing it. But no one can will it without having it. And one cannot have it at all except by grace. Therefore just as no one acquires it without a prevenient grace, so too no one preserves it except by subsequent grace. Clearly, though it is preserved by free choice, nevertheless its retention should be attributed more to grace than to free choice, since free choice only has and preserves it owing to the prevenient and subsequent grace.

Moreover, grace so follows upon its previous gift that it never fails to go on giving the gift unless free choice abandons it by willing something different. For this uprightness is never severed from the will unless it wills something else which is not in accord with this uprightness. This happens, for example, when someone receives the uprightness of voluntary sobriety and then rejects it by choosing the pleasure of drinking to excess. When people actually do this, they do so by their own free will, and they lose the grace they have received through their own fault. In addition grace assists free will when it is prevailed upon to surrender the received uprightness. This it does either by mitigating or wholly removing the power of the temptation which assails it or by increasing its love of the uprightness in question. Furthermore, since all things are subject to God's disposing, whatever happens to a person by way of aiding free will either to receive or maintain the aforesaid uprightness must all be attributed to grace.

I have said that justice is in every case uprightness of will maintained for its own sake. Whence it follows that everyone who has this uprightness has justice and is just, since everyone who has justice is just. Nevertheless I notice that eternal life has not been promised to all who are just, but to those only who are just without any injustice. For the latter are properly and unqualifiedly called just and upright of heart. For there are people who are just in one respect and unjust in another, for example both chaste and envious. The beatitude of the just is not promised to such people, since just as true beatitude is not marked by any imperfection, so too it is bestowed only on one who is just without any injustice. This is so because the beatitude promised to the just shall be just like that of God's angels. Just as there is no injustice in the good angels, so no one with any injustice shall be grouped with them. It is not my present purpose to show how people become free of all injustice. However, we do know that this is possible for a Christian by holy pursuits and the grace of God.

5

If my observations are carefully weighed, it is clearly evident that when Sacred Scripture says something in favour of grace it does not at all exclude free choice, and in turn when it speaks in favour of free choice it does not dismiss grace, as though either grace alone or free choice alone is sufficient for salvation, as it seems to those who are the occasion of this disquisition. Assuredly (with the exception of what I said about the salvation of infants) the divine sayings are to be recognized as saying that neither grace alone nor free choice alone effects a person's salvation.

Not surprisingly, when the Lord says: 'Without me, you can do nothing' [John 15: 5], he is not saying: 'Your free choice is of no use to you,' but 'It is of no use to you without my grace.' And when we read, 'it is not of the one who wills, nor of the one who runs, but of God, who shows mercy' [Rom. 9: 16], there is no assertion that the free choice of one who wills or runs is of no avail at all. The text is saying that the fact that one wills and runs should be attributed to grace rather than to freedom of choice. For when it says 'it is not of the one who wills, nor of the one who runs', the implication is, 'The fact that one wills and the fact that one runs'. Similarly, when people give a garment to a naked man to whom they owe nothing and who cannot on his own acquire a garment, even though the latter has the power personally to use and not to use the garment he has received, still, if he does use it, the fact that he is clothed should not be credited to him but to the one who gives him the garment. So we may put it as follows: 'The fact that he is clothed is not due to him but to him who shows mercy, that is, by giving the garment.' Indeed this might be asserted with much better reason, if the one who gave the clothing had also given the power to maintain and use it. This is exactly the case when God, by giving the often mentioned uprightness, also gives the power to maintain and use it, since he has previously given the free choice to maintain and use it. If the garment were not a gift to the naked man to whom nothing was owed, or if he freely threw it away after receiving it, surely his nakedness would be imputed to no one but himself. Thus when God gives willing and running to someone conceived and born in sin to whom he owes nothing but punishment, this is not 'of the one who wills, nor of the one who runs, but of God, who shows mercy'. As for those who do not accept the same grace of righteousness or reject it after receiving it, it is owing to them and not to God that they persevere in their brazenness and sin.

We should put the same interpretation (namely that free choice is not being excluded) on other passages when Scripture speaks about grace. Likewise when the divine verses are expressed so that they seem to attribute human salvation to free choice only, they are in no way to be understood as isolating it from grace. To use a comparison, though natural intercourse does not procreate offspring without a father but only by means of a mother, still saying this is not understood as denying a role in the generation of a child to either father or mother. In the same way grace and free choice are not in conflict but work together to justify and save the human being.

6

In those passages in which Scripture is seen to invite free choice to will and act rightly the question arises why it invites people to will rightly and why it blames them when they fail to obey, since no one is able to have or receive this uprightness except by the gift of grace. The following reflection should be weighed. Without any cultivation on our part the soil brings forth countless plants and trees which fail to nourish us and sometimes even kill us. But it is only when associated with great toil and a grower along with seedlings that the earth produces those things which are especially needed to nourish us. Similarly on the one hand human hearts without learning or intellectual activity spontaneously sprout, as it were, thoughts and volitions which are of no avail to salvation or are even harmful. On the other hand, however, it is only by their own sort of seed and assiduous cultivation that they at all conceive and germinate those without which we cannot advance toward the soul's salvation. That is why St Paul calls those persons to whom the task of such cultivation is entrusted 'God's husbandry' [1 Cor. 3: 9]. And the seed of this cultivation is the word of God—or rather, not the word itself, but the meaning which is grasped through the word. Obviously mere sound without meaning establishes nothing in the mind. And not only is the meaning of God's word a seed of willing rightly but so too is every perception or understanding of uprightness which the human mind conceives whether by hearing or reading or reflection or any other way.

Obviously no one can will something not first conceived in the mind. Moreover, to will to believe what ought to be believed is to will rightly. Therefore no one can will rightly without knowing what ought to be believed. And so after St Paul's premiss: 'Whosoever calls upon the name of the Lord shall be saved,' he added, 'How then shall they appeal to one in whom they have not believed? Or how shall they believe in one of whom they have not heard? Or how shall they hear without a proclaimer? How indeed shall there be proclaimers unless they are sent?' [Rom. 10: 13–15]. And shortly thereafter: 'Therefore belief follows upon hearing, and hearing by word about Christ.' However, when he says that belief follows upon hearing, he should be understood to mean that belief comes from what the mind conceives through hearing. And, furthermore, he should not be understood to say that a mental concept alone creates belief in a person. He is saying that the concept is an essential condition for belief. It is when the righteousness of willing is added to the concept that belief is created by grace. For one believes what one hears. 'And hearing follows upon the word about Christ,' that is, by the word of those who proclaim Christ. In fact there are no proclaimers unless they are sent. Moreover, their very sending is a grace. It follows that their proclamation is also a grace because what flows down from grace is a grace. And the hearing is a grace and the understanding which issues from the hearing is a grace and the righteousness of the will is a grace. Yes, the sending, the proclamation, the hearing and the understanding are ineffective until the will wills what it understands, and this it cannot do without receiving righteousness. For in fact it wills rightly when it wills what it ought. Consequently what the mind conceives upon the hearing of the word is the proclaimer's seed, and the uprightness is the 'growth', the gift of God, without which 'neither the one who plants nor the one who waters accomplishes anything, but only God who gives the growth' [1 Cor. 3: 7].

Therefore, just as at the beginning God marvellously, without cultivator or seeds, created grain and other terrestrial things to nourish people, so too he marvellously, without human learning, made the minds of prophets and apostles and, above all, the Gospels, rich with seeds for our salvation. These are the source of whatever we sow salutarily, in God's husbandry, for the nourishment of our souls, just as what we cultivate for the nourishment of our bodies derives only from the original seeds of the earth. In fact we proclaim what is useful for the salvation of souls only what Sacred Scripture, made fecund by the marvellous activity of the Holy Spirit, has produced or contains in its womb. For if at times we assert by a process of reasoning a conclusion which we cannot explicitly cite from the sayings of Scripture or demonstrate from the bare wording, still it is by using Scripture that we know in the following way whether the affirmation should be accepted or rejected. If the conclusion is reached by straightforward reasoning and Scripture in no way contradicts it, then (since just as Scripture opposes no truth so too it abets no falsehood) by the very fact that it does not deny what is inferred on the basis of reason, that conclusion is accepted as authorized by Scripture. But if Scripture indubitably opposes our understanding, even though our reasoning appears to us to be impregnable, still it ought not to be believed to be substantiated by any truth at all. It is when Sacred Scripture either clearly affirms or in no wise denies it, that it gives support to the authority of any reasoned conclusion.

Let us now see by way of example how the word is a seed. When those to whom it is addressed hear the phrase: 'If you are willing and heed me' [Isa. 1: 19], they realize and consider what the words 'will' and 'attend' mean, that is 'to obey'. For one who attends and does not obey is said not to attend. But they cannot obey unless they will to. But to will to obey is to will rightly. In fact no one is able to will rightly without uprightness of will, which none of us has without grace. But uprightness of will is only granted to one who has the intelligence to will and understands what ought to be willed. We conclude then from the phrase 'If you are willing and attend to me' that the seed is not one which bears fruit all by itself without the addition of uprightness, and, further, that the uprightness itself is not granted except by means of seeds. Likewise when God says: 'Turn back to me' [Isa. 45: 22], the seed fails to sprout as long as God does not turn the human will toward willing the kind of turning which people grasp when they hear the order to turn back. Without this seed no one can will so to turn. God also keeps saying 'Turn back' to those who have turned back either so that they turn even more or preserve the turning achieved. Now those who pray 'Convert us, O Lord' [Ps. 85: 4] are already converted to some degree because they have an upright will when they will to be converted. In which case they are praying by means of what they have already received that their turning be increased, like those believers who prayed 'Increase our faith' [Luke 17: 5]. It is as if both the former and the latter were praying: 'Increase in us what you have bestowed; complete what you have begun.' What I have shown in these examples should also be applied in other similar ones.

So just as the soil does not by nature bring forth without seeds those things on which our bodily health depends, neither does the soil of the human heart bring forth the fruit of faith or uprightness without the seeds needed for this. And though God does not give growth to every seed, our farmers do not stop sowing in the hope of a fair-sized harvest. And even though God does not cause every single seed of this kind to grow, still he orders his farmers to sow his word urgently in hope. We have shown, I think, that it is not pointless to invite all people to faith in Christ and in all that this faith demands, even though all do not accept this invitation.

7

I have said that we may also ask why those who do not accept the word of God are held accountable since they cannot do so unless grace propels their wills. For the Lord says in regard to the Holy Spirit: 'He shall convict the world of sin because they do not believe in me' [John 16: 8–9]. Although it may be hard to reply to this question, I ought not to be silent about what I can do with God's help. We ought to observe that a helplessness owing to one's own fault does not excuse the powerless one as long as the flaw abides. Hence in the case of infants in whom God looks to humanity for the state of justice which it received in our first parents together with the power to preserve it on throughout its entire progeny, the inability to possess that justice does not excuse humanity since it was by its own sin that it fell into this helplessness. Indeed the very fact that humanity does not have that which left on its own it cannot recover constitutes its inability to acquire that state of justice. The human race fell into this helplessness precisely because it freely abandoned what it had the power to preserve. And so because by sinning it abandoned the state of justice, the impotence it created for itself by sinning is imputed to it as sin. And in those who are not baptized not only the incapacity to acquire justice but also the inability to comprehend it is similarly imputed as sin since it is equally the result of sin. We can also maintain the imputation of sin to the deprivation and depravity which followed upon the original state of human excellence and strength and beauty. Indeed humanity thereby detracted, as far as it could, from God's praise and glory, because naturally the wisdom of a craftsman is lauded and proclaimed according to the excellence of his work. Consequently the more that humanity essentially diminished and defiled in itself the precious work of God from which he should have received glory, the more it dishonoured God by its sin. And that is accounted against humanity as so heinous a sin that it is expunged only by the death of God.

Indeed sacred authority sufficiently testifies that the consequences of original sin are accounted as sinful, namely those disorders and appetites to which we are subject like brute animals because of Adam's sin. St Paul calls them 'flesh' and 'concupiscence' [Rom. 7: 7–8], and makes clear that he undergoes them unwillingly when he says: 'What I hate, that I do' [Rom. 7: 15]—that is, 'I lust against my will.' For, of course, when the Lord says of the passion alone of anger apart from deed or word, 'He who harbours anger against his brother shall be on trial at the Judgement' [Matt. 5: 22], he clearly shows that it is no venial sin which so serious a condemnation follows, namely a sentence of death. It is as if he were to say: 'Those who do what people ought not to do, and what they would not be doing if they had not sinned, ought to be removed from the race of human beings.' Paul also says about those who against their will experience 'the flesh', that is fleshly lusts: 'There is no condemnation at all of those who are in Christ Jesus, who do not walk according to the flesh' [Rom. 8: 1]—that is, those who do not voluntarily consent to it. Here he is undoubtedly implying that condemnation ensues for those who are not in Christ, as often as they experience 'the flesh' even though they do not walk according to it. For human beings were created in such a state that they were not due to experience lust, as I said with regard to wrath. If, then, people carefully weigh my remarks, they should be in no doubt at all that those are justly blamed who are unable to receive the word of God because of their own sin.

8

Moreover, in the case of those who receive the grace of Christian faith, just as baptism banishes the original state of injustice in which they are born, so too it pardons any guilt attaching to their incapacity and all the corruption they incurred because of the sin of their first parent and which dishonours God. For after baptism they are not blamed for any of the guilt within them before baptism, even though the corruption and appetites which are the penalty for sin are not immediately wiped away in baptism. And no offence is charged against them except for one they voluntarily commit. So it is clear that the corruption and the evils which were the penalty for sin and remain after baptism are not sinful in themselves. For only the state of injustice is intrinsically sinful, while the evils which follow upon it are adjudged sinful because of their cause, until the state itself is forgiven. For if they were by themselves sinful, they would be effaced in baptism, in which all sins are washed away by the blood of Christ. Furthermore, if they were called sins in the strict sense, they would be sins in the condition of brute beasts after whose likeness our human nature is burdened with those evils as a consequence of sin.

There is also something else which can be recognized in humanity's first sin and which ought much to be feared. Since people are as 'a wind which departs not to return' [Ps. 78: 39], after they voluntarily fall—to speak now only of voluntary sins—they cannot in any way rise again unless raised by grace. And if they are not upheld by God's mercy, they drown as they deserve in sin after sin into a bottomless pit of sin, that is a measureless deep, in such manner that they even hate the good and are heading for death. For that reason the Lord says to the apostles: 'If the world hates you, know for sure that it hated me before you' [John 15: 18]. And St Paul says: 'We are a fragrant incense rising to God; in some cases an aroma of death into death, in others an aroma of life into life' [2 Cor. 2: 15–16]. And that is why we say of God that 'He shows mercy where he wills but also hardens where he wills' [Rom. 9: 18]. But it is also true that God does not show mercy to the same degree to all who receive mercy, and he does not harden to the same degree all those he hardens.

9

Yet another question is: why does the penalty of sin endure in us in this life after the sin has been erased? I have a brief response to the question, although I did not propose to address it now. If baptism or martyrdom immediately immunized the faithful against their subjection to corruption, then merit would perish and people would be saved without any role for merit, except for those first human beings who would believe without previous experience of corruption. There would be no role for faith and hope without which nobody gifted with intelligence can merit the kingdom of God. Obviously the objects of faith and hope are things that are unseen. For since people would see those converts to Christ instantly passing into incorruptibility, there would be no one who could even will to withdraw from the overwhelming happiness to be seen. Therefore in order to attain the more gloriously to the happiness we desire by meritorious faith and hope, we remain, as long as we are in this life, in a condition which is no longer accounted as sin even though it resulted from sin.

Finally, we are not promised in baptism and faith the happiness which Adam enjoyed in Paradise before his sin. Instead we are promised the happiness which he would have when the number to be taken up to form the heavenly citizenry would be complete. This company shall be populated by angels and human beings, though the latter shall not procreate as they would have done in Paradise. If, then, the converted to Christ were quickly to pass into the state of incorruptibility, there would not be people from whom that destined number could be gathered, since no one could help rushing to happiness seen. I imagine that this is what St Paul means when he says of those 'who have worked at justice through faith' that 'they all, though approved because of the witness of their faith, did not receive the promise, since God is preparing some greater good for us, lest they make up a total without including us' [Heb. 11: 33, 39–40]. For if we ask what greater good God shall have provided for us from their not receiving the promise, I do not see the possibility of a response more apt than what I said above. That is to say, if the happiness promised to the just were not delayed for those who have won approval, there would be no role for merit in those who would know of it not by faith but by actual experience. The propagation of human beings by which we are born would also cease, for they would race to that incorruptibility they would see occurring without delay. And so God has provided a great good for us in delaying the reception of the promise to the saints approved by the witness of their faith. This he does so that we would keep being propagated and the faith would abide by which we would merit the promise together with them and would reach a consummation simultaneously with them.

There is also another reason why the baptized and the martyrs do not immediately become incorruptible. Suppose that a master harshly scourges a slave whom he had planned to endow one day with high honours. The slave has committed an offence for which he could not on his own make satisfaction. Also suppose that the master, after the scourging, is about to thrust the slave into a dreadful dungeon for a fixed period where he would be tortured with very painful punishments. Suppose furthermore that someone influential with the master makes satisfaction for the servant and thereby reconciles him. The strokes the guilty one deservedly received while still at fault and before the satisfaction are not thereby made to disappear as if they had never occurred. But the greater torments into which he had not yet been thrust are warded off by the intervening reconciliation. And the honours which he was about to receive in due time if he had not sinned (honours which he would lose after his offence were there no reconciliation) are, by the perfect satisfaction, now restored to the degree previously intended without any change. Obviously, if he had already been disinherited of those honours (as he was to be disinherited beyond redemption after his offence in the absence of a reconciliation), no sort of reconciliation would be able to assist him. But since he could not be disinherited from an honour which he did not yet possess and to which he had no right, reconciliation can intervene against the impending disinheritance and prevent it—on condition (first) that the slave, while weak and recovering from the scourging, honestly vows loyalty to his master and a change of behaviour, and (second) that the slave fulfils his promise.

The situation between God and the human race is something like this. In fact after humanity sinned it was 'whipped' with a penalty such that it would only physically produce offspring as we find infants are at birth, and after this life it would be exiled forever in the underworld, excluded from the kingdom of God for which it was created, unless someone were to reconcile it, something which it could not do by itself alone. But Christ alone is able to reconcile humanity. Therefore in the case of all infants physically begotten, human beings are born under 'the whip'—a sinful state. When people gain access to reconciliation, the 'whip' incurred before reconciliation deservedly stays in place. But in the case of those redeemed by Christ, those torments which humanity was to suffer in the underworld are remitted and many are gifted with the kingdom of God which they were to receive in due time after a period of intimacy with God in the earthly Paradise—on condition that they persevere right up to the end in the faith they promise at baptism.

10

There are people who think that experience proves that free choice is worthless, seeing that many either strive to live virtuously with immense effort but then make no progress at all because of some impossibility in their path, as they claim, or else do advance somewhat only to fall back beyond recovery. But their thinking does not refute what I have reasonably argued, namely that free choice is effective with the help of grace. In my judgement, the lack of progress in those who strive, or their falling back after an advance, are not caused by an impossibility but by a sometimes serious, sometimes easily surmountable, difficulty. Indeed we are very often accustomed to claim that something is impossible for us which we can only accomplish with difficulty. For if one carefully examines the operations of one's own will, one shall realize that we never forsake the uprightness of will received by grace except by willing something which cannot coexist with it. Surely one does this not through any failure of the ability to preserve one's uprightness, an ability which is the will's very freedom, but rather because of the will's failure to preserve what does not fail of itself, which one does, as I said, by a contrary will to expel it.

11

Since the reflection just offered especially concerns the will, I think I ought to say something in greater depth which will be very helpful in my way of thinking. We have bodily members and five senses, each of which was equipped for its special purpose, and which we use as tools. For example, the hands are designed for seizing, the feet for walking, the tongue for speaking, and sight for seeing. So, too, the soul possesses certain powers which it employs like tools for appropriate functions. The soul, for instance, has the power of reason which it employs as its special tool for reasoning, and a will which it employs for willing. Neither the reason nor the will is the whole of the soul; each is something within the soul. Therefore since the distinct tools have their distinct natures, abilities and functions, let us distinguish in the will upon which we are now focusing the tool along with its aptitudes and its functions. In the case of the will we can call these aptitudes affectivities. An affectivity is truly a tool of the will in exercising its own aptitudes. That is why the human soul when it passionately wills something is said to be emotionally moved to will it (or to will it affectionately).

Undoubtedly the word 'will' appears to be used equivocally with three different senses: one as the tool of the will's action, another as the affectivity of the tool, and yet another as the using of the tool. The will's tool is that power of the soul we use for willing, just as reason is the tool for reasoning we use when we reason and sight is the tool we use for seeing. The affectivity of this tool is that by which the tool itself is so swayed toward willing some object, even when one is not thinking about what one is willing, that it comes to mind either immediately or when the time is right. For example, the will's tool is so disposed toward willing health, even when one is not thinking about it, that when it comes to mind, one immediately wills it. And it is so disposed toward sleep, even when one is not thinking about it, that when it comes to mind one wills it at the right time. For the will is never disposed either to will sickness at any time or else to will never to sleep at all. Likewise too in the case of the just person, the will's tool is disposed toward justice, even when the person is asleep. The person wills it as soon as thinking of it. Now the actual use of the will's tool is something which we have only when we think of the will's objective.

The word 'will' then is applied to the will's tool, to its disposition and its actual use. We in fact call its tool the 'will' when we speak generally of directing it toward a variety of objectives, for example, now the will to walk, now to sit, and at another time to will this or that. People always possess this tool even though they are not always using it, just as they have sight, the tool for seeing, even when they are not using it, as when they sleep. And when they do use it they turn it now to seeing the sky, now to seeing the earth, and again to something else. It is like our always having the tool for reasoning, the faculty of reason, which we are not always using and which when reasoning we direct to a variety of matters. But the disposition of the will's tool is called 'will' when we say that people always will their well-being. In this case it is actually the disposition of that tool toward willing their well-being that we call their 'will'. The same is true when we say of saints that they possess unceasingly the will to live rightly even when sleeping and not thinking about it. However, when we say that one person has a greater will to live rightly than another we are only using the term 'will' of that disposition of the tool itself according to which one wills to live rightly. For the tool itself is not greater in one individual and less in another. Now the actual employment of that tool is termed 'will' when someone says: 'Right now I have a will to read,' or 'Right now I do will to read.' Or else: 'Right now I have a will to write,' or 'Right now I do will to write.' For just as seeing is making use of sight (the tool for seeing), and its employment is called 'vision' or 'sight' when used as a synonym for 'vision' (for 'sight' also signifies the tool itself), so, too, 'willing' is the employment of the will as designating the will's tool, and that employment is called 'will' only when our minds are actually engaged with the object of our will.

Therefore there is only one 'will' when the word signifies and refers to the tool, that is, a person has only one tool for willing, just as there is only one reason, that is, one tool for reasoning. But when the word 'will' refers to that which disposes the tool, then such disposing is of two kinds. Just as sight has several abilities (an ability to see light, and one to see shapes by means of the light and thereby to see colours), so the tool for willing has two abilities which I term affectivities: one is for willing what is advantageous, the second for willing what is right. To be sure, the will's tool wills only what is either advantageous or right. For whatever else it wills, it does so in view of its usefulness or rightness, and even if it is mistaken, it deems itself to be willing what one does in relation to these two aims. Indeed when disposed to will their own advantage, people always will their gratification and a state of happiness. Whereas when disposed to will uprightness, they will their uprightness and a state of uprightness or justness. And in fact they will something on the grounds of its advantage, as when they will to plough or toil to insure the means to preserve their livelihood or health, which they regard as advantages. But they are disposed to will on the grounds of uprightness, for instance, when they will to learn by hard work to know rightly, that is, to live justly. When, however, the word 'will' signifies the employment of that often mentioned tool, it refers only to the case when someone actually has an object of will in mind, as has been said. We may discriminate among many characteristics of 'will' in this sense which we shall not address now, but perhaps elsewhere. So you see that the word 'willing' is equivocal as is the word 'seeing'. For indeed just as people are described as 'seeing' when they are using their sight and also when not doing so, but possess the ability to see, so also 'willing' is attributed to people when they are employing the will's tool while thinking of what they will, and when they are not actually using it because they do not possess the disposition or inclination to will to act.

We can also realize that the will as tool, as its disposition, and as its actual use are all different by means of the following example. If a just person, even when asleep and not thinking at all, is said to have the will to live justly, whereas the unjust person when asleep is said not to have the will to live justly, one and the same thing is denied to the unjust person that is attributed to the just. Plainly, however, that is because when we deny a will to live justly to the sleeping unjust person we are not denying to that person a will as tool whether awake or asleep since every human will always has that. Since the will, then, in our example, is the same which is affirmed of the good person but denied to the evil one, we are not insisting on the presence of will as tool in the good person. Rather, we are insisting on the presence of a particular disposition of will. Now there is no doubt that the actual use of the will is absent in sleepers unless they are dreaming. Similarly, when the will to live justly is said to be present in a sleeping just person, the will as actual use is not intended. Therefore the will as a disposition is not the same as the will as a tool or the will as its actual use. Moreover, everyone knows that the will as tool is not the will as its actual use, for when I say that I do not have the will to write, no one concludes that I do not have the will as tool. We conclude, therefore, that the will as a tool, as a disposition, and as its use, are not the same.

The will as a tool moves all the other tools which we freely use—both those which are internal to us, for example our hands, tongue and sight, as well as those which are external, such as a pen or an axe. It also produces all the movements of the will even as it moves itself by its own dispositions. It can therefore be called a tool that moves itself. I say that the will as tool causes all the movements of the will. Yet on deeper reflection, God is more truly said to produce all that nature or human will produce, for God creates nature and the will as tool along with its dispositions—without which it accomplishes nothing.

12

All human merit, whether good or evil, come from the two dispositions termed 'wills'. These two 'wills' also differ in that to will one's own advantage is unavoidable while to will what is right was avoidable, as I have said above, for the angels and our first parents, and is avoidable for those who remain in this life. But they also differ in that the disposition to will the advantageous is not itself what it 'wills', whereas the one to will uprightness is uprightness. In fact no one wills uprightness without possessing uprightness, and no one can will uprightness except by uprightness. Plainly this uprightness is a property of the will as tool. It is uprightness of this sort that I am talking about when I define 'justice' as 'the will's uprightness when the latter is sought for its own sake'. This type of uprightness is also that 'truth' of the will in which, as the Lord charged, the devil failed to remain steadfast. I treated this point in my work *On Truth*.

Now we ought to consider the way in which, as I said, a person's merits, whether unto salvation or condemnation, derive from these two 'wills' which I call 'aptitudes' or 'affectivities'. Uprightness in essence is not the cause of any evil, and is the mother of every good merit, for it is an ally of the spirit in its zealous contention with the flesh [Gal. 5: 17] and shares the spirit's delight in 'God's law in accord with the inner man' [Rom. 7: 22], namely, in accord with the same spirit. Moreover, if evil sometimes appears to follow from uprightness, the evil does not really follow from it but from something else. It was precisely due to their uprightness that the apostles were 'a fragrant aroma rising to God' [2 Cor. 2: 15]. The fact that they were for some people an 'aroma of death leading to death' resulted not from the justice of the apostles but from the sinfulness of those with bad will. As a matter of fact that other 'will' which wills what is advantageous is not bad except when it consents to the flesh lusting against the spirit [Gal. 5: 17].

13

In order to understand this matter more clearly we must examine the reason why the latter 'will' is so flawed and prone to evil, for we should not think that God created it such in the case of our first parents. For when I stated that it was due to sin that humanity was subject to corruption and appetites characteristic of brute beasts, I did not say how the 'will' prone to evil first arose in people. Obviously corrupt appetites are one thing, quite another a corrupt will consenting to such appetites.

So I think we must ask how such a will befell humanity. The cause of such a will as this one shall be readily plain to us if we consider the original state of the rational creature. As we know, it was God's intention to create his rational creature just and happy so that it might enjoy him. But it could not be either just or happy without its willing both justice and happiness. Now the will to be just is actually justice itself, but the will to be happy is not happiness itself because not everyone who wills it has it. Moreover, all agree that happiness, whether that of angels or the kind which Adam enjoyed in Paradise, consists of a sufficiency of appropriate advantages without any deprivation. Although the happiness of angels is greater than that which Adam and Eve enjoyed in Paradise, that is no reason for denying the happiness they did enjoy. Similarly intense heat as such is free of all cold, yet nevertheless there can be another instance of greater heat. Likewise coldness as such is without any cold, and yet there can be a greater coldness. In the same manner there is no reason to deny that Adam enjoyed happiness in Paradise without any deprivation, although the happiness of the angels was the greater. Surely to enjoy something less than another does is not the same as deprivation, but to lack something which one ought to have is to be deprived, which was not true in the case of Adam. In fact where there is deprivation, there is unhappiness. Moreover, God did not create human beings (creatures he created to know and love him) unhappy antecedent to their sin. So he created them happy with no deprivation. For this reason his rational human creatures received all at once the will to be happy, happiness itself, and the will to be just (the uprightness which is the very state of justice) and freedom of will as well, without which they could not preserve that state.

Now God so ordained these two 'wills' or 'affectivities' in order that the will as a tool would employ the will to justice for commanding and ruling under the tutelage of the spirit, that is, the mind or reason, and the second one for obeying without any difficulty. Indeed God gave people happiness, not to say the angels, as an advantage, whereas he gave them justice for the sake of his own glory. He gave justice in such manner that people could abandon it while, should they not do so but rather persevere in preserving it they would be advanced to the company of the angels. However, should they abandon it, they would in no way be able to recover it on their own. They would not attain to the happiness of angels and would be deprived of that which they had, and falling into the likeness of brute beasts would be subject like them to physical corruption and the oft-mentioned appetites. However, the will to be happy would stay on, so that by reason of the deprivation of the benefits they had lost, they would be justly punished with grievous unhappiness. Therefore, once they abandoned the state of justice, they abandoned happiness. And the will which they received as good and for their own good, still seethes with a longing for the advantages which they cannot help but want. And because they cannot recover the lost genuine advantages befitting a rational creature, they turn to the spurious advantages which befit brute animals and characterize bestial appetites. And so when they will those advantages unlawfully, they either rebuff righteousness so that it is not accepted when offered or else expel it after receiving it. But when they will the advantages lawfully they do not act in this way.

In this way, then, the will as a tool was created good in respect to its being. It was also created just, and able to preserve its received righteousness. However, it became evil by its free choice—evil not in regard to its existence, but inasmuch as it became unrighteous owing to the absence of the righteousness it freely abandoned, a righteousness which it was intended to maintain forever. It now also became powerless to will the justice it had abandoned. For one cannot will justice if one does not have it, though one can preserve it when one has it. The will to one's advantage was also created good as regards its existence, but it became in a certain way evil, that is unjust, because it was not subordinate to justice without which it ought to will nothing. Therefore since the will as a tool freely became unjust once it abandoned justice, its operation necessarily remains unjust and the handmaid of injustice. For it is unable by itself to return to justice and without the latter it is not in any circumstances free, since in its absence the natural free choice is useless. It also became the handmaid of its own disposition toward the advantageous, because in the absence of justice the will as tool can only will what the former dictates. Moreover, I describe both the tool and its disposition as 'wills' because both the tool and its actual disposition are modes of willing. Indeed both are fittingly so called because the tool wills what it is disposed to will and the disposition also wills as it moves the will as a tool. In the same way the person who sees by sight is said to be seeing, and the sight by which one sees is also said to see. Hence we can quite reasonably say that the dispositions of that will which I call a tool of the soul are, as it were, tools of that tool, because the latter does nothing without them. Therefore once its 'tool', its disposition to will justice or righteousness, has been lost, the will as tool can in no way will justice unless the latter is restored by grace. Therefore since the will as tool should only will something justly, whatever it wills without righteousness it wills unjustly. Now none of the appetites, all of which St Paul calls 'flesh' and 'lust', are evil or unjust in respect to their existence but are said to be unjust because they are present in a rational creature where they ought not to be. In brute beasts they are not evil or unjust because they ought to be there.

14

From what has been said above, we can now conclude that people do not always possess the justice which they ought always to have because they cannot in any way attain it or recoup it on their own. It is also plain that God is active in good works with his own goodness alone as their source; it is that goodness which is the Creator of the human will with its freedom of choice and which endows it with the state of justice to empower its activity. But that God is active in evil ones is the fault of the human being alone; for God would not be active in human evil deeds unless people were freely willing to do them. Still God does cause the fact that they exist, since he created the human will which people employ when they lack the state of justice. It is therefore the fault of people when their actions are evil. It is not the fault of the God who created that will endowed with freedom of choice and bestowed uprightness upon it that it might will justice only. It is the fault of human beings that they abandoned the state which they had the power to preserve. Therefore God is involved in good works both because their existence is good and because their righteousness is good. God is involved in evil works only insofar as they have goodness simply by being. God is not responsible for the evil which they have insofar as they lack justice which they ought to have—for a lack is not something which has existence. People, however, are involved in their good deeds in that they are not evil—because when they could abandon righteousness and do evil, they do not do so. No, they preserve it by their free choice and by the initial and subsequent gift of the grace of God. But in the case of evil deeds people are the sole cause of their evilness because they do them by their independent, unjust choice alone.

I think I may now fittingly conclude my treatment of the three difficult inquiries which I began in the hope of God's assistance. If I have in this treatise somehow said what ought to meet the needs of any inquirer, that is no credit to me since it is not I but the grace of God in me which is responsible. I shall, however, say this much. When I was looking into these same questions and my own inquiring mind was groping about for a satisfactory account, if someone had given me the responses which I have now written, I would have been grateful because he would have satisfied me. So, since what I subsequently learned by God's enlightenment was powerfully pleasing to me, and confident that it would please some people if I were to write it down, I wanted as a gift to impart to those who ask for it that which I have received as a gift.

PHILOSOPHICAL FRAGMENTS

A. *The four senses of 'to will'* (SM 334–5)

1. It should be borne in mind that we sometimes will in such a fashion that, if we can, we actually do so that what we will is the case, e.g. when the sick man wills his own health. For he actually does so that he is healthy, if he can; but if he cannot, then he would do so, if he could. This is the type of willing which can be called *effective*, to the extent that if he can he does so that that which is willed is the case.

2. But sometimes we will that which we are capable of doing, but without actually doing it; but nevertheless, if it happens to be done, we are thereby pleased, and we approve. Thus if a poverty-stricken unclothed person says to me that I am unwilling to clothe him, and this is because his nudity comes about as a consequence of my wishing him to be unclothed or because I am unwilling that he should be clothed, then my reply is that I am willing that he should be clothed and that he should not be unclothed, and that I much rather approve of his being clothed as opposed to his being unclothed, notwithstanding my not doing so that he is clothed. This is the type of willing which is exemplified in my thus willing that he should be clothed, and which may be designated as *approbative*.

3. There is yet another type of willing, as when a creditor is willing to excuse a debtor, and to accept barley in place of the corn that the debtor is unable to restore to him. This we may designate as willing of the merely *concessive* sort. The creditor would prefer the corn, but on account of the poverty of the debtor he concedes that the latter should restore barley.

---

* The translation is from the version presented in R. W. Southern and F. S. Schmitt (eds.), *Memorials of St Anselm* (coded as 'SM', with page-numbers immediately following). In the present translation the verb '*facere*' has invariably and deliberately been translated as 'to do', and the composite '*facere esse*' has been rendered as 'to do so that', so as to reflect the central position of these locutions in Anselm's system. This explains the slight degree of clumsiness of expression at the various relevant points in the English version.

4. There exists also a common usage according to which a person is said to will that which he neither *approves* nor *concedes*, but merely *permits*, it being in his power to prevent it. Thus, when a ruler is not willing to take measures against thieves and robbers in his kingdom, we proclaim that because he is willing to permit them, he wills the evils which they do, even though those evils displease him.

It seems to me that this fourfold classification embraces every type of willing. Thus in terms of these four diverse types of willing, that particular type which I have called the *effective* involves not only the doing (insofar as the agent can) of what is willed, but also its *approval*, *concession*, and *permission*.

However, he who wills in the *approbative* manner does not do that which he wills, but merely *approves* of it, as well as *conceding* and *permitting* it.

In contrast, he who wills in the *concessive* manner neither does nor *approves* that which he wills (except in some oblique sense), but merely *concedes* and *permits*.

Finally, he who wills in the *permissive* manner, neither *effectuates* nor *approves* nor *concedes* that which he wills, but merely *permits* it in a non-approbative manner.

B. *Scriptural uses of the senses of 'to will' related to the styles of 'to do'* (cf. section G below)

All these various fashions of willing are exemplified in Holy Scripture, and so I now supply a few examples.

Thus when, of God, it is said 'He has done whatsoever he has willed' and 'Therefore has he mercy on whom he will', here 'to will' is used in the effective sense, and has the form of the first mode of *willing that there is* . . . , after the manner of *doing so that there is* . . . : this is because he wills that very thing that he is being said to will.

But when the text reads, 'whom he wills, he hardens', then this involves permissive willing, and it is in the second mode of *willing that there is* . . . , given that he is here said to will that there is a hardened person on the ground that he does not will that there is not a hardened person (in the effective sense of willing); that is, he does not will to do so that there is not a hardened person. If, however, we assert that he wills to make hard on the ground that he does not will to make soft, then the sense will be preserved, and will involve the same permissive import, but now it is in the fourth mode of willing that there is . . . This is because he is said to will that hardening should occur because it is not the case that he wills that there is something other, namely, that there is softening. For he who softens, both does so that there is softening, and also does so that there is not hardening.

On the other hand, when we hear that 'God wills that all men should be saved', then the *approbative* sense of willing is in question, and, as in the case of *willing to harden* the second mode of *willing that there is* . . . will be involved, because he does not will to do so that there is not a saved person; alternatively, the fourth mode will apply, because he does not will so that there is something other, that is, he does not will that a man should be damned (in the effective sense of willing), which amounts to: he does not will to do so that a man is damned. This remark is added in order to oppose those who say that the will of God is the cause which brings it about that some are not just but rather unjust, and hence that they are not saved; in fact, however, the wrongdoing on account of which they are damned originates from them, and does not stem from the will of God.

Should we assert that God wills that the single life should be adhered to, then in respect of those who are influenced by him to thus adhere, the type of willing involved is *efficient*, and is in the first mode of *willing that* . . . In respect of other persons, however, the type of willing is *approbative*, on the ground that he does not will (in the effective sense) that they should not adhere (and then the second mode of willing is in question). Alternatively, we have: he does not will that the single life should be forsaken, and this is in the fourth mode.

C. *Four senses of 'something'* (SM 336–7)

We use the word 'something' in four ways.

1. We use the word 'something' in its proper sense when that which is indicated by the name and which is thought of in the mind does in fact exist, as in the cases of a stone or a log of wood. These latter

are not only named by their corresponding words, and thought of by the mind, but exist also in reality.

2. That which has a name, and has a mental concept, but which does not truly exist, is also said to be something, as in the case of a chimera. For by its name is signified a certain mental concept, which involves a resemblance to an animal, when such a thing does not exist in the reality of things.

3. We also make use of the word 'something' in respect of that which merely has a name, but without the name's in any way corresponding to a mental concept, and without any implication of its being a being, e.g. injustice and nothing. For we say that injustice is something when we assert that he who is punished because of an injustice is punished on account of something. Again, we say that nothing is something when we say things such as 'Something is nothing or something is not nothing'; this is because if a proposition is thus true or false, we are asserting that either something is affirmed of something, or something is denied of something. Injustice and nothing have no corresponding mental concepts, although they do settle the understanding in the same way as do negative names. It has to be stressed that *settling the understanding* is not the same as *settling something in the understanding*. For 'non-man' settles the understanding, since it brings it about that the hearer understands that *man* is not contained within the meaning of this utterance, but rather that he is removed therefrom. For it does not settle something in the understanding as being the significate of this utterance, in the way that 'man' does settle some concept of that which is the significate of this name. Thus 'injustice' puts aside any appropriate justice, without positing any other thing, and similarly 'nothing' puts aside something, without positing anything in the understanding.

4. We also give the name 'something' to that which neither has its own name, nor a concept, nor any existence in reality, as when we assert of a non-existent that it is something, and that a non-existent exists. Thus when we assert that the non-being of the sun above the earth brings about the non-existence of the day, and if it is declared that every cause is something and every effect something, then we are not in a position to be able to deny that the non-being of the sun above the earth and the non-existence of day are each something, on

the ground that the one is the cause and the other the effect. On the other hand we make an assertion that non-being is a being when, in respect of someone who has been denying that something is the case, we declare that things are the way he says they are; in this case, were we to express ourselves properly, we should rather declare that things are not in the way in which he says they are not.

Thus, there are four ways in which 'something' is said to apply: in one of these ways, it is properly applied, but in the others we are dealing, not with something, but only with quasi-something, on the ground that we use speech in respect of them as though they are something.

D. *The totally general function of 'to do'* (SM 337–8. Note that some parts are repeated in section G below)

The verb 'to do' customarily acts as a place-holder for no matter which verb, whatever its meaning, be it complete in form or incomplete, and even for 'not to do'. For when it is asked concerning someone 'What is he doing?' then exact research will show that 'doing' is there being put in the place of any verb which can occur in the reply, and whichever verb may thus be involved in the reply is a substituend for 'doing'. For in reply to someone who queries, 'What is he doing?' no verb can rightly be used in which 'he does ...' is not understood in respect of the person concerning whom the question is raised. Thus should the reply be, 'He is reading', or 'He is writing', then this amounts to the same as saying, 'He is doing this, namely, reading', or 'He is doing this, namely, writing'.

In fact just every verb can thus be used in reply to such a query. This is obvious enough in the majority of cases such as 'He is singing' and, 'He is dictating', but doubts may perhaps be raised in cases like 'He is ...', 'He lives ...', 'He is able ...', 'He owes ...', 'He is named ...', or, 'He is called ...'. But no one can find fault if, in reply to the query, 'What is he doing?' the reply is given that he is in the church, or that he lives in the manner of a good man, or that he is able to have his own way throughout his town, or that he owes a lot of money, or that he is named as being better than his neighbours, or that he is called before all others, wherever he may be.

Hence every verb may at some time or another constitute an

appropriate reply to the query, 'What is he doing?', provided there is someone who knows how properly to arrange this. Thus whatever the verbs may be which are used in reply to someone raising the 'What is he doing?' question, such verbs are, as I remarked, actually put in the reply as substituends for that 'doing', and the 'doing' in the question stands as their place-holder; this is because that concerning which the question is raised is supplied in the reply, and that which is supplied in the reply is that concerning which the question is raised.

'To do' is also often a place-holder for negative verbs, and even for 'not to do'. For example, he who *does not* have virtue and who *does not* hate vice, *does* evil, and he who *does not* that which he ought not to do, *does* well. It is in this fashion that 'to do' acts as a place-holder for every verb, be it positive or negative, and every verb is a doing-word.

Yet again, every thing of which some verb is predicated, is in some sense a cause of that being the case which the verb signifies, and according to the common course of utterance, every cause is said *to do so that there is* that of which it is the cause. And so every thing of which some verb is predicated *does so that there is* whatever is signified by the verb in question. I need not dwell upon those verbs the signification of which obviously involves doing (e.g. running and the like), but it still is the case that other verbs which at first sight appear remote from this characteristic of doing, obviously fit in with what I am asserting. For it is in this fashion that he who sits, *does so that there is* sitting, and he who undergoes, *does so that there is* undergoing; for were it not that there were someone who undergoes, there would be no undergoing, nor would there be anything which is named, were it not that there was some thing which was named, nor is there any way in which something may be said to be so-and-so, unless that object which is said to be so-and-so is first had in mind.

Thus when it is asserted '*Man* is so-and-so' or '*Man* is not so-and-so', then it is that name's significate which is first conceived by the mind, and which is asserted to be so-and-so, or not to be so-and-so, and hence it is that which is conceived which is the cause of its being said to be so-and-so. Thus, were we to assert '*Man* is *animal*', then *man* is the cause of his being *animal*, and of his being said to be animal. Now I am not here maintaining that *man* is the cause of animal's existing, but merely that *man* is the cause of his being animal and of his being said to be animal. For it is the whole man which is signified and brought to mind by this name, and it is within this whole that there is *animal* as a part. Here, therefore, it is in this sense that the part follows upon the whole, for where there is the whole, the part must necessarily also be. Since therefore, it is the whole man which is conceptually associated with the name 'man', it is the former which is the cause that he is animal, and is said so to be, for it is the concept of the whole thing which is the cause of the part's being embraced within that concept and of its being asserted of the whole. In this style, whether being is asserted of whatever is in question in the truncated manner, as with '*Man* is . . .', or with due completion, as with '*Man* is *animal*', or 'healthy', then in either case it is the foregoing concept which is the cause of the thing's being said to be (or not to be), and which ensures the understanding of what is asserted.

Since it turns out that on the basis of the foregoing argument whatever the thing may be of which some verb is predicated, that thing is signified as *doing* whatever is the import of the verb in question, it follows that it is not altogether unreasonable for a certain manner of speaking to be allowed, according to which 'does' acts as a place-holder for every verb, and according to which every verb is said to involve doing. Indeed, the Lord also uses 'to do' (or 'to act', which amounts to the same thing) in the place of every verb, when he says, 'Everyone who acts in an evil fashion hates the light' [John 3: 20], and 'He who does the truth comes to the light' [John 3: 21].

For indeed, he who does that which he ought not to do acts in an evil way, and thus likewise all verbs may be interpreted. For he who is where or when he ought not to be, or who sits or stands where or when he ought not to do so, and he who is not or sits not or stands not where or when he ought to do so, acts in a wrong fashion. On the other hand he does the truth who does what he ought to do, as well as he who does not do what he ought not to do. In like manner he who is or sits or stands where or when he ought, and he who is not or does not sit or does not stand where or when he ought not, does the truth. It is in this fashion that the Lord comprises every verb, positive or negative, within the ambit of *doing*.

E. *On causes and their relation to doing* (SM 338–40)

Some causes are said to be efficient, as is the workman (he does so that his work is done), and as is wisdom (it does so that there is a wise person) but others, contrastingly, may not be called efficient, as in the cases of the matter out of which something is done, and place and time, within which are done things which are located and timed. Although these thus vary, nevertheless all causes are equally said (each in their several ways) to involve doing, and everything which is adjudged to involve doing is named a cause.

Every cause *does* something. But there is one sort of doing which is a cause such that that which is said to be done really is the case, be it affirmatively or negatively, yet there is another sort of doing which does not bring it about that what it is said to do really *is* the case, but only that it is *said* to be the case. Thus both the executioner and Herod are equally said to have killed John [the Baptist], since each of them did and was the cause such that there came about that which they are said to have done.

Another example: because, during his infancy and childhood, the Lord Jesus interacted with Joseph as though he were his son, he brought it about in a causal sense, not that he really *was*, but that he *was called*, the son of Joseph. God willing, I shall first make some remarks about that sort of cause which does so that that which it is said to do actually comes about; of the other contrasting varieties I shall speak later.

Thus, as far as causes of this first-mentioned sort are concerned, some of them are proximate, in that they do directly that which they are said to do, with no other intermediate causes intervening between them and the effect which their doing brings about. But there are also remote causes, which are such that they do not do directly that which they are said to do, but only thanks to the intervention of one or more other causes. Thus the fire, as well as he who lights the fire, and also he who commands that the fire should be lit, all do so that there is burning, but it is the fire which does it directly, without the intervention of any other cause between it and the effect. For indeed he who lights the fire does so that there is burning, with fire as the sole intermediary between him and the effect, whereas he who commands that the fire should be lit does so that there is burning by means of two other intermediate causes, namely the fire and the person who lights the fire. Thus there is a distinction between those causes which directly do that which they are said to do, as contrasted with those which do something else which nevertheless suffices to bring about the same effect, in which case the cause is remote.

It also sometimes happens that the effect is attributed to a cause which in fact does so that something else is, as opposed to that which in fact does so that the effect comes about directly. For example, we attribute to an agent's power that which in fact issues from his command and authority, and it is a like situation when, in the case of someone who does so that he gets killed, we assert that he has killed himself rather than saying that he was killed by someone else.

Some efficient causes operate directly to do that which they are said to do, whereas some operate remotely, by an intermediary, and the same contrast applies when causes other than the efficient ones are concerned. For the iron is the proximate cause of the sword, and in its own indirect manner does so that this exists without the intervention of any intermediate cause; again, the ore, whence is extracted the iron, is the sword's remote cause, doing so that this exists, but indirectly, i.e. by means of that intermediary which is the iron. Each cause has causes which extend to the supreme cause of all things, namely God, who (since he is the cause of all things which are anything at all) himself has no cause. Again, every effect has many and diverse sorts of cause, with the exception of the prime effect, brought about when the supreme cause alone created all things. In contrast, in the case of the killing of one man, he who killed him is a cause, he who commanded this is a cause, as also are the reason for his being killed, the place and the time (without which nothing is done), and many other things.

Causes are also said to do something, in some cases by actually doing, in others by not doing, and sometimes not merely by not doing, but even by not existing at all. Thus there is the way in which he who does not prevent evils is said to do so that they are, and he who does not do good things is asserted to do so that they are not, and likewise in the case of teaching, which, when it occurs, in the same way as it does so that there are good things, and does so that bad things are not, so also, when it does not occur is said to do so that there are evils and to do so that good things are not, owing to its absence. But causes of this sort are included among those which in the course of their not doing something are said to do.

Although it most often happens that causes are said to do something in an oblique manner, and not directly, in that they operate through an intermediary, so that they may hence be called remote, nevertheless every cause has its own proximate effect, this being that which it brings about directly, and of which it is the proximate cause. For he who lights a fire is the proximate cause of the fire, and using the fire as a means he does so that there is the conflagration, of which he is the remote cause. When, therefore, he is the proximate cause, then he is rightly said to do a given thing, since he does it directly; when, however, he is the remote cause, it is because he does something other than that thing that he is said to do something.

Every cause is either an entity or a non-entity, and every effect is likewise either an entity or a non-entity, given that every cause either brings about being or brings about non-being. Now I describe as *being* every cause covered by utterance without negation (regardless of whether one or many utterances are involved), and I describe as *non-being* that which is covered by negative utterance. Thus when the sun is named, the allusion is to some sort of being, although it is not as yet designated as being a cause. Likewise, when I say '. . . shines', I allude to something, but without going on to signify its being the effect of anything. When, however, I assert, 'The sun shines', then the sun is the cause and . . . shines the effect, and each of these is a something and a being, given that the sun has its own being and does so that the light exists. In this case, therefore, one has a causing by being, and also being as an effect. In contrast, were I to say 'The sun does so that the non-being of the night ensues', then in this instance the cause is a being and the effect is a non-being. A like complex analysis applies in the case of being itself. For the sun's being above the earth is a something, and it does so that there is both the being of the day and the non-being of the night. In this case being does so that both being and non-being ensue. Again, the sun's not being above the earth does so that there exists both the being of the night and the non-being of the day. In the case of this example, non-being does so that both being and non-being ensue.

In the same way as that which is said to *do* something is obviously the cause, so also that which in some way or other is said to be a cause *does so that* that of which it is asserted to be the cause ensues. Thus if one were to say, 'It is because of the presence of the sun that the day exists and that there is no night' or, 'It is because of the absence of the sun that the night exists and there is no day', this amounts to the same as saying, 'The presence of the sun *does so that* both the day and the non-being of the night ensue', and, 'The absence of the sun *does so that* both the being of the night and the non-being of the day ensue'. So also he who says, 'My knees have been weakened by fasting and my flesh has been transformed because of the oil' [Ps. 108: 24] is saying the same thing as, 'Fasting weakened my knees; the oil transformed my flesh', but the fasting does this because it is present, and the oil because it is absent, i.e. it is not present. For often a cause is said to do something or not to do something on the basis of its presence or absence, even though the presence or absence is not overtly mentioned. Thus, were it to be said, 'The sun does so that the being and the non-being of the day ensues, as well as doing so that both the being and the non-being of the night ensue', then in the one case the doing is in virtue of presence, and in the other in virtue of absence.

F. *Problems of modality* (SM 341–2)

Student. There are lots of things to which I have for a long time wanted your reactions. Among these are capability, incapability, possibility and impossibility, necessity and freedom. Since the concept which embraces these seems to me to involve their overlapping, I enumerate my queries all together. In connection with these I may make clear what troubles me as far as they are concerned, so that when you will have satisfactorily dealt with these for me, I may be able to advance more easily towards other items which interest me.

For we sometimes assert a capability in an instance wherein no capability exists. For no one would deny that every thing which is capable is capable because of a capability, so that when we assert that that which does not exist is capable of existing, we predicate a capability of that which does not exist, and this I cannot understand; an example of this occurs when we say that a house which does not yet exist is capable of existing, whereas no capability can be attributed to that which does not exist.

Again, that which does not exist has no capability, and as such has neither the capability for existing nor the capability for not existing. From this it follows that that which does not exist is neither capable of being nor capable of not being. Now the first of these two negative consequences, namely, 'That which does not exist is not capable of being' has as attendant consequences that that which does not exist is not a possible existent, and hence is a thing whose existence is impossible, and hence necessarily is not. In contrast, if we adopt the other negative result, namely, 'That which does not exist is not capable of not being', then we find that that which does not exist is not a possible non-existent, and hence it is a thing the non-existence of which is impossible, so that it necessarily exists.

The final consequence is that that which does not exist at all, because of its incapacity for existing, is a thing the existence of which is impossible, and which thus is necessarily non-existent; on the other hand, since such a non-existent is equally incapable of not existing, it is hence impossible for it not to exist, and so it necessarily exists.

Again, that which cannot be has no capacity for being, and that which has no capacity for being is incapable of being. Likewise, that which cannot not be has no capacity for not being, and that which has no capacity for not being is incapable of not being. Whence that which does not exist neither is capable of being, nor is it capable of not being; it is both incapable of being and incapable of not being. But in like manner, that which is incapable of being is incapable of not being, and that which is incapable of not being is capable of being. Thus that which does not exist is both capable and incapable of being; likewise, it is capable [and incapable] of not being. It therefore has equally the capacity and the incapacity for both being and not being.

But all these results are quite silly, for the following pairs are each never true [in the same respect]:

it is impossible to be and it is impossible not to be;
it is necessary to be and it is necessary not to be;
it is capable of being and it is incapable of not being;
it is capable of not being and it is incapable of not being.

Hence if these couples represent impossibilities, that principle whence they follow is likewise impossible, namely, that that which does not exist is neither capable nor incapable of being, since it has no capabilities at all. Yet I just cannot understand how this principle is false.

Then there are theses in connection with impossibility and necessity which also disturb me, namely that it is impossible for God to do a certain thing, such as to utter a lie, and also that God is something or other of necessity, such as his being just. For impossibility connotes impotence, and necessity compulsion. But in God there is neither impotence nor compulsion, for if he adheres to the truth because of an impotence, or if he is just from compulsion, then neither his veracity nor his justice are founded upon freedom. If, now, you reply that this impossibility and that necessity signify an insuperable strength where God is concerned, then I still want to know why this strength is designated by names which signify weakness.

These points, and perhaps some others, push me into certain problems of meaning in connection with capability, and possibility, and with their opposites, as well as with necessity and freedom. Although these doubts of mine may be childish, I ask you to equip me so that should someone question me about them, I may know what to reply, for I am aware that I do not know how so to do.

Teacher. Even though your queries may seem childish to you, nevertheless it seems to me that their resolutions are not at all so simple as to permit me to view those queries as simple-minded. Indeed, I have already for a long time looked forward to your persuading me to go into greater detail, were I to begin to make reply. Indeed, I must not attempt to escape from doing what I can, God willing, even though I may not be able to cover every item you query. However, in order to deal with the point you have raised, I consider it necessary to preface my discourse with some remarks about the verb 'to do', and about what is rightly attributable to someone, as otherwise I may be compelled to interpose a digression concerning these topics when they come up in the course of the discussion. For your part, you must remember to keep within the bounds of your queries.

S. I have nothing against whatever you may propose, provided that you will bring us round to what we are looking for.

G. *Doing and its styles* (SM 342–7. Cf. Section D above)

T. The verb 'to do' customarily acts as a place-holder for no matter which verb, whatever its meaning, be it complete in form or incomplete, and even for 'not to do'. For when it is asked of someone,

'What is he doing?', then exact scrutiny will show that 'doing' is there being put in the place of any verb which can occur in the reply, and whichever verb may thus be involved in the reply is a substituend for 'doing'. For in reply to someone who queries, 'What is he doing?' no verb can rightly be used in which 'he does . . .' is not understood in respect of the person concerning whom the question is posed. Thus should the reply be, 'He is reading', or, 'He is writing', then this amounts to the same thing as saying, 'He is doing this, namely reading', or, 'He is doing this, namely writing'.

In fact, just every verb can thus be used in reply to him who poses the question. This is obvious enough in many cases such as, 'He is singing', and, 'He is dictating', but doubts may perhaps be raised in cases like 'He is . . .', 'He lives . . .', 'He is able . . .', 'He owes . . .', 'He is named . . .', or 'He is called . . .'. But no one can find fault if, in reply to the query, 'What is he doing?' the reply is given that he is in the church, or that he lives in the manner of a good man, or that he is able to have his own way throughout his town, or that he owes a lot of money, or that he is named as being better than his neighbours, or that he is called before all others, wherever he may be.

Hence every verb may at some time or another be used as an appropriate reply to the query, 'What is he doing?', provided there is someone who knows how to properly arrange this. Thus whatever the verbs may be which are used in reply to someone raising the 'What is he doing?' question, such verbs are (as I remarked) actually put in the reply as substituends for that 'doing', and the 'doing' in the question stands as their place-holder; this is because that concerning which the question is raised is supplied in the reply, and that which is supplied in the reply is that concerning which the question is raised.

But further, every thing of which some verb is predicated is in some sense a cause of that which the verb signifies as being the case, and according to the common course of speech, every cause is said to do so that there is that of which it is the cause. And so every thing of which some verb is predicated does so that there is whatever is signified by the verb in question. I need not dwell upon those verbs the signification of which obviously involves doing (e.g. running and the like), but it is still the case that other verbs which at first sight appear remote from this characteristic of doing, obviously fit in with what I am asserting. For in this fashion, he who sits, *does* so that there is sitting, and he who undergoes *does* so that there is undergoing; for were it not that there was someone who undergoes, there would be no undergoing, nor would there be any thing which is named, were it not that there was some item which was named, nor is there any way in which something may be said to be so-and-so unless that object which is said to be so-and-so is first had in mind.

Therefore, given that by the foregoing argument whatever the thing may be of which some verb is predicated, that thing is signified as *doing* whatever is the import of the verb in question, it thence follows that it is not altogether unreasonable for the verb 'to do', according to a certain manner of speaking, to be a place-holder for every verb.

S. What you say is obvious enough to anyone who is willing to understand, although I myself do not yet understand what is the point of your assertions.

T. You will understand in the course of what is to follow.

There is a further point to be noted in connection with the verb now in question, namely, the number of styles of occurrence of '*to do*' in the current course of utterance. Although the classification of these is manifold and exceedingly complex, I will still say something about them; this will, I think, support what we have been saying, and at the same time will not be altogether worthless when it comes to helping someone who may want to follow the matter through in greater detail.

Although some causes may be said to be efficient (as with he who does the writing) and others, in contrast with these, are not called efficient (as with the material out of which something is made), nevertheless, every cause, as I have already said, is asserted to do something, and everything which is adjudged to do something is called a cause.

Now whatever is said to do something either does so that there is something, or does so that it is not that there is something. Hence every case of *doing* can be asserted to involve either *doing so that . . .* or *doing so that not . . .*, these two being contrary affirmations. Their respective negations are 'not doing so that . . .' and 'not doing so that not . . .'. However, the affirmative 'doing so that . . .' sometimes takes the place of the negative, namely 'not doing so that not . . .', and conversely, 'not doing so that not . . .' replaces 'doing so that . . .'. Likewise, 'doing so that not . . .' and 'not doing so that . . .' replace each other. Thus sometimes he is said *to do* so that there are evils on the ground that he *does not do* so that they are not, or he is said *not to do* so that evils are not on the ground that *he does* so that they are, or he is said *to do* so that good things are not on the ground that he *does not* so that they are, or he is said *not to do* so that there are good things because he *does* so that they are not.

Let us now bring *doing* under some sort of classificatory control. Now since *doing* is always *doing so that* . . . or *doing so that not* . . . , as was noted above, we are going to have to add 'so that . . .' and 'so that not . . .' to the individual styles of doing, in order that they may be clearly distinguishable.

Hence we distinguish six styles of *doing*:

The first two of these obtain when the cause does so that that very thing is which it is said to do or when the cause does not so that it is not that that very thing is which it is said to do.

Then come the contrasting four cases, in which the cause either does so that, or does not so that some thing other than that which it is said to do either is or is not.

For we say of any thing that it does so that something or other is the case either

1. because it *does so that* that very thing which it is said to do really *is*, or
2. because it *does not so* that that very thing *is not*, or
3. because it *does so that something other* than that very thing really *is*, or
4. because it *does not so that something other* than that very thing really *is*, or
5. because it *does so that something other* than that very thing is *not*, or
6. because it *does not so that something other* than that very thing is *not*.

1. The first of these styles is exemplified when someone killing a man with a sword is said to do so that he is dead. This is because he precisely does that very thing which he is said to do.

2. I have no example of doing so that he is dead in the second style, unless I posit someone who can revive the dead, but who

refuses so to do. Were this to be the case, he would be said to do so that so-and-so is dead in the second style, on the ground that he would not do so that so-and-so is not dead. There are plenty of examples in other contexts, as when we say that someone does so that evils are, in the event of their not doing so that they are not (when they could do so).

3. The third style is exemplified when someone or other is said to have killed someone else, i.e. when they have done so that so-and-so is dead, either because of their having ordered the killing, or because of their having arranged for the killer to have the sword, or because they brought accusations against the victim. (Or he who gets killed may be said to have killed himself because he did something on account of which he was killed.) These cases, however, do not precisely involve the doing of that very thing which is said to be done, that is, the agents do not kill or do so that a dead or killed person is, but rather, by doing something other, through an intermediary, they do that which they are said to do.

4. The fourth style is exemplified when we assert that someone has killed, either because he did not reveal weapons to the person who was killed before he was killed, or because he did not impede the killer, or because he did not do something which is such that, had he done it, the killing would not have occurred. Here also we have agents who do not kill precisely, but who, by not doing so that there is something else, do that thing which they are said to do.

5. The fifth style is exemplified when someone is adjudged to have killed either because by taking away the arms he did so that the person killed was not armed, or because, by opening the gate he did so that the killer was not closed up in the place where he was being detained. Here also they who are said to have killed did not kill precisely, but in an oblique sense, by doing so that something else is not.

6. The sixth style is that in accordance with which he is guilty of having killed who either did not do so that by the taking away of the arms the killer was not armed, or who did not remove the person to be killed, so that he would not be in the presence of the killer. In these cases the killing is not done precisely, but obliquely, i.e. by not doing so that something else is not.

The same sort of classificatory scheme can be applied to *doing so*

that not . . . For whatever is said to do so that something is not, is
said so to do either

1. because it does so that the very thing in question is not, or
2. because it does not so that that thing is, or
3. because it does so that something other is, or
4. because it does not so that something else is, or
5. because it does so that something else is not, or
6. it does not do so that something else is not.

Examples of these can be followed through using the instance of
a man's being killed, as was propounded in the cases of *doing so
that* . . .

1. In the case of he who kills, even as he does so that so-and-so is
dead in the first style of doing so that . . . so also in the first style of
doing so that . . . is not, he does so that the living being is not.

2. In the second style, however, I can adduce no example of 'doing
so that the living being is not' unless (as before) I posit someone who
can revive the dead. For should he be unwilling so to do, then he can
be said in this second mode to do so that the living being is not
because he does not do so that the living being is. Now it has to be
admitted that being dead is not the equivalent of not being living.
For after all many things are not living which are not deprived of life,
as in the case of a stone. Still, even as killing is equivalent to doing
so that there is a dead being, as well as being equivalent to doing so
that the living being is not, so also restoring to life is the same as
doing so that there is a living being, and doing so that the dead being
is not. However, in other subject-matters there are plenty of examples of this second mode. For he is certainly said to do so that good
things are not who, when he can do so, does not do so that they are.

In the four styles which next ensue, and which involve doing or
non-doing so that there is something other or so that there is not
something other, the examples which were propounded under *doing
so that* . . . will suffice.

Next it should be noted that although *doing so that there is* . . . and
not doing so that it is not that there is . . . can be mutually replaced,
nevertheless they do differ. For in fact he *does so that there is* . . . in
the proper sense who does so that there exists that which previously
did not exist; contrastingly, however, *not doing so that it is not that*

there is . . . no more properly applies to the person who does so that there is . . . than to the person who neither does so that there is . . . nor does so that it is not that there is . . .

Likewise, there is the difference between *doing so that it is not that there is* . . . and *not doing so that there is* . . . For in the proper sense he *does so that it is not that there is* . . . who does so that it is not that there is that which previously was; contrastingly, however, *not doing so that there is* is equally applicable to the person who does so that that which was is not, and to the person who neither does so that there is . . . nor does so that it is not that there is . . .

Now it is important to note that I made use of examples involving efficient causes to illustrate *doing so that there is* . . . and *doing so that it is not that there is* . . . This I did simply because they best served to illustrate the points I wished to make. However, in the same way as the above-described sixfold styles apply to instances of the efficient cause, so also they will be found to apply where instances other than those involving efficient causes are in question, should anyone be willing to undertake detailed research into their cases.

The negative forms (i.e. *not doing so that there is* . . . and *not doing so that it is not that there is* . . .) are classifiable in a like manner. This may be made apparent if, in the examples proposed for the various styles of *doing so that there is* . . . and of *doing so that it is not that there is* . . . the affirmative cases are transformed into negatives and the negative cases into affirmatives. However, should one want to use the examples proposed above in the same original order, then in the four styles following upon the first two one should propound affirmatively in the third that which I used negatively in the fourth, and negatively in the fourth that which was propounded affirmatively in the third; in like manner the fifth becomes the sixth and the sixth the fifth. It should further be noted that in the negative styles the first case sheerly negates, without any intimation of anything further, whereas the five following cases use the negative form for the opposites of their affirmatives. Thus he who restores someone to life is said in the second case not to do so that there is a dead thing, in place of being said to do so that there is not a dead thing, and one puts 'not to do so that it is not that there is a living thing' instead of 'to do so that there is a living thing'.

In contrast, he who either

1. in accordance with the third style does so that he who is threatened with killing is armed (by giving him arms), or
2. does not do so that he is not armed (in accordance with the sixth style), when he is capable of performing the deprivation of arms, or who
3. does so that the intending killer is not armed (in accordance with the fifth mode) by removing the arms, or who
4. in this case refuses to provide the arms,

does not do so that that the person in question is armed in the sense of the fourth style.

If it is denied that he does so that there is a dead thing or that he does so that it is not that there is a living being, then he being understood to perform to the best of his capacity, he does so that it is not that there is a dead thing, as well as doing so that there is a living thing.

The same principle of classification proposed for *doing so that there is* . . . or *doing so that it is not that there is* . . . may be applied when any further verb is likewise adjoined to *doing*. Examples would be, 'I do so that you do', or 'I do so that you write something', or 'I do so that something is done', or 'I do so that something is written'.

The styles which I have propounded in respect of *doing* may also be found to obtain in respect of other verbs, in a similar sort of fashion. However, although not all verbs function in all the styles, some or all of those styles apply in individual instances, especially where those verbs are concerned which are transitive in respect of other verbs, as in the instances of *being obliged to* . . . and *being able to* . . . For these are definitely transitive in respect of other verbs, as when we say 'I am able to read' (or '. . . to be read'), and, 'I am obliged to love' (or '. . . to be loved').

There are also verbs which are transitive towards some thing, as opposed to being transitive to verbs, as in the instances of eating bread or lighting a fire.

There are, in addition, certain verbs which involve no transitivity, as with lying down and sleeping, although there are some among these which still present the appearance of making a transition to a verb, as do those in the assertion, 'The people sat down to eat and to drink, and they rose up to play' [Exod. 32: 6]. But this appearance is false. For there is no analogy such that 'The people sat down to eat and to drink, and they rose up to play' is like in form to 'He wants to eat and to drink and to play'. This is because the former should be analysed as, 'The people sat down in order to eat and in order to drink, and they rose up in order to play'.

The verb 'to be' also exhibits some of the foregoing styles. Of these the first two are easily recognizable, whereas the four following, which involve doing or not doing so that something else either is or is not so, are more difficult to bring under systematic control, since there are very many ways in which they involve doing or not doing so that something else either is or is not so. However I shall say a little on the subject, some likes of which you may then be able to detect in the Scriptures or in the common course of utterance, but which I shall not have covered.

It looks to me as though, when a name or a verb is improperly applied to something, the thing to which it is applied may be related to the thing to which it properly applies thus: either as being similar, or as cause or as effect, or as genus, or as species, or as whole, or as part, or as equivalent, or as the symbol or the symbolized (even though every symbol has a likeness to the thing that it symbolizes, the symbol and that which is symbolized are not altogether alike), or (as I was on the point of saying) in some way other than by way of the symbolic, as by signifying that thing whose name (or verb) applies to it, and this either as its significate or by way of being incidental to it; alternatively, the converse of the latter may hold, as when that of which the part of speech is properly used is incidental to that of which it is improperly used; alternatively they are related in the manner of the user and the thing which is used in a context where doing is asserted.

H. *Doing and its analogues* (SM 347–9)

Now all these styles which I have attributed to the verb 'to do' are to be found in other verbs also, although not all of them in individual cases, but at least one or more. Thus every verb, if it is properly predicated of some thing which actually does that which is asserted by the verb, is being used in the first mode, as in the instances of 'He throws', 'He sits', or 'He runs' (where in the latter case he does this by means of his feet), or 'He builds a house' (when he does this with his own hands), or 'The day exists', or 'The sun shines'.

However, if it is not the case that someone does that very act which is propounded, as when someone is said to build a house, but merely gives the order for it, or if we say that so-and-so runs a string of horses, when in point of fact he does not run, but arranges for the running of the horses, then in such cases the doing is in a style other than the first. To the extent, therefore, that we hear some verb predicated of some thing which does not do that very thing which is asserted of it, then a careful researcher will find that the verb is being used in some one or other of the five styles which follow upon the first.

There is no doubt that when someone says to me, 'I ought to be loved by you', then his form of speech is awry. For if he ought then he is under an obligation that he should be loved by me. Hence he ought to take it upon himself that he should be loved by me, and if he does not take on that which he ought to do, then he does wrongly. However, he does not himself understand the situation in this way, even though he thus propounds it. It is therefore because he imposes upon me an obligation to love him that it is said that he ought to be loved by me. For if he deserves this, then he puts me under an obligation so to do; even if his deeds are such as to deprive him of merit, just the fact that he is a human being is reason enough in itself why I can be under an obligation to love him.

In the same way, therefore, as he who does not is said to do, but in some one or other of the aforementioned styles is a cause of someone else's doing, so also of he who is not obliged, it is asserted that he ought, although it is only in a certain manner that he brings it about that someone else is obliged, insofar as he is the cause of the latter's being obliged.

It is in like fashion that it is said of the poverty-stricken that they ought to receive help from the rich, when in fact the poor are not themselves obliged at all, but are something other, namely poor, and it is this which is the cause whereby they impose an obligation upon the rich, namely that the latter should give help.

We also say of ourselves that we are not obliged [*non debere*] to sin, instead of saying that we are obliged not [*debere non*] to sin. For if one thinks strictly about the matter, not everyone who does what they are not obliged to do need be a wrongdoer. For in the same way as 'to be obliged' is equivalent to 'to be under an obligation', so also 'not to be obliged' amounts to 'not to be under an obligation'. But a man does not invariably sin when he does that which he is not obliged to do. For indeed, a man is not obliged to get married, because it is licit for him to adhere to the single life. Hence it follows that he is not obliged to marry, and yet if he does so, he does not do anything wrong. Hence it is not the case that that man sins who does what he is not obliged to do, given the proper analysis of 'not to be obliged'. And yet no one denies that a man ought to get married. Hence he both ought to and ought not. However, in the light of what was said above, in the same way as we say 'not to do so that . . .' instead of 'does so that not . . .', so also we say 'not obliged to do . . .' instead of 'obliged not to do . . .'; hence where 'to be obliged not to sin' covers the case, we instead use 'not to be obliged to sin'. This is a usage which is so prevalent that the latter is understood as nothing other than 'to be obliged not to sin'.

In the form of speech propounding that a man ought to marry, if he wants to, the 'ought to marry' is used instead of 'it is not that he ought not to marry', and this in the same way as I showed above that 'does so that there is . . .' is used instead of 'does not so that . . . is not'. In like fashion, then, in the same way as we say 'not to be obliged to do' instead of 'to be obliged not to do', so also we say 'to be obliged to do' instead of 'not obliged not to do', although the 'to be obliged to do' that we have here could be understood in the same sense as that in which we say that God ought to be above all things. For God is under no obligation to anyone; rather, all things are obliged to be subject to him. Hence the reason why it is said that God ought to be above all things is that he is the cause of everything's being obliged to be subject to him, even as I asserted that the poor ought to receive help from the rich because intrinsic to the poor is the cause of the rich peoples' having to assist them. Hence also it is in this sense that it can be said that a man ought to take a wife. For everything which rightly pertains to someone should be subject to his will. Now it rightly pertains to every man that he may choose whether or not to take a wife (on the assumption that he is not vowed to the single life). Hence the decision as to whether or not he marries ought to be in accordance with his will, and it is on this basis that it is said that should he so will, then he ought to marry, and should he not so will, then he ought not.

However, when we pray to God that he will put aside our sins, it is not appropriate that he should bring about what is suggested by our words. For if he puts aside our sins, he neither wipes them out nor does he lift them from us. Rather, when we pray that our sins may be put aside, we do not pray that the sins in question should themselves be put aside, but rather the indebtedness that we incur on account of our sins. Given that the sins are the cause of, and that they bring about, our indebtedness, it is the latter which we must needs have put aside, and in this respect when we ought to pray that our indebtednesses may be put aside, we in fact pray that the sins may be put aside. In so doing we are not expressing a preference that it should be our sins which are put aside, but rather that this should apply to the indebtedness which they can bring about. This is evident in the [Latin version of the] Lord's Prayer, when we say, 'put aside our indebtednesses'.

Hence also it is the case that it is in accordance with usage that someone says to the person who has burned down the former's house, or who has brought about some inconvenient harm, 'Make good the harm that you have done' whereas the person who burned down the house says, 'Put aside the harm that I did to you'. However, the harm cannot be restored or put on one side, but it is rather that which was taken away by the harm which is to be made good, and it is understood that that which one asks to be put aside is the thing that should be restored on account of the harm done.

In like manner the Lord says [Luke 6: 38] that those whom we compassionately forgive, and to whom we compassionately give, 'will give to us in our bosom a good measure, pressed down and shaken together and running over'. For it is those to whom the compassion is dispensed who are the cause of the dispensers being given something in return, and hence the former are said to give it back.

A likeness to the verb 'to do' is to be found in the verb 'to have'. For someone who lacks eyes is said to have eyes, not because he does have eyes, but rather because he has someone else who does for him what the eyes do. Again, he who has no feet is said to have feet, because he has something else which takes over the role of feet as far as he is concerned.

The verb 'to be' also imitates the verb 'to do'. For something is said to be that which it is not, and this is not because it is that which it is asserted to be, but rather because there is something else which is the ground of its being said to be thus. For example, someone's foot is said to be lame, and their eye to be blind, not because there exists that which is said to be qualified in these ways, but rather because there exists something which takes the place of the foot and the eye. Further the life of the just, involved as it is in many strivings on account of the desire for eternal life, is said during their lifetime to be happy, not because it actually is so, but because it is the cause of their being happy at some time.

The following remarks have to do with the foregoing:

Student. I now see clearly.

Teacher. I used those examples involving efficient causes because in their case the point I wish to make comes across more clearly. Thus efficient causes in the five modes following upon the first do not do that which they are said to do, given that the second involves the cause's *doing not so that there is not* that which in the first mode it *does so that there is*, and in the third mode we have *doing so that something other is*, and in the fourth *doing so that something other is not*, and in the fifth *not doing so that something other is*, and in the sixth *not doing not so that something else is not*; thus also therefore analogously, as I have often shown by means of examples, even as such efficient causes are said to do what the first does, so also non-efficient causes are said to do in the same modes. There are proximate causes of that which they are said to do being the case, even though they are non-efficient, and there are other remote causes which do not so that there is what they are said to do, but so that something other is. Thus the window which does so that the house is bright is a proximate cause of there being that which it is said to do, although it is not an efficient cause, but one which brings something about by means of the light. This is because it is a direct rather than an oblique cause of its being so. This exemplifies the first mode of doing, because in its own fashion it does so that there is that very thing which it is said to do. If, however, the window is not there, or if it is closed, and it is then said to do so that the house is dark, then this is in the second style, since the window is said to do so that there is darkness on the basis of its not doing so that that darkness is not. If, on the other hand, he who did the making of the window is said to do so that the house is bright, or he who did not do the making of the window is said to do so that it is dark, or if someone says that his land feeds him, then remote causes are involved, because they do not do directly; rather it is the man who does by means of the window which he makes, or which, when he ought to do so, he does not make, and the earth which does the feeding by means of the fruit which it provides.

Hence these causes, be they efficient or non-efficient, which involve the first or second styles of doing, may be said to be proximate; the others, in contrast, are remote.

Now we may deal with 'to do so that it is not that . . .', which I had declared also to comprise six styles. These styles are all the same as those which are comprised in 'to do so that . . .', but now we are bringing under 'to do so that it is not that . . .' that which earlier came under 'to do so that . . .'.

1. The first style is the one which applies when the thing is said *to do so that not* because it *does so that* the thing in question (i.e. that the non-being of which it is said to effectuate) *is not*. For he who kills a man is said to do so that he is not living, because he does that very thing which he is said to do.

2. The second style applies when something is adjudged *to do so that not* because *it does not so that* the thing in question (i.e. that the non-being of which it is said to effectuate) is. I am unable to use the example of the living man to illustrate both *to do so that* . . . and *to do so that not* . . . unless I suppose someone who can do so that a dead person is alive. Under such a supposition, if he does not do this, he may be said *to do so that* the dead person is *not* living, because he *does not so that there is* a living person. In other subject-matters, however, there are plenty of examples. Thus if he whose nightly responsibility it is to do so that the house is illuminated does not do what he ought, then he is said *to do so that* the house is *not* illuminated because he *does not* so that it is illuminated.

3. The third style applies when *to do so that not* is said of someone because he *does so that* there obtains *something other* than that which he is adjudged to do so that it is not. For example, we say that someone has *done so that* someone else is *not* alive because he *did so that* the killer had a sword.

4. The fourth style applies when someone is said *to do so that not* because he *does not so that* something other is the case. For example, someone is said to have *done so that* someone else is *not* alive, because before the killing he *did not do so that* the victim was armed.

5. The fifth style applies when someone is said *to do so that* something is *not* because he *does so that* something other is not. For example, someone is said to have done so that someone else is not alive because he did so that before the killing the victim was not armed.

6. The sixth style applies when someone *does so that* something is *not*, because he *does not so that* something other is *not*, as when he does not do so that the killer is not armed by taking away his arms, given that he then has it in his power so to do.

We use 'to will . . .' in the same six styles as those of 'to do so that . . .' Likewise we use 'to will so that not . . .' in as many different ways as 'to do so that not . . .'

Sometimes we will something for its own sake, as when we will health; sometimes we do so on account of something else, as when we will to have bitter medicine for the sake of health.

The will is spoken of ambiguously . . . It is in the permissive style when we allow something to be done which nevertheless is displeasing to us.

INDEX

The Oxford World's Classics Website

www.worldsclassics.co.uk

- Information about new titles
- Explore the full range of Oxford World's Classics
- Links to other literary sites and the main OUP webpage
- Imaginative competitions, with bookish prizes
- Peruse the Oxford World's Classics Magazine
- Articles by editors
- Extracts from Introductions
- A forum for discussion and feedback on the series
- Special information for teachers and lecturers

www.worldsclassics.co.uk

American Literature

British and Irish Literature

Children's Literature

Classics and Ancient Literature

Colonial Literature

Eastern Literature

European Literature

History

Medieval Literature

Oxford English Drama

Poetry

Philosophy

Politics

Religion

The Oxford Shakespeare

A complete list of Oxford Paperbacks, including Oxford World's Classics, Oxford Shakespeare, Oxford Drama, and Oxford Paperback Reference, is available in the UK from the Academic Division Publicity Department, Oxford University Press, Great Clarendon Street, Oxford OX2 6DP.

In the USA, complete lists are available from the Paperbacks Marketing Manager, Oxford University Press, 198 Madison Avenue, New York, NY 10016.

Oxford Paperbacks are available from all good bookshops. In case of difficulty, customers in the UK can order direct from Oxford University Press Bookshop, Freepost, 116 High Street, Oxford OX1 4BR, enclosing full payment. Please add 10 per cent of published price for postage and packing.